CORPORATE GOVERNANCE

CORPORATE GOVERNANCE

Economic, Management, and Financial Issues

Edited by
KEVIN KEASEY, STEVE THOMPSON,
and MIKE WRIGHT

Oxford University Press

Oxford University Press, Great Clarendon Street, Oxford OX2 6DP

Oxford New York

Athens Auckland Bangkok Bogotá Buenos Aires Calcutta
Cape Town Chennai Dar es Salaam Delhi Florence Hong Kong Istanbul
Karachi Kuala Lumpur Madrid Melbourne Mexico City Mumbai
Nairobi Paris São Paulo Singapore Taipei Tokyo Toronto Warsaw
and associated companies in
Berlin Ibadan

Oxford is a registered trade mark of Oxford University Press

Published in the United States by
Oxford University Press Inc., New York

British Library Cataloguing in Publication Data
Data available

Library of Congress Cataloging in Publication Data
Corporate governance: economic and financial issues/edited by Kevin
Keasey, Steve Thompson, Mike Wright.
Includes bibliographical references.
1. Corporate governance—Cross-cultural studies.   2. Corporations—
Finance—Cross-cultural studies.   I. Keasey, Kevin.   II. Thompson,
Steve.   III. Wright, Mike, 1952- .
HD2741.C775 1997 97-3700 658.4—dc21
ISBN 0-19-828991-X (Pbk)
ISBN 0-19-828990-1

10 9 8 7 6 5 4 3 2

Printed in Great Britain by
Biddles Ltd., Guildford & King's Lynn

PREFACE

It is clear from the attention that corporate governance is receiving from news-papers, business magazines, and the broadcast media that the subject has thoroughly entered the public domain. The large number of conferences devoted to a corporate governance theme also testifies to the strength of interest among academics and corporate professionals. It is the case, of course, that contributions to these discussions may be drawn from a variety of disciplinary backgrounds, including sociology, law, political science, game theory, etc.

The purpose of this volume is to offer students and practitioners of corporate governance a series of 'state of the art' reviews of key topics in the area. It is based primarily—but not exclusively—on economic and financial analyses of governance issues. The contributors, who for the most part work as economists, or finance or management specialists in business schools, have each set out to review the arguments and supporting evidence from the literature on their particular topic. In its coverage the book might be considered as complementary to texts such as J. Charkham, *Keeping Good Company* (Oxford, 1994), N. Dimsdale and M. Prevezer (eds.), *Capital Markets and Corporate Governance* (Oxford, 1994), J. E. Parkinson, *Corporate Power and Responsibility* (Oxford, 1993), D. Prentice and R. Holland (eds.), *Corporate Governance* (Oxford, 1993), and R. Monks and N. Minow, *Corporate Governance* (Oxford, 1995).

In compiling this volume we would like firstly to thank our co-authors for the timeliness and quality of their contributions which made our editorial task manageable. Authors of individual chapters make their own thanks to those who have provided comments on earlier drafts. Secretarial support from Margaret Burdett is acknowledged with thanks, as is financial support for the Centre for Management Buy-out Research from Deloitte and Touche Corporate Finance and BZW Private Equity. We would also like to thank David Musson of Oxford University Press for his encouragement, support, and forbearance throughout the project.

CONTENTS

LIST OF FIGURES

LIST OF TABLES

NOTES ON THE CONTRIBUTORS

LYNN ASHBURNER is a Lecturer in the Centre for Health Planning and Management at the University of Keele.

RICHARD BOSTOCK is a researcher in corporate governance in the Business School at Leeds Metropolitan University.

ALISTAIR BRUCE is Senior Lecturer in Industrial Economics in the School of Management and Finance at the University of Nottingham.

TREVOR BUCK is Senior Lecturer in Industrial Economics in the School of Management and Finance at the University of Nottingham.

PETER J. BUCKLEY is Professor of International Business in the School of Business and Economic Studies at the University of Leeds.

THOMAS CLARKE is Professor of Corporate Governance in the Business School at Leeds Metropolitan University.

MARTIN J. CONYON is a Research Fellow in the Centre for Corporate Strategy and Change of Warwick Business School at the University of Warwick.

MAHMOUD EZZAMEL is Professor of Accounting in the Department of Accounting and Finance at the University of Manchester.

IGOR FILATOTCHEV is Lecturer in the Economics of Transition of Central and Eastern Europe in the School of Management and Finance at the University of Nottingham.

ROBERT E. HOSKISSON is Professor of Management in the Department of Management, College of Business Administration and Graduate School of Business, Texas A & M University, College Station, Texas.

KEVIN KEASEY is the Leeds Permanent Building Society Professor of Financial Services and Director of the Centre for Financial Services in the School of Business and Economic Studies, University of Leeds.

HICHEON KIM is Assistant Professor of Management in the Department of Strategic Management and Public Policy, School of Business and Public Management, The George Washington University, Washington; and Assistant Professor in the College of Business and Economics, Han Yang University, Seoul.

STUART OGDEN is Professor of Management Accounting in the School of Business and Economic Studies at the University of Leeds.

PAULINE O'SULLIVAN is formerly Lecturer in Accounting in the School of Management and Finance at the University of Nottingham.

KEN ROBBIE is Senior Research Fellow and Deputy Director of the Centre for Management Buy-out Research, University of Nottingham.

HELEN SHORT is Lecturer in Accounting and Finance in the School of Business and Economic Studies, University of Leeds.

STEVE THOMPSON is Professor of Managerial Economics in the School of Management and Finance at the University of Nottingham.

ROBERT WATSON is Professor of Finance and Accounting in the School of Business and Economic Studies at the University of Leeds.

MIKE WRIGHT is Professor of Financial Studies and Director of the Centre for Management Buy-out Research in the School of Management and Finance at the University of Nottingham.

INTRODUCTION: THE CORPORATE GOVERNANCE PROBLEM— COMPETING DIAGNOSES AND SOLUTIONS

Kevin Keasey, Steve Thompson, and Mike Wright

The owner of a business, when contemplating any change, is led by his own interest to weigh the whole gain that it would probably bring to the business, against the whole loss. But the private interest of the salaried manager, or official, often draws him in another direction: the path of least resistance, of greatest comfort and least risk to himself, is generally that of not striving very energetically for improvement; and of finding plausible excuses for not trying an improvement suggested by others, until its success is established beyond question.

(Alfred Marshall, *Industry and Trade*)

1. Introduction

Corporate governance has become a focus of attention because of widely articulated concerns that the contemporary monitoring and control of publicly held corporations in the UK and USA is seriously defective. These concerns are frequently coupled with unfavourable comparisons of Anglo-American economic and social development with that obtaining elsewhere in Europe and in Japan, with the implicit or even explicit conclusion that the adoption of, say, German or Japanese governance structures would deliver superior national performance. In turn the defenders of the Anglo-American corporate form object that such reforms would, in practice, weaken the market discipline upon senior managers leading to a diversion of resources into unprofitable uses and to outcomes which are the opposite of those the reformers intend. Therefore the subject of corporate governance has become a keenly contested debate. The participants in this debate draw their arguments from very different analyses of the nature and purposes of the modern quoted corporation. Such disagreements cover positive issues concerning how institutions *actually* work and normative ones such as what *should* be the firm's purpose?

In this chapter we take the view that to make sense of the corporate governance debate it is necessary to consider the principal analytical backgrounds or approaches from which the participants begin. This is so because, as will be seen, much of the extensive discussion in the literature of the effectiveness of particular institutional devices takes place without agreement on how those arrangements ought to function.

2. Competing Diagnoses and Solutions

The term 'corporate governance', although now commonplace, was rarely encountered before the 1990s. Unfortunately, its subsequent rapid adoption has not been accompanied by consistent usage. Different writers vary widely in where they draw the boundaries of the subject. In its narrowest sense, the term may describe the formal system of accountability of senior management to the shareholders. At its most expansive the term is stretched to include the entire network of formal and informal relations involving the corporate sector and their consequences for society in general. For the purposes of this volume we define corporate governance to include 'the structures, process, cultures and systems that engender the successful operation of the organisations' (Keasey and Wright 1993).

The absence of any real consensus on the definition of 'corporate governance' in the rapidly growing literature on the subject is symptomatic of the whole debate on governance reform. It is a debate in which the participants have entirely different analyses of the problem and therefore offer markedly different solutions. Fundamental disagreements cover key questions: for example, does the effectiveness of a firm's governance arrangements have implications which go beyond those for its shareholders and, if so, does this justify public policy intervention? Should any such intervention be concerned with distributional issues as well as those of efficiency? What is the nature of the shareholder's ownership claim? And what, if any, restrictions should be placed upon the shareholder's contractual freedom, as a resource owner, to maximize his financial reward from such resources?

The underlying problem of corporate governance as recognized by a long tradition of scholars stretching back from the present day via Berle and Means (1932) and Marshall (1920) to Adam Smith (1776) lies with the separation of beneficial ownership and executive decision-making in the joint-stock company. All analysts agree that such a separation allows—if it does not actually encourage—the firm's behaviour to diverge from the profit-maximizing, cost-minimizing ideal. However, the corporation's theorists disagree profoundly on the significance of this separation. To illustrate this we will summarize four competing perspectives, using a typology loosely adapted from Blair (1995), each with its own diagnosis of the faults in the Anglo-American governance model and each with its own prescription for improvement.

The Principal–Agent, or Finance, Model

The principal–agent, or finance, model is the dominant academic view of the corporation and is perhaps most clearly articulated by Hart (1995a,b). It rests on the premises that markets—particularly the markets for capital, managerial labour, and corporate control—provide the most effective restraints on managerial discretion, and that the residual voting rights of shareholders should ultimately commit corporate resources to value-maximizing ends. It sees a firm's existing corporate governance arrangements as the outcome of a bargaining process which has been freely entered into by corporate insiders and outsiders. It therefore tends to oppose any *ex post* external interventions as at best unhelpful and at worst distortionary. This model recognizes that monitoring and bonding expenditures paid out to align the behaviour of the manager-agents with the interests of owner-principals represent costs to the economic system. However, rather than justifying public intervention, it suggests that such costs provide the incentive for innovations in corporate governance. Thus recent developments in the managerial labour market, such as executive stock options, and the market for corporate control, e.g. leveraged and management buy-outs (Thompson and Wright 1995), are seen as *responses* to institutional deficiencies.

The principal–agent, or finance, model of the corporation starts from the position that in the absence of explicit impediments—most obviously monopoly power or negative externalities—profit-maximizing behaviour by firms is a sufficient condition for (Paretian) social welfare maximization. The separation of ownership and control is important inasmuch as it may allow managers to deviate from shareholder value—i.e. profit—maximization. However, such behaviour is widely predicted and, following Jensen and Meckling (1976), is expected to be fully anticipated when an owner-manager sells equity to outsiders. Therefore the owner bears the full cost of equity dilution. That he or she decides to proceed *despite* this fall in value suggests that the benefits of flotation—i.e. wealth diversification and/or the gains from professionalizing the management function (Fama and Jensen 1983a,b)—are sufficient to outweigh the costs of any separation of ownership from control. This *ex ante* anticipation and evaluation of the agency relationship is important to the argument. It suggests to supporters of the principal–agent model that the imposition of additional obligations on the corporate board—for example, to employees as 'stakeholders'—would simply discourage the original owners from taking on outside equity holders.

In the principal–agent, or finance, model the basic institutions of corporate governance—a board accountable to shareholders, elected non-executive directors, independent auditors, etc.—may be considered to be products of this initial sale of external equity. That is, by committing future managers to particular monitoring and accountability procedures the original owner-manager is able to increase the marketability of claims to the firm's future profits and hence maximize the sale price of the equity issue. In the typical publicly quoted Anglo-American corporation the role for individual shareholder *voice* is strictly limited. The access to liquid stock markets gives the shareholder virtually unrestricted, low-cost *exit* opportunities. Therefore given the high costs associated with collective action by shareholders—particularly among dispersed small shareholders—exit dominates voice.

Notwithstanding the limited role for shareholder voice in the finance model, one important source of power is seen as remaining with shareholders—namely the right to vote. Easterbrook and Fischel (1983) have pointed out that despite widespread criticisms of the actual level of shareholder participation, equity claims almost invariably come with voting rights. Furthermore, in the United States and United Kingdom—although not necessarily in continental Europe—there is general adoption of a one-share–one-vote decision rule. Easterbrook and Fischel and others have argued that it is the equity owners' position as residual claimants that explains why they alone enjoy voting rights in typical Anglo-American firms. Since their interest in the firm is anonymous and limited to the residual itself, the equity holders have an unbiased interest in value maximization. However, should the firm experience financial difficulties, which would leave equity investments exposed, the shareholders might develop incentives to back high-risk strategies. In such circumstances other groups of factor suppliers, most obviously preference shareholders and/or debtholders, may receive voting rights.

Of the several issues upon which shareholders might vote, most discussion has centred upon just one, namely the right to vote on takeover approaches. Since Manne (1965), the market for corporate control hypothesis has held that the shareholders' ability to vote control to that managerial team which offers the most for residual claims represents the single most important constraint on managerial behaviour. Hart (1995*b*) has shown how a one-share–one-vote rule offers equity holders the best opportunity to avoid minority shareholder coercion and to secure maximum gains from the takeover process, under normal circumstances.

Supporters of the finance model acknowledge that corporate governance failings occur, but argue that these are best addressed by removing restrictions on factor markets—see Fama (1980)—and the market in corporate control. For example, Jensen (1986) has argued persuasively that diffusely owned firms located in profitable but low-growth markets frequently lack worthwhile reinvestment opportunities. Jensen suggests that rather than pay out this 'free cash flow' as extra dividends to their shareholders, these firms may engage in unprofitable expenditures, particularly upon preferred diversifications and R & D. To Jensen (1989), the debt-financed takeovers and leveraged buy-outs of the late 1980s represented a response to this problem which functioned primarily by committing the firm's cash flow in advance to meet high levels of debt interest, thus reducing the agent's discretion to harm the principal's interests.

Whilst supporters of the principal–agent, financial, model do not dismiss the possibilities of shareholder gains via improved corporate governance arrangements and many would endorse the introduction of a voluntary code such as Cadbury, they tend to be suspicious of legislative changes which impose costs or obligations upon either the firms themselves or their major shareholders. In general it is argued that if it is possible to introduce some governance improvement which will raise the profits and hence the value of the firm, it will be adopted without compulsion. Many studies exist within the financial literature which have tried to estimate the shareholder wealth effects of the introduction of such governance devices as golden parachutes, executives' share options, non-executives' director appointments, etc. (Brickley *et al.* 1985; Lambert and Larcker 1985*a,b*).

Attempts to encourage relationship investor behaviour by *imposing* obligations or restrictions upon institutional investors are also viewed with concern from the principal–agent position. First, anything which locks the investors into long-term positions may damage the market's liquidity. Second, encouraging a greater involvement by institutional shareholders is sometimes seen as an encouragement to insider dealing, which is illegal and widely—but not universally—seen as a threat to outsider participation. Finally, as indicated above, when all such impositions are evaluated *ex ante*, the introduction of extra shareholder costs will depress the flotation price to the detriment of new owners seeking outside equity.

The Myopic Market Model

Many of the sternest critics (e.g. Charkham 1994; Sykes 1994) of the Anglo-American model of corporate governance argue that it is fundamentally flawed by an excessive concern with the short term, which is itself a consequence of capital market failure (see Blair 1995 for a more detailed discussion of this critique). Those holding such a view do not necessarily dissent from the principal–agent position that the *purpose* of the joint-stock company is to maximize the well-being of its shareholders, although many would endorse a rather wider maximand. However, the myopic market school contends that a goal such as shareholder welfare is not synonymous with share price maximization because the market systematically undervalues certain long-term expenditures—particularly capital investment and R & D spending. Therefore the market's myopia forces otherwise diligent managers into taking decisions with regard to the current share price, or else risk a heightened threat of hostile takeover. It follows that supporters of the myopic market view see the challenge of corporate governance reform as one of providing an environment in which shareholders and managers are encouraged to share long-term performance horizons.

There are a number of complementary strands to the myopic market argument; not all of which are endorsed by individual supporters of the approach. These strands may be considered in turn:

1. It has been argued—especially in the USA in the 1980s (McCauley and Zimmer 1989)—that the cost of capital is simply too high, certainly by comparison with the bank-based systems of Germany and Japan. A higher cost of capital necessarily means that rational managers in London or New York would reject projects considered acceptable in Tokyo or Frankfurt. However, the globalization of capital markets implies that such differences should disappear through arbitrage unless maintained by institutional restrictions or via macroeconomic factors, such as variations in the level of real interest rates. The cost of capital argument appears to have become less important in the 1990s, with some convergence of real interest rates between the economies (see Blair 1995).

2. Irrespective of the 'true' cost of capital, some argue that financial accounting practices within the firm give rise to unnecessarily high rate of return requirements or, alternatively, unrealistically short pay-back periods (Sykes 1994). This is sometimes attributed to an executive labour market which rewards and appoints on the basis of short-term performance. It has also been linked to the meagre managerial role of scientists and engineers in US and UK companies, certainly by comparison with Japan and Germany, and the correspondingly greater power of accountants.

3. The previous argument is usually supported by the view that the stock market is overly concerned with short-term performance. Share trading is dominated by institutional fund managers, whose own investment performance is judged on a relatively short-term horizon. Therefore it is suggested that the market is over-concerned with earnings data and short-term forecasts. (Of course, precisely because the market is dominated by institutions, the argument has the unfortunate corollary that the 'successful' fund manager who sells on an over-priced share—i.e. a share whose long-term earnings potential is lower than that implied by its current price—is generally doing so to another fund manager, whose performance will suffer in the future through his or her lack of foresight.)

4. It is argued that the stock market itself routinely misprices assets. It has been argued that stock markets experience fashions and fads (Shiller 1989). Furthermore, it is widely suggested that major market changes—such as the October 1987 Wall Street collapse—occur without any correspondingly proportionate changes in underlying fundamentals. (For a review of the evidence, see Copeland 1989.)

5. It has already been noted that the hostile takeover plays an important role in the Anglo-American model, but not elsewhere. However, if the company's share price is no longer seen as a useful—or even unbiased—indicator of fundamentals, the market for corporate control ceases to be an efficient natural selection mechanism. The transfer of assets from the control of managers of an underpriced company may or may not improve the effectiveness of their deployment. Instead there is a danger that the *threat* of hostile takeover becomes both a distortion and a distraction from the true task of value creation.

Support for the myopic position leads proponents to advocate reforms that would increase shareholder loyalty and voice, and correspondingly reduce the ease of shareholder exit. Policy prescriptions frequently include the encouragement of 'relationship investing' by seeking to lock institutions into long-term positions, restrictions on voting rights for short-term shareholders, and the empowerment of offer groups—employees, suppliers, etc.—presumed to have long-term relationships with the firm. These may be supplemented by restrictions on the takeover process.

The difficulty for corporate governance reforms is that the above changes are precisely those which are seen as most damaging by the principal–agent school. On the latter view the proposals raise the costs of shareholder exit and hence make the owners more vulnerable to managerial self-serving. Similarly, they impede the takeover process and so further weaken the sanction against such behaviour. Gibbs (1993) and Markides (1995), for example, provide evidence which suggests that the threat of takeover is associated with corporate restructuring attempts.

To resolve these difficulties it is necessary to ask whether the empirical evidence supports the notion of market myopia. Certainly comparisons of the costs of corporate capital in the 1980s suggested that Germany and Japan probably enjoyed an advantage (e.g. McCauley and Zimmer 1989). However, such results are largely driven by the levels of real interest rates, which are themselves determined by fiscal and monetary factors rather than governance ones. Furthermore, as indicated, they appear to have become less important as real interest rates have converged in the 1990s (see Blair 1995 for a review) and may be expected to become irrelevant with the globalization of international capital markets (Kester and Luehrman 1992). Studies which have addressed the market's own hypothesized dislike of long-term spending have usually produced little supportive evidence (see Marsh 1994 for a review). Such work, which has generally adopted an event study design and examined the impact of capital investment or R & D spending announcements on share prices (e.g. McConnell and Muscarella 1985; Woolridge 1988), reports no general allergic reaction to R & D spending (Woolridge 1988) but suggests that the market's response depends critically on the apparent technological potential of the industry concerned (Chan *et al.* 1990).

The Abuse of Executive Power

A section of the participants to the corporate governance debate—and one by no means restricted to the popular press—hold to the view that the principal problem rests in the abuse of power by corporate élites. The basic argument is that the status quo leaves excess power in the hands of senior management, some of whom abuse this in the service of their own self-interest (see e.g. Hutton 1995). The result is damaging for shareholders, for the industrial system, and for society as a whole. Supporters of such a view suggest that the current institutional restraints on managerial behaviour—as provided by elected non-executive directors, the audit process, the threat of takeover, etc.—are simply inadequate to prevent corporate assets from being used in ways dictated by the managerial interest. Shareholders, protected by liquid assets markets and largely operating as managers of other people's money, can afford to be uninterested in all but the most substantial abuses. Even devices such as share options, which the principal–agent school views as a means of aligning shareholder well-being and manager behaviour, are interpreted as symptoms of the breakdown of governance—a means through which managers can legitimize abnormal inflation of their own remuneration.

Kay and Silberston (1995) explicitly reject the principal–agent analysis as a realistic description of the control process in modern corporations. They argue that most quoted companies are effectively dominated by a board which functions as a self-perpetuating oligarchy. They dismiss the existing governance arrangements as inadequate, and liken senior management to the governing élite of a political dictatorship. They suggest that we should not be surprised if self-serving behaviour—and even corruption—are encouraged in such an environment. Others, including Hutton (1995), suggest that the emphasis on enterprise culture or unrestrained free markets since the 1980s may have exacerbated this problem by weakening traditional ethical constraints.

The debate over executive pay has become a particular focus of interest. The publication of research suggesting that senior executive remuneration has risen sharply by comparison with average earnings is less damaging than the apparent failure to find any robust pay–performance relationship. (See e.g. Gregg *et al.* 1993; Conyon *et al.* 1995; although it is debatable how far the literature has adjusted for the role of executive share options—see Chapter 4, by Bruce and Buck, in this volume.) This fuels the suspicion that senior management have written themselves contracts in the form of an each-way bet: remuneration rises by options gains if the share price grows and by other means if it doesn't. Or, as Kay and Silberston (1995) express it: 'the only restraint on executive pay and perks appears to be the modesty of executives themselves, and that is a commodity in increasingly short supply' (p. 85).

Those believing that Anglo-American industry suffers from the abuse of executive power argue for statutory changes in governance. Kay and Silberston, for example, propose a series of changes designed to weaken what they see as the entrenched position of the senior corporate élite. These include fixed four-year terms for chief executive officers, independent nomination of non-executive directors, greater powers for non-executive directors, etc.

The Stakeholder Model

The most fundamental challenge to the principal–agent approach comes from supporters of the stakeholder model of the firm. This view is presented in numerous ways: sometimes as a descriptive theory, sometimes as an instrumental or predictive one, and often as a normative theory (Jones 1995). However, the central proposition at the heart of the stakeholder approach is that the purpose—the objective function—of the firm should be defined more widely than the maximization of shareholder welfare alone. In particular it holds that there should be some explicit recognition of the well-being of other groups having a long-term association with the firm—and therefore an interest, or 'stake', in its long-term success. These groups are usually taken to include suppliers, customers, and, particularly, employees. Whilst issues of distribution and efficiency interact in the stakeholder literature—and are sometimes treated very loosely in its more popular presentations—it is also a central plank of the stakeholder model that a wider objective function is not merely more equitable but also more socially efficient than one confined to shareholder wealth.

The efficiency case for the stakeholder model has been developed in two principal ways. First, it has been demonstrated that many firms which develop a reputation for the ethical treatment of suppliers, clients, and employees are able to build up trust relations which support profitable investments and mutually beneficial exchanges; and second, proponents of the stakeholder view have pointed to Japan and Germany—both economies with extensive stakeholder involvement with the firm and where corporate goals are typically defined fairly widely—as examples of successful industrial societies which reject the principal–agent model. More recently, Blair (1995) and Acs *et al.* (1996) have developed a generalized case for stakeholder involvement based on the appropriability problems associated with co-specialized assets. This approach subsumes the previous arguments as particularly institutional solutions to a general problem.

It has long been recognized that ethical behaviour reduces the costs of social association. Arrow (1972), for example, describes truth-telling as a public good: lying may produce individual gain but, if prevalent, it raises the costs of information-gathering for all. More specifically, economic relationships typically have a co-operative game or prisoner's dilemma characteristic: full co-operation maximizing the participants' joint pay-off but 'cheating'—i.e. exploiting any contractual incompleteness to one's own advantage—remaining the dominant strategy in a one-shot game. Firms which build a reputation for ethical collaborations over a long period are able to substitute co-operative outcomes for unsatisfactory cheating ones. These relationships—the internal and external 'contractual architecture' of the firm, to use Kay's (1994) terminology—may be the source of considerable competitive advantage (Jones 1995). Furthermore, firms which have established such a reputation (for example, Sainsbury's, Marks & Spencer, or Boots) will enjoy an advantage in attracting new trading partners—whether as customers, suppliers, or employees—precisely because the latter know that the former can be expected to maintain their reputations.

It appears to us that there is nothing in the preceding paragraph which is at all in conflict with the principal–agent model. Indeed, Hill and Jones (1992) provide an initial attempt at developing a stakeholder-agency theory. If ethical behaviour is the strategy that maximizes long-term profits, then shareholder-principals should encourage their manager-agents to practise it. (A more interesting ethical issue for shareholders occurs in industries, generally characterized by unrepeated opportunities, where cheating is the most profitable strategy.) However, if rational, self-interested behaviour involves ethical contracting we have no need of the stakeholder model. To sustain the latter it is necessary to argue that more tangible associations between the firm, its trading partners, and its employees are necessary to build the trust relationships and permit long-term contractual associations. These are next examined in the Japanese and German cases.

In each of the German and Japanese cases there appears to be agreement among commentators (e.g. Charkham 1994; Schneider-Lenne 1992) that corporate goals are defined more widely than shareholders profits. Charkham, for example, suggests that German companies are under a social obligation to employees and the local community (p. 10) whilst Japanese firms are particularly concerned with size and market share (p. 73). In both countries the corporation is viewed as an enduring social organization. (This view is a more sustainable position in countries where mergers are relatively few and hostile acquisitions are almost unknown.) In both countries suppliers and major customers may be linked to the firm via interlocking shareholdings and cross-directorates. In Japan these associations are familiar within major industrial groups or keiretsu (Acs *et al.* 1996) which also encourage the exchange of technical information and specialist personnel. In both countries the banks play a much closer role in financing expenditure and in its governance of the firm (Corbet 1994; Prevezer and Ricketts 1994).

Finally, in both Germany and Japan the interests of labour receive particular safeguards in decision-making. The German co-determination system involves workers as participants in works councils. It also requires, at least for firms employing 20,000 or more, that employees enjoy 50 per cent representation on the supervising board of directors (*Aufsichtsrat*), a body which in turn nominates the members of the managerial board (*Vorstand*). Japanese workers, at least those in the larger-firm sector, enjoy the traditional lifetime employment guarantee. They face promotion opportunities in what remains a strictly internal labour market. Furthermore, they share some of the demand fluctuation risk with shareholders through a remuneration system which contains a large annual bonus element.

In short, whilst the German and Japanese systems display many differences, they share the characteristic that decisions are traditionally made under the assumption that employees' interests will be safeguarded. In this regard they differ strongly from the Anglo-American model, where strategic decisions are frequently made to cut labour costs. For example, hostile mergers are typically followed by cuts in wages and/or non-pecuniary benefits (Shleifer and Summers 1988) and often accompanied by white-collar job losses (Bhagat *et al.* 1990).

Blair (1995) has recently argued that within the nexus of contracts that constitutes the firm the most important will typically involve co-specialized investments. Thus a typical supplier–user relationship might involve the development of specific physical capital and human and organizational skills. It is well recognized in the literature that such assets generate quasi-rents but also give rise to a potential hold-up problem—i.e. participants may be tempted to engage in an opportunistic post-contractual ploy to secure an increased share of the quasi-rent (Klein *et al.* 1978). A whole literature has grown up in the vertical integration or vertical contracting fields which examines how these problems are overcome. In a corporate governance context, inter-firm relations involving investment in co-specialized assets may be regularized by interlocking shareholdings and directorates, and strategic alliances. Thus in part the German (and much of the continental European) and Japanese systems can be interpreted as facilitating inter-firm co-operation. In the UK and USA such associations are far less common and—in the USA at least—may even be unlawful under certain circumstances.

Cultural and antitrust difficulties aside, the above governance arrangements can be used, in principle, to administer inter-firm relations involving co-specialized assets. Much greater difficulties attach to labour. As Blair (1995) points out, job-specific human capital is also a co-specialized asset. Furthermore, it gives rise to important quasi-rent streams within the firm leading, amongst other things, to big insider–outsider wage differentials. In modern labour economics efficiency wages and seniority wage profiles are interpreted as ways of encouraging the recruitment and retention of workers where job-specific skills matter. However, employees enjoying wages above the opportunity cost—i.e. the next best employment—for their labour also face a risk. In the Anglo-American corporate environment their specific human capital investments do not figure in the firm's decision-making.

Blair (1995) and Acs *et al.* (1996) argue that this failure to represent the employees' interests can lead to an under-investment in job- and firm-specific skills. They argue that in their separate ways the Japanese (via lifetime employment and consensus-based decision-making) and the Germans (via co-determination) encourage the acquisition of firm- and job-specific skills. This, they suggest, is reflected in high labour productivity—particularly in quality-adjusted labour productivity, an outcome which is reflected in Germany's competitive advantage in high-quality manufacturing.

3. Discriminating between the Competing Hypotheses: The Structure of this Book

The validity of each of the competing schools of thought on corporate governance depends ultimately upon the supporting empirical evidence. Moreover, as hinted earlier, while aspects of each school may be viewed as competing, they also contain elements of complementarity. In reviewing the economic and financial evidence, the chapters in this book draw on both quantitative and qualitative approaches to shed light on the contribution of these schools of thought to various aspects of corporate governance.

Primarily using Anglo-American evidence, the first half of the book (Chapters 2–7) examines the contribution of both 'voice' and 'exit' aspects of governance, concerning in particular the roles of institutional shareholders and non-executive directors, the links between executive remuneration and performance, the role of the market for corporate control, and new developments such as leveraged buy-outs which combine voice and exit mechanisms. The second half of the book looks at corporate governance in particular contexts, notably international dimensions and particular organizations.

Chapters 2 and 3 examine two sets of actors whose roles have received increasing attention in the corporate governance debate. In Chapter 2, Short and Keasey address the abilities and incentives of institutional shareholders to enhance governance in larger publicly quoted companies. Both the Cadbury and the Greenbury reports have suggested that institutional shareholders have an important role to play in ensuring that companies adhere to certain principles of corporate governance as laid down by the respective reports. This chapter identifies the objectives of institutions with respect to their ownership and investment behaviour, examines their incentives in terms of monitoring management behaviour, and considers whether incentives can be altered such that a more proactive corporate governance role can be achieved. The chapter concludes that institutional shareholders have few incentives to alter fundamentally their investment and ownership behaviour within the current financial market environment.

In Chapter 3, Ezzamel and Watson highlight the conflicting control and management roles of non-executive directors and the consequent implications for corporate governance. By failing to resolve these conflicting requirements, they argue that the Cadbury proposals did little or nothing to improve the independence or incentives for non-executive directors to take seriously their monitoring duties. They argue that if the Cadbury Committee proposals regarding the greater roles of non-executive directors are to have credibility with stakeholders, to whom both theory and law suggest they have a responsibility, a more fundamental reform of the process of their nomination, appointment, and performance evaluation is necessary.

Chapters 4 and 5 address the highly controversial area of executive remuneration. First, Bruce and Buck, in Chapter 4, review the available literature, focusing in particular on the links between remuneration and performance. They highlight the need to identify appropriate measures of remuneration and show that much of the evidence concerning a weak pay–performance link may be attributable to a failure to take fully into account the variable element in remuneration packages. They provide evidence that when executive stock options are included as part of the measure of remuneration, the relationship with performance is strengthened significantly. Second, Conyon, in Chapter 5, provides a complementary analysis of the institutional arrangements for setting directors' compensation. He shows marked evidence of increasing compliance with best practice as set out in the Cadbury Code, especially in relation to the usage of remuneration committees to decide executive pay and nominations committees to select non-executive directors. However, he also finds that chief executives play a major role in remuneration committees that determine their own pay. Conyon points out that the available evidence derived primarily from survey data conceals the richer and highly important processes by which boards operate, arguing that there is a need for further case-study research of the behavioural dynamics within the board of directors.

Chapters 6 and 7 focus on developments, especially relevant in Anglo-American systems, of the governance role of the market for corporate control. In Chapter 6, O'Sullivan examines the evidence concerning the market for corporate control in terms of evidence relating to traditional takeovers and more recent studies which address such areas as dual class recapitalizations, the effects of takeover defences, and failed takeover bids. Her review of the empirical evidence shows that governance by exit does not confer clear benefits to shareholders. Apart from the potential problems of managerial short-termism and infringement of contractual relations, the adoption of defensive tactics can entrench management and make takeovers an expensive mechanism to execute. She argues, however, that suggestions to impede the functioning of the market for corporate control may have a detrimental effect on the process of corporate governance. Takeovers, for example, can play a vital role in compelling reluctant managers to exit from industries with excess capacity arising from changing technological or market conditions. She stresses that governance by voice and by exit are complementary devices, pointing out that an important aspect of the future role of the market for corporate control is likely to be its interaction with the adoption of new forms of internal governance such as suggested by the Cadbury Report.

The problem of governance involving investor voice in a system where the threat of exit plays an important role has to some extent been addressed by the development of new organizational forms, predominantly leveraged and management buy-outs. Wright, Thompson, and Robbie consider the contribution of the governance mechanisms in such organizations in Chapter 7. They show that buy-outs involve governance mechanisms which include a combination of direct and significant managerial equity ownership, active investor participation by venture capitalists and other financial institutions, and high leverage. The commitment to service high levels of debt bonds management to perform to predetermined levels. They provide evidence of significant performance improvements following buy-outs and highlight the crucially greater importance of insider equity ownership rather than debt bonding in generating post-buy-out gains.

Chapters 8 to 11 provide international dimensions to the corporate governance debate. An important issue is the effectiveness of internal organizational structures and processes which may vary between systems, and these are addressed in Chapters 8 and 9. Kim and Hoskisson compare financial governance systems and managerial labour market differences among US and Japanese firms employing multi-divisional (M-form) structures. They argue that US governance structures are market-oriented while Japan's are management-oriented, and suggest that this difference creates an advantage in monitoring costs among Japanese in comparison to US M-form firms. This, they contend, is primarily due to low ownership concentration and ineffective internal governance structures in the USA. The lack of strong internal governance mechanisms in the USA creates the need for external governance mechanisms, but these also lead to potential over-diversification of acquiring firms. In Japan, in contrast, the market for corporate control as a governance tool for M-form firms is largely unnecessary because of financial institutional involvement and a collective orientation associated with internal governance mechanisms. The chapter also concludes that Japanese M-form firms have advantages for retaining talented managerial resources over smaller U-form firms. However, because of managerial labour market differences, US M-form firms would have difficulties in retaining high-performing middle managers, who are likely to move to smaller U-form firms. This dilutes the managerial talent pool in US M-forms relative to Japanese M-forms. These governance and managerial labour market differences are expected to have an impact on the performance of corporate diversification strategy and M-form organization.

Buckley, in Chapter 9, examines the governance problems faced by multinational enterprises operating in several countries by analysing the nature of costs involved in such instances. Of the four costs involved in managing internal markets, that is the resource costs of managing internal markets, communications costs, management costs, and potential discrimination against foreign owned firms, only the last is specifically international. He argues that although there are undoubtedly learning effects which reduce the cost of cross-border governance over time and in repeated international ventures, it is not possible to claim that the costs of such governance will ever fall to zero.

Major corporate governance issues are raised as part of the transition to a market system of the economies of Central and Eastern Europe. As Wright, Filatotchev, and Buck show in Chapter 10, the act of transferring ownership of assets from the public to the private sector does not of itself establish the conditions for enhanced corporate governance, which in turn will generate greater enterprise efficiency. Problems arise partly because of the conflicting objectives of privatization, especially where political and social justice arguments have often meant that ownership of assets is transferred 'free' to incumbents through voucher schemes without the introduction of other outside governance mechanisms being established. In addition, undeveloped institutional and legal frameworks may mean that important necessary conditions for effective corporate governance, such as bankruptcy codes, effective financial institutions, etc., are absent. Wright, Filatotchev, and Buck, in examining the differing approaches adopted in Central and Eastern Europe, emphasize the importance of taking a life-cycle view of the development of corporate governance in enterprise in these countries.

In the final of the four chapters dealing with international aspects of corporate governance, Chapter 11, Clarke and Bostock examine the changing parameters of the governance system of German enterprises. They argue that although the German system of corporate governance with its supervisory board, industrial groupings, implicit contracting and extensive cross-shareholdings is in many ways superior to the Anglo-American system, it has some inherent problems. In particular, the Germanic system ignores the interests of small shareholders, is over-secretive and lacking in information and transparency, and is especially ill-designed to cope with the pressures of international investment or the global market for companies.

The last two chapters address corporate governance issues in organizations which until quite recently were subject to traditional public sector administration, but where greater openness to market forces has been associated with major changes in corporate governance. Ogden, in Chapter 12, examines corporate governance in privatized utilities, focusing in particular on the problem of executive remuneration in the water industry. He argues that despite considerable public criticism of the remuneration of senior executives in the industry, it is misleading to think of their behaviour as simply opportunistic. Ogden demonstrates that there are three important areas of managerial discretion whereby the activities and decisions of senior executives can have considerable effects on corporate profitability: relations with the regulator, improving internal efficiency, and diversification. Moreover, the publication of performance indicators required by the Regulator enhances scrutiny by analysts, which may mean that senior executives may be subject to greater active monitoring than those in many other firms in the private sector. When the extensive compliance with the Cadbury Code found in the industry is also taken into account, it is arguable that solutions to alleged problems with executive remuneration in the water industry need to be addressed through reform in general corporate governance arrangements rather than further specific regulatory intervention.

Ashburner, in Chapter 13, examines corporate governance in organizations remaining in the public sector, taking the National Health Service as a major case involving problems in the development of corporate governance. Ashburner examines how the private sector board model has been implemented in the NHS and finds that the regulations controlling the operation of NHS boards are far greater than those for the private sector. What emerges, she argues, is a hybrid form rather than a direct transfer from the private sector. A major issue is that the notion in the public sector that boards are either democratically accountable or managerially effective needs to be challenged if their development is not to be limited by narrow thinking. She identifies an opportunity for the emergent hybrid form to integrate both of these requirements.

REFERENCES

Acs, Z., Gerlowski, D. A., and FitzRoy, F. R. (1996), 'Ownership and Control', University of St Andrews mimeo.

Arrow, K. (1972), *The Limits of Organization* (New York: Norton).

Berle, A., and Means, G. (1932), *The Modern Corporation and Private Property* (New York: Commerce Clearing House).

Bhagat, S., Shleifer, A., and Vishny, R. (1990), 'The Hostile Takeovers in the 1980s: The Return to Corporate Specialization', *Brookings Papers on Economic Activity: Microeconomics*, 1–72.

Blair, M. (1995), *Ownership and Control: Rethinking Corporate Governance for the Twenty-First Century* (Washington: Brookings Institution).

Brickley, J., Bhagat, S., and Lease, R. C. (1985), 'The Impact of Long-Range Compensation Plans on Shareholder Wealth', *Journal of Accounting and Economics*, 7: 115–50.

Charkham, J. (1994), *Keeping Good Company: A Study of Corporate Governance in Five Countries* (Oxford: Oxford University Press).

Chan, S., Martin, J. D., and Kensinger, J. W. (1990), 'Corporate Research and Development Expenditures and Share Value', *Journal of Financial Economics*, 26: 255–76.

Conyon, M., Gregg, P., and Machin, S. (1995), 'Taking Care of Business: Executive Compensation in the UK', *Economic Journal*, 105: 704–14.

Copeland, L. (1989), 'Market Efficiency before and after the Crash', *Fiscal Studies*, 3: 12–23.

Corbett, J. (1994), 'An Overview of the Japanese Financial System', in Dimsdale and Prevezer (1994).

Easterbrook, F. H., and Fischel, D. R. (1983), 'Voting in Corporate Law', *Journal of Law and Economics*, 26: 395–427.

Fama, E. (1980), 'Agency Problems and the Theory of the Firm', *Journal of Political Economy*, 88: 288–307.

—— and Jensen, M. C. (1983a), 'Separation of Ownership and Control', *Journal of Law and Economics*, 26: 301–26.

—— —— (1983b), 'Agency Problems and Residual Clamis', *Journal of Law and Economics*, 26: 327–52.

Gibbs, P. (1993), 'Determinants of Corporate Restructuring: The Relative Impact of Corporate Governance, Takeover Threat and Free Cash Flow', *Strategic Management Journal*, 14(S): 51–68.

Gregg, P., Machin, S., and Syzmanski, S. (1993), 'The Disappearing Relationship between Directors' Pay and Corporate Performance', *British Jouranl of Industrial Relations*, 31: 1–10.

Hart, O. D. (1995a), *Firms, Contracts and Financial Structure* (Oxford: Clarendon Press).

—— (1995b), 'Corporate Governance: Some Theory and Implications', *Economic Journal*, 105: 678–89.

Hill, C. W. L., and Jones, T. M. (1992), 'Stakeholder-Agency Theory', *Journal of Management Studies*, 29: 131–54.

Hutton, W. (1995), *The State We're In* (London: Cape).

Jensen, M. C. (1986), 'Agency Costs of Free Cash Flow, Corporate Finance and Takeovers', *American Economic Review*, 76: 323–9.

—— (1989), 'The Eclipse of the Public Corporation', *Harvard Business Review* (Sept.–Oct.), 61–74.

—— and Meckling, W. (1976), 'The Theory of the Firm: Managerial Behavior, Agency Costs and Ownership Structure', *Journal of Financial Economics*, 3: 305–60.

Jones, T. M. (1995), 'Instrumental Stakeholder Theory: A Synthesis of Ethics and Economics', *Academy of Management Review*, 20: 404–37.

Kay, J. (1994), *Foundations of Corporate Success* (Oxford: Oxford University Press).

—— and Silberston, A. (1995), 'Corporate Governance', *National Institute Economic Review*, 84 (Aug.), 84–97.

Keasey, K., and Wright, M. (1993), 'Issues in Corporate Accountability and Governance', *Accounting and Business Research*, 91a: 291–303.

Kester, W. C., and Luehrman, T. A. (1992), 'What Makes you think that US Capital is so Expensive?', *Journal of Applied Corporate Finance*, 5: 29–41.

Klein, B., Crawford, R. G., and Alchian, A. A. (1978), 'Vertical Integration, Appropriate Rents and Competitive Contracting Process', *Journal of Law and Economics*, 21: 297.

Lambert, R., and Larcker, D. (1985a), 'Executive Compensation, Corporate Decision-

Making and Shareholder Wealth: A Review of the Evidence', *Midland Corporate Finance Journal*, 2: 6–22.

—— —— (1985*b*), 'Golden Parachutes, Executive Decision Making and Shareholder Wealth', *Journal of Accounting and Economics*, 7: 179–204.

McCauley, R. N., and Zimmer, S. A. (1989), 'Explaining International Differences in the Cost of Capital', *Federal Reserve Bank of New York Quarterly Review*, 14: 7–28.

McConnell, J. J., and Muscarella, C. (1985), 'Corporate Capital Expenditure Decisions and the Market Value of the Firm', *Journal of Financial Economics*, 14: 399–422.

Manne, H. G. (1965), 'Mergers and the Market for Corporate Control', *Journal of Political Economy*, 73: 110–20.

Markides, C. (1995), 'Diversification, Restructuring and Economic Performance', *Strategic Management Journal*, 16/2: 101–18.

Marsh, P. (1994), *Market Assessment of Company Performance*, in Dimsdale and Prevezer (1994).

Marshall, A. (1920), *Industry and Trade* (London: Macmillan).

Prevezer, M., and Ricketts, M. (1994), 'Corporate Governance: The UK Compared with Germany and Japan', in Dimsdale and Prevezer (1994).

Schneider-Lenne, L. (1992), 'Corporate Control in Germany', *Oxford Review of Economic Policy*, 8: 11–23.

Shiller, R. J. (ed.) (1989), *Market Volatility* (Cambridge, Mass.: MIT Press).

Shleifer, A., and Summers, L. (1988), 'Breach of Trust in Hostile Takeovers', in A. Auerbach (ed.), *Corporate Takeovers: Causes and Consequences* (Chicago: University of Chicago Press).

Smith, A. (1776), *An Inquiry into the Nature and Causes of Wealth of Nations* (repr. New York: Random House, 1937).

Sykes, A. (1994), 'Proposals for Internationally Competitive Corporate Governance in Britain and America', *Corporate Governance*, 2/4: 187–95.

Thompson, S., and Wright, M. (1995), 'Corporate Governance: The Role of Restructuring Transactions', *Economic Journal*, 105: 690–703.

Woolridge, J. R. (1988), 'Competitive Decline: Is a Myopic Stock Market to Blame?', *Journal of Applied Corporate Finance*, 1: 26–36.

2

INSTITUTIONAL SHAREHOLDERS AND CORPORATE GOVERNANCE IN THE UNITED KINGDOM

Helen Short and Kevin Keasey

1. Introduction

Within the general UK corporate governance debate, there is an increasing emphasis on the need for institutional shareholders to play an active role in the governance of companies. For example, the Cadbury Report (1992) notes that, 'Because of their collective stake, we look to the institutions in particular, with the backing of the Institutional Shareholders' Committee, to use their influence as owners to ensure that the companies in which they have invested comply with the Code' (para. 6.16). However, in many of the discussions of the need for an increased involvement by institutions in corporate governance issues there has been a distinct lack of consideration given to the objectives of institutions and their willingness and ability actively to govern corporations. In particular, it is not clear that institutions, at least on an individual basis, have incentives to devote resources to active monitoring. Agency problems existing between the ultimate beneficiaries of institutional funds and the fund managers responsible for the investment of those funds may act to emphasize short-term profits at the expense of the longer-term corporate governance issues. Furthermore, it is unclear that the role of institutions as shareholders can be easily reconciled with their role as investors where there is a duty to maximize the return for the beneficiaries of the funds that they invest.

The purpose of this chapter is to identify the objectives with respect to their ownership and investment behaviour, to examine their incentives in terms of monitoring management behaviour, and to consider whether their incentives can be altered such that a more proactive role becomes worth while. This chapter is structured as follows. Section 2 provides a brief summary of the level of institutional shareholdings in the UK. Section 3 provides a general overview of the objectives and incentives of institutions in respect of their shareholdings in UK companies. A discussion of the willingness and ability of institutions to become actively involved in the governance of corporations is presented in Section 4. Section 5 evaluates the methods by which institutions can intervene in governance matters. The empirical evidence relating to the ability of institutions to monitor and control companies successfully is evaluated in Section 6. Finally Section 7 provides a summary and conclusions.

2. Institutional Shareholdings in the UK

Over the 1980s and 1990s individual equity ownership has continued to decrease in terms of the total percentage of equity owned from 54 per cent in 1963 to less than 18 per cent in 1993. The corollary to the declining proportion of total equity held by individual shareholders has been an increasing dominance of institutional shareholders. Table 2.1 indicates that financial institutions held approximately 62 per cent of ordinary shares in 1993, this percentage having more than doubled since 1963.

The major growth in institutional shareholders is mainly the result of the growth in pension funds and, less significantly, insurance funds. Both have grown as a result of the increase in private retirement savings, in the form of occupational or private pension schemes and long-term life insurance or assurance. As personal pensions often take the form of investment plans operated by life insurance

Table 2.1. The pattern of share ownership in the UK, percentage distribution by sector 1963–1993 (% of total equity owned at 31 December)

Beneficial owner	1963	1969	1975	1981	1989	1990	1991	1992	1993
Pension funds	6.4	9.0	16.8	26.7	30.6	31.6	31.3	35.1	34.2
Insurance companies	10.0	12.2	15.9	20.5	18.6	20.4	20.8	16.7	17.3
Unit trusts	1.3	2.9	4.1	3.6	5.9	6.1	5.7	6.2	6.6
Other financial institutions (incl. investment trusts)	11.3	10.1	10.5	6.8	2.7	2.3	2.3	2.5	3.1
Banks	1.3	1.7	0.7	0.3	0.7	0.7	0.2	0.5	0.6
Total financial institutions	30.3	35.9	48.0	57.9	58.5	61.1	60.3	61.0	61.8
Industrial and commercial companies	5.1	5.4	3.0	5.1	3.8	2.8	3.3	1.8	1.5
Individuals	54.0	47.4	37.5	28.2	20.6	20.3	19.9	20.4	17.7
Overseas	7.0	6.6	5.6	3.6	12.8	11.8	12.8	13.1	16.3
Other personal sector	2.1	2.1	2.3	2.2	2.3	1.9	2.4	1.8	1.6
Public sector	1.5	2.6	3.6	3.0	2.0	2.0	1.3	1.8	1.3
TOTAL	100.0	100.0	100.0	100.0	100.0	100.0	100.0	100.0	100.0

Note: Figures may not add up to 100.0 due to rounding.

Source: CSO (1994).

companies, a significant proportion of investment by life insurance companies represents pension funds.

Thus a large part of the growth in institutional shareholdings represents an indirect growth in equity investment by individuals, as pensions and life insurance are merely a vehicle for long-term personal savings. As Table 2.2 illustrates, life insurance and pension funds, valued at £694.8 billion, accounted for approximately 49 per cent of the financial assets of the personal sector at the end of 1992; whereas direct holdings of UK securities accounted for only 10.9 per cent of personal financial assets. One of the reasons why the pension fund vehicle is favoured as opposed to personal portfolios of shares is the tax advantages presently accruing to pension contributions and pension benefits, as compared to personal equity holdings.

Given that the pension funds are the largest form of institutional investor (in terms of net asset value) and, furthermore, that UK ordinary shares make up over half of their total portfolio of assets, it is not surprising that UK equity holdings make up a significant proportion of the net assets of institutional investors (see Table 2.3). Only in the smaller institutions (general insurance and investment trusts) are UK equities not the largest class of assets. Clearly, then, the performance of UK equities is a key determinant of the performance of the various institutions, and this in itself might lie behind the belief that the institutional investors should have, from a pure self-interest perspective, a role to play in the more effective governance of UK corporations. It is at this very juncture, however, that a key issue for consideration arises; namely, why has corporate governance become such a major issue at a time when institutional shareholdings have increased?

Table 2.2. Personal sector financial assets: amounts outstanding at end of period

Personal sector financial assets	1988		1992	
	£billion	%	£billion	%
Life insurance and pension funds:				
Self-administered	267.4	27.5	382.0	27.1
Administered by insurance company	176.6	18.2	302.9	21.5
Central government funds	9.8	1.0	9.9	0.7
Total	453.8	46.7	694.8	49.3
Units trusts	17.8	1.8	23.8	1.7
UK company securities	119.1	12.3	153.8	10.9
Overseas securities	11.4	1.2	12.6	0.9
Deposits with banks and building societies	246.3	25.4	356.3	25.3
Other	122.5	12.6	168.3	11.9
Total financial assets	970.9	100.0	1,409.8	100.0

Source: Adapted from CSO, *Financial Statistics* (Aug. 1994).

Table 2.3. Portfolio holdings of institutions at the end of 1992: market value

Portfolio holdings of institutions	Pension funds		Insurance				Unit trusts		Investment trusts	
			Long-term		Other than long-term					
	£million	%	£million	%	£million	%	£million	%	£million	%
Short-term assets (net)	13,487	3.5	14,824	4.5	3,477	6.4	2,502	4.1	574	2.0
British government Securities	25,188	6.6	51,009	15.6	8,378	15.4	659	1.1	739	2.6
Local authorities securities	34	0.0	667	0.2	49	0.1	1	0.0	—	—
UK company securities:										
Ordinary shares	202,148	52.9	122,055	37.3	7,356	13.5	32,903	54.3	12,799	44.6
Other	6,068	1.6	22,242	6.8	2,978	5.5	1,713	2.8	814	2.8
Overseas securities	75,592	19.8	40,894	12.5	8,407	15.4	22,820	37.7	13,398	46.7
Loans and mortgages	273	0.1	8,295	2.5	977	1.8	—	—	246	0.9
Unit trusts	10,322	2.7	27,907	8.5	146	0.3	—	—	72	0.2
UK property	19,914	5.2	30,074	9.2	2,299	4.2	—	—	69	0.2
Other	28,998	7.6	9,488	2.9	20,431	37.5	−8	0.0		0.0
Total net assets	382,024	100.0	327,455	100.0	54,498	100.0	50,590	100.0	28,711	100.0

Source: Adapted from CSO, *Financial Statistics* (Aug. 1994).

3. General Overview of the Objectives and Incentives of Institutions

Part of the emphasis of the Cadbury Report on institutional investors as a means of improving corporate governance seemingly rests on the premiss that because of their very size, they have the ability to influence the actions of companies. The Report places emphasis on the ability of market solutions rather than on external regulation to solve corporate governance problems, and relies on shareholders (institutional investors) to shake off their traditional apathy and take a more active interest in the companies they own. In order for institutions to adopt a proactive monitoring role, it is necessary that institutions view themselves as owners of UK corporations rather than viewing equity shares as short-term investment vehicles. Charkham (1990) argues that because many institutions view shares as 'commodities' with no intrinsic qualities other than that they can be readily tradable in an active market, the system of corporate governance as laid down in the Companies Act breaks down because directors cannot be accountable to shareholders who refuse to accept their role as shareholders.

Institutional investors are responsible to the owners of the funds that they invest. The institutional investing arrangements that exist in the UK mean that, with the exception of insurance companies investing their own insurance funds, funds are in general invested by fund managers rather than the beneficial owners of those funds. The trustees of pension funds, for example, have a fiduciary relationship with the beneficiaries of the pension fund, and must act in their best interests. In a similar vein, quoted insurance companies (such as the Prudential) have a responsibility to their own shareholders. In this context, institutional investors have a duty to maximize their investment returns. An important question to ask is whether the role of institutions as major shareholders in UK companies can be reconciled with their role as investors of funds, etc. The Cadbury Report expects institutions, in their role as major shareholders, to take on the role of the large shareholder, who will monitor company management on behalf of smaller shareholders. Hence, in this context, institutions are expected to take a long-term view of their shareholding positions, and, where necessary, incur expense in intervening to correct mismanagement. However, in their role as investors, institutions need to be free to move funds around in order to find the best return for the beneficiaries of those funds. In this respect, it is difficult, certainly in the current ideological free market climate, to argue that institutions should continue to hold equity positions in problem companies and incur additional expense by intervening in management, particularly when there are no guarantees that intervention will be successful. Indeed Drucker (1976) argues that, 'The pension funds are not "owners", they are investors. They do not want control. . . . The pension funds are trustees. It is their job to invest the beneficiaries' money in the most profitable investment. They have no business trying to "manage". If they do not like a company or its management, their duty is to sell the stock' (p. 82). From an alternative viewpoint, Hutton (1995) argues that, 'Pension funds and insurance companies have become classic absentee landlords, exerting power without responsibility and making exacting demands upon companies without recognising their reciprocal obligation as owners' (p. 304).

As shareholders, it is, however, the right of institutions to appoint directors and, it could be argued, their 'moral duty' to ensure that companies are governed in the interests of shareholders. However, whilst Hutton suggests that institutions have obligations as owners, it is not clear, certainly under company law, what those obligations are, if indeed they do have obligations as owners. Furthermore, as will be argued in detail in Section 4, all shareholders are faced with a potential free rider problem. If, for example, an institution took costly action to intervene in company management while other institutions simply did nothing, the intervening institution would report lower returns, to the detriment of its beneficiaries or shareholders, at least in the short term. If the intervening institution is a fund manager investing funds on behalf of external pension funds, given the increasing competition in fund management, the intervening manager is likely to lose clients. On the face of it, it is difficult to see what incentives there are for institutions to bear a private cost for a public good (for other shareholders, both private and institutional, and for the economy as a whole).

Cadbury (1990) argues, however, that while free riding may be an option for individual institutional investors, for institutions collectively this situation is becoming less tenable as the proportion of equity they own increases. It is argued that institutions are effectively becoming locked into companies in which they invest and are, furthermore, becoming locked into the UK economy. While institutions are increasing the proportion of total assets invested in overseas equities (for example, World Markets reports that pension funds have increased the proportion of total assets invested in overseas securities from 17 per cent in 1983 to 24 per cent in 1993), the majority of their total assets is invested in UK securities. As they clearly cannot divest on any major scale from UK companies, it would seem that the long-term performance of British companies is of paramount importance to them. The classic public-good dilemma, therefore, arises in that because individual shareholders (institutions) do not have the appropriate mix of incentives to become involved in the detailed governance of corporations, the emphasis is on short-term gains at the expense of long-term corporate performance. The different types of institutions may, however, have varying time frames for their investment portfolios. For example, pension funds, which should have a long-term perspective because of the nature of their business, are more likely to emphasize the importance of achieving long-term corporate performance.

With regard to the investment behaviour of institutions, Charkham (1994a) presents two contrasting stances of active institutional investing, which he labels Type A and Type B. These types illustrate the opposite ends of the investment spectrum on which all institutions can be placed. The differing characteristics of Type A and Type B investors with regard to their investment policies are presented in Table 2.4.

Table 2.4. Charkham's contrasting stances of institutional investment behaviour

Characteristic	Type A	Type B
Portfolio make-up	Concentration on fewer stocks	Wide diversification
Stakes in companies	Large	Small
Communication with companies	Close	Superficial
Loyalty to companies	High	Virtually non-existent
Dealing activity	Fewer dealings and less freedom to deal due to high stake	Frequent dealing
Interest in corporate governance issues	High	Virtually non-existent

As Table 2.4 illustrates, a Type A fund manager places emphasis on the long-term performance of a relatively small portfolio of companies. In contrast, Type B fund managers emphasize the short-term performance of a relatively large portfolio of companies. Charkham suggests that the type of approach adopted by a particular institution is dependent not only on the purpose of the investment, but also on a complex mixture of factors relating to the management of those funds, such as the motivation and ability of the individual fund managers. Therefore, while pension funds, as long-term investments, would appear most likely to adopt a Type A approach, this may not be followed if the fund managers were motivated, particularly by virtue of their reward structure, to follow a Type B approach.

These contrasting types of investment behaviour concentrate on a fund manager's approach to active investing. Over recent years, however, passive institutional investing has grown in the form of index-matched funds. As index-matched funds have, by their very nature, a buy and hold policy, such fund managers should be willing to take a longer-term perspective. None the less, a long-term investment horizon does not necessarily lead to increased monitoring and intervention. The use of index-matched funds obviously removes the pressure on fund managers to beat the index. However, as competition in terms of return has largely been removed in the case of indexed funds, this emphasizes competition in terms of the cost of managing such funds. While it may be argued that intervention will improve performance of companies and hence the return on the index as a whole, it is again difficult to see what incentives individual fund managers would have to follow this course of action. As they are assessed on relative returns as against a matched index, any difference between the fund's return and the index is the result of management costs. Monitoring and intervention increases management costs for the individual fund managers, while potentially improving the performance of non-intervening index-matched funds. The result of this is that the intervening fund manager faces higher costs while all other index-matched funds show higher returns at lower cost. In this situation, the higher costs cannot be passed on to the beneficial owners without risk of their simply moving to a lower-cost fund manager. This takes us to the crux of the problem: fund managers are not the beneficial owners of the shares and hence do not substantially share in the increased profits to be gained from intervention. Unless there is collective intervention by all fund managers, the costs of intervention simply reduce the individual fund manager's profits.

When examining the objectives of institutions and of their investment managers, the general investment environment in the UK needs to be considered. The nature of ownership in the UK is essentially short-term with equity shares seen as commodities (Charkham 1990). However, institutions are not the only shareholding party to view holdings in equity in this way—small private shareholders are also likely to view holdings in equity merely as investment vehicles, particularly given the emphasis on equities as tax-efficient investments, for example in the form of PEPs and pensions. Note also that the privatization issues were sold on the basis that small investors would earn a substantial return in the early days of trading—the notion of the purchase of equity as a stake in the long-term performance of British industry was rarely mentioned. Similarly, the relationship between the City and British industry has been essentially one of arm's length investment. The market for funds (both equity and debt) is seen essentially from a short-term perspective, with both sides of the funding transaction seeing the transaction in terms of price and availability. The arm's length market nature of the system promotes an emphasis for both sides of the system that militates against active, direct governance from the providers of finance: the logic of the system is a market based upon 'exit' rather than 'voice' (in Hirschman's (1970) terms). However, it is within this system that the institutions are expected to have the motivation and ability to adopt active and direct governance.

However, despite the fact that the nature of the market would seem to discourage monitoring, there are many examples of institutions having intervened in the management of problem companies (see Black and Coffee, 1994, for examples of institutional intervention and the circumstances surrounding such interventions). However, as Black and Coffee note, such intervention is usually carried out in private rather than in the public arena and, moreover, usually as a last resort in times of crisis. Furthermore, as Ball (1990) comments, 'As presently conducted, there is more VOICE being exercised than is commonly supposed, and this has certainly increased in the 1980's. Nevertheless, the nature of this VOICE is unsatisfactory. It is not systematic. It takes place behind closed doors. The process itself is not subject to any kind of monitoring' (p. 24). Hence, by its very covert nature, it is not presently possible to examine the degree to which institutions intervene in the governance of corporations, nor the effect of any intervention.

To summarize, it is clear that a problem exists in attempting to reconcile the role of institutions as shareholders with their role as investors of funds. Although, in the long-term and at a collective level, the objectives of institutions as both shareholders and investors should be to improve corporate performance (brought about, it is assumed, by improving the standards of corporate governance), in the short-term and at an individual level, it is not clear that institutions' objectives from the investment perspective can be met by improving their role as shareholders.

4. The Willingness and Ability of Institutions to Intervene in the Governance of Corporations

There is much anecdotal evidence to suggest that institutional shareholders do not adopt a monitoring role, preferring to sell their holdings in 'problem' companies rather than intervening in the management of that company (to exit rather than use voice). There are several reasons why institutions may adopt such a stance. First, if they intervene publicly, they are effectively drawing to public attention the difficulties the company is facing. This is likely to be perceived as 'bad news' by the market, resulting in a fall in share price and a reduction in the value of their investment. Second, if they become involved in the management of such problem companies, they become privy to inside information and unable to trade in those shares, potentially compounding their losses. Finally, effective monitoring is costly in terms of time and money, especially for institutional investors which hold diverse portfolios. To counter the above, it may be argued that the option of exiting becomes more problematic as institutional investors increase their stakes in public companies and as the number of institutional players in the market decreases. Selling large blocks of shares in a problem company is likely to be extremely difficult, particularly as the potential buyer is likely to be an alternative institution with knowledge of the potential problems which exist in the company.

In this section, the factors which affect the willingness and ability of the institutions to intervene to correct corporate governance failures (to use voice rather than exit) are evaluated. Specifically, this section considers the agency problems arising at all levels of the fund management relationship; the effect of the size of institutional equity holdings on the incentives of institutions to intervene; the public-good nature of active monitoring and the associated problem of free riding; and finally, the conflicts of interests faced by institutions when considering whether intervention is worth while.

Agency Problems Arising between Institutions and Beneficiaries

At this stage, a number of crucial and related aspects of institutional investment and particularly occupational pension fund arrangements need to be outlined, in order to understand fully the objectives and incentives which institutions face when considering their investment and ownership stance. First, due to the structure of the fund management arrangements of occupational pension funds, agency problems arise at every level in the relationship between the ultimate beneficiary of the pension fund (the current or past employee) and the fund manager. Second, the method and timing of the performance measurement of the fund and of the fund manager will have an important effect on the incentives of the fund manager, and may increase agency problems between the parties.

Because the mechanics of institutional investment management mean that there is often a division between voting control of shares and the ultimate beneficial owner, agency problems of ownership and control arise at every level of the relationship between the beneficiary and the fund manager. Such agency problems may lead to a fund being managed using, in Charkham's (1994*a*) terms, a Type B approach when a Type A approach is more appropriate. As an example, Figure 2.1 outlines the relationships which may exist between an externally managed company pension fund and its fund manager. While the current and past employees are the ultimate beneficiaries, the fund trustees are those who have legal control over the assets of the fund. Conflicts may arise between the interests of employees and those of the company, particularly if the trustees are also directors of the company, as is often the case. Trustees or directors may wish to maximize the value of funds in order to minimize the company's contributions and possibly use any pension fund surplus to inflate company profits. The Maxwell affair is an extreme example of the problems which may arise between beneficiaries and trustees or directors.

Furthermore, pension fund trustees can delegate investment management to an external fund manager to invest under a management contract. Within the market-place for such business there is a great deal of competition among fund managers and, not surprisingly, much emphasis is placed on 'annual league tables' of fund performance. Two performance measurement services, the World Market company and Combined Actuarial Performance Services (CAPS), produce performance figures for individual fund managers and also produce median figures for the fund managers they survey. Not surprisingly, therefore, fund managers are under a great deal of pressure to perform better than the median fund.

Thus agency problems may arise between the pension funds and a fund management institution if the trustees have incentives to maximize the long-term value of the fund but fund management performance is evaluated on a short-term basis. However, Marsh (1990) argues that concern expressed over the measurement of fund managers' performance on a quarterly basis reflects a misconception of the activities of the fund managers and the performance measures. Essentially, he

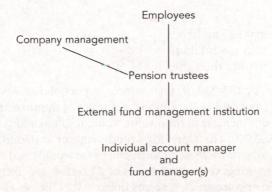

Fig. 2.1. The relationship between pension funds and fund managers

suggests that whilst a fund's performance may be monitored on a quarterly basis, the performance of a fund manager is not evaluated on the basis of even a few quarters' performance data. Similarly, institutional evidence presented to the Trade and Industry Committee on Competitiveness of UK Manufacturing Industry (1994) suggested that, whilst performance was monitored on a quarterly basis, performance was assessed over a longer period. In addition, a survey by CAPS (1993) found that, of pension funds that changed their investment manager in 1993, the mean and median period of tenure of the outgoing manager was seven years. Furthermore, data presented by Philips and Drew Fund Management in 1995 found that the average holding period of equities by pension funds was approximately five years in 1994.

However, whilst figures such as these are used to refute the argument that the measurement of fund management performance has led to an emphasis on the short-term performance of fund managers (see e.g. Marsh 1990), it may be argued that they do not provide conclusive evidence of the long-term emphasis taken by fund managers. For example, a turnover period in fund managers of seven years may not be indicative of long-term attitudes of trustees and fund managers if those fund managers that retain the longest contracts are those that practice short-termism. In a similar vein, relatively long holdings periods for equities are not proof of long-term attitudes by fund managers if the companies whose equity shares are held are adopting short-term strategies and attempting to maximize short-term performance to suit the wishes of fund managers. If, in general, all players in the market are short-termist in outlook (for whatever reason), the performance of all companies will be affected by short-termism. If this is the case, then fund manager turnover rates and equity holding periods become meaningless as proof of long-term attitudes.

These agency problems are enhanced when the compensation awarded to the fund manager is structured in such a way that, in the event of the fund manager taking corporate governance actions, he or she bears the cost of intervention but the beneficial owner gains the benefit. As an illustration of the problems which arise as a result of the fee structure of fund managers, consider the fee structure of a UK fund manager. The annual fee scale is calculated on the fund's market value as follows:

0.5 per cent on the first £25 million,
0.3 per cent on the next £50 million,
0.2 per cent on the balance thereafter,

subject to a minimum of £75,000. If, for example, a portfolio of £1 billion was increased in value by 1 per cent (£10 million) as a result of improved monitoring by the fund manager, this increase in fund value would result in additional annual management fees of £20,000. Therefore, for a fund manager to undertake significant monitoring activities, its increased management fee would need to outweigh the costs of such monitoring. Given that funds of £1 billion are likely to spread across a large portfolio of companies, it seems unlikely that the benefits of monitoring and intervention to the fund manager in the form of increased fee income would exceed the costs. Coupled with the potential costs of lost business from the management of the offended companies (the fund manager may also be currently managing their pension funds or be a future contender), it would seem clear that there are few incentives for intervention at the level of the fund manager. This again takes us to the crux of the problem: fund managers are not the beneficial owners of the shares and hence do not substantially share in the increased profits to be gained from intervention. Unless there is collective intervention by all fund managers, the costs of intervention simply reduce the individual fund manager's profits.

Effect of the Size of Institutional Holdings on Incentives

The Cadbury Report suggests that, by virtue of the size of their holdings, institutional investors have the potential to exercise considerable control over the actions of the board of directors—potential which is rarely available to other (small) shareholders. From a rational perspective, one aspect of the governance of corporations is that the costs of intervening must be less than the probable benefits if governance actions are to be effected. Given potential scale economies in accessing corporate data and a positive relationship between the value of shareholdings and increased corporate performance, larger shareholders have greater incentives to become involved in governance issues than smaller shareholders. As Stiglitz (1985) argues, individual shareholders with relatively small holdings have little incentive to gather and bear the relatively fixed costs of collecting information to enable them to monitor and control the behaviour of the board. Alternatively, large shareholders may have sufficient incentives to obtain the information necessary to control management effectively if the benefits of such monitoring outweigh the associated costs. However, Stiglitz does note that control by large shareholders may have a cost; if such shareholders are limited in terms of their diversification, then their objectives may conflict with those of small shareholders. Furthermore, Stiglitz suggests, large controlling shareholders and managers may co-operate in the diversion of resources from remaining shareholders.

Notwithstanding the desirability of governance via large institutional shareholders and the fact the benefit–cost ratio is likely to be more favourable for large as compared to small shareholders, there still remains the issue whether the probable benefits of governance are likely to outweigh the mostly certain costs for large shareholders. Given the general direction of the relationships between firm size and benefits–costs, and the highly firm-specific nature of any individual relationship, this issue boils down to a consideration of whether given percentages of shareholdings enable institutions to alter the actions of corporations and thereby the probable benefits they receive. Although this is difficult to answer in the absolute, it is possible to form an impression from the current holdings of the UK institutions. While institutional investors as a collective own the majority of equity in UK companies, on an individual basis their shareholdings are mostly in the region of 2–3 per cent of issued shares. Clearly, institutional investors will be unwilling to take on substantially larger holdings of equity in a single company as that would effectively lock them in to that company, and potentially present liquidity and portfolio diversification problems.[1] While a shareholding in the region of 2–3 per cent is large relative to individual shareholders, in comparison to the size of the company and the size of institution's total portfolio it is small and may not warrant the expense which has to be incurred in actively monitoring management. The direct issue to be considered here, however, is whether shareholdings of this size are sufficient to control or guide the actions of management. Certainly Hanson's shareholding of 2.5 per cent in ICI was seen as enough of a threat to spark major changes in the corporation. However, a share position of that level taken by institutions may not have the same effect as they are unlikely to have the same (assumed) motives as Hanson of takeover and divestment.[2] Nevertheless, a shareholding by an individual institution needs to be taken in the context of City relationships and the potential to influence other institutions or shareholders. This issue reflects the importance of the nature of the overall distribution of shares for the potential influence of any individual shareholding. For example, part of the influence of a 3 per cent shareholding will depend on the ability of an institution to marshal the support of other shareholders, and this in turn is a complex function of the distribution of the size of other shareholders and their diversity of interests (the next section's review of the free-rider problem in the context of institutional investment attempts to throw some light on these issues). However, given the difficulties of determining the potential influence of a particular block of shares, and in the absence of fully understanding the institutional dynamics of the City, it is a brave step to conclude that institutional investors have the potential to exercise considerable control over the actions of boards.

The picture of the potential influence of institutional shareholders is yet further clouded by the relationship between institutions, such as company pension schemes, that are the beneficial owners of the shares and institutions that act as fund managers for such pension schemes. Fund managers often manage funds on a full discretionary basis, which means that they have control over the composition of the fund portfolio and, in many cases, over the voting rights attached to the shares which make up that portfolio. Therefore, it is likely that the amount of shareholdings under the control of institutional investors is significantly greater than the amount of their beneficial holdings. Nevertheless, it would still appear to

---

[1] Black and Coffee (1994) report that Prudential Portfolio Managers Ltd., the investment subsidiary of the Prudential, own a stake of 5 per cent or higher in about 200 companies, but become concerned about illiquidity at ownership stakes in the region of 10 per cent. However, the Prudential is the UK's single largest institutional investor, owning over 3 per cent of the stock market. Smaller institutions would clearly be required to take smaller stakes in the larger companies in order to maintain liquidity.

[2] Although, a large shareholding by an institution may provoke management into improving standards of corporate governance and performance if management believe that such an institutional shareholder may encourage a hostile bid if performance is not improved. These arguments are particularly relevant with respect to the Granada takeover of Forte, in which it has been surmised that Mercury Asset Management (a major shareholder in both Forte and Granada) may have encouraged Granada to mount its hostile bid (see e.g. *Financial Times* 1996: 19).

be a bold step to conclude that shareholdings of even 5 to 6 per cent would be sufficient to affect the actions of corporations. The argument so far has, however, ignored the actual size of the institutions and their general ability to influence general impressions within the share-buying market.

There is no doubt that many of the financial institutions are large as measured by any yardstick. For example, the Prudential had a market value of £5,436 million in June 1994, placing it in the top thirty companies quoted on the London Stock Exchange in terms of market value. Postel (the pension fund of British Telecom and the Post Office, recently renamed Hermes) alone has £25 billion in funds under its control. This gives them a voice, via their impact upon the media, of considerable volume and a potential ability to influence general perceptions. For example, in June 1994 Ross Goobey of Postel instigated a campaign against directors' rolling contracts of longer than three years by taking the highly unusual step of writing publicly to the chairmen of the top 100 companies. This break in the tradition of 'behind the scenes' negotiation naturally produced a great deal of media interest (with virtually all media commentators being in support of Postel's stance) and has brought the issue to the attention of individual shareholders and the public in general. Interestingly, however, it would rarely pay an institution to voice negative opinion publicly because of the potential impact upon share prices. Furthermore, many institutional investors feel that the public stance taken by Postel is damaging to the relationships between institutional investors and the companies in which they invest. A member of the investment committee of the Association of British Insurers was quoted in the *Financial Times* as saying 'We want to try to contain the damage that has been done. There is general concern on our committee that we do not want to damage relationships with companies' (*Financial Times*, 17 Aug. 1994: 13). However, the potential for such public voice translates into private influence and the seeming willingness of corporations to manage specific sessions for institutional shareholders. The obvious benefits to be gained by corporations and institutional shareholders in ensuring that 'control' is in the private rather than the public domain is one reason why it is difficult to gauge the influence of institutional shareholders. Thus, there is an argument which suggests that the large institutional shareholders may be able to influence the affairs of a corporation over and above their nominal shareholdings. This then moves us on to consider why the institutions bother monitoring the actions of individual companies when they can free ride on the actions of others.

The Free Rider Problem

The above sections have mentioned the free rider problem facing individual institutions. This section considers, in more detail, the merit of applying free rider type arguments to institutional investors. The free rider problem is commonly seen as the problem of public goods, for example the failure to supply street lighting because of the potential of individuals to free ride off the actions of others. Similarly, an absence of governance by institutions because of the potential for individual institutions to benefit from the actions of others is also indicative of a free rider problem. Since the benefits of any collective action go to every individual in a group whether or not that individual has borne any of the costs of the collective action, it follows that, unless the group is small or meets certain other special conditions, the collective good will *not* be provided through market mechanisms or other straightforward and voluntary arrangements. Given that institutional investors are subject to such free rider problems, it may be more relevant to examine why institutions ever engage in collective action when there are so many factors counting against such actions. For example, as Black and Coffee (1994) note, the absence of a generally accepted mechanism for cost-sharing amongst institutions that undertake collective action presents a major obstacle to such collective action.

An analogy which may be applied to institutional investors to illustrate the nature of the conflict which might lie between private and collective benefits–costs is the classic Prisoners' Dilemma. This relates the tale of two prisoners who have been caught in a joint crime. Each prisoner is interviewed separately by the judge and told, 'I have enough evidence to send both of you to prison for a year if neither of you confess. However, if you alone confess, I'll send you to prison for just three months, whilst your partner will receive a ten-year sentence. If you both confess to the crime, you'll both be sentenced to five years in prison.' As neither prisoner knows what action the other prisoner will take, the likely outcome is that both prisoners will confess (avoiding the risk of a ten-year sentence), whereas the optimal solution (from the prisoners' collective point of view) would be for neither prisoner to confess.

However, there are major differences between the Prisoners' Dilemma and the framework within which institutions operate which may help to overcome the seemingly insurmountable free rider problems facing institutional investors. But before examining these differences in detail, it is necessary to note the environment in which the institutions operate. Another peculiar feature of the UK market for funds is its spatially concentrated nature within London's Square Mile. Historically, the investing institutions have a well-developed network of informal communication. Thus, one of the problems of trying to analyse and understand institutional governance in the UK is that it seemingly operates via a series of well-developed informal networks, usually behind closed doors. Thus although there may be a lack of publicly noted governance, this does not mean that governance actions do not occur. Therefore, when analysing the actions of institutions, it is necessary to take into account the nature of the relationships within the Square Mile. Moreover, from a corporate governance perspective, there are two ways of viewing the investing institutions' market-place: as a no-holds-barred competitive situation or as a competitive market underpinned by orderly conduct. All the available evidence (see e.g. Holland 1994) points to the latter being the most appropriate description. This suggests that, although the governance actions of institutions may be seen as being conditioned by a free rider problem, the informal systems of the City allow collective solutions to be found. Thus, although the institutions may be seen as operating arm's length investment policies, the history and nature of the City may allow governance issues to be confronted in 'relational' rather than pure arm's length market terms.[3]

One feature of collective action to consider is whether the size of the group of institutional investors is an important factor in determining collective action. Specifically, would a sufficiently small group of institutional investors be able to overcome free rider problems? The conclusion usually drawn from the Prisoners' Dilemma model is that even groups of only two members normally fail to obtain a collective good. It is only when two individuals repeat that Prisoners' Dilemma game a large number of times that they are able to achieve the gains from co-operation. In any single game (or in any set of games where the players know in advance how many games will be played), the dominant strategy for each player is to defect and not co-operate.

A crucial aspect of the Dilemma is that the prisoners are denied communication and hence the opportunity to make mutually advantageous deals. Clearly, such a situation does not exist within the City, where there are well-developed networks (including the so-called 'old boys' network') and codes of practice and behaviour which have arisen from the City's long history of trading. Furthermore, within the context of the Prisoners' Dilemma, co-operation derives from the repeated play of a two-person game. Given that relationships which exist between the various institutions are generally long-term, there are incentives for institutions to take a long-term view of co-operation in corporate governance matters. For example, institutions may take turns to play the role of 'lead institution' when intervention in a company becomes necessary (see Black and Coffee 1994 for a summary of the process of forming coalitions of institutions to confront management). If individual institutions refuse to play their part, it would seem likely that other institutions will withdraw their goodwill towards that institution and refuse to co-operate in future interventions. Hence, the existence of communication networks and the long-term nature of mutually advantageous relationships between City institutions may contribute towards an environment in which co-operation can take place and free riding is reduced.

However, within the context of the Dilemma, the tendency towards co-operation is diminished as group size increases. In a sufficiently large group where no single member gets no more than a small share of the benefits of a collective good, the incentive to co-operate with other potential beneficiaries of the collective good disappears. In support of this, Black and Coffee (1994) note that when institutional coalitions do form, they are usually small in terms of the number of institutional participants but relatively large in terms of collective shareholding. However, although the communication and interaction networks within the City may appear to reduce free riding, the increasing number of institutions within the

---

[3] This reflects a style of regulation which is firmly within the tradition of 'British policy style' which emphasizes consultation, persuasion, co-operation, and accommodation between 'reasonable people' rather than compulsion and conflict. See Jordan and Richardson (1982) for a discussion of this style of negotiation.

City may help to break down the old codes of conduct and means of doing business.

Although coalitions between institutions do form, those coalitions still face free rider problems from institutions who do not form part of the coalition. In the majority of situations, it is likely that institutions involved in collective action against an individual firm will not be rewarded by substantial future profits from that firm. Furthermore, when the costs of taking such public action and the possibility that any action will be unsuccessful are taken into consideration, there remains the question why institutions undertake such action when the benefits of doing so appear to be so small, if indeed any benefits exist. Public action is likely to be more costly than private action, as the very fact that public action has been taken suggests that previous 'behind the scenes' attempts to influence boards have failed. In addition, the particular institutions involved in such public action risk a loss of reputation if they are unable to force their desired outcomes. Given that public action is taken, albeit rarely, this suggests that there are some benefits to be gained, although these benefits may not be directly associated with the immediate action being taken against an individual firm. Rather, it is likely that action is taken to act as a deterrent to other companies' boards and to signal to the corporate community in general that intervention by institutions remains a credible threat.

Therefore, although it may be first assumed that institutions have very little incentive to become involved in the monitoring activities that corporate governance demands, it would appear that the relationships which exist between institutions act to limit free-riding behaviour. If collective action by institutions were to be viewed as a single play of the Prisoners' Dilemma game, it is clear that such collective action would be unlikely to take place due to the prevalence of free riding. However, given the City context in which the institutions operate, repeated play of the Prisoners' Dilemma is the more appropriate analogy to make, where co-operation between institutions becomes worth while. Furthermore, in the context of private versus public action, it would seem that, in the majority of cases, private action on the part of institutions would be the most appropriate course for institutions to take. However, when public action does occur, it is likely to be motivated by the need to enforce the notion that institutional intervention remains a credible threat.

Therefore, in summary, the public-good nature of corporate governance actions and the associated incentives for free riding would suggest that monitoring would not be provided. However, the rationality arguments do not take into account the institutional framework of the Square Mile that has evolved over a number of centuries. The institutional investors in the UK form a highly concentrated network, often operating in the confines of the Square Mile with a well-developed history of relationships and communication. This facilitates the operation of relational dynamics and the possibility of concerted focused action. In this form of society, it may, of course, be extremely difficult to identify actions directly that could be definitely categorized under the banner of governance; actions taking place through gentle persuasion and the knowledge that the potential public disclosure of opinions can be extremely damaging. In fact, the tendency to work behind closed doors in the UK reinforces the strength of any potential threat to 'go public'. Such a threat, of course, is only likely to be credible if the companies believe it is in the interests of the institutions to publicly voice their concerns. It is clear, however, that the nature of governance within the UK is such that it is difficult to determine visibly how far it is in operation. In addition, the problems of co-ordinating collective action mean that such actions occur only in extreme circumstances.

Conflicts of Interest

Whilst there may be informal mechanisms in place which mean that institutions do have incentives to take governance actions (albeit in private rather than public), there are additional factors which provide disincentives to institutional monitoring and intervention. This section examines the possible conflicts of interests that certain institutions may face as a result of other (actual or potential) relationships with the company.

Pound (1988) presents three different hypotheses which may explain the relationship between institutions and their incentives to intervene in corporate governance: the efficient monitoring hypothesis, the conflict of interest hypothesis, and the strategic alignment hypothesis. The efficient monitoring hypothesis suggests that institutional shareholders are more informed and able to monitor management at lower cost than small shareholders. Alternatively, the strategic alignment hypothesis suggests that institutional shareholders and the board may find it mutually advantageous to co-operate on certain issues. In a similar vein, the conflict of interest hypothesis suggests that institutional shareholders may have current or potential business relationships with the firm which make them less willing actively to curb management discretion.

Pound's hypotheses that the extent of institutional intervention will depend on the relationship between the institution and the company may be used to explain Postel's campaign against directors' three-year rolling contracts, a campaign which was unusual in that attempts to impose governance standards on companies were carried out in public, rather than using the generally preferred 'behind the scenes' method. Postel represents only two pension funds, the Post Office and British Telecom pension funds and acts as their in-house fund manager. They are not open to business from any other sources and therefore do not have conflicts of interest which may preclude them from actively opposing management. Other pension fund managers such as merchant banks and insurance companies may have other business interests with the companies in question and hence are less likely to oppose management actively for fear of jeopardizing those interests. In addition, fund management is a highly competitive business, and fund managers may understandably feel wary of criticizing the very directors of a company whose pension fund management business they may be seeking in the future. It is notable that at the start of their campaign, Postel could not get open support from the umbrella organizations, the Association of British Insurers (ABI) and the National Association of Pension Funds (NAPF), although this has changed, particularly since the publication of the Greenbury Report (1995). Furthermore, many of the institutional investors are themselves quoted companies and have directors on three-year rolling contracts (a good example at the time was the Prudential). Hence, it could be argued, in line with Pound, that not only do such institutions face conflicts of interest, but directors of institutions have reasons for aligning themselves with company management over certain issues for fear of specific practices, which they themselves adopt, becoming unacceptable. In addition, institutions may face conflicts of interest by virtue of their own ownership structure. In particular, certain fund-managing institutions are subsidiaries of investment banks. For example, Schroders Investment Management, which has notifiable interests in many quoted companies, is a subsidiary of Schroders, an investment bank which acts directly or through its other subsidiaries as investment adviser to many such companies. In such situations, conflicts of interest may arise between the institution and its parent with regard to corporate governance matters. Actions to curb management discretion by the institution may have long-term consequences for its parent if it has current business relationships with the firm or is likely to act as an adviser to the firm on future matters such as takeovers, rights issues, etc.

However, although there are obvious disincentives as a result of conflicts of interest to institutions becoming involved in governance issues, there are examples of direct involvement which suggest that the disincentives are not insurmountable and institutions do find it worth while to voice their concerns. For example, Postel is a particularly useful example of an institution that finds the benefits of open intervention outweigh the costs. As Britain's largest in-house pension fund investor, it is estimated to own 1.5 per cent of British industry and owns shares in a large percentage of all quoted companies. Therefore, the cost to firms of large compensation payments in the event of a director's loss of office as a result of three-year rolling contracts directly affects the fund's revenues. Its campaign focuses on one issue which is common to all companies and hence the costs of intervention are much less than if it campaigned on individual firm-specific issues.

Pension funds such as Postel have characteristics which are similar to Coffee's (1991) notion of the 'optimal corporate monitor'. Coffee suggests that the optimal corporate monitor should be relatively free from conflicts of interest such that its monitoring and control activities are not biased by opportunities to earn other income from the company in question. It should also have a long-term investment horizon and its stake in the corporation should be large enough to justify the expenditure of significant monitoring costs. Coffee argues that pension funds are in a better position than other institutions to perform this role. However, while this is true of in-house managed pension funds such as Postel, the position is not so clear in the case of externally managed pension funds. As discussed earlier, the agency problems arising between pension funds and external fund managers may prohibit monitoring by pension funds. Furthermore, large pension funds tend to be highly diversified with relatively small holdings in any one company, which places constraints on the amount of monitoring activity which can be undertaken in terms of both cost and in-depth knowledge of management. In addition, the trustees of pension funds managed internally may face pressure from their own company's management to form strategic alliances with the management of the companies in which they invest. Their own companies may be faced with corporate governance problems to which they would rather not draw attention. Thus the point to note is that the institutions themselves are organizations where there is a separation between management and owners, and hence the same potential governance problems are as likely to apply here as they are to corporations; essentially, in promoting institutions as a partial solution to the governance problem, there is an inherent belief that institutions themselves are less prone to governance issues than corporations.

Whilst there has been much debate concerning the ability of institutions to monitor corporate management effectively, relatively little attention has been paid to the monitoring of institutions themselves. Jenkinson and Mayer (1992) argue, 'Why precisely managers of institutional funds are supposed to be so much better at administrating non-financial enterprises than the management of these enterprises themselves, or why similar problems of corporate governance do not afflict the funds themselves are questions that are never very clearly answered' (p. 2). Indeed, Coffee (1991) suggests that there are reasons to believe that some institutional investors are less accountable to their owners than are corporate managers to their shareholders and argues that the usual mechanisms of corporate accountability are limited or unavailable at the institutional level. The extent of the problem depends of the nature of the institution concerned. For example, self-administered occupational pension schemes are obviously immune from mechanisms such as takeovers. In addition, their beneficiaries, the company's employees, are not in the position to sell their stakes in the pension fund if the fund underperforms. Furthermore, discipline in the form of monitoring by debtholders does not affect self-administered occupational pension funds. However, given the obvious lack of external market discipline available to control such funds, statistics from WM show that on average these funds perform better than externally managed funds and have lower activity rates. In addition, it is these types of funds that have recently taken a more interventionist attitude to corporate governance, as Postel's stance against directors' three-year rolling contracts illustrates.

A crucial aspect of the debate which is often ignored is the relationship between the fund manager, the occupational pension fund, and the sponsoring company. As noted, the trustees of an occupational pension fund usually include directors of the sponsoring company. Throughout the above discussion, the pressures placed on the fund manager to maximize performance have been stressed, pressure which is in part placed on the fund manager by the sponsoring company. As Charkham (1994a) argues, 'All company managers want their own shareholders to belong to the type A school. If they put pressure on their own pension fund managers for short-term results they push them toward type B' (p. 103). The pressure that companies place on their pension funds to perform well in the short-term has important implications for the corporate governance debate and the accusations levelled at fund managers that they are responsible for the short-temism which prevails in the market. Blake (1992), on the topic of hostile takeovers, argues strongly that,

This aspect of short-termism is a direct consequence of the companies themselves demanding that their own pension funds beat the average, when no more than half of them can do this. They cannot really complain when fund managers capitalise on the large price rises resulting from takeover bids by selling their stakes in an attempt to beat the average, knowing that if the bid fails, the share price will sink back again. (p. 86)

Hence, it may be argued that companies themselves are, at least in part, responsible for institutional behaviour of which they are then highly critical. This highlights the agency problems and conflicts of interest which are inherent in the occupational pension fund arrangements which operate in the UK. It is notable that in Germany and Japan, countries which are often highlighted as having fewer corporate governance problems than the UK and USA, pension funds are not significant players in the ownership of equity. This suggests that a fundamental review of the operation of occupational funds is required. As Blake (1992) notes, 'Pension scheme members are entitled to expect that their pension funds do not act in a way that destabilises the very companies for whom they work' (p. 94).

   In summary, institutions face conflicts of interest in their dealings with companies as a result of their role as shareholder–investor and current or potential business service provider that possibly inhibit their willingness to apply pressure to company management in the event of corporate governance deficiencies. Furthermore, it is clear that the institutions themselves are not immune from corporate governance problems and may be unwilling to draw attention to these problems by criticizing the companies in which they invest. Finally, a related issue is the relationship between occupational pension funds and their sponsoring companies, which is likely to affect the way those fund managers act towards other companies.

5. Methods of Intervention

The above sections have drawn attention to the lack of incentives faced by institutions with regard to active monitoring and intervention. Furthermore, if as discussed in Section 4, the problems of co-ordinating collective action can be overcome, the question what action institutions can take remains. The system of corporate governance in the UK operates through the Companies Act and recognizes the power of the shareholder via their right to vote at the AGM. Whilst this is may be the obvious way for institutional shareholders to exercise their power over company management, as discussed below such public action is usually eschewed by institutions. However, there are a number of other actions which, although not available to individual shareholders, are available to institutional shareholders in their role as relatively large shareholders. In this section, the actions which institutions can take to intervene in the management of a company are discussed. However, given the limitations of this actions (discussed below), the section evaluates arguments which suggest that institutions need to take more public action in the form of exercising their right to vote.

Within the 'outsider' system of corporate governance existing in the UK, institutional investors have a number of governance actions available to them. However, as will be discussed, the ability of institutions to act publicly is constrained by the possible adverse effects of those actions. Hence, it is the *threat* of public action which is the most powerful weapon open to institutions, although there are times when such threats have to be carried through for such actions to remain credible.

An obvious first course of action open to institutions is to refuse to partake in rights issues when companies come to the market to raise additional equity funding. Institutional shareholders are at their most powerful in such situations, for the onus is on management to negotiate with the institutional shareholders. Institutions may make the provision of additional finance subject to governance changes within the company, for example, by demanding board changes, etc. Because management are appealing to institutions to support them at the time of the rights issue, many of the usual problems of organizing collective action will not arise, in particular the cost of such action to institutions will be lower as they do not have to initiate the action themselves. However, this source of power obviously arises only when companies require additional equity finance; hence other forms of governance action are required in other circumstances.

The second course of action open to institutions is to make adverse public comment, which may damage the firm in terms of its share price and its overall business reputation. The problem with this form of action is that it risks damaging the investing institution and other investing institutions as well. Hence, when, in June 1994, Postel publicly criticized some companies' executive compensation contracts, it did not receive the warmest of responses from the companies concerned or from other institutions. Part of the problem with such an approach is that the institution puts itself in a light of being 'whiter than white' and hence leaves itself open to increased public scrutiny. Furthermore, although the relationship may be essentially arm's length, the institution needs the continued support of the firm if it is to access firm-specific data on a timely basis. For these reasons, the institutions may prefer to comment privately; in this way, the firm, the institution, and relationships with other institutions are not damaged. If this form of 'quiet' policing works, then it is to the benefit of all concerned as it avoids the costs of excess volatility. In a sense, the system is a hybrid between a public arms length system (the USA) and a closed relationship system (the German system). The problem with the UK system, as compared to the German system, is that a large part of the shareholding in a firm is not privy to the discussions which take place behind closed doors and, therefore, there must always be a lingering doubt about whose needs are being served.

The third potential action open to institutions is the removal of directors via a general meeting, an example being the removal of Maurice Saatchi from his post as chairman of Saatchi and Saatchi plc by a consortium of mainly US institutions in December 1994. However, this form of action suffers from many of the problems already discussed, and it seems likely that it is used in only the most extreme of circumstances. A slightly less public form of action is the threat of selling a firm's shares, with the consequent damage upon share price and general reputations. Again, this action suffers from the fact that it will damage other institutions, and hence it opens up the potential for retaliatory action.

The most obvious course of action open to institutions is to exercise their right as shareholders to vote at a company's AGM. The ISC (Institutional Shareholders' Committee) (1991) recommended that institutional shareholders should make positive use of their voting rights and should register their votes wherever possible on a regular basis. Furthermore, the Cadbury Report (1992) stated that, 'Voting rights can be regarded as an asset, and the use or otherwise of those rights by institutional shareholders is a subject of legitimate interest to those on whose behalf they invest. We recommend that institutional investors should disclose their policies on the use of voting rights' (para. 6.12).

The empirical evidence on the level of institutional (fund manager) voting is limited, but that which is available suggests that voting levels are low. The NAPF undertakes an annual survey of occupational pensions; Table 2.5 documents the voting policy of the investment managers of pension schemes who responded to this survey for the period 1990 to 1994. As the table illustrates, there has been an increase in the percentage of investment managers who always vote if practicable, but overall there has been no significant change in the voting policies of investment managers. While the 1994 survey reports that 60 per cent of fund managers would be expected to vote on contentious issues, the level of voting in general would appear to be rather low. This is in spite of the calls made by numerous bodies, such as the ABI, the NAPF, and the ISC, as well as the Cadbury Committee, for institutional shareholders to exercise the voting rights of the shares they control.

Possibly as a reflection of the current state of play regarding voting by fund managers, there have been calls for institutional investors to be required to exercise the voting rights of the shares they control. In particular, the Labour Party is

Table 2.5. National Association of Pension Funds: survey of voting policy (%)

	1990	1991	1992	1993	1994
Vote at all times if practicable	20	21	26	26	28
Vote only on contentious issues	33	34	34	31	32
Not vote	23	24	22	24	21
Other (had no policy or did not know if their managers voted)	24	21	18	19	19

Source: NAPF (1990–4).

currently considering proposals to include an obligation to vote in the fiduciary duties of pension funds and to require fund managers to justify their voting decisions to trustees.[4] Davies (1993) argues that mandatory voting would be 'a useful discipline to monitoring if institutions were obliged to formulate and express a view on all issues put to a vote at shareholder meetings' (p. 92). However, Davies does recognize that mandatory voting would have to accompanied by an obligation that the votes were informed. Similarly, other commentators (e.g. Cadbury 1992; Mallin 1995) have suggested that institutions would have to publish statements detailing their voting policies. However, while mandatory voting coupled with the publication of voting policy may at first seem to make the voting process more transparent and force institutions to take a more active interest in corporate governance issues, it is not clear that such a policy would translate into real changes in fund managers' and pension trustees' attitudes. While it is possible to place a legal obligation on institutions to vote, placing a legal obligation on institutions to vote in a sensible and informed manner is likely to be a practical impossibility. If 'informed' voting were made mandatory, it is unclear how the subsequent voting behaviour of institutions would be policed. It is doubtful whether pension fund trustees, in general, are qualified to undertake a detailed evaluation of the external fund manager's voting decisions. Given the diversity of company resolutions on which they would be voting, fund managers' voting policy statements would necessarily be broad statements, and unlikely to commit institutions to specific actions. For example, it is unlikely that institutions would publish statements committing themselves to vote against the re-election of directors if a company had less than the three non-executive directors (as recommended by the Cadbury Report) when there are a number of very successful companies which do not abide by these recommendations (for example, W. M. Morrison, etc.). In a similar vein, drafting voting policies on the issues such as remuneration increases would be difficult in the extreme.

If institutions were obliged to produce very detailed voting policy statements, there will always be instances when, in the interests of beneficiaries, institutions should vote contrary to their policy statements. In such circumstances, institutions could be obliged to publish justifications of their actions, but, without detailed knowledge of the circumstances, it may be impossible for pension trustees or regulators to judge whether the institution's action was actually justified. Clearly, mandatory 'informed' voting would impose costs on the institutions. Furthermore, such legislation may have the opposite effect to that intended. If institutions find themselves in the position of having to vote, in the interests of good corporate governance, contrary to their policy statement, rather than endure the ramifications of this they may instead vote in accordance with their published policy (to the detriment of their beneficiaries), or they may simply sell their holdings.

While the imposition of mandatory voting does have initial attractions in appearing to force institutions to take a more active governance role in the

---

[4] See e.g. *Accountancy* (1995: 12), reporting Dr Jack Cunningham's comments at a Fabian Society seminar on corporate governance, and *Financial Times* (1995: 16).

companies in which they invest, the above discussion suggests that it is unlikely to produce these desired benefits. While it is possible to ensure that fund managers and/or trustees vote their shares, ensuring that they vote in an 'informed' way is impossible to police, particularly given the difficulties is defining 'good' corporate governance practices. Furthermore, given that pension fund trustees are often officers of the sponsoring company, they have little incentive to enforce voting policies (particularly on contentious issues) which may affect the sponsoring company in the future.[5]

A perceived benefit of mandatory voting is that the costs of maintaining highly diversified portfolios would increase, potentially forcing fund managers to change their investment behaviour. Given that the costs of voting will, however, differ between different types of fund management arrangements, it is likely that, in the long term, pension funds will be channelled into lower-cost arrangements, particularly 'pooled funds', while still maintaining highly diversified portfolios (see Short and Keasey 1997 for a discussion of these points).

Hence, while the introduction of legal obligations for pension funds to exercise their voting rights may at first seem an attractive option, it is unlikely to produce the desired benefits of increased monitoring. Given that institutions prefer to exercise any control they deem necessary in private, the introduction of mandatory voting may simple lead to lip-service being paid to the voting procedure, without any changes to the underlying ethos of investment and ownership policy. If the desired result is to increase monitoring by shareholders, it would seem necessary to create a new breed of long-term institutional owners, holding much larger stakes in their portfolio companies and hence dependent on the long-term performance of those companies.[6] There are some indications that institutions are reviewing their role in the governance of companies in which they invest. For example, RailPen (the occupation pension fund for railway employees) has recently issued a new governance policy which not only details their views on typical governance issues, such as directors' remuneration, but also instructs its fund managers to take a more active interest in strategic and firm performance issues (reported in Lewis 1995). Such developments are to be welcomed, but mandatory voting on its own is unlikely to produce such a change in investment ethos.

6. Governance by Institutional Shareholders: Empirical Evidence

The empirical evidence regarding governance and institutional shareholders is discussed as follows. First, evidence regarding the supposed short-termism of

---

[5]   For example, pension fund trustees are unlikely to press their fund managers to vote against companies with a combined chair–CEO if the sponsoring company has a combined chair–CEO.

[6]   An approach advocated by Charkham (1994*a*,*b*). For more radical proposals to improve the relationship between companies and institutions, see Sykes (1994).

institutions and the subsequent effect on R & D expenditure is outlined. Second, evidence regarding the relationship between firm performance and institutional shareholders is examined. Finally, this section discusses the evidence relating to the impact of institutions on directors' remuneration.

Short-Termism

One criticism which has emerged in the governance literature is that institutional shareholders are only interested in short-term gains, and moreover, given their large ownership positions in UK firms, they have been responsible for the short-termism which the capital market as a whole is supposed to exhibit. Indeed, it is the alleged desire by institutional investors for short-term gains which is often blamed for the extent of takeover activity in the UK and the relatively poor performance of the UK in industrial and economic terms. The argument that institutions are short-termist is essentially a criticism of the efficiency of the capital market; that is, the external capital market undervalues long-term investments. As Marsh (1990) states, 'The crime of which the stock market stands accused is that of mispricing shares.' The evidence to support these criticisms is largely anecdotal. Very little empirical evidence exists which directly tests whether UK stock market valuations of companies is 'short-term'. However, that which does exist (Nickell and Wadhwani 1987; Miles 1993) suggest that long-term cash flows are discounted at much higher rates than shorter-term cash flows.[7] While such findings are open to criticism regarding model assumptions (as indeed are all efficient market studies), they do present results which are difficult to reconcile with market efficiency. In contrast, Stapledon (1994) concludes there is little in the way of argument and/or evidence to suggest corporations have been short-termist. In fact, he even questions whether the corporations have misinterpreted the objectives of the institutions. He does argue, however, that rather than the system being actively short-term, there is a lack of incentives to look long-term. In the present arm's length market system there is no real emphasis on the gains to be made from long-term commitments, in contrast to the relational systems of Germany and Japan. Hence, the problem is seen not so much as a consequence of the purposeful actions of individuals and organizations but rather a result of the inherent emphasis of the system as a whole.

One often cited consequence of institutional short-termism is that UK companies under-invest in R & D relative to their international competitors. Lack of investment in R & D is often blamed for the poor performance of the UK economy. However, the empirical evidence available for the USA does not support this argument. Studies by McConnell and Muscarella (1985), Woolridge (1988), and Jarrell and Lehn (1985) indicate that announcements of long-term investment expenditure are regarded as good news by the market and result, on average, in positive abnormal returns. Overall, there is substantial evidence to support the contention

[7] See also dissenting comment by Satchell and Damant (1995) and the reply by Miles (1995).

that the market does not systematically discriminate against companies that undertake above-average expenditures in R & D (Marsh 1990). However, the lack of discrimination against companies undertaking R & D expenditure does not mean that the market is able to distinguish between R & D expenditure which will yield future positive net cash flows and that which will not. It remains to be seen whether market players are, on average, capable of correctly evaluating investment opportunities in certain highly technical industries and hence pricing the shares of such firms correctly. In a similar vein, Charkham (1994*a*) argues that many fund managers are not equipped to act as long-term (Type A) investors as their primary understanding is of short-term markets rather than industry.

The empirical research which examines the effect of institutional shareholdings on R & D expenditure, however, has produced mixed results. Hansen and Hill (1991) argue that there are two alternative hypotheses which may explain the potential relationship between institutional investors and R & D expenditure. The first, the myopic institutions theory, argues that institutions sell in response to a short-term decline in earnings. This results in a drop in the share price and an increase in the probability of a hostile takeover bid. This theory essentially argues that the external capital market is inefficient, undervaluing long-term investments. As a consequence, management cut back on long-term investments, specifically R & D expenditure, to inflate short-term earnings. Hence the myopic institutions theory predicts a negative relationship to exist between institutional shareholdings and R & D expenditures. Alternatively, the efficient markets theory argues that all shareholders approve of investments which increase the future cash flows of the firm. Rational investors are not led by short-term profits and will approve of R & D expenditure which enhances future cash flows and may sell shares if a firm over- or under-invests in R & D. The efficient markets theory therefore predicts that no relationship between institutional shareholdings and R & D expenditure will be observable. While Graves (1988) found evidence to support the myopic institutions hypothesis, Hansen and Hill (1991) and Jarrell and Lehn (1985) found no evidence of a negative relationship between R & D expenditure and institutional shareholders. Indeed, Hansen and Hill found a weak positive relationship to exist between institutional shareholdings and R & D expenditure, a result which they interpreted as being inconsistent with the efficient markets hypothesis as it suggests that the presence of institutions encourages greater R & D expenditure.

The crux of the problem, in terms of R & D short-termism, would seem to be twofold. Institutions do not appear to be able to analyse 'correctly' such investment decisions and companies often do not provide the information that would enable them to make at least a reasonable attempt to do so. If, as Zechauser and Pound (1990) suggest, institutions are unable to monitor and control management activities in technically based companies effectively, it would suggest that there is a serious problem of information asymmetry existing between such companies and institutions. From a commercial perspective, however, companies are in a difficult position. Detailed information concerning R & D expenditure is proprietary information. As such, it is difficult to value without being fully revealed, but the act of disclosure risks sacrificing its value. It may be argued that the nature of ownership and control is to some degree responsible for the unwillingness of companies to reveal such information to institutional investors. If the information is price-sensitive, it cannot be revealed to institutions without making a public announcement, unless those institutions forgo the opportunity to trade in the company's stock. As a result, institutions are unwilling to be a party to such inside information. From an alternative perspective, it may be argued that management use investment in assets such as R & D in order to entrench themselves in the company (see Shleifer and Vishny 1989). In conclusion, if all the arguments concerning short-termism are brought together, there is some doubt whether it can be seen as a direct consequence of the purposeful action of individuals and/or organizations, or rather as a result of the nature of the systems of communication which exist between the institutional shareholders and corporations.

Firm Performance

Empirical investigation of the relationship between ownership or control structure, in terms of the identity of shareholders, and firm performance essentially attempt to test the managerial or agency theory propositions that different ownership or control structures result in differing performance (see Short 1994 for a review of the relevant literature). Furthermore, it is assumed that if certain shareholders are acting as monitors of management behaviour (either actively or by virtue of their mere presence), performance will be better than in firms where monitoring does not occur (assuming that managers will not operate efficiently if monitoring does not take place). Much of the empirical literature utilizes ownership stakes of institutional shareholders as a proxy for their willingness and ability to undertake monitoring activities. Ideally, the level of institutional activity with respect to intervention in board decision-making etc. and its subsequent effect on corporate performance should be examined, but such information is rarely publicly available. However, when examining the empirical evidence on the effect of institutions on corporate performance, it is essential that the limitations associated with such research are borne in mind when attempting to draw conclusions from such work.

There are a number of empirical papers which examine the relationship between firm performance and large shareholders in general (of which institutional investors may be seen as one identifiable group). With respect to the effect of large external shareholders on firm performance, the evidence is inconclusive. Holderness and Sheehan (1988), Murali and Welch (1989), and Denis and Denis (1994) found no evidence to suggest that performance differed between majority-owned firms and diffusely owned firms. McConnell and Servaes (1990) found blockholder ownership to have an insignificant effect on performance when considered independently of other ownership interests. However, when blockholder ownership and director ownership were combined, a significant relationship was reported. Overall, their results do not support the notion that large block ownership plays an important role in monitoring management. However, Zeckhauser and Pound (1990) reported results which suggested that the technical nature of the industry in which the firm operates had an effect on the ability of large shareholders to provide effective monitoring.

Little empirical evidence exists which examines the role of institutional shareholders in monitoring the board of directors, and that which does exist has produced conflicting results. Investigating proxy contexts, Pound (1988) reported results which suggested that institutions did not act as efficient monitors, providing evidence to suggest that institutions were more likely to vote in favour of management. This suggests that institutions either face conflicts of interest or find it worth while to strategically align themselves with the current management. Alternatively, Brickley *et al.* (1988, 1994) examined institutional voting patterns in management-initiated anti-takeover amendments and found institutional opposition to be greatest when the proposal reduced shareholder wealth. In addition, their results suggested that institutions that are less subject to management influence, such as mutual funds and public pension funds, are more likely to oppose management than institutions, such as banks and insurance companies, who may have current or potential links with the firm. Therefore, although these findings are consistent with the efficient monitoring hypothesis, they do suggest that the conflict of interest hypothesis may hold for certain institutional shareholders. McConnell and Servaes (1990, 1995) found the percentage of shares owned by institutions to be positively and significantly related to Tobin's Q and that institutional ownership acted to reinforce the positive effect of directors' shareholdings on firm performance, a result they suggested was consistent with the efficient monitoring hypothesis. However, Chaganti and Damanpour (1991) found institutional ownership to have a significantly positive effect on the return on equity but not on other measures of firm performance (return on assets, price earnings ratio, and total stock return).

In response to the largely US-based literature, we conducted an empirical project for the Institute of Chartered Accountants of England and Wales on the relationships between corporate performance, executive remuneration, and institutional shareholdings within the UK (see Short and Keasey 1995). The research was based on a random sample of 225 firms quoted on the Official List of the London Stock Exchange for the period 1988 to 1992. The overall conclusion to be drawn from the analysis was that although the relationship between corporate performance and institutional shareholdings is complex and difficult to disentangle, a number of specific results could be detailed. First, when considered independently of other ownership interests, institutional shareholders seemed to have little impact on corporate performance. However there was some evidence to suggest that the presence of institutional shareholders affected the relationship between directors' ownership and performance: namely, a significant and positive relationship was found to exist between directors' ownership and firm performance only when an individual institutional shareholder owned a larger percentage of equity than the directors. Furthermore, institutional shareholders appeared to have a significant effect on performance only when there were no other large external shareholders, suggesting that, where possible, institutions rely on other large external shareholders to provide monitoring. Overall, the results suggest that a complex relationship exists between the various ownership interests with regard to their impact on firm performance. However, all of the above conclusions were mainly derived for accounting measures of performance. In general, the ownership variables were found to have little impact on market-based measures of performance. One conclusion to be drawn from such a mixture of results is that although greater alignment of ownership and control has a positive impact on short-term profits, the market has not yet positively reacted to the changes. Indeed, the impact of the ownership variables on accounting measures of performance is relatively small compared to the effects of size and growth. Given this interpretation of these joint results, therefore, it is perhaps not surprising that the ownership effects are swamped in market assessments of actual and expected corporate performance. Another interpretation, however, is that the market perceives the accounting measures of performance to be open to manipulation by directors and accordingly discounts their value; which interpretation is correct awaits further investigation.

In summary, it is clear that the empirical analysis of the relationship between institutional shareholders and performance has produced conflicting findings, a likely result of the exceedingly complex web of interrelationships existing between the various ownership interests. Furthermore, empirical problems exist in attempting to model the relationship between institutional ownership and firm performance; for example, much research is constrained by the use of publicly available data on institutional ownership.[8] In addition, by focusing on the presence of institutional shareholders and/or the percentage of shares owned by institutions, there is an inherent assumption that a certain level of institutional shareholding is associated with a certain level of monitoring activity.

Executive Remuneration

In recent times there has been a lot of media attention on the perceived excessive level and growth in the pay of directors in a period of recession in the UK economy. The general perception would appear to be that directors are free to award themselves excessive remuneration without fear of interference from shareholders. In particular, institutional shareholders have been frequently criticized for their lack of apparent intervention on this issue. Furthermore, the Greenbury Committee (1995) stated that institutional shareholders should act to ensure that companies implemented the recommendations set out in their Code of Best

---

[8] In the UK, companies have to disclose external ownership interests amounting to 3 per cent or more (5 per cent or more prior to 1990) in their annual report. While a complete record of shareholders' equity interests can be obtained from a company's register, problems associated with processing such a large amount of data normally prohibit its use. However, very recently, commercial organizations have started to produce shareholder lists on CD-ROM, detailing ownership interests in excess of, for example, 0.25 per cent.

Practice regarding the determination of directors' remuneration. Relatively few studies have, however, examined the relationship between ownership structure, performance, and executive remuneration. Even fewer studies have examined the impact of institutional shareholders on executive remuneration. For the USA, Bilimoria (1992) found a significantly positive relationship to exist between institutional shareholdings and the link between executive remuneration and performance, while Mangel and Singh (1993) found a significant negative relationship to exist between executive compensation and the percentage of shares held by institutions. For the UK, a paper by Conyon and Leech (1994) found no significant relationship to exist between the level and growth in the pay of the highest-paid director and the presence of pension fund and insurance company shareholders. However, the papers by Mangel and Singh (1993) and Conyon and Leech (1994), by investigating the relationship between pay and institutional ownership, appear to be based on the assumption that, left to their own devices, directors will award themselves excessive remuneration. Therefore, the presence of large institutional shareholders who have the incentives and ability to control the board of directors should be associated with a lower level of remuneration or a reduced level of growth in remuneration. This assumption then leads to the conclusion that the insignificance of variables denoting institutional ownership suggests that these shareholders do not perform an effective monitoring role in this context (see e.g. Conyon and Leech 1994).

However, the finding that the presence of institutional shareholders does not lead to significantly lower remuneration does not necessarily mean that these shareholders are failing in their assumed role as corporate monitors. There are two separate issues to be considered here: the effect of ownership structure on the level or growth in remuneration, and the effect of ownership concentration on the relationship between remuneration and performance. If large shareholders are able to enforce monitoring devices such as performance-related remuneration, their presence should result in remuneration being more closely related to performance; a similar argument is employed by Main and Johnson (1993) in respect of the existence of remuneration committees. It therefore does not follow that large monitoring shareholders will automatically decrease the level of directors' remuneration; indeed in certain circumstances, they may increase it. It is necessary to examine the interaction between institutional shareholdings and the relationship between performance and remuneration, rather than simply the relationship between institutional shareholdings and remuneration. The results of Short and Keasey (1995) indicate, however, that the presence of an institutional shareholder has little effect on either the level of executive remuneration or the relationship between pay and performance.

7. Summary and Conclusions

There are clearly many factors which act to provide incentives for institutions *not* to involve themselves in corporate governance issues. Whilst the level of monitoring by institutions is greater than that commonly supposed, such monitoring tends to be carried out in private and, as Black and Coffee (1994) note, 'for most British institutions, activism is crisis driven'. Furthermore, it is unlikely that 'behind the scenes' monitoring is satisfactory, particularly from the point of view of the public, as it enhances the belief that institutions and company management are all simply part of the same 'old boy network', a belief illustrated by the debate concerning the high level of directors' remuneration. However, on an individual basis, competition in the market means that institutions do not have incentives to partake in detailed and costly monitoring. From a collective position, however, it is clear that institutions do have incentives to monitor and intervene to improve the long-term performance of companies. The missing link in the debate is how collective incentives can be translated into collective action by individual institutions. Given the current market and institutional arrangement, it is unlikely that institutions can be voluntarily persuaded to take on a more public monitoring role. If changes in corporate governance are to brought about, a more fundamental change to the market and institutional arrangements existing in the UK is required.

Many commentators (e.g. Coffee 1991; Charkham 1994*a,b*; Sykes 1994) suggest that enhanced monitoring by institutions can only come about if institutions reduce the number of companies in their portfolios and take on long-term ownership positions in the companies that remain. Clearly, a major factor acting against increased monitoring is the number of companies held in institutions' portfolios. Sykes (1994) advances radical proposals for institutions to group together to form long-term 'relationship' investors whereby they would agree to remain as shareholders for approximately five years. In a similar vein, Coffee (1991) suggests limiting the number of holdings of any one institution. However, whilst there is much debate over the merits of diversification,[9] it is doubtful whether proposals to limit the number of companies in an institution's portfolio would be acceptable at the City and political level. Moreover, whilst institutional long-term investment is likely to increase the level of monitoring, such a change in investment stance is likely to affect the working of the stock market. If institutions adopt more long-term positions and reduce their trading activity, this may cause liquidity problems in the market and consequently the markets would be in danger of becoming inefficient. This illustrates the need for any changes in institutional behaviour to be viewed in the context of the market in which they operate.

Given that the government is unwilling to take steps to significantly alter the structure of the corporate governance in the UK, a crucial question to ask is why should institutional investors take on the burden of providing a public good. As Artus (1990), group chief investment manager of the Prudential, noted, 'Where

---

[9] It has been argued (see Charkham 1994*b*) that a widely diversified portfolio does not provide any additional benefits in terms of risk diversification than a more concentrated portfolio. It has been shown that most of the benefits of diversification can be achieved from a randomly selected portfolio of about fifteen to twenty stocks (see e.g. Wagner and Lau 1971; Fama 1976). If a portfolio is comprised of carefully selected stocks, a smaller efficient portfolio may be constructed. Therefore, the benefits to be gained from a widely diversified portfolio are questionable and transaction or monitoring costs are obviously higher.

the authorities take the view that the national interest and public policy does not justify their intervention in the market process, it is unrealistic to believe that the fragmented investment community could somehow take a different view and effectively impose it' (p. 17).

Whilst there may be general agreement that institutions are acting as 'absentee owners' (Sykes 1994), and that this is resulting in corporate governance failures, this does not mean that institutions are to 'blame' for the situation. Throughout the 1980s individuals have been encouraged to act as individuals, as encapsulated in the famous Thatcher statement that 'there is no such thing as society'. Collective action has been discouraged (for example, the Conservative government's actions against trade unions and collective bargaining, and the moves towards individually negotiated contracts in the public sector). At all levels, individuals have been encouraged 'to fight their own corner'. Yet this same government expects institutions to take *collective* action to correct corporate governance problems. This notion of collectivity is an important issue, because, as discussed above, institutions individually rarely own a large enough stake in any one company to make intervention worth while from a cost–benefit analysis point of view. The accusation that institutions are passive whilst individual shareholders are powerless (Sykes 1994) assumes that institutions have the power to control management. However, whilst this may be true at the collective level, it is rarely true at the individual institutional shareholder level.

A further point to note is that many of the institutions themselves are listed companies and hence subject to the market for corporate control. Moreover, as witnessed by a number of recent takeovers of UK institutions by overseas institutions, that market for corporate control acts internationally (although, given the relative lack of regulation of takeovers in the UK, UK institutions are more at risk from takeover by overseas companies than vice versa). If UK institutions set aside the fact that, in the short term, the most profitable action to take when faced with an underperforming company is to sell the stake rather than to bear the cost of intervention, it is likely to have an adverse impact on their own share price if this practice is carried out on a regular basis. As a result, this may make the institutions subject to takeover, particularly by overseas institutions.

In summary, it is clear that the 'so-called' short-term attitudes of institutions with regard to their ownership and investment positions are in part a rational response to the market, institutional, and corporate arrangements which exist in the UK. Unless calls for institutions to change their behaviour and undertake monitoring in a more widespread and public manner are coupled with a fundamental review of the ways the whole market system works, there is unlikely to be a significant change in the level of monitoring undertaken. However, the changes in the market, institutional, and corporate systems operating in the UK are extremely difficult to identify in isolation and, moreover, would be difficult to bring about given the current state of the capital market with its emphasis on arm's length funding and liquidity. As Artus (1990) notes, 'Any conceivable increase in [monitoring] activity will not amount to a major new element of accountability in our system matching that of the bank-based economies, since share ownership unaccompanied by the additional involvement in providing finance and other services will never provide the depth of knowledge and commitment that arises with the combination of banking and proprietary interests' (p. 14). Hence, a change in emphasis on the stock market as the means of raising long-term funds and a greater reliance on debtholders to provide the monitoring function may be required. In conclusion, it would seem clear that, given the present system of arm's length equity investment, it is unlikely that institutions are willing or able to change fundamentally their own investment and monitoring behaviour, without, as Davies (1993: 96) notes, 'a wholesale restructuring of the UK's financial system'.

REFERENCES

Accountancy (1995), 'Harder Line from Labour' (Oct.).

Artus, R. E. (1990), 'Tension to Continue', in *Creative Tension?* (London: National Association of Pension Funds), 12–17.

Ball, J. (1990), 'Financial Institutions and their Role as Shareholders', in *Creative Tension?* (London: National Association of Pension Funds), 18–26.

Bilimoria, D. (1992), 'Perspectives on Corporate Control: Implications for CEO Compensation', *Proceedings of the Academy of Management Best Papers.*

Black, B. S., and Coffee, J. C. (1994), 'Hail Britannia?: Institutional Investor Behaviour under Limited Regulation', *Michigan Law Review*, 92/7: 1997–2087.

Blake, D. (1992), *Issues in Pension Funding* (London: Routledge).

Brickley, J. A., Lease, R. C., and Smith, C. W. (1988), 'Ownership Structure and Voting on Antitakeover Amendments', *Journal of Financial Economics*, 20: 267–91.

—— —— —— (1994), 'Corporate Voting: Evidence from Charter Amendment Proposals', *Journal of Corporate Finance*, 1: 5–31.

Cadbury, A. (1990), 'Owners and Investors', in *Creative Tension?* (London: National Association of Pension Funds).

—— (1992), *Report of the Committee on the Financial Aspects of Corporate Governance* (London: Gee).

CAPS (Combined Actuarial Performance Services) (1993), *Pension Fund Investment Performance: General Report 1993* (Leeds: Combined Actuarial Performance Services).

Chaganti, R., and Damanpur, F. (1991), 'Institutional Ownership, Capital Structure and Firm Performance', *Strategic Management Journal*, 12: 479–91.

Charkham, J. P. (1990), 'Are Shares just Commodities?', in *Creative Tension?* (London: National Association of Pension Funds), 34–42.

—— (1994a), 'A Larger Role for Institutional Investors', in N. Dimsdale and M. Prevezer (eds.), *Capital Markets and Corporate Governance* (Oxford: Clarendon Press).

—— (1994b), *Keeping Good Company* (Oxford: Oxford University Press).

Coffee, J. C. (1991), 'Liquidity versus Control: The Institutional Investor as Corporate Monitor', *Columbia Law Review*, 91/6: 1277–368.

Conyon, M. J., and Leech, D. (1994), 'Top Pay, Company Performance and Corporate Governance', *Oxford Bulletin of Economics and Statistics*, 56/3: 229–47.

CSO (Central Statistical Office) (1994), *Share Register Survey Report End 1993* (London: HMSO).

Davies, P. L. (1993), 'Institutional Investors in the United Kingdom', in D. D. Prentice and P. R. J. Holland (eds.), *Contemporary Issues in Corporate Governance* (Oxford: Clarendon Press), 69–96.

Denis, D. J., and Denis, D. K. (1994), 'Majority Owner-Managers and Organisational Efficiency', *Journal of Corporate Finance*, 1: 91–118.

Drucker, P. F. (1976), *The Unseen Revolution: How Pension Fund Socialism Came to America* (London: Heinemann).

Fama, E. F. (1976), *Foundations of Finance* (New York: Basic Books).

Financial Times (1996), 'At the Centre of the City Web', 19 Jan.

—— 'Labour Attacks Investors' Secrecy', 5 June.

Graves, S. B. (1988), 'Institutional Ownership and Corporate R & D in the Computer Industry', *Academy of Management Journal*, 31: 417–28.

Greenbury, R. (1995), *Directors' Remuneration: Report of a Study Group Chaired by Sir Richard Greenbury* (London: Gee).

Hansen, G. S., and Hill, C. W. L. (1991), 'Are Institutional Investors Myopic? A Time-Series Study of Four Technology-Driven Industries', *Strategic Management Journal*, 12: 1–16.

Hirschman, A. O. (1970), *Exit, Voice and Loyalty: Responses to Decline in Firms, Organisations and States* (Cambridge, Mass.: Harvard University Press).

Holderness, C. G., and Sheehan, D. P. (1988), 'The Role of Majority Shareholders in Publicly Held Corporations: An Exploratory Analysis', *Journal of Financial Economics*, 20: 317–46.

Holland, J. (1994), 'Corporate Governance and Financial Institutions', Working Paper, University of Glasgow.

Hutton, W. (1995), *The State We're In* (London: Jonathan Cape).

ISC (Institutional Shareholders' Committee) (1991), *The Role and Responsibilities of Institutional Shareholders in the UK* (London: Institutional Shareholders' Committee).

Jarrell, G. A., and Lehn, H. (1985), *Institutional Ownership, Tender Offers, and Long-Term Investments* (Washington: Office of the Chief Economist, Securities Exchange Commission).

Jenkinson, T., and Mayer, C. (1992), 'The Assessment: Corporate Governance and Corporate Control', *Oxford Review of Economic Policy*, 8/3: 1–10.

Jordan, G., and Richardson, J. (1982), 'The British Policy Style or the Logic of Negotiation?', in J. Richardson (ed.), *Policy Styles in Western Europe* (London: Allen & Unwin).

Lewis, W. (1995), 'RailPen Tightens Governance Policy', *Financial Times*, 14 Dec.

McConnell, J. J., and Muscarella, C. J. (1985), 'Corporate Capital Expenditure Decisions and the Market Value of the Firm', *Journal of Financial Economics*, 14: 399–422.

—— and Servaes, H. (1990), 'Additional Evidence on Equity Ownership and Corporate Value', *Journal of Financial Economics*, 27: 595–612.

—— —— (1995), 'Equity Ownership and the Two Faces of Debt', *Journal of Financial Economics*, 39: 131–57.

Main, B. G. M., and Johnston, J. (1993), 'Remuneration Committees and Corporate Governance', *Accounting and Business Research*, 23/91A: 351–62.

Mallin, C. (1995), *Voting: The Role of Institutional Investors in Corporate Governance* (London: Research Board of the Institute of Chartered Accountants in England and Wales).

Mangel, R., and Singh, H. (1993), 'Ownership Structure, Board Relationships and CEO

Compensation in Large US Corporations', *Accounting and Business Research*, 23/91A: 339–62.

Marsh, P. R. (1990), *Short-Termism on Trial* (London: Institutional Fund Managers' Association).

Miles, D. (1993), 'Testing for Short Termism in the UK Stock Market', *Economic Journal*, 103: 1379–96.

—— (1995), 'Testing for Short Termism in the UK Stock Market: A Reply', *Economic Journal*, 105: 1224–7.

Morck, R., Shleifer, A., and Vishny, R. W. (1988), 'Management Ownership and Market Valuation: An Empirical Analysis', *Journal of Financial Economics*, 20: 293–315.

Murali, R., and Welch, J. B. (1989), 'Agents, Owners, Control and Performance', *Journal of Business Finance and Accounting* (Summer), 385–98.

NAPF (National Association of Pension Funds) (1990–4), *Annual Survey of Occupational Pension Schemes* (London: National Association of Pension Funds).

Nickell, S., and Wadhwani, S. (1987), 'Myopia, the Dividend Puzzle and Share Prices', LSE Centre for Labour Economics, Discussion Paper No. 272.

Pound, J. (1988), 'Proxy Contests and the Efficiency of Shareholder Oversight', *Journal of Financial Economics*, 20: 237–65.

Satchell, S. E., and Damant, D. C. (1995), 'Testing for Short Termism in the UK Stock Market: A Comment', *Economic Journal*, 105: 1218–23.

Shleifer, A., and Vishny, R. W. (1989), 'Management Entrenchment: The Case of Manager-Specific Investments', *Journal of Financial Economics*, 25: 123–39.

Short, H. (1994), 'Ownership, Control, Financial Structure and the Performance of Firms', *Journal of Economic Surveys*, 8/3: 203–49.

—— and Keasey, K. (1995), 'Institutional Shareholders and Corporate Governance in the UK: Arguments and Evidence', Report for the Research Board of the Institute of Chartered Accountants of England and Wales.

—— —— (1997), 'Institutional Voting in the UK: Is Mandatory Voting the Answer?', *Corporate Governance*, 5/1, 37–44.

Stapledon, G. P. (1994), 'Controlling the Controllers of Public Companies: A Study of the Role of Institutional Shareholders in Corporate Governance in the United Kingdom and Australia', University of Oxford Ph.D. thesis.

Stiglitz, J. E. (1985), 'Credit Markets and the Control of Capital', *Journal of Money, Credit and Banking*, 17/2: 133–52.

Sykes, A. (1994), 'Proposals for a Reformed System of Corporate Governance to Achieve Internationally Competitive Long-Term Performance', in N. Dimsdale and M. Prevezer (eds.), *Capital Market and Corporate Governance* (Oxford: Clarendon Press), 111–27.

Trade and Industry Committee (1994), *Competitiveness of UK Manufacturing Industry*, Second Report, 41.I (London: HMSO).

Wagner, W. H., and Lau, S. C. (1971), 'The Effect of Diversification of Risks', *Financial Analysts' Journal*, 27: 48–53.

Woolridge, J. R. (1988), 'Competitive Decline: Is a Myopic Stock Market to Blame', *Journal of Applied Corporate Finance*, 1: 26–36.

Zeckhauser, R. I., and Pound, J. (1990), 'Are Large Shareholders Effective Monitors? An Investigation of Share Ownership and Corporate Performance', in R. G. Hubbard (ed.), *Asymmetric Information, Corporate Finance and Investment* (Chicago: University of Chicago Press).

3

WEARING TWO HATS: THE CONFLICTING CONTROL AND MANAGEMENT ROLES OF NON-EXECUTIVE DIRECTORS

Mahmoud Ezzamel and Robert Watson

1. Introduction

The central legal responsibilities of the UK's 'unitary' boards of directors are fairly clear, namely to manage the business collectively in accordance with its constitution for the benefit of its shareholders and to comply with the financial reporting and other disclosure requirements stipulated by company law. For UK companies then, the 'unitary' board of directors fulfils two main, and apparently incompatible, functions. First, the board is the enterprise's supreme executive body. It is legally responsible for formulating and implementing business strategy on behalf of shareholders and for ensuring that all business activities are conducted in a manner which complies with company law and other legal requirements. Second, the board has crucial governance functions to perform. The board is the primary institutional mechanism by which the shareholders render the executives appointed to manage the assets on their behalf accountable for their stewardship.

Traditionally, these two functions have been reconciled in company law by relying upon the system of 'accountability through disclosure'. There are two essential elements to this system of accountability: shareholder rights and information disclosure. Briefly, the rights of shareholders consist of the right to vote at the annual general meeting (AGM) and any other shareholder gatherings that may be called throughout the year to appoint and/or dismiss from office any or all directors and to determine the conditions of employment, terms of office, and remuneration of the board. Of course, without adequate information regarding the performance and financial consequences of the board's stewardship, these shareholder rights are probably meaningless. Hence, UK company law requires the board to produce and make available to shareholders prior to the AGM 'independently' audited financial statements. These financial statements are presumed to contain sufficient information for shareholders to assess the adequacy or otherwise of the board's stewardship over the period, thereby facilitating informed voting.

The greatly increased size and complexity of companies in the 100 years or so since this 'accountability through disclosure' system was first introduced has, however, seriously undermined its ability to provide an adequate solution to the governance responsibilities of the unitary board. The increased size of companies and the much greater complexity of many of the transactions undertaken creates financial reporting problems not evident when the system was devised. Today, a multitude of 'creative accounting' practices which exploit the inevitable ambiguities and many alternative methods of reporting the financial effects of transactions are both available and routinely used by boards to mislead rather than inform shareholders (see Smith 1992). Few informed commentators now believe that, despite the greatly increased financial reporting regulations and/or the supposed 'independence' of the auditors of the financial statements, the system is able to prevent effectively a determined board of executives from adopting reporting practices which greatly hinder accountability. Moreover, with the growth of widely held firms, the recipients of the information disclosed, individual shareholders, lack any strong incentive to expend resources on either analysing the financial information provided or otherwise monitoring managerial performance.

Recently, however, the highly influential Cadbury Report (1992*b*) into the financial aspects of corporate governance argued that the UK unitary board system is still capable of reconciling its two conflicting functions. The Cadbury Report focused on the composition of the unitary board and the monitoring role of non-executive directors in relation to the executive board members. Cadbury made the point that, though the distinction is without any legal foundation in company law, the boards of most large UK companies actually consist of two types of director: first, those who, in addition to being members of the board, have full-time executive responsibilities and, second, those directors, normally part-time, who have no executive responsibilities with respect to the enterprise's day-to-day operations. In the academic literature, these two groups are usually referred to as 'insiders' and 'outsiders' respectively.

As will be discussed later, the non-executive (or outside) board members, are not homogeneous in terms of expertise, function, or affiliation. A useful sub-division of these non-executive directors is into those individuals who owe their place on the board primarily to some pre-existing business connection with the firm (e.g. former executives and representatives of the firms' banking partners, suppliers, or customers) and directors without any other contractual relationship with the business other than their fees and (possibly) their ownership of shares. The first group are normally referred to as 'affiliated outsiders', whilst the latter group are referred to as either 'non-affiliated outsiders' or, as in the Cadbury Report, 'independent non-executives'. In this chapter, unless otherwise stated, the term 'non-executive' will normally refer only to the independent, or non-affiliated, board members.

The Cadbury Report viewed the non-executive board members as having a major role in improving the accountability of executives to their shareholders. The Report, though recognizing that non-executive directors legally have exactly the same duties as other board members for the conduct of the business, emphasized their role as independent monitors of senior executives.[1]

We argue below that the Cadbury Report represents a missed opportunity and that its proposals to enhance the monitoring roles of non-executives are unlikely to have much of an impact upon the governance of UK companies.[2] This is because the Cadbury Committee restricted its proposals to what could be achieved without fundamentally altering the legal responsibilities of non-executives, the basic structure of the unitary board, or the UK's 'accountability through disclosure' system. It is argued that the retention of the unitary board in its current form can be expected to inhibit severely the ability and incentives of even highly independent-minded non-executive directors to fulfil adequately *either* of their management or monitoring roles. Indeed, the proposals do nothing either to reduce the freedom of action and influence of executives over appointments or to increase the incentives of shareholders to be actively involved in the choosing, monitoring, and disciplining of either class of director. We argue, therefore, that the implementation of the Cadbury proposals to establish new board subcommittees and the disclosure of additional information are highly unlikely to result in a material improvement in the influence or independence of non-executive board members.

The remainder of the chapter is structured as follows. In Section 2 we examine the problem of corporate governance from an incomplete contracting perspective, focusing particularly upon the agency problems associated with the separation of ownership from control and the lack of incentives for individual shareholders of widely held companies to monitor the decisions supposedly made on their behalf by the senior executives. This section also critically reviews the literature which has suggested that these agency problems can be wholly or partly overcome by an appropriately structured board of directors and the disclosure of independently audited financial information. In Section 3 the legal position of UK boards, their composition, and the various functions they have to perform are examined. The conflicting management and monitoring roles of non-executive board members, the process by which they are appointed, and the (lack of) incentives for them to voice any doubts regarding executive actions or otherwise act in shareholder interests when these clash with those of executives are also examined.

The Cadbury proposals to enhance the 'policing' role of non-executives by setting up audit and remuneration committees, whilst retaining the main elements of the existing system of UK corporate governance, are reviewed in Section 4. In the fifth section, the available empirical evidence from the UK and elsewhere regarding the influence of non-executives upon corporate policy-making and

---

[1] Similar arguments also appeared in the more recent Greenbury Report (1995) into the setting of executive pay.

[2] We focus exclusively upon the issue of accountability and not on whether different corporate governance systems produce (or are associated with) 'superior' economic performance.

improving accountability of executives to shareholders is examined. This section includes some of the results of the first post-Cadbury study of UK companies into the composition and functioning of the newly introduced audit and remuneration committees. The final section summarizes the arguments and evidence and discusses the main policy implications and possible future developments for the UK system of corporate governance.

2. Incomplete Contracting: The Separation of Ownership from Control and the Board of Directors

Executives are primarily employed to use their skills, experience, and judgement on behalf of shareholders to make and implement decisions regarding strategy, major investment, and financing plans and to manage other labour, supplier, and customer contracts with the firm. In order for them to undertake these (largely non-programmable) aspects of their job adequately, senior executives' employment contracts must necessarily allow them a significant element of discretion. This relative freedom of action is, of course, vital to enable executives to use their entrepreneurial skills and expertise to take advantage of new market opportunities for increasing shareholder wealth. Clearly though, in the absence of institutional means by which executives can be 'called to account' for their actions, such freedom can be, and often is, abused.

This raises a number of familiar, though fundamental, questions for both academics and regulators, such as: 'In whose interests is (or should) this discretion be exercised?' 'Do executives use their freedom of action to further their own agenda and economic interests (as many public choice writers contend) or do competitive pressures in the product, financial, and managerial labour markets effectively constrain executives and thereby ensure that only economically efficient practices and organizational arrangements survive (as assumed by most agency theory models)?' 'What organizational constraints and incentives currently exist, can be improved upon, or can be devised to ensure that actions are taken in the interests of those groups and individuals that bear the cost of executive decisions (the residual claimants)?'

Clearly, the central practical problem for the governance of companies is finding and operating a set of institutional arrangements which strike the right balance between executive freedom of action and accountability to other stakeholders. On a more theoretical level, corporate governance, how the discretionary actions of executives are exercised in a manner consistent with the interests and rights of other stakeholders, is of economic importance only in a world characterized by agency costs and incomplete contracts (Hart 1995). An incomplete contract exists whenever the contracting parties are unable *ex ante* to specify fully the actions to be taken in every possible future 'state of nature'. Every long-term labour contract which does not fully specify an employee's duties is an obvious and common example of an incomplete contract. With such contracts, it is implicit that the employee will frequently be required to undertake activities which, due to the inability to specify what these will be *ex ante*, are not explicitly detailed in the contract.

In a similar fashion, debt contracts are necessarily incomplete because although the contract may, in addition to the repayment terms, specify many restrictions, such as dividend and debt or equity caps, the firm's actions are not perfectly controlled. It is possible (and indeed is quite common in practice) for a firm to comply fully with all of the restrictions contained in its debt agreements whilst still being able to undertake many changes in corporate policy which will nevertheless have an influence upon the debtholder's wealth. As Garvey and Swan (1994) have noted in respect of bond prices,

so long as such explicit promises are fulfilled, the bondholders bear any losses and enjoy any gains that may flow from changes in corporate policy. This simply says that bond prices will move for reasons other than exogenous realisations of 'states of nature'. The firm's actions are not perfectly controlled but only loosely guided by rules negotiated in arms-length markets, and the costs and benefits of such actions are not borne entirely by shareholders. (p. 141)

This incompleteness exists despite the fact that, at the time of the drawing up of a contract, the parties are able to incorporate (i.e. price) their expectations regarding the most probable and important possible future events that are likely to affect their interests materially. Even contracts which incorporate the most complex and detailed set of rules, and which have low monitoring and enforcement costs, will be incomplete because expectations may, nevertheless, be confounded by events which were not even conceived of *ex ante*. Clearly a contract cannot incorporate the inconceivable, and in this situation one or more of the contracting parties will have freedom of action (i.e. discretion). Hence, from an incomplete contracting perspective, corporate governance concerns the management and accountability of executive discretion in relation to the non-programmable aspects of the firm's contracts with labour, capital, and other input suppliers and its customers.

In widely held public companies individual shareholders and executives will generally own only a tiny proportion of a firm's equity. This separation of ownership[3] from control also implies that the executives no longer have the same financial incentives as an owner-manager to increase the value of the firm. Even so, if the monitoring and control of executive actions was costless to shareholders, then there is no reason to suppose that managerial discretion would not continue to be exercised in the interests of shareholders. Under UK company law, the formal powers of shareholders are fairly extensive and (costlessly observed) underperforming executives could, in principle, easily be disciplined and/or be replaced. However, as both the agency and public choice literatures have emphasized, in

---

[3] In UK law, though the shareholders enjoy many of the benefits usually associated with ownership, they are not strictly the owners of the firm (see Kay and Silberston 1995).

practice the separation of ownership from control can be expected to result in value losses to shareholders.

There are two main reasons for this. First, executives will normally have a significant advantage over diffused shareholders in that it is costly for the latter to find out whether the apparently poor performance of a firm is due to poor management and, if so, to evaluate the relative merits of alternative management teams. Second, apart from cases where an individual has a large proportion of their personal wealth invested in the firm, even when the benefits of improved monitoring in terms of increases in shareholder wealth greatly outweigh the costs of monitoring, diversified shareholders will still typically lack incentives to monitor and control managerial actions.[4]

As discussed in Chapter 2, by Short and Keasey, even shareholders with relatively large holdings, such as financial institutions, are also unlikely to have strong incentives to monitor and discipline poor managerial performance, not least because these institutions are themselves controlled by professional managers and can, therefore, also be expected to suffer from similar agency problems. The existence in the UK of heavily traded, and therefore highly liquid, secondary markets for corporate securities, coupled with the difficulties associated with intervention, also provides institutional and other investors who harbour serious doubts regarding corporate policies with the less costly option of simply exiting (selling their shares).

If it is indeed the case that there is an absence of committed shareholders who find it to be in their interests to monitor and control managerial actions, then what is there to prevent executives from using their significant discretionary powers to follow their own agenda even when this conflicts with the interests of shareholders? Not surprisingly, then, researchers and regulators alike have focused on what incentives and institutional arrangements are required to ensure that managerial discretion is in fact exercised in ways which further shareholder interests.

A number of external and internal monitoring and control mechanisms have been suggested; the market for corporate control (hostile takeover bids), the managerial labour market, shareholder (particularly, institutional shareholder) activism, debt bonding, incentive mechanisms, and changes in the composition and functioning of the board of directors. As noted earlier, shareholder activism

[4] The 'public good' characteristics (joint supply and non-excludability) of monitoring and control imply that, whilst only one shareholder need incur the monitoring costs, other shareholders cannot be excluded from the resulting beneficial consequences of this monitoring. Thus, the shareholder that monitors can appropriate only a tiny proportion of the increase in wealth due to his or her monitoring activities and all other shareholders can 'free ride' and still benefit in direct proportion to their shareholdings. In addition, collective cost sharing agreements between shareholders with regard to monitoring are likely to be severely inhibited since organizing and policing such collective agreements between dispersed shareholders are likely to be far from costless. Hence, each shareholder has an incentive to free ride and it becomes irrational for an individual shareholder to devote resources to becoming better informed and to voting intelligently. Consequently, in the absence of collective provision, there are likely to be insufficient resources devoted to managerial monitoring (see Grossman and Hart 1980; Stiglitz 1985).

is distinctly limited by information and free rider problems. In terms of ensuring that executives act in shareholders' interests, the other external, market-based control mechanisms mentioned above can also be expected to be of limited effectiveness (see Forbes and Watson 1993 for a review).

The theoretical arguments of Fama and Jensen (1983*a,b*) address the agency cost properties associated with the composition and control characteristics of the board of directors. Fama and Jensen make the distinction between 'decision management' (the initiation and implementation of decisions) and 'decision control' (the ratification and monitoring of decisions). They argue that where there is a separation of ownership (residual risk bearing) from control, arising from organizational complexity and information costs, agency costs will be minimized only when decision control is the responsibility of the residual claimants (the shareholders). Economically efficient outcomes are guaranteed only if organizations are structured in such a way as to ensure that the residual claimants are responsible for decision control since any costs associated with decisions to undertake non-value-maximizing behaviour will be borne by the residual claimants themselves. This, they believe, explains the 'survival value' of both owner-managed and widely held firms.

Fama and Jensen's case is that, by definition, owner-managed firms efficiently combine both decision management and decision control because both functions are undertaken by the sole residual claimant, the owner-manager. In widely held public companies, however, the two control functions should be undertaken by two distinct groups. The initiation and implementation of decisions (decision management) should be the responsibility of the salaried executives since they have the requisite information and expertise, whilst the ratification and monitoring of these managerial decisions (decision control) should be overseen by a board of directors directly elected by the shareholder group (the residual claimants).

In order for Fama and Jensen's argument to provide a justification for the economic efficiency of actual widely held public companies, empirically the board of directors has to represent shareholders' interests accurately and be truly independent of the executives. The extent to which this is so in practice and the factors which compromise this independence are discussed in the next section. On a more theoretical level, the argument assumes a world of complete contracts because only then is it tenable to view shareholders as being the sole residual claimants.

From an incomplete contracting perspective, residual risk bearing is inescapable in an *ex post* sense for all parties contracting with the firm. The incompleteness of contracts means that, though only shareholders are entitled to the residual profits after all other legally binding claims to other parties have been met, in terms of economic consequences any differences in the residual claimant status of the various contracting parties is simply a matter of degree. Kay and Silberston (1995) have summarized the situation thus:

If a company is not 'owned' by its shareholders, and the shareholders are simply one of a number of stakeholder groups, each of whom enjoy claims against it, then there is no particular reason to think that the interests of shareholders do or should enjoy priority over the interests of these other stakeholders. From a legal perspective, even the rule that shareholders have exclusive claim to the residual assets in the event of liquidation (established in 1962) was reversed by the 1985 Companies Act, which entrenches the interests of employees and imposes on directors an explicit duty to strike a balance between their interests and those of other members. (p. 88)

This is just as true in the case of an owner-managed firm, where a single individual owns 100 per cent of the firm's equity. Contractual incompleteness implies that the owner-manager is not the sole residual claimant and his or her actions will have unanticipated (and, therefore, unpriced) economic consequences for other (non-equity) stakeholders such as employees, debtholders, and suppliers. This is also well recognized in UK company law since even owner-managed firms are subject to various forms of external regulation to protect the residual claimant status of creditors and employees, particularly in the event of financial distress (see Keasey and Watson 1994). Hence, the agency theory-based literature generally fails to address the implications of incomplete contracting since typically only the firms' shareholders are deemed to be the residual claimants.

This restricted definition of who is and who is not a residual claimant leads inevitably to the view that economically efficient outcomes consist simply of maximizing the returns to shareholders and that the sole objective function of executives and the board of directors should be to act in ways which further the interests of shareholders. Recognition that shareholders are not the sole residual claimants would tend to suggest that in order for the decision control role of the board of directors to be economically efficient, the board should represent a much broader range of interests than simply that of shareholders. The incomplete contracting approach, as Garvey and Swan (1994) have stated, 'suggests that a more explicitly "political" view of corporate objectives is appropriate, since members of the firm besides shareholders are affected by executive decisions' (p. 148).

As will be apparent in the following section, empirically the boards of UK companies typically include representatives of several contracting parties (residual claimants), i.e. executives, shareholders, major suppliers, and customers, and (occasionally) employee representatives. However, though board representation of residual claimants is perhaps a *necessary* condition for efficient governance, in itself it is far from being *sufficient*. What is far more vital is the influence and independence from management of these non-executive board representatives, the resources available to them, and their incentives to challenge executive actions that appear to run counter to their constituency's financial interests.

Though, to date, there is little theory or direct empirical evidence to indicate just how effective the non-shareholder constituencies are in influencing corporate policy decisions, there is a wealth of studies which show that senior debtholder, creditor, and employee concerns in some circumstances appear to be an important consideration in determining corporate policy (for a review, see Garvey and Swan 1994). Thus, the incomplete contracting model of corporate decision-making, and the characteristics of an economically efficient governance structure for widely held public companies, have much more in common with the 'political bargaining' and 'dominant coalition' models of Cyert and March (1963) and Pennings and Goodman (1977) than is immediately apparent from the writings of agency theorists.

3. The Composition and Functioning of UK Boards

In the UK the legal responsibilities of both the executive and non-executive board members are wide-ranging and encompass strategic and day-to-day management of the company, information disclosure, and other governance functions. In many other countries the examples of German and Japanese companies where separate 'supervisory boards' are charged with the governance and decision control functions, are commonly cited in this context. Since in both the UK and the US separate 'supervisory boards' are rare, the composition and functioning of the unitary board of directors has, somehow, to reflect these multifaceted roles. The primary issues are, therefore, the extent to which the structure and the decision processes of unitary boards are such that UK companies are able to balance and undertake these diverse functions simultaneously.

Despite the presence of non-executives, it is widely recognized that the boards of directors of UK companies are generally dominated by executives. For example, a study by Hemmington-Scott (1992) of 1,612 commercial and industrial UK listed companies found that on average 63 per cent of board members were executives of the firm and that the majority of the non-executives were in fact executives of other listed companies. These findings are almost identical to an earlier UK study (Cosh and Hughes 1987), which indicated that typically executive directors outnumbered non-executive board members by two to one and that the majority of the non-executives were either retired executives of the firm or currently executive directors in others large firms. The Hemmington-Scott study reported that approximately 25 per cent of all company chairmen were also the chief executive, the proportion being much greater for the smaller listed firms. This concentration of boardroom power in many UK companies is a further cause for concern since many of the recent and highly publicized instances of failures of corporate governance in the UK and elsewhere have stemmed from a lack of countervailing influence on boards dominated by an over-mighty chief executive (see the review by Short 1996 for additional evidence on the concentration of power on UK boards).

Not only do the executives dominate in terms of numbers, but also as full-time incumbent executives they have privileged access to and control of internal information and of appointments, dismissals, and payments to auditors and other (executive and non-executive) directors. As noted in the previous section, neither individual nor institutional shareholders appear to have strong incentives to be active in monitoring or disciplining poorly performing executives. Despite their formal legal right to vote to change corporate policy and personnel at the AGM, voting intelligently (i.e. in terms of having a clear idea of the consequences of various options) would require shareholders to become informed and organized regarding alternative policies and management teams.

Not surprisingly, then, proxy fights are rare in the UK and the AGM is normally a perfunctory affair. Few shareholders bother to turn up and vote, or even to sign the proxy forms assigning voting power to another shareholder or director. Thus, as recently indicated by the failed attempt in June 1995 by the small investors of British Gas plc to overturn the large increases in its chief executive's pay, the board of directors usually has a built-in and unassailable majority for approving its own policies and slate of directors. Davis and Kay (1993) have provocatively described the situation as follows:

Imagine a system of government in which there are annual elections, but these are almost never contested. Whenever they are, the incumbent government wins by an overwhelming majority. All the information about the state of the nation which the voters receive is controlled and distributed by the government and is glossy and self-congratulatory in tone. Changes in the senior leadership do take place, normally through an orderly process of retirement in which the incumbent leaders select and groom their successors. Occasionally there is more violent change. Sometimes this takes the form of an internal *coup d'état*. Or it may occur as a result of the intervention of the hostile government of another state. This is not a description of Eastern Europe before perestroika and glasnost. It is a description of the system by which public companies in Britain are controlled and governed. (p. 200)

Whilst this quotation deliberately overstates the situation, it accurately indicates that the board of directors can normally expect to get its own policies and personnel voted through without having to worry unduly about adverse shareholder reactions. This much remarked upon feature of UK boards may not necessarily imply in itself that executives themselves control the board and are able to pursue their own agenda no matter how inimical this may be to shareholders' interests. If the non-executives on the board are independent of the executives, have reserved functions and powers, and/or are highly organized and motivated with access to sufficient resources seriously to monitor executives, then their influence may be much greater than their small numbers may suggest.

The appointment of other executives to the board to act as non-executives, many of whom have a pre-existing business relationship with the firm (affiliated outsiders), is clearly fairly widespread. Though there is no necessity for advisers and consultants to be members of the board, this appears to be the main function of these directors, i.e. providing industry specific, financial, and other expertise. Of course, if they are representatives of major suppliers, customers, etc., they are also in some sense residual claimants and may have a claim to be involved in the decision control process. Nevertheless, being executives themselves and business acquaintances of the executive members of the board, they can hardly be expected to be independent of the executives that appointed them. Clearly then, whatever their specific skills and value as advisers, affiliated non-executives cannot be expected to perform the primary monitoring and control roles required to protect shareholders' interests (see also the discussion in Chapter 7 by Wright, Thompson, and Robbie).

The combining of both monitoring and management functions into one agency (in his case the non-executives), as Fama and Jensen (1983*a*,*b*) have argued, is not recommended where expertise and information are asymmetrically distributed. They argue that non-executive directors on the boards of public companies have an overriding incentive to be independent of the executives and to monitor their activities efficiently in order to ensure that shareholders' interests are being maintained. They argue the case that outside board members with multiple directorships have an incentive to act in shareholders' interests because of their high investment in establishing and maintaining their reputations as 'decision experts'. Thus, although opposing, say, a value-decreasing proposed takeover may be detrimental to a non-executive's position on the bidder's board, the cost of not opposing it may be much greater if it results in significantly reducing his or her reputational capital in the market-place for decision experts.

Note, however, that this 'reputational capital' argument relies upon an informationally efficient market with regard to the performance of non-executives. Of course, if such an informationally efficient market existed, then there is no reason to suppose that a similar market would not also exist in relation to executives. It is precisely because shareholders have few incentives to monitor executives that non-executive board members are needed. Unfortunately, it is unclear why or how shareholders should find it any easier or have greater incentives to monitor the performance of non-executives. As Short (1996) has argued, since it is the executives that actually do the hiring, an external labour market for non-executives is simply likely to lead to a high value being placed on non-executives with a reputation for 'not rocking the boat'. Thus, without some guarantee of independence from the executive board members, coupled with direct incentives to act in shareholders' interests, the combining of the management and monitoring functions that non-executives have to undertake violates Fama and Jensen's most basic principle of separation of decision rights.

The combining of these two functions can, in practice, be expected to restrict significantly the effectiveness of non-executives in performing their monitoring role. As part of the management team, non-executives have to work closely with the executives in formulating and implementing company policy and it is unreasonable to expect them also to be independent monitors when they themselves share the responsibility for company policy equally with executives. The inconsistency in these functions, coupled with the fact that there is no mechanism through which non-executives can be held accountable to shareholders in respect of their monitoring duties, does nothing to strengthen their independence or to instil confidence in their monitoring capabilities (see Main and Johnston 1993 for a similar concern).

Indeed, a survey in 1991 by PA Consulting and Sundridge Park (cited in Bell 1994) into the nomination and selection process of non-executive directors revealed that 70 per cent of non-executives were personal acquaintances of the company's chairman. Davis and Kay (1993: 212) sum up the predicament succinctly:

Non-executives are in general picked by the executives, owe their salary to the executives, and commonly share social and other business connections with the executives. They rely on executives for information and advice, and their principal duties are carried out in the presence of the executives. It is hardly surprising that changes in executive management are more frequently the product of expensive, external action through take over than consequences of the activities of non-executive directors.

Similar concerns have been raised in the USA. For example, Milgrom and Roberts (1992: 434) have suggested that non-executive directors

are effectively nominated by the CEO, they must rely on the executives for most of the information they receive, and they need good relationships with the officers if they are to func tion well in guiding corporate policy. Often, directors share similar backgrounds and interests with the firms' executives. Frequently, they themselves are senior executives in other firms. Moreover, outside directors who are not CEOs of other firms may well derive a significant portion of their incomes from their directorship.

Jensen (1989: 64), in sharp contrast to his earlier and highly optimistic (theoretical) work with Fama which argued strongly in favour of independent board monitors, had been even more pointed, suggesting that in practice the notion that 'outside directors with little or no equity stake in the company could effectively monitor and discipline the managers who selected them has proven hollow at best'. As we indicated earlier, however, the unitary board of directors has multiple functions to perform and will, therefore, require a mix of technical expertise, outside (non-equity) stakeholder and capital market representation, and independence from management. Too great an emphasis upon the monitoring role may, of course, diminish the board's ability to carry out its managerial functions. In practice, whatever their formal legal responsibilities, if the monitoring role is to be taken seriously, non-executives' *actual* duties should be fairly tightly constrained, being confined to certain areas where executives' and shareholders' interests are most likely to diverge. In this respect, the preferences of shareholders and executives relating to such matters as the initiation of (or response to) takeover bids, information disclosure, executive remuneration, and board composition decisions may fundamentally differ, particularly when executives do not have significant shareholdings. Allowing executives unfettered discretion in these areas is, therefore, unlikely to produce outcomes which are in the best interests of shareholders.

Moreover, because such decisions do not normally involve issues directly relating to an executive's technical expertise, it is unclear that executives, rather than professional monitors or shareholders' representatives, will necessarily be either the best placed or most expert individuals to make decisions in these areas. It seems that these are the types of decision where non-executives' influence and monitoring abilities should be greatest. We examine the role of non-executives in relation to the remuneration of executives and their financial disclosure review functions in a later section. Below, we briefly review the (fairly limited) evidence relating to the role of non-executives in relation to takeover decisions and the effects of board composition upon shareholder wealth.

Takeover activities, either as a bidder or as a target, is an area where the interests of executives may differ from those of shareholders, employees, and existing suppliers. Executives may be motivated to launch takeovers for empire-building reasons, personal prestige, or enhanced remuneration rather than because the acquisition is expected to increase the value of the firm. Similarly, owing to fears of losing their jobs, executives may fight a takeover bid (using shareholder funds to do so) even though the bid premium inevitably leads to significant gains to its shareholders. In general, the empirical evidence points to significant gains to the shareholders of the target firm, whilst the shareholders of the bidding firm tend at best not to gain from the acquisition, evidence which is consistent with the phenomenon of the 'winner's curse', in which successful bidders overestimate the value of the target. Clearly, this is an important area where non-executive directors could exercise a significant monitoring role. Does the empirical evidence, however, suggest that they do?

Empirical evidence from the US (Rosenstein and Wyatt 1990) indicates that shareholder wealth increases significantly at the time of the appointment of an additional outside director. However, a more recent US study by Byrd and Hickman (1992) into the effects on tender offer bids indicated that, in this context at least, whilst shareholders appear to gain from more effective monitoring by independent outside directors, it is possible to have too many independent monitors. This study also found that shareholder gains were subject to diminishing returns as the proportion of outside directors on the board went above 60 per cent. Further evidence regarding the capital market's perception of the effectiveness of monitoring by independent non-executives in relation to takeover decisions and the importance of maintaining a balance between executives and outsider comes from the study by Kini *et al.* (1995). This study found that two general effects were associated with 'disciplinary takeovers' (takeovers where the target was an underperforming firm): '(1) for inside dominated targets, the number of inside directorships decreases while the number of outside directorships remains about the same; and (2) for outside-dominated boards, the number of inside directorship increases while the number of outside directorships decreases. As a result, the board is recomposed toward a more even balance between inside and outside directorships' (p. 383). These research findings suggest that the effects upon shareholder wealth of takeover decisions may be related to the characteristics of the board, its balance of inside and (affiliated and independent) outside directors, and that underperforming firms that are taken over appear to have had an unbalanced mix which is subsequently redressed after takeover. Clearly then, independent non-executives appear to be an important ingredient of this mix. This, however, also suggests that they should restrict their role to that of monitor since the above research findings indicate that, even in respect of takeover decisions, the relative absence of executives and other affiliated outsiders can adversely affect firm performance and shareholder wealth.

4. Recent Institutional Developments in the UK

Inadequate corporate accountability can be expected to lead to value losses to a wide group of stakeholders. That is to say, poor corporate governance has significant externalities and, therefore, it is not surprising that the state has always had an important role in this area. As Jonathan Charkham, recently retired adviser to the Governors of the Bank of England, has written:

There is no doubt that, except in the short term, corporate governance does matter. In my view, it matters to everyone in the community, especially because it is an important aspect of the interface between the City and the corporate sector, but this does not mean that it should be the responsibility of the central bank to monitor and reform it. The responsibility for this lies with the government, and currently with the Department of Trade and Industry (1993: 390).

This quotation conveys what has now become a commonplace in discussion of corporate governance in the UK—that responsibility for ensuring the operation of an effective form of governance in UK companies is ultimately vested in the government. However, other major institutions, such as the Bank of England, the Stock Exchange, and the professional accounting and institutional shareholder bodies, as mediators between the suppliers and users of capital and financial information, are expected to contribute to the debate.

The Bank of England has for some time been concerned to explore ways and pioneer means by which corporate governance in the UK might be improved. For example, in the early 1970s the Bank was instrumental in the establishment of the Council of Security Investors and the Institutional Shareholders Committee in order to mobilize the involvement of institutional shareholders in corporate governance. In the late 1970s the Bank turned its attention to the composition of boards of directors with a view to strengthening the role of non-executives in order to combat what it perceived as 'lack of proper control' of management of companies facing financial distress at that time (Charkham 1993). This culminated in the setting up of the 'Professional Non-Executive Director' (PRO NED) programme in 1981.

PRO NED had two main tasks: (1) to promote the employment of more and better non-executive directors (NEDs) as a means of improving corporate control; and (2) to provide companies seeking advice with additional names of NEDs. Within a few years PRO NED's contribution was reflected in fifty appointments on company boards per year. This belief in the crucial role that NEDs could play in rendering corporate governance more effective was given increased impetus in 1992 by the recommendations and subsequent implementation of the proposals contained in the Cadbury Report. The Cadbury Committee was set up jointly by the Stock Exchange Council and the Financial Reporting Council in the wake of a spate of highly publicized financial scandals and corporate failures. The Report of the Committee stated that: 'The Committee believes that the calibre of non-executive members of the board is of special importance in setting and maintaining standards of corporate governance . . . an essential quality which non-executive directors should bring to the board's deliberations is that of independence of judgement' (paras. 4.10 and 4.12). Unfortunately, the Cadbury recommendations with respect to non-executive directors virtually fails at the first hurdle, for it does nothing to resolve the problem in UK law regarding the conflicting roles expected of them. Indeed, the Cadbury Report simply re-emphasizes, without any recognition of the potential conflicts involved, that non-executives are expected to wear two hats: 'The emphasis in this report on the control function of non-executive directors is a consequence of our remit and should not in any way detract from the primary and positive contribution which they are expected to make, as equal board members, to the leadership of the company.' The Cadbury Report stipulates that each public company should employ a minimum of three independent non-executive directors. In this context, the notion of 'independence' is somewhat formal since the Report simply defines the notion in terms of having no pre-existing business relationship with the firm (para. 2.2). Even the holding of shares in the firm is seen as non-essential and, indeed, the Report suggests that such shareholdings may even compromise the non-executive's independence. Nevertheless, the dual roles required of non-executive directors can be expected to undermine any initial 'independence of judgement' before to long, particularly since the proposals do not increase either the power or the incentives to oppose executives when the latter appear to be acting contrary to shareholders' interests.

The influence and independence of non-executive directors is, however, presumed to be strengthened through the establishment in each of these companies of three subcommittees at board level; the nominations committee (to advise on the appointment of new directors), the audit committee (to advise on the audit and to have free access to company financial information and its auditors), and the remuneration committee (to advise on directors' emoluments and service contracts). With respect to executive compensation, the Cadbury recommendations state that the total emoluments of directors and those of the chairman and the highest-paid UK director should be fully disclosed and split into their salary and performance-related components and the basis by which the latter is determined should also be explained. Moreover, executive directors' remuneration should be subject to the recommendations of a remuneration committee made up wholly or mainly of non-executive directors.[5]

The establishment of these board subcommittees clearly offers more scope for non-executive directors to discuss financial disclosure and remuneration policy options and to influence management collectively than was previously the case. For example, establishing a remuneration committee with non-executive members could, *in principle*, avoid the conflict of interest which inevitably exists when executives are permitted to determine their own rewards. Similarly, having an audit committee comprising solely of non-executives could, *in principle*,

---

[5] The Greenbury Report went further and recommended that the remuneration committee should consist *solely* of non-executives.

improve financial disclosure practices, communications with shareholders, and the independence of the firm's auditors by discouraging their dependence upon the executives who employ and pay them.

There remain, however, several plausible reasons to doubt the overall efficacy of these developments. First, the Cadbury Report does not spell out what precisely the new subcommittees are meant to achieve, what their terms of reference are to be, and how, other than simply by attending meetings, the non-executives are to hold executives more accountable through these new committees. This vagueness regarding purposes and means is most obvious with respect to the audit committee. The independent audit suffers from a serious structural problem which has led to an 'expectations gap' amongst users (i.e. the difference between what an audit actually achieves and what users believe it can or should achieve). On the one hand, competitive pressures encourage firms both to minimize the costs of the audit and to present financial results which meet the perceived expectations of their shareholders. On the other hand, the diversity of accounting rules allows auditors, who also face competitive pressures, have close relationships with executives, and are appointed and paid by the executives, to adopt a strategy of evasion by not seriously questioning the figures produced by management. In the wake of the Caparo case,[6] the credibility of the auditing process has declined significantly since it is now also unclear what exactly the objectives of the independent audit are. The Caparo case is important 'because it exposed two misconceptions: first that the audit report is a guarantee of the accuracy of the accounts and the soundness of the company; second, that anyone can rely on the audit' (Stanley 1993: 55). Moreover, unlike the duties of directors, the Companies Acts are silent in respect of the duties of the auditors. Without a clear idea of what a properly conducted audit can actually achieve, the 'expectations gap' is likely to persist, which can only further undermine the credibility of the audit irrespective of the activities and diligence of the audit committee.

Second, the establishment of subcommittees does not resolve the inherent conflict of interest caused by non-executive directors being both an integral part of the management team and also monitors of their executive colleagues on the board. It is clear that the commitment to the unitary board system is what forced the Cadbury Committee to combine these two inherently conflicting roles. The Cadbury Report believed that the UK system of corporate governance was basically sound and that its efforts were, therefore, primarily directed at increasing its effectiveness rather than attempting to restructure it fundamentally (para. 1.7). The independence of non-executives could have been more readily achieved if the Cadbury Report had considered more radical solutions such as seeking a change in UK company law to restrict the duties of non-executives to that of monitor, and/or introducing a two-tier board structure with the non-executives serving

---

[6] In 1990 the Caparo case established in UK law that the auditors did not owe a duty of care to third parties (i.e. non-shareholders) who may have relied upon the audited financial statements for decision-making purposes, such as whether or not to make a takeover bid (as was the situation in the Caparo case). See O'Sullivan (1993) for further discussion of the case and its implications.

solely on the supervisory board without any formal executive responsibilities.[7] The Cadbury Committee rejected legislative changes of any kind and its centre-piece, the code of best practice, is entirely voluntary. As with all voluntary codes, it lacks any effective sanctions which can be applied to firms which fail to comply. As Stanley (1993) has noted, 'voluntary proposals like these will mean nothing unless they change corporate culture. If boards continue to appoint non-executive directors who are "one of us" (as in the Blue Arrow Affair) rather than independent watchdogs, then the sensible reforms of the Cadbury Committee will have been in vain' (p. 53).

Given this commitment to the existing regulatory regime, albeit supplemented by a voluntary code, the lack of any institutional means for appointing truly independent non-executive directors and for ensuring that they remain independent of management, whilst also rejecting any attempt to increase directly the incentives of shareholders themselves to be more active monitors, the Cadbury Committee could only simply endorse, and ultimately legitimize, current 'best practice' in the UK corporate sector.

A third reason to doubt the efficacy of the new subcommittees concerns the actual implementation and working practices adopted. As will be indicated below, in practice the three board subcommittees rarely appear to function simply as forums free of executive influence and/or more direct interference. It is to these issues we now turn our attention.

5. The Functioning of the Board's Subcommittees: Some Empirical Evidence

In this section, we examine the available evidence regarding the composition and functioning of the board subcommittees recommended by the Cadbury Report relating to the overseeing of the annual independent audit and the remuneration of executives. Chapter 5, by Conyon, also presents additional postal survey evidence broadly consistent with the studies reported below.

Board Subcommittee Composition and Functions

The three board subcommittees, i.e. the nomination, remuneration, and audit committees, recommended by the Cadbury Report are meant to give non-

---

[7] The two-tier board issue is somewhat controversial. Discussions regarding its desirability are often confused with whether or not it promotes, or is associated with, superior economic performance (see e.g. Owen 1995). We are simply arguing that it is likely to produce greater accountability than the current unitary board structure. Though we doubt that this greater accountability will lead to a deterioration in company performance, even if it did, this would not affect the accountability characteristics of the system, but would merely indicate that it imposes some costs on one or more of the groups contracting with the firm. Moreover, problems, such as 'excessive' employee entrenchment, a

executive directors greater scope to exercise their independent influence on the way executives manage certain aspects of a company's affairs. As the discussion above indicated, the dual roles expected of non-executives, and the political and organizational constraints within which the committees have to operate, are likely to result in outcomes far removed from the rhetoric and aspirations contained in the Cadbury Report. The voluntary nature of the Cadbury proposals and the vagueness of the terms of reference of the new committees allows firms considerable flexibility in implementing the proposals. For example, it is now well known that the formal terms of reference for remuneration committees vary considerably across different companies, ranging from, at one extreme, being solely concerned with the remuneration of the chairman and senior executives to, at the other extreme, ensuring the matching of personnel policy to business strategy, overseeing succession planning and share schemes, and the remuneration of all employees (see Bell 1994). Clearly, if the board subcommittees have wide, largely managerial, terms of reference, then this can be expected to inhibit the monitoring function. In this situation, the non-executives become more closely involved with managerial concerns and the committees' time and other resources get dissipated in dealing with matters which have little to do with ensuring that executives act in ways that are not detrimental to shareholders' interests.

Accounts given by several commentators (e.g. Bell 1994; Davis and Kay 1993) also make clear that a significant proportion of companies do in fact look for management leadership from their non-executive directors. For example, Bell (1994: 9), in commenting on companies' desire for the remuneration committee to perform the dual role of watchdog and contributor to management, has pointed out that,[8] 'In order to fulfil the latter role, companies seek directors who have a strong record of managing a company, so that they can bring this expertise in their role as non-executive director.' But there are also additional issues of concern, in particular the composition of committee membership and *how* the committees function in practice. Ezzamel and Watson (1995a) conducted an empirical investigation of committee membership in the first year after the Cadbury proposals were implemented for a sample of 224 UK companies with year ends December–January 1992–3. Their examination of the membership of the three main committees indicated that, in the majority of cases, executives were members of the committees, and indeed often chaired the committee. To the extent that membership of committees offers scope for influencing deliberations, then executive directors in UK companies can still be seen to have ample scope to do this.

'slowness of response' to environmental changes, insufficient information flows to and/or from meetings of the supervisory board and other external regulations, are often attributed to the two-tier board system when in fact they are not essential features of the two-tier board system itself, though clearly they are of some importance in the current German context. For recent thinking on these issues, see the contributions by Charkham (1994), Demb and Neubauer (1992), Dimsdale and Prevezer (1994), and Edwards and Fischer (1994).

[8] This tendency is actually reinforced by organizations supposedly concerned with mitigating the evident weakness of existing arrangements for corporate governance. Thus, PRO NED require those who enlist on their register as potential non-executives to have served on the main board of a quoted company and to be under 60.

Also, as we have already suggested, given the conflicting roles of non-executive directors and their close associations with executive directors, the added constraint of having executives working alongside them on what are meant to be monitoring committees is unlikely to encourage them to use their 'independence of judgement' or to be conductive to seeing their primary role as guardians of shareholders' interests.

Indeed, accounts of how committees, such as the remuneration committee, are *managed* (Bell 1994) indicate that:

- Remuneration committee meetings are held immediately before or after board meetings, lasting just about an hour, and allowing little time for detailed discussion.
- In many companies, executive directors either chair or are members of the remuneration committee. But even when the chief executive officer is not a member of that committee, he almost invariably attends the meeting, leaving the meeting while his own pay is discussed.
- In summary, Bell (1994: 12) argues: 'Our discussions suggest that whether or not the chief executive is technically a member of the committee has little significance. In either case, the CEO will take a full part in the discussions and decisions are rarely, if ever, arrived at through a vote of the members.'

Remuneration Committees and Executive Pay

The question of executive pay in public companies has been a controversial one, both in the USA and in the UK, as evidence has repeatedly indicated that executive pay is not very sensitive to changes in corporate performance (see Pavlik *et al.* 1993 and Conyon *et al.* 1995 respectively for reviews of the US and UK evidence on this issue).[9] If executives dominate the board, then this should not be surprising since they clearly have the opportunity to design their own remuneration packages without reference to shareholders. Nevertheless, the evidence relating to the lack of a powerful relationship between pay and firm performance may not necessarily be indicative of executive opportunism. Designing and monitoring senior executive pay packages is a complex task, and simply focusing upon incentive alignment with shareholder wealth may have dysfunctional consequences, particularly if executives are forced to bear excessive and firm-specific non-diversifiable risk (see Forbes and Watson 1993 for a review of the issues).

Evidence from both the UK and the USA (where remuneration committees are almost universal) strongly suggests that, not only do non-executive directors typically have close ties with the executive directors they are meant to be monitoring, but they are also no less likely to award large pay rises which bear little relation to company performance.

A study by Main and Johnston (1993) of 220 large listed UK firms, sixty-three

---

[9] See also, Chapter 4, by Bruce and Buck.

of which had remuneration committees, indicated that, even after controlling for differences in firm size and performance, the level of pay awarded to chief executives when the firm had a remuneration committee was significantly higher than for firms without such committees. Main and Johnston suggest that on average remuneration committees award an additional 17 per cent to 21 per cent, or some £56,000 per annum, to their CEOs. However, as the authors point out, the main purpose of a remuneration committee is not to hold down, or for that matter to increase, pay levels, but rather to tie pay more closely to company performance. In this respect then, Main and Johnston's results regarding the breakdown between pay in cash and pay in the form of stock options, which showed that 'there was no discernible effect that could be attributed to the existence of a remuneration committee', indicates that there was little evidence that the UK's pre-Cadbury remuneration committees were having a significant impact upon the strength of the relationship between executive pay awards and shareholder wealth measures.[10]

O'Reilly *et al.* (1988) focused on the 'strong social influence considerations' that affect the pay awards granted by remuneration committees in the USA. O'Reilly *et al.* and Main and Johnston's results both suggest that the remuneration received by non-executive directors in their own companies largely conditions (or, to use Tversky and Kahneman's (1974) terminology, 'frames') what is deemed to be a 'reasonable' pay award when serving on the remuneration committee of other companies.

Indeed, the suspicion that a 'cosy collusion' exists between executive and non-executive directors, who sit on each other's remuneration committees and thereby bid up executive earnings, appears to be widespread amongst the business community. For instance, Tatton (1992) states that 'remuneration committees don't control pay at all, because they are effectively setting their own pay levels', whilst the *Financial Times* (20 April 1993) talked of 'tame non-executive directors sitting on malleable remuneration committees advised by tame pay consultants'.

Inevitably, given the lack of expertise of non-executives and the need to work closely with their executive colleagues on the board, the decisions of remuneration committees regarding executive pay are largely driven by the recommendations of outside pay consultants. Equally inevitably, if only from a recruitment and retention concern, external labour market conditions will be an important factor in the recommendations of outside consultants, whose 'expertise' is presumably largely based upon comparisons with the pay levels and practices of other, similar firms. Hence, whilst there may be some element of pay related directly to firm performance (i.e. profits, growth, and shareholder returns), empirically it can also be expected that the decisions of remuneration committees will be strongly related to (external) market rates of pay irrespective of either the individual's or his firm's performance.

---

[10] However, using a more comprehensive measure of pay changes than used in previous (US and UK) studies since it incorporated changes in the value of an executive's total share option holdings, Main *et al.* (1994) discovered that the assumed weak relationship between changes in pay and shareholder wealth was in fact very strong.

Whilst one might reasonably expect remuneration committees to increase the pay of executives who appear to be significantly underpaid relative to the market, it is less than obvious that outside pay consultants would recommend (or that the remuneration committee would seriously consider such a recommendation) that executives who appear to be overpaid should have their pay reduced and/or suffer smaller pay increases over time. Of course, if apparently underpaid executives have their pay increased and apparently overpaid executives do not suffer any downward movement in their pay, then the general level of executive pay can be expected to rise significantly over time. This is the basis of the complaint by share-holder groups that remuneration committees simply result in 'bidding up' pay. Note, however, that this bidding up argument is based upon the upward biases in pay comparisons largely introduced by the outside pay consultants (though, usually, simply 'rubber-stamped' by the committee); it does not directly rely upon the assumption that non-executives lack independence, though clearly a lack of independence would be expected to result in a higher incidence of the bidding up phenomenon.

An empirical investigation of the impact of the Cadbury recommendations on CEO pay and a direct test of the empirical validity of the bidding up hypothesis was recently undertaken by Ezzamel and Watson (1995*a,b*). Their results relating to CEO changes in pay between 1992 and 1993 indicated strong support for the bidding up hypothesis (i.e. relatively underpaid executives in 1992 experienced an additional increase in pay in 1993 which was approximately 50 per cent of the previous year's deviation from the estimated market rate). This result was robust to changes in the previous period comparison pay levels, various measures of firm performance, and the inclusion of other explanatory variables in the model.

In general, then the existing research suggests that the effectiveness of remuneration committees in linking CEO pay to performance is fairly limited. As we stated earlier, however, the existence of a closer relationship between executive pay and external market pay levels rather than firm performance measures need not necessarily imply that executive pay should be made more responsive to changes in shareholder wealth. Pay determination is a complex area, not least because it involves several trade-offs between rewards for past performance, incentives to perform well in the future, risk sharing, recruitment and retention considerations, etc. Hence, it is perhaps unreasonable to expect executive pay to be very sensitive to changes in firm performance. In addition, it is unclear from an incomplete contracting perspective that it would be economically efficient to attempt to make executive pay more dependent upon shareholder wealth measures. Shareholders are not the only residual claimants, and encouraging executives to believe and behave as though they were may have deleterious and economically inefficient consequences for other stakeholders.

Even so, the issues raised above concerning the lack of independence of remuneration committees in particular and non-executive directors in general has done nothing to add credibility to the process of executive pay determination. Indeed, what is clear from the evidence to date is that the establishment of remuneration committees made up of part-time management appointees largely dependent upon the recommendations of outside pay consultants certainly does not appear to have provided the neat and widely accepted solution hoped for by those who drafted the Cadbury Report.

6. Conclusions

The main purpose of this chapter has been to examine the structure and functioning of UK boards and the role of non-executives in reconciling the dual, and apparently contradictory, management and governance duties UK company law places on boards of directors. Owing to relatively poor economic performance, a number of well-publicized management 'excesses', and unexpected corporate collapses, the UK's unitary board structure and the accountability through disclosure system has been heavily criticized. Improving executives' accountability to shareholders has come to be seen as an urgent priority amongst many sectors of the business community in the UK, though not to the extent that substantial changes in company law are routinely advocated or supported. Consequently, proposals for reform have generally focused upon increasing the numbers, quality, and powers of non-executive directors and on exhortations to institutional shareholders to become 'more active'.

The Cadbury Committee proposals intended to enhance the monitoring capabilities of non-executives in respect of their executive board colleagues were also critically reviewed. Briefly, by failing to resolve the conflicting requirements associated with the dual executive and monitoring roles expected of non-executives, it was suggested that the Cadbury proposals did little or nothing to improve their independence or incentives to take seriously their monitoring duties. Moreover, the Cadbury Report simply assumed that accountability to shareholders was the primary objective of good corporate governance. Both UK company law and the theory of incomplete contracting suggests, however, that the usual agency theory focus upon shareholder wealth maximization and the need to make executives accountable only to shareholders is misplaced since all those contracting with the firm are, to varying degrees, residual claimants.

Even though executives have a legal obligation to be trustworthy stewards of shareholder funds, this does not imply that shareholders' interests should be the sole criterion by which to judge executive decision-making. As Kay and Silberston (1995) have stated: 'Commercial life necessitates many incomplete and implicit contracts, and we make such contracts with firms as employees, as customers, and as suppliers. Ownership confers the right to determine the unresolved terms of these contracts. If the governance structure of the firm allows, or indeed requires, all such incomplete terms to be resolved in favour of the shareholders, we will be reluctant to make such contracts, or indeed to do business with the firm at all' (p. 90). In order to manage efficiently the contractual relationships that make up the firm, executives therefore have also to take account of other stakeholders' interests. Hence, empirical evidence that executives do not always act in share-holders' interests, that they appear to be 'entrenched', or that their pay is not closely related to changes in shareholder wealth is not sufficient to conclude that economic inefficiencies and managerial opportunism are serious problems. Though such evidence is consistent with this view, it is also consistent with the idea that executives manage the business in the interests of a much wider range of constituencies. To date, however, empirical models have not been sufficiently developed to enable us to distinguish between these alternative explanations.

What is clear, however, is that executives have their own economic interests, and that if the firm is to be managed in a way that takes account of the interests of other stakeholders, some institutional means has to exist whereby these interests can effectively influence corporate policy-making. Though executives dominate in terms of numbers and influence, the boards of UK companies do often contain non-executives who are clearly representatives of important interested parties, though the majority of non-executives are probably formally 'independent' of such interests. The board of directors has several functions to perform, and the appointment of individuals with managerial expertise is probably essential for firms to maintain both their competitive edge and the support of important business contacts such as suppliers, customers, and the financial markets. Nevertheless, the control function which was quite rightly emphasized by the Cadbury Report probably cannot be truly effective within the unitary board structure characteristic of UK companies.

If executives are to be adequately supervised, then clearly the non-executive board members need to be independent monitors. Their dual role as both managers and monitors within the unitary board structure just as clearly compromises this independence, assuming (a touch unrealistically) it even existed when they first joined the board. In addition, mechanisms are required which ensure that individuals, such as employee representatives, who are not so obviously linked to executives in terms of economic and social interests are appointed to non-executive positions. We would agree with Bell (1994: 10) that more radical solutions, such as the creation of 'supervisory boards, where the function is clearly control and not management, and where the members clearly represent the appropriate constituencies of shareholders and employees', need to be seriously considered. Given their strong opposition to the tone of the Cadbury Committee's interim report (1992*a*), which talked of non-executives' 'policing role', such a solution would, however, most likely be strongly opposed by UK executive directors.

Some of these concerns were confirmed when we examined the empirical findings relating to the implementation of the Cadbury proposals and the functions, membership, and decisions of the new board subcommittee. The empirical findings revealed that the terms of reference of the board subcommittees, especially the remuneration committees, vary widely across companies and in many cases are demonstrably 'management committees'. An examination of the membership of the remuneration, audit, and nominations committees indicates that typically executive directors are strongly represented on all these committees.

Even when they are not members or chairs of these committees, the independence of the committees is still called into question given the major influence executive directors have on appointing and determining the remuneration of non-executive directors.

The empirical results relating to the changes in executive remuneration suggest that changes in executive pay are largely driven by external market executive pay comparisons, at least in respect of executives who appeared to be relatively under-paid. Although firm performance was found to be of some importance in explaining changes in executive pay, particularly when pay was defined to include both salaries and cash bonuses, the explanatory power of the bidding up phenomena dominated the empirical results. Once again, it is worth emphasizing that these results do not necessarily imply that executives are simply exploiting the situation and furthering their own interests at the expense of other stakeholders. However, although alternative explanations are possible, the lack of transparency in the pay-setting process and the doubts regarding the independence of the non-executive board members clearly invites such an interpretation.

Evidently, if the Cadbury Committee proposals regarding the greater roles of non-executive directors and remuneration committees are to have any credibility with stakeholders and the general public, then a more fundamental reform of the process of nomination, appointment, and performance evaluation of non-executive directors will need to be instituted. In the absence of such reforms and/or other institutional changes which encourage greater stakeholder use of 'voice' mechanisms, the remuneration committee is likely to be increasingly seen as little more than a legitimizing device whereby senior executives continue to set their own pay (albeit via the appointment of 'reliable' pay consultants) without any more accountability to other stakeholders. Without these more fundamental reforms, the Cadbury proposals are unlikely to have much impact upon either the setting of managerial remuneration or the central, practical concern of corporate governance: how to improve the accountability of executives to those groups most seriously affected by their decisions whilst still giving them enough freedom of action and incentives to allow their firms to compete effectively in an increasingly global and competitive market-place.

REFERENCES

Bell, D. (1994), 'Setting Pay at the Top', Focus Report, *Incomes Data Services*, 5–16.

Byrd, J. W., and Hickman, K. A. (1992), 'So Outside Directors Monitor Managers?', *Journal of Financial Economics*, 32: 195–221.

Cadbury, A. (1992a), *Draft Report of the Committee on the Financial Aspects of Corporate Governance* (London: Gee).

——(1992b), *Final Report of the Committee on the Financial Aspects of Corporate Governance* (London: Gee).

Charkham, J. (1993), 'The Bank and Corporate Governance: Past, Present and Future', *Bank of England Quarterly Bulletin* (Aug.), 388–92.

—— (1994), *Keeping Good Company* (Oxford: Oxford University Press).

Conyon, M., Gregg, P., and Machin, S. (1995), 'Taking Care of Business: Executive Compensation in the United Kingdom', *Economic Journal*, 105: 704–14.

Cosh, A., and Hughes, A. (1987), 'The Anatomy of Corporate Control: Directors, Shareholders and Executive Remuneration of Giant US and UK Corporations', *Cambridge Journal of Economics*, 11: 285–313.

Cyert, R., and March, J. (1963), *A Behavioural Theory of the Firm* (London: Prentice-Hall).

Davis, E., and Kay, J. (1993), 'Corporate Governance, Takeovers, and the Role of the Non-Executive Director', in M. Bishop and J. Kay (eds.), *European Mergers and Merger Policy* (Oxford: Oxford University Press), ch. 5.

Demb, A., and Neubauer, F. (1992), *The Corporate Board* (Oxford: Oxford University Press).

Dimsdale, N., and Prevezer, M. (eds.) (1994), *Capital Markets and Corporate Governance* (Oxford: Clarendon Press).

Edwards, J., and Fischer, K. (eds.) (1994), *Banks, Finance and Investment in Germany* (Cambridge: Cambridge University Press).

Ezzamel, M., and Watson, R. (1995a), *Corporate Governance and Managerial Remuneration*, an end of award report (London: Institute of Chartered Accountants in England and Wales).

—— —— (1995b), 'An Empirical Investigation of the Relationship between Executive Remuneration and Corporate and Human Capital Characteristics', Paper presented at 'Beyond Accounting, Finance and Management', Waikato, New Zealand, July.

Fama, E., and Jensen, M. C. (1983a), 'Separation of Ownership and Control', *Journal of Law and Economics*, 26: 301–26.

—— —— (1983b), 'Agency Problems and Residual Claims', *Journal of Law and Economics*, 26: 327–52.

Forbes, W., and Watson, R. (1993), 'Managerial Remuneration and Corporate Governance: A Review of the Issues, Evidence and Cadbury Committee Proposals', *Accounting and Business Research*, 23: 331–8.

Garvey, G., and Swan, P. (1994), 'The Economics of Corporate Governance: Beyond the Marshallian Firm', *Journal of Corporate Finance*, 1: 139–74.

Greenbury, R. (1995), *Report of the Committee on Executive Remuneration* (London: Gee).

Grossman, S., and Hart, O. (1980), 'Takeover Bids, the Free-Rider Problem and the Theory of the Corporation', *Bell Journal of Economics*, 11: 42–64.

Hart, O. (1995), 'Corporate Governance: Some Theory and Implications', *Economic Journal*, 105: 678–89.

Hemmington-Scott (1992), 'Non-Executive Director Statistics', *Corporate Register* (Mar.), (Hemmington-Scott), 5–9.

Hirshleifer, D., and Suh, Y. (1992), 'Risk, Managerial Effort, and Project Choice', *Journal of Financial Intermediation*, 2: 308–45.

Jensen, M. C. (1989), 'The Eclipse of the Public Corporation', *Harvard Business Review* (Oct.), 61–74.

Kay, J., and Silberston, A. (1995), 'Corporate Governance', *National Institute Economic Review* (Aug.), 84–97.

Keasey, K., and Watson, R. (1994), 'The 1986 UK Insolvency and Company Directors' Disqualification Acts: An Evaluation of their Impact upon Small Firm Financing Decisions', *Small Business Economics*, 6: 257–66.

Kini, O., Kracaw, W., and Mian, S. (1995), 'Corporate Takeovers, Firm Performance and Board Composition', *Journal of Corporate Finance*, 1: 383–412.

Main, B. G. M., and Johnston, J. (1993), 'Remuneration Committees and Corporate Governance', *Accounting and Business Research*, 23/91A: 351–62.

——— Bruce, A., and Buck, T. (1994), 'Total Board Remuneration and Company Performance', University of Edinburgh Department of Economics Discussion Paper.

Milgrom, P., and Roberts, J. (1992), *Economics, Organization and Management* (Englewood Cliffs, NJ: Prentice-Hall).

O'Reilly, C., Main, B., and Crystal, G. (1988), 'CEO Salaries as Tournaments and Social Comparisons: A Tale of Two Theories', *Administrative Science Quarterly*, 33: 257–74.

O'Sullivan, N. (1993), 'Auditor's Liability: Its Role in the Corporate Governance Debate', *Accounting and Business Research*, 23/91A: 412–20.

Owen, G. (1995), *The Future of Britain's Boards of Directors: Two Tiers or One?* (London: ICAEW).

Pavlik, E., Scott, T., and Tiessen, P. (1993), 'Executive Compensation: Issues and Research', *Journal of Accounting Literature*, 12: 131–89.

Pennings, J., and Goodman, P. (1977), *New Perspectives on Organisational Effectiveness* (New York: Jossey-Bass).

Rosenstein, S., and Wyatt, J. (1990), 'Outside Directors, Board Independence and Shareholder Wealth', *Journal of Financial Economics*, 26: 175–92.

Short, H. (1996), 'Non-Executive Directors, Corporate Governance and the Cadbury Report: A Review of the Issues and Evidence', *Corporate Governance*, 4/2: 123–31.

Smith, T. (1992), *Accounting for Growth* (London: Century Business).

Stanley, C. (1993), 'An Approach to the Internal Regulation of the Corporation: A Critical Analysis of the Recommendations of the Cadbury Committee', *Journal of Financial Regulation and Compliance*, 2: 48–58.

Stiglitz, J. (1985), 'Credit Markets and the Control of Capital', *Journal of Money, Credit and Banking*, 17: 133–52.

Tatton, A. (1992), 'Top People's Pay is Called to Account', *Independent on Sunday*, 20 Sept., 21.

Tversky, A., and Kahneman, D. (1974), 'Judgement and Uncertainty: Heuristics and Biases', *Science*, 185: 1124–31.

4

EXECUTIVE REWARD AND CORPORATE GOVERNANCE

Alistair Bruce and Trevor Buck

1. Introduction

Academic interest in the study of executive remuneration has increased significantly in recent years. In part, this reflects concerns within business, political, and popular circles that, in many cases, levels of executive compensation are excessive in both absolute and relative terms and that they frequently appear both unrelated to corporate performance and at odds with the fortunes of other corporate stakeholders, such as other employees, shareholders, suppliers, and customers. A further stimulus has been the continued development of interest in the set of issues which comprise the corporate governance debate and the reward of executive agents in this context. Equally, and relatedly, innovations in remuneration policy and particular instruments of remuneration have prompted analysis of their impacts on aggregate executive compensation and corporate performance. These innovations have frequently sought to adjust the balance between long-term and more immediate forms of remuneration, or between certain and performance-contingent elements. Finally, and more practically, activity in this area reflects the development of new, and application of existing, analytical frameworks which facilitate such investigation.

The objective of this chapter is to examine the relationship between executive remuneration and corporate governance in general, to focus more specifically on a particular innovation in executive remuneration, the executive share (or stock) option (ESO) and to assess the significance of such modified forms of remuneration for corporate governance. ESOs are given special emphasis as an incentive device capable of aligning more closely the interests of executives and shareholders. The chapter is structured as follows. Section 2 introduces and explains the theoretical frameworks which may be most appropriately employed in analysing executive rewards in general and the ESO in particular. This allows an understanding of how executive remuneration may be located within the corporate governance debate. Specifically, the potential contribution which the ESO and related instruments may offer as instruments of governance is compared to alternative mechanisms for internal control, both established and recently developed. Section 3 begins by explaining the fundamental characteristics of the ESO and its significance within the context of the 'standard' components of executive remuneration. The growth in popularity of the ESO is demonstrated and analysed and the regulatory and legal contexts within which it has developed are explained. Section 4 provides a basis for reviewing the empirical analysis of the ESO and related remuneration instruments by discussing, in general terms, some of the more significant methodological challenges posed by this area of investigation. Specific attention is devoted to the issues raised by studies which probe the link between executive reward and corporate performance. This is followed, in Section 5, by a critical review of both the broader remuneration literature and the more specific ESO-related work, inasmuch as it relates to issues within corporate governance. This section concludes with a discussion of those issues and areas which seem to justify further enquiry.

2. Executive Rewards: Theoretical Frameworks and the Link with Corporate Governance

It could be argued that contemporary academic interest in the remuneration of corporate executives has its roots in the managerialist reformulation of the theory of the firm in the 1950s. Recognition of an identifiable managerial class of decision-makers at the core of the modern corporation found expression via a series of theories based on alternative premisses regarding the motivation and objectives of managers and consequent alternative predictions regarding their decision-making behaviour. A central feature of the managerial theories was their recognition of the divorce of corporate ownership and control and their discarding of the traditional assumption, embedded in the notion of profit maximization, of decision-maker as residual claimant. This said, profit was generally not wholly discarded as a managerial concern in these theoretical reformulations; instead, the managerial theories tended to relegate profit to the status of a constraint within the managerial utility function, rather than the central focus of the managerial decision. The link between the managerialist reformulation and the study of alternative remuneration instruments is evident in the first detailed empirical investigation of remuneration effects by Lewellen (1968) and Lewellen and Huntsman (1970), which tested the basis for Baumol's (1967) theory of sales revenue maximization. Interest in the relationship, and potential conflicts of interest, between corporate owners and decision-makers provided one of the stimuli for the development, in a more general context, of agency theory. Unsurprisingly, therefore, agency theory offers an appropriate and persuasive framework for the study of executive compensation and its effects, a potential first recognized by Ross (1973) and most recently explored by Garen (1994). A central question here addresses the

challenge of reducing agency costs by aligning the interests of corporate principals, whose return to ownership relates entirely to their position as residual
claimants, and agents, whose return is largely or wholly independent of the residual generated, but rather dependent, in large part at least, on an *ex ante* negotiated
sum. Coughlan and Schmidt (1985) dispute the origin of agency costs by suggesting that costs are a function of information asymmetry associated with delegated authority rather than of the divorce of ownership and control *per se.*
Potential divergence of interest between principals and agents in this context may
manifest itself via a variety of forms. Lewellen *et al.* (1987), for example, point to
the potential for differential propensities for risk exposure, different time horizons, and attitudes to work effort on the part of the agent. Specifically, they argue
that the behaviour of executives whose remuneration is predominantly independent of corporate performance (and shareholder wealth) may be characterized by
greater risk-aversion, shorter time horizons in appraising decisions, and diminished effort.

A number of approaches have been developed which attempt to address the
divergent goals of shareholder principals and their executive agents within the
corporation. Each embodies the recognition that the monitoring of individual or
collective executive effort by owners is costly and difficult. For the modern corporation, the difficulty of establishing an effective monitoring system is, in large
part, a function of diffuse ownership, which carries with it a significant free rider
problem as individual shareholders are reluctant to devote resources to managerial monitoring. These difficulties are compounded by those associated with organizing joint legal action where executive negligence is apparent, where the
uncertainty and potential costs associated with a civil action are prohibitive. If
monitoring were not a problem, then, as Abowd (1990) notes, traditional instruments of remuneration in conjunction with monitoring could adequately resolve
potential conflicts of interest between principals and agents.

In broad terms, we may distinguish between those measures to promote goal
congruence between shareholders and managerial agents which are essentially
institutional or structural and those which involve a reframing of the executive
contract. Each of these types of measure is now considered in turn.

In dealing, first, with institutional measures, one such arrangement involves the
appointment to the board of non-executive directors to represent shareholders'
interests. Large UK corporations typically appoint several non-executive directors. Their role, according to Davis and Kay (1993), is threefold. First, they may
bring to the board particular skills or experience; second, in legal terms they are
decision-makers, forming part of a unitary board, members of which, in law, are
not distinguished according to whether or not they perform an executive role.
Finally, and most pertinently in the context of governance, the non-executive
directors have a monitoring role, observing at close quarters the decision-making
performance of executive directors and evaluating such performance in the light
of shareholders' interests. In practice, the effectiveness of the monitoring role is
open to question, however. There is, for example, limited sanction against the non-
executive who neglects the proper execution of the roles described. Even where

non-executive directors attempt to pursue their roles actively, their effective contribution to or influence on the activity of the board may remain extremely limited. Non-executives are likely to be disadvantaged relative to executive directors, in terms of access to detailed and specific decision-relevant information and of the consequent difficulty in raising and pursuing legitimate reservations about a course of action. The typical profile of the non-executive director calls into question their ability to perform an effective, independent monitoring role. The majority of non-executive directors are themselves directors in other companies, 'sharing the culture of those they monitor' (Davis and Kay 1993: 212). Cosh and Hughes (1987), in a study which offers an interesting comparison of US and UK ownership and board structures, also note the prevalence of interlocking directorships and the fact that 15 per cent of UK non-executives sampled were former executive directors in the same company. Equally, the appointment of non-executive board members by the executive directors, rather than by the shareholders, is viewed as compromising their ability to challenge the actions of those executives. Under such circumstances, perhaps the most plausible outcome is a tacitly collusive relationship, wholly at odds with the notion of effective monitoring. The weakness, in practice, of the non-executive director as a guarantor of robust governance is well established in the literature (see e.g. Monks and Minow 1995; Milgrom and Roberts 1992; Mangel and Singh 1993; Forbes and Watson 1993), and this weakness is particularly relevant to executive pay as non-executives dominate boards' remuneration committees and the determination of executives rewards, as discussed below. In a discussion of the weakness in general of internal corporate control systems, Jensen (1993) goes beyond the limitations of non-executive directors by questioning the effectiveness of the board system *per se* as a control mechanism. The failure of the board is seen as residing in its propensity to reward consent and discourage conflict and a 'limitation on information [which] severely hinders the ability of even highly talented board members to contribute effectively to the monitoring and evaluation of the CEO and the company's strategy'.

A further institutional device involving non-executives which, it has been suggested, could act as a brake on the self-serving behaviour of senior management is the appointment of a separate non-executive chairman and chief executive officer. The argument behind this practice, which has become increasingly common in UK corporations, though less so in the USA, is that it avoids an over-centralization of power. In practice, it seems implausible that this separation between senior executives with, presumably, similar personal and corporate interests would effectively address the governance issue. After all, the effective decision-making power continues to reside with the board with either split or unified roles.

A variant, and in a zsense a formalization, of the role of the non-executive director in relation to remuneration issues has been the recent development, most extensively in the USA, of remuneration committees, comprising non-executive directors, whose function is to approve the terms of executive reward, bearing in mind corporate performance and the interests of shareholders. In theory, again, the remuneration committee offers a safeguard against self-serving abuse of executive power in setting their own terms of engagement. In practice, however, remuneration committees share many of the disadvantages associated with the role of the individual non-executive director noted above, and it is far from clear that the wider shareholder interest is necessarily safeguarded by their existence. Main and Johnston's (1992) analysis of remuneration committee composition, encourages scepticism regarding the effectiveness and independence of the device, while Main and Johnston (1993) point to the frequent practice whereby executive directors serve on remuneration committees in their own companies.

As an alternative to increasing shareholder 'voice' through non-executive directors, another institutional mechanism with the potential to align executive and shareholder interests is the promotion of what Jensen (1993) terms 'active investors'. Active investors are substantial, often institutional, shareholders who have large enough shareholdings to justify the costs of influencing (or being invited to participate in) the firm's strategic direction and the monitoring of directors. As Jensen notes, however, the potential contribution of these groups has not generally been exploited as 'they have been shut out of board rooms and firm strategy by the legal structure, by custom and by their own practices'.

Certainly, in the UK, the role of potential active investors such as the pensions funds and insurance companies is generally not viewed as part of the internal governance of the corporation. Rather their role remains more comparable to that of an external pressure group. In this context, the institutional investors' representative bodies have been active in establishing guide-lines regarding use of performance-contingent executive rewards. These are discussed below. It should also be noted here that though institutional shareholders with substantial holdings in a company may initially appeal as a potentially powerful brake on executive excess or inefficiency, their influence in practice is likely to be limited by a reluctance to express dissatisfaction through either 'voice', which could adversely affect share values, or 'exit', where the disposal onto the market of substantial quantities of shares could be problematic.

It seems uncontroversial to suggest that there is, at the very least, scepticism regarding the effectiveness of the above governance mechanisms, involving non-executive directors and active investors. Executive directors' influence and resilience to internal control appears substantially unaffected by adjustments to board structure or personnel. Their privileged access to company-specific information, allied to their control over appointments to non-executive posts and the 'outsider' status of institutional shareholders, constitute powerful barriers to the building of effective systems of governance.

The difficulties associated with designing robust governance structures may be regarded as an important factor behind the reappraisal of the contractual relationship between principal and agent. The development of new forms of executive compensation can be seen as representing an alternative approach to the reduction of agency costs. Various modifications to the terms of executive engagement, retention, and reward have been developed in this context. Firms may choose to sharpen the link between executive and corporate interests by increasing the significance of profit-related bonuses, encouraging executive shareholding (see, in this context, Benston 1985), or demonstrating a clear commitment to corporate performance in their policies relating to recruitment, retention, promotion, and dismissal of executives (see Jensen and Murphy 1990). The ESO, the mechanics of which are discussed in detail in the following section, represents a more systematic attempt to align the interests of individual executives and shareholders, agents and principals (see Milgrom and Roberts 1992; Reitman 1993). A key requirement of any new form of contractual arrangement is that its design addresses and overcomes both the 'participation' and 'incentive compatibility' constraints at the heart of the principal–agent issue. That is to say, agents must be induced both to engage in the contract and, once engaged, to invest effort in those areas which benefit the principal (see, for further discussion of the nature of the principal–agent problem, Kaplan 1982; Grossman and Hart 1983; Guesnerie 1992; Rosen 1992). ESOs attempt to achieve this by aligning a part of the executive's reward to a variable (share price) which is also positively correlated with shareholder wealth. In theory, this appears a positive step towards a congruence of objective between owners and executives, though two caveats must be applied. First, the effectiveness of such a mechanism demands that share price movements reflect reliably the performance of management. Secondly, there is evidence to suggest that an effective alignment of objectives may require considerable attention to the *details* of share option scheme operation, including factors such as eligibility for award, policy regarding the frequency and extent of option award, and the origin of shares bought as a result of options being exercised. In other words the mere establishment of an option scheme is not, of itself, sufficient to harmonize the interests of principal and agent. Nevertheless, the ESO can be viewed as a signal from boards on the sort of executive they seek or from executives on their expected performance.

It is important to note that the interest in the modification of methods of remuneration is not confined to developments, such as ESOs, which aim principally to adjust the balance between longer-term, performance-contingent reward and more short-term pay components. A related area which has received considerable attention recently concerns 'tournament' mechanisms in executive remuneration. Here, the emphasis focuses on the relative incentive effects of extended and compressed executive pay structures, rather than the comparative merits of contingent and non-contingent components. To the extent that investigation of tournament impacts may point the way to mechanisms for enhanced executive performance, this is clearly an area that has implications for governance issues, though the focus of this chapter on long-term or short-term, contingent or non-contingent pay elements suggests that a more comprehensive discussion of tournaments is not appropriate here (but see, for a recent review of tournament issues, Main *et al.* 1993).

In summarizing this section, there is a variety of governance measures which attempt to align the interests of corporate executives and shareholders. It is generally acknowledged, however, that structural or institutional devices such as remuneration committees may, in practice, be extremely limited in effect.

Innovations to the executive contract, and in particular the incorporation of performance-contingent pay forms such as the ESO, offer an alternative potential basis for the resolution of governance issues, though it will become clear that their ability to control agency costs may also depend on the effective monitoring of their use. Section 3 addresses specifically the potential contribution of the ESO.

3. The Executive Share Option: Context and Development

As a basis for charting the evolution of the ESO and related instruments as elements of executive remuneration, it is important initially to develop an understanding of the various components of the 'typical' executive's aggregate remuneration package. Though this, in turn, invites some discussion of the appropriate definition of the executive, for the purposes of this chapter the definition adopted is that of a main board director with a full-time contract of employment.

In simple terms, executive reward comprises three elements. The first is what might be termed the executive's 'base' pay, which comprises fees, salary, and any bonuses; secondly, there are additional benefits, comprising, for example, perquisites, pensions rights, and compensation agreements, and thirdly there are ESOs. The first two components are relatively straightforward in terms of how they operate and how they are valued, and each is subject to disclosure in the UK under the terms of the 1985 Companies Act, albeit in a form which is less than wholly transparent. For example, apart from the highest-paid director, fees are generally not attributable to individual directors and values of fees are only reported as falling within given bands. Given the relative unresponsiveness of fees, salaries, bonus, and other benefits to company profit, it is often asserted that they create dissonance between executives and shareholders, specifically encouraging relative risk aversion compared with the risk neutrality of shareholders with perfectly diversified portfolios.

In contrast to base and bonus pay elements, the third component, ESOs, is inherently more complex. Assigning a value to ESOs is considerably more problematic and the disclosure rules in the UK are even less stringent than for the other elements (for a summary of disclosure requirements, see Egginton *et al.* 1993). The valuation and data assembly problems associated with these latter two characteristics are discussed in greater detail in the following section, which addresses methodological problems of option investigation.

For the purposes of the current discussion, it is important to explain briefly the fundamental characteristics of the ESO. In general terms, the granting of an option confers on a recipient executive the right to buy, at some future date, a share in his or her company at a price, the 'exercise price', close to the market price at the time of the grant. The value of the share option increases as the market price increases above the exercise price, during the period in which the option is eligible for exercise. In the UK this period normally begins three years after the grant of the option and ends ten years after the grant, thereby creating a seven-year exercise 'window'. The exercise of an option and the immediate subsequent sale of the associated share generates a return to the executive equal to the difference between current market price and exercise price, less transactions costs. This return is subject to taxation as a capital gain. In practice, the exercise of an option and sale of the associated stock are frequently conducted via a single composite transaction, which is typically facilitated by the provision of short-term bridging finance by the company. At any one time, executives involved in Inland Revenue-approved schemes are restricted to an option holding of four times their annual base remuneration, where options are valued in terms of their exercise price. As noted above, under circumstances where the company performance is particularly high, this multiple can rise to eight.

Clearly, sustained growth in the market price of a share over a number of years has the capacity to generate significant returns to the recipient of the associated option. On the other hand, should the share price remain below the exercise price ('under water') throughout the eligible exercise period, the executive enjoys no gain, though equally suffers no actual loss. This is not to deny that the executive may experience a sense of loss, however, especially where the share price had previously exceeded the exercise price, and the potential motivational effect of this is worth noting, particularly given that the vagaries of share price movement may at times be unrelated to an individual company's performance or, more pertinently, an individual executive's effort or performance.

Eligibility for the award of options is generally confined to a small number of senior executives and, increasingly, the decision regarding the granting of options lies with the company's remuneration committee, comprising non-executive directors of the company. Remuneration committees have become more common as companies have become sensitive to suggestions that executives were effectively awarding themselves significant increases in remuneration via options, though, as is observed above, the effectiveness of remuneration committees is open to question.

The executive share option as an element of executive remuneration owes its popularity over the last two decades to a number of factors. Fundamentally, it may be seen as one of several instruments of compensation which seek to address the conflict of interest embedded in the relationship between corporate owners and decision-makers, principals and agents, by effecting a closer congruence of interests between the two groups. More mundanely, or pragmatically, the early uptake of ESO schemes in the UK was often associated with their tax efficiency relative to other means of reward, though tax advantages in the UK (and USA) have been substantially weakened in recent years. For example, in the UK the harmonization of the higher-rate income tax and the capital gains rate in 1987 removed most of the tax advantages of the ESO.

Continuing from a UK perspective, the strong growth in the development of ESO schemes throughout the 1980s probably reflected also the desire of larger UK corporations not to be disadvantaged in international executive labour markets, where American firms had been the pioneers in developing such schemes. As ESOs became established among the larger British firms, so it seems likely that their continued uptake was sustained by followship behaviour. In the three years from March 1985, during the peak years of scheme inception in the UK, over 2,700 ESO schemes were approved by the Inland Revenue.

Though one explanation of the continued popularity of the ESO in the 1990s in the UK is the fact that they are now regarded as an essential, or standard, component of reward in competitive labour markets, an additional factor may relate to the sensitivity associated with large baseline or 'headline' pay settlements, particularly during an era of relatively very modest pay settlements in general. The award of ESOs allows the prospect of substantial, but fairly covert, enhancement to aggregate remuneration, without the prospect of generating negative reaction. The reasons for this are threefold. First, the award of options involves no immediate realizable gain because, as noted above, options cannot be exercised before a three-year period has elapsed. Actual exercise may be as remote as ten years from award, and this type of option is non-tradable. Secondly, the actual value of options to the executive is only finally verifiable on exercise. Though estimates of value can be developed in advance of exercise, these necessitate fairly sophisticated mathematical procedures which are themselves somewhat controversial (see Section 4). Thirdly, the regulations relating to disclosure of option award are such that they are not readily visible to other interested parties, such as shareholders.

It is this latter characteristic in particular which has focused the attention of shareholder groups on the potential for ESOs to present a further avenue for the expression of self-serving behaviour by opportunistic executives. This reintroduces the critical role of an effective monitoring system, this time in a more specific context. As a result, institutional shareholders have seen the need to establish codes of good practice in the operation of schemes. These guide-lines, issued in the UK jointly by the Association of British Insurers (ABI) and the National Association of Pension Funds (NAPF), include explicit requirements regarding the pricing and terms of award of options. To some extent, the guide-lines reflect what has been seen as the abuse of option schemes by early adopters of this form of remuneration, granting themselves benefits unavailable to shareholders in general. Among the issues of concern to institutional shareholders is the practice of reissuing, at a lower exercise price, options which, as a result of market developments and/or poor performance by executives, were 'under water'. A related concern is the practice of discounting option exercise price significantly below market price. Current UK guide-lines permit only a modest discount and that only where the company also operates an all-employee share ownership scheme. A third, and significant, concern relates to the possible dilution of incumbent shareholders' equity by the issue of new shares to satisfy executives wishing to exercise their options. Whether or not dilution occurs is largely a function of whether the company buys and sets aside its own equity to satisfy option-related demand, or merely issues new shares. Tax considerations are generally a major consideration in the mode of option provision. In the former case, clearly, dilution is not a problem (see Egginton *et al.* 1993).

Concern may also relate to the potentially negative impact of ESO schemes on the level of corporate dividends, as noted by Lambert *et al.* (1989). Using a sample of 221 large US firms and a dividend expectation model, they observed a significant decline in dividend levels following ESO scheme inception.

Finally, institutional shareholders have lobbied for the development of guidelines to try to ensure that ESOs are earned by executives, in terms of reflecting enhanced corporate performance. The clearest example of this is the condition required for Inland Revenue-approved schemes in the UK for the multiple of option award to rise from four to eight. For this to operate, the minimum holding period on the additional options is five years and companies must demonstrate a growth in earnings per share which places it in the highest quartile of the FTSE 100 index.

The development of the ESO in the UK lags behind the experience in the USA by at least a decade. The American stock option is, in many important respects, similar to the UK version. Its development was motivated by a similar blend of tax efficiency incentives and a more fundamental desire to realign potential conflicts of interest within the corporation. At the same time, there are conspicuous differences, however. These include, for example, the relative transparency of stock option dealings in the USA, a feature which has encouraged UK shareholder groups to press for more robust disclosure procedures. On the other hand, the liberal approach towards the disclosure of option award in the USA is mirrored in the relative lack of official or shareholder restrictions on the terms attached to either the number or the value of options awarded to individual executives.

4. Research Questions and Methodological Challenges

Empirical analysis of the motivations for and impacts of new forms of remuneration has generated a significant volume of academic output. The aim of this section and Section 5 is to assess the implications of this analysis for governance issues. This necessarily implies a selective discussion of the literature, with the primary focus being those studies which explore the relationship between alternative payment structures and corporate performance. It is this relationship which lies at the heart of the governance debate by testing the alignment of executive reward with the interests of shareholders.

Whilst Section 5 reviews the results of empirical investigations in the USA and UK, this section introduces and explains the significance, in a general sense, of the some of the more important methodological challenges which are raised by investigation in this area.

Causality and Related Issues

An immediate problem which presents itself in examining the pay–performance link is that of the direction of causation. This is perhaps most acute where the impact of profit-sensitive remuneration components is under scrutiny. Thus, for example, an innovation in the structure of incentives which is followed by improved performance, though suggestive of a causal link, may in fact reflect inception of a scheme by corporate executives *in anticipation of* improved performance and, thereby, consequent lucrative returns to eligible executives (see Tehranian and Waegelein 1985). Event analyses (see e.g. Brickley *et al*. 1985; see also Warner 1985) which chart performance around the point of scheme inception may, additionally, be frustrated by the announcement of intention to launch a scheme some time in advance of its official establishment; hence the 'event' is not uniquely identifiable as relating to a specific point in time.

A further problem with investigation of the link between performance-related remuneration and corporate performance is the tautology inherent in a procedure which investigates the relationship between, for example, the share-price-determined value of ESOs on the one hand and market-based measures of company performance on the other. It may still be pertinent, however, to measure and test the strength of any association between company performance and executive rewards despite the mechanical relationship between the appreciation of share values and ESO gains. Indeed, this form of investigation is arguably of no less value than the majority of existing studies which measure correlations between company turnover and base pay narrowly defined plus sales-contingent bonuses. Ultimately, it should be recognized that it is the relationship between executive pay *in aggregate* and corporate performance which is of primary interest in the governance debate. As such, the most informative results should emerge from the most comprehensive pay measure employed.

Given that one of the alleged motivations for the establishment of performance-contingent elements in aggregate pay is the expectation of enhanced performance, an important issue in the longitudinal monitoring of companies with newly established pay systems is how to differentiate between improved performance which merely reflects improved operating conditions for all firms (or all firms in a sector) and that which is specific to the firms under scrutiny. Clearly, for example, through the middle years of the 1980s, many large UK companies were performing extremely well in terms of market measures irrespective of whether they had recently established ESO schemes. It may be necessary under such circumstances to develop a yardstick or baseline performance model against which abnormal performance by payment system innovators may be identified (see, in this context, Egginton *et al*. 1989). Relatedly, it must be acknowledged that any performance advantages which appear to flow from a new payment system may rather be accounted for by some other firm-specific variable, such as size, which is common to firms which are innovative in remuneration policy.

Temporal Factors and Environmental Change

A further consideration in interpreting empirical investigation of innovations such as the ESO is that they are still, in the mid-1990s, a comparatively novel phenomenon in executive remuneration, particularly in the UK. Though this is, of course, one of the reasons for economists' interest in their impacts, time-series analysis of ESO activity is likely to incorporate 'novelty' effects during the earlier part of the series. In other words, it is arguably only now becoming viable to monitor ESOs as an *established* feature of the broader remuneration package. It seems reasonable to suggest that both companies and individual executives may react differently towards ESOs now, compared with in the early years of their popularity, when a degree of familiarization and learning was likely to influence behaviour on both sides.

Additionally, identification of clear trends in the use of ESOs in the last fifteen years has been compromised by the substantial changes in the market, legal, and institutional contexts within which ESOs have developed. Clearly, trends in general stock market activity influence the potential value of ESOs as an instrument of executive reward. In the UK, for example, the 1980s witnessed a period of sustained stock market growth ending abruptly with the crash of October 1987, which wiped millions of pounds from the 'paper gains' of option-holding executives. Furthermore, in both the USA and UK, the tax status of ESOs has been subject to a variety of modifications, which could be expected to have influenced materially the attractiveness of ESO schemes to both companies and eligible executives. For example, in the UK the 1987 Finance Act markedly reduced the tax efficiency of the ESO by removing the distinction between higher-rate income tax and capital gains tax. Most studies which probe the corporate motivation for scheme implementation acknowledge the difficulty of stripping out the 'tax effect' from less pragmatic, more philosophically rooted motivations.

In addition to fiscal changes, modifications to the guide-lines issued by institutional shareholders frustrate straightforward comparison of early and late period ESO activity, whilst, in a similar way, the rapid development, through the last decade, of remuneration committees by larger corporations (Conyon and Leech 1994) has meant that the internal governance structures against which option award has taken place have changed significantly.

Both longitudinal and cross-sectional studies need to take account of the fact that, within the aggregate set of ESO schemes operated by firms, there are arguably at least two subpopulations. On the one hand, there are what might be termed ESO 'pioneers', firms which were philosophically attracted to a restructuring of the portfolio of executive reward and which were early implementers of schemes. In this category, firms such as the Burton Group in the UK, with individually tailored ESO schemes, were prolific in the award of options. More recently, as ESO schemes have become a standard feature of executive remuneration, the schemes themselves have become increasingly 'standard' and the decision to operate a scheme is less associated with a fundamental enthusiasm for new forms of reward, and more a function of the need to remain competitive in the executive labour market. As such, the researcher should be aware that cross-sectional comparison is comparison between schemes implemented by pioneers and those designed for followers. Equally, aggregations of firms' ESO experience should take account of such differences.

ESO-Specific Issues

Data Availability   Turning more specifically to the problems of investigating the ESO, one of the more significant areas of difficulty, particularly in the UK, is that associated with data availability. As has been observed, the disclosure requirements relating to executive remuneration in UK companies are extremely weak, by comparison with the USA. Whilst some summary information is carried in annual reports, this generally relates only to base remuneration and bonus and, in any case, as was noted in Section 2, the anonymity of individual directors is protected by the nature of the summarization. Details of executive share option awards to executives do not appear in annual reports. Technically, however, they are open to public scrutiny via the requirement in the Companies Act that Directors' Registers, which contain details of each individual's holding and exercise of options, must be made available on request. In practice, though, Directors' Registers provide at best a rather opaque source of information relating to share options. Gaining access to registers, despite the legal requirements, frequently requires repeated approaches to companies. Interpreting the information in the registers is confounded by often poor standards of information presentation. Many registers continue to be compiled in handwritten form and the balance and value of options held and their exercise price may be subject to adjustments in the event of rights issues or related financial restructuring. Precise measurement of individual executives' gains from the exercise of options and subsequent sale of shares is frequently complicated by devices such as the lodging of sale proceeds in trust funds. Nevertheless, in the absence of alternative sources, it is argued that Directors' Registers offer the best basis for developing a picture of companies' use of option schemes and individual directors' gains from options and hence a more accurate insight into aggregate remuneration. This view is based on the authors' compilation of a database of all option awards and exercise by executives in the largest 100 UK companies between 1980 and 1990.

The same problems of data accessibility do not apply to studies based on US option experience. As was noted earlier, US disclosure requirements are markedly more stringent. Despite this, in 1995 the Federal Accounting Standards Bureau (FASB) is under strong pressure to require companies to provide valuations of option benefits. Similar pressures are, to a lesser extent, reflected in the attention given to the issue by the Accounting Standards Board in the UK.

Valuation   Studies which seek to develop valuations of outstanding options held by executives encounter the need to apply an appropriate valuation procedure. A common approach in such studies has been to utilize the Black–Scholes option pricing model (1973). The Black–Scholes method was developed as a measure of the value of 'traditional' options, which differ from share options principally in terms of their much shorter life (three months versus seven years) and their tradability. Nevertheless, its use in valuing share options is generally regarded as reasonable (see e.g. Foster *et al.* 1991 and, for a wider review of valuation issues, Hull 1993). The Black–Scholes valuation takes account of the dividend forgone in holding the option rather than the underlying share by applying the Merton (1973) version of the formula. It could be argued, additionally, that where the ESO is awarded, in effect, in lieu of some alternative component of aggregate remuneration, account should be taken of this forgone alternative. In practice, however, this 'opportunity cost' of receiving options is likely to defy precise identification.

Focus of Investigation   A further issue confronting those studies which seek to understand the relationship between remuneration and corporate performance is how tightly to focus on the executive core of the company. It has been common until recently in the UK to focus on the highest-paid director's experience. Though it could be argued that this constitutes a reasonable proxy for the experience of the board as a whole, the main reason for this focus is the availability of data relating to the highest-paid director, relative to the rest of the board. More recent work (e.g. Main *et al.* 1994) argues that the appropriate focus is the board of directors as a whole, this reflecting the authority invested in the directors collectively. As Jensen (1993) observes: 'The board, at the apex of the internal control system, has the final responsibility for the functioning of the firm.'

5. Remuneration and Governance: An Empirical Survey

As was noted above, the most significant empirical studies in relation to governance issues are those which seek to understand the implications of various remuneration structures for corporate performance and shareholder wealth. It is these studies, therefore, which form the basis for this review. It should be acknowledged, however, that considerable attention has also been given to other types of impact. These include the impact of performance-contingent reward on dividend policy, the effect on executive motivation as revealed, for example, through attitude surveys, and the impact of innovative pay systems on the absolute size of executive pay. Though each of these further areas of empirical work may impact on governance issues, they are not addressed directly here. Table 4.1 provides a summary presentation of the main studies discussed in this section.

Remuneration, Corporate Performance, and Shareholder Wealth

Much of the investigation, both in the UK and USA, into the links between executive pay and corporate performance has been set in a wider context whereby additional firm variables, such as size and growth rate, are also considered as potential correlates of executive pay. It should become apparent that the results of this

Table 4.1. Empirical analyses of the impact of ESOs and related instruments: a selected chronology

Author(s), date	Nature of sample	Results
Lewellen, Huntsman (1970)	50 US companies 1942–63	Including long-term elements has little effect on reward–performance link
Cosh (1975)	1,601 UK companies 1969–71	Size more important than profitability in determining narrowly defined pay
Meeks, Whittington (1975)	1,008 UK companies 1969–71	Sales the best determinant of pay, but profit's significance reaffirmed
Murphy (1985)	73 US companies 1964–81	Performance more significant than size in explaining executive reward
Deckop (1988)	108 US companies 1977–81	Profit–sales ratio most powerful explanatory pay determinant
Benston (1985)	29 US companies 1970–75	Stronger performance–reward link when stock-related elements included
Leonard (1990)	20,000 executives, managers in 439 large US companies 1981–5	Link between long-term executive plans and return on equity. No ESO data
Abowd (1990)	16,000 managers in 250 US companies 1981–6	Correlation between pay and degree of sensitivity between previous year's pay and market performance
Jensen, Murphy (1990)	1,688 executives, 1,049 US companies 1974–86	Weak relationship between performance and remuneration. Incomplete ESO measure
Szymanski (1992)	51 UK companies 1981–91	Weak pay–performance link, but ESO valuation unclear
Gregg, Machin, Szymanski (1993)	288 UK companies 1983–91	Weak pay–performance link; strong pay–growth link. No ESOs
Conyon, Gregg (1994)	170 highest-paid UK directors 1985–90	Sales growth significantly more important pay determinant than performance. No ESOs
Conyon, Leech (1994)	294 highest-paid UK directors 1983–6	Weak pay–performance link. No ESOs
Main, Bruce, Buck (1994)	59 UK companies, aggregate board, and highest-paid directors 1982–9	Inclusion of ESOs significantly increases pay–performance link

empirical work, taken together, fail to offer a strong consensus on the nature of the remuneration–performance relationship. This may in part reflect different approaches to the resolution of the methodological issues discussed above.

As noted above, one of the earliest attempts to investigate the relationship between pay elements and performance is provided by the analysis of Lewellen (1968) and Lewellen and Huntsman (1970). This was an analysis of fifty US companies over a twenty-two-year period. One of the more important conclusions to emerge was that the performance–pay relationship was relatively unaffected by the incorporation of long-term remuneration instruments. It seems fair to suggest that Lewellen and Huntsman's conclusions, based on a substantial sample, were influential in subduing interest in the pay–performance link in the USA for over a decade. In the UK, meanwhile, empirical analysis was pioneered by Cosh (1975) and Meeks and Whittington (1975). Cosh's analysis, covering 1,601 firms which, collectively, accounted for approximately two-thirds of the UK's industrial and commercial assets in 1971, focused on a fairly narrow definition of highest-paid directors' (HPD) remuneration, details of which had become available following the 1967 Companies Act. Contrary to Lewellen's US findings, Cosh identified firm size as the major determinant of executive reward, with the addition of the profit coefficient offering only marginal explanatory improvement. To some extent, the contrast with the US results could reflect both the lagged uptake of profit-contingent elements in UK pay as well as the fact that Cosh's pay measure excluded them from his analysis.

Using a similarly narrow pay measure, Meeks and Whittington (1975) analysed HPD experience in 1,008 companies. Again, size offered a more powerful explanation of pay than profit. Growth and profit appeared similarly influential, with the caveat that growth appeared to have a ratchet effect on executive reward, whilst profit levels were more symmetrical in influence. Meeks and Whittington acknowledged the continued significance of profit in contrast with the dismissive managerialist view. Coughlan and Schmidt (1985) identify a positive relationship between the real rate of change in executive salary plus bonus and stock price performance, using 597 observations from 249 companies between 1978 and 1980, but their results fail to identify a significant relationship between sales growth and performance.

Murphy's (1985) longitudinal analysis of individual executives covers the experience of 461 individuals in seventy-two firms over the period 1964–81. He notes that the failure of many earlier studies to identify strong pay–performance links is accounted for by their failure to incorporate and analyse the less accessible performance-sensitive elements of pay. Accordingly, Murphy's most comprehensive pay variable, total compensation, computed on a pre-tax basis, includes *ex ante* (Black–Scholes) value of stock options, as well as deferred components of compensation and various fringe benefits. Utilizing a shareholder return performance measure, Murphy's results offer strong support for both the pay–performance and the pay–sales growth links and argue strongly against the reliability of cross-sectional analysis, given the significance of firm- and individual-specific variables. The sharp distinction between Murphy's pay–sales growth results and those generated by Coughlan and Schmidt is rationalized by the latter in terms of the distinctly different types of dataset used. Specifically, Coughlan and Schmidt suggest that their data include a greater number of executives who are near the beginning or the end of their careers and that sales-sensitive remuneration packages are less likely to be employed for such individuals.

Deckop (1988), analysing US CEO base plus bonus for a minimum of 108 companies between 1977 and 1981, finds profit as a percentage of sales to be the most powerful explanatory variable, rather than sales *per se*. He also notes the significance of industry-specific effects in determining the relationship between executive reward and performance or size variables.

Abowd (1990), utilizing data on 16,000 managers in 250 US companies between 1981 and 1986, tests the relationship between the sensitivity of remuneration to performance within a year and the subsequent year's performance and identifies some evidence for a correlation when market, rather than accounting-based, performance measures are employed.

Jensen and Murphy's (1990) study analyses the remuneration of 1,688 executives in 1,049 US companies between 1974 and 1986. The results indicate a positive but weak relationship between salary plus bonus and shareholder wealth, though the incorporation of past performance increases the sensitivity somewhat, as does extension of the pay variable to incorporate all except stock option elements of remuneration. Extending their study to incorporate stock option effects, Jensen and Murphy take a sample of the experience of 154 CEOs over a fifteen-year period. Combining gains from new option awards during the year and change in the value of existing option holdings (each using Black–Scholes) and adding profits from option exercise (based on an assumption of exercise at the highest available price, hence giving an upper-limit value) yields a figure for total option-related gain per year. The resultant option-related incentives were significantly higher than those associated with other pay elements. For each $1,000 dollars of increased shareholder wealth, option-related returns increase by 14.5 cents, compared with only a 3.3 cent increase for the comprehensive (excluding options) pay measure and a 1.35 cent increase using the base plus bonus measure (all values in 1986 prices). The rationale offered for a pay–performance relationship which is both weak and declining is that public and private political forces constrain greater sensitivity.

Panel data for directors of fifty-one UK companies between 1981 and 1991 forms the basis for Szymanski's (1992) investigation. Using a relatively broad measure of executive remuneration, cross-sectional analysis suggests a far greater significance for size than profitability in each year. Longitudinal analysis amplifies the size–pay relationship, indicating a strong link between sales growth and pay. The nature of the data used raises some questions, however. In particular, the origin of the data on ESOs and the basis for their inclusion and valuation is not clearly explained, and the weak pay–performance link suggests that ESOs, which had become a significant element of pay in UK companies by the mid- to late 1980s, may not have been reliably incorporated.

Similar results are generated by Gregg et al. (1993), who chart HPD remuneration for 288 large UK companies over a similar period. They argue that a weak pay–performance relationship, discernible until 1988, breaks down completely thereafter. Growth again emerges as the most important pay determinant. Significantly, however, this study excludes ESOs, using instead a simple base plus bonus measure of pay which represents a narrow perspective on the nature of recent executive remuneration.

Conyon and Gregg (1994), again employing a base plus bonus pay measure for 170 HPDs of UK companies, report unsurprisingly similar results, with sales growth an important pay predictor, market performance a weak predictor, and accounting performance negligible in impact. Their comparison of executive reward between organically and acquisitively growing firms generates more interesting results, with clear rewards to the acquisitive executive.

A rather different focus is adopted by Conyon and Leech (1994), who examine the relationship between various governance structures and HPD pay as well as the more usual pay–performance link. The results question the effectiveness of institutional mechanisms of governance. Once again, the pay–performance link is weak, though the partial nature of the pay measure (base plus bonus) compromises the significance of the results.

Main *et al.* (1996) employ a more comprehensive measure of remuneration in exploring the relationship between total board remuneration and company performance. Incorporation of data on all ESO awards and exercises for executives in fifty-nine of the largest UK companies during the 1980s generates results which indicate a significantly greater sensitivity of pay to performance than that observed using the more usual and narrower base plus bonus pay measure. These results hold not merely for boards as a whole, but also for HPDs and chief executives. Thus, a 10 per cent increase in shareholder wealth generates immediate increases of 8.94 per cent and 7.2 per cent in the pay of HPDs and chief executives respectively. By contrast the sales–pay relationship using the comprehensive pay measure is generally weak.

Literature Summary and Future Directions

Taking the literature as a whole, the dominant theme emerging from the empirical analysis of the remuneration–performance relationship is that the link is relatively weak. In general, stronger evidence emerges for a correlation between remuneration and sales or sales growth. Put simply, the managerialist perspective appears to be supported and the concerns of shareholders which stem from an awareness of potential agency costs imposed by self-serving managers appear well grounded. To the extent that this dominant impression is acceptable, it is not difficult to rationalize. Executives are able to pursue objectives which conflict with shareholders' interests because of the costs and free rider problems associated with monitoring, the general ineffectiveness of shareholder 'voice', and the constraints on the 'exit' sanction which apply in particular to larger shareholders. None of the potential restraints on executive power which shareholders may impose appears sufficiently robust to overcome the established and informationally privileged position of the executive director. In terms of the acknowledged weakness of governance structures in large UK and US corporations, the results appear to make sense. Yet many of the studies which have been reviewed and which contribute to the establishment of consensus are methodologically questionable, principally in relation to their partial measure of executive remuneration. It has been observed that a commonly neglected component of executive remuneration in these studies is that relating to the returns to ESO schemes. In other words, an important component which, *by design*, attempts to tie executive return to shareholder enrichment is frequently absent from the analysis. It is therefore even less surprising that a divergence of executive and shareholder interests emerges as a well-corroborated result. Though such an exclusion remains methodologically unjustifiable, it is at the same time understandable, given the elusive nature of option-related data noted above. Where the returns to ESOs have been incorporated into analysis of the determinants of executive pay, different results have emerged, suggesting a much stronger pay–performance link and a measure of success for ESOs in aligning the interests of principals and agents. It therefore seems important that further comprehensive studies of the determinants of executive pay are conducted to clarify the nature of the pay–performance link.

It seems highly probable that the innovative spirit which has characterized executive remuneration on both sides of the Atlantic in the past two decades will continue to occupy those who design and implement executive pay regimes. As such, academic interest in assessing the impact of new forms of executive pay is likely to be sustained. It also seems probable that the academic analysis of the correlates of executive pay will be the subject of increasing scrutiny by employee and shareholder groups, and the business and general media. This wider interest reflects current concerns, particularly in the UK, that executive remuneration is excessive both in absolute terms and relative to other groups of employees, substantially unrelated to corporate performance, and outwith the control of shareholders. It is these types of concern which gave rise to the establishment, in the UK, of the government- and CBI-backed Greenbury Committee to investigate executive pay.

The future of the ESO more specifically is likely to depend in part on how influential the recommendations of the Greenbury Committee are in modifying the use of ESO schemes. In the UK the substantial ESO-related gains made by executives of recently privatized utility companies have brought the instrument into disrepute, where profits and thus ESO gains may result from natural monopoly power in product markets rather than board performance. Nevertheless, the emerging academic view of ESOs is that they have the potential to effect closer alignment of shareholder and executive interests. The key arguably lies in realizing the potential, which in turn demands careful attention to the details of ESO scheme operation. There is little doubt that ESO schemes, as noted above, can provide a vehicle for opportunistic and self-serving behaviour by executives. On the other hand, more stringent requirements relating to details such as allowable discounts on issue price, terms of reissue, the need for shareholder consent, and the transparency of award and subsequent gains could curb excessive behaviour in relation to ESOs and capture more effectively the potential benefits. Conyon *et al.* (1995) identify three key requirements: greater transparency of details of ESO award, enhanced independence of remuneration committees, and the establishment of an effective mechanism of regulatory control.

In the area of disclosure requirements, the Urgent Issues Task Force of the UK Accounting Standards Board in late 1994 reiterated the spirit of the earlier Cadbury Report in recommending much greater transparency of ESO award terms. The recommendations of the Greenbury Committee, published in July

1995, provide, *inter alia*, for more stringent disclosure requirements, more explicit justification of amendments to remuneration, and a 'tightening up' of the composition of remuneration committees (see Chapter 5 in this volume, by Conyon, for a discussion of the Greenbury Report). Such recommendations, if acted upon, could silence more radical calls for the abolition of the ESO.

Recent attention in the USA has focused on the accounting treatment of stock options and the disclosure requirements relating to them. The Federal Accounting Standards Board recommended in 1992 that the award of options by companies should be recorded in their profit and loss statements. The recommendation received little support, even from institutional shareholders, however, and was rejected by the US Senate in 1994. The shareholding community, taking its lead from the representations of the Council of Institutional Investors, has focused attention on the need for comprehensive mandatory disclosure of option details to facilitate independent valuation of options by outsiders (see Monks and Minow 1995: 51–5).

6. Conclusion

The aim of this chapter has been to locate the significant recent literature relating to executive remuneration within the broader corporate governance debate. At the conceptual level, agency theory offers a fertile framework for addressing the link between remuneration and governance and comparing the capabilities of alternative reward systems in aligning shareholder and executive interests. Equally, there has been a reasonably full discussion of the possible contribution of institutional governance structures in this context. At the empirical level, a consistent impression which emerges from the substantial body of literature is that this is an area of enquiry attended by a variety of methodological problems which frequently compromise the reliability of empirical results. Arguably the most significant enduring problem for work in this area is the difficulty associated with establishing comprehensive measures of executive reward as a basis for testing for correlation with corporate performance. To this end, the current pressures for stricter disclosure requirements reported above may lead to the development of a more reliable and balanced analysis of the possibilities and limitations of ESOs and related instruments in establishing stronger systems of corporate governance.

REFERENCES

Abowd, J. M. (1990), 'Does Performance-Based Managerial Compensation Affect Corporate Performance?', *Industrial and Labor Relations Review* (special issue), 43: 52–73.

Accounting Standards Board Urgent Issues Task Force (1994), *Disclosure of Directors' Share Options* (London: Accounting Standards Board).

Association of British Insurers (1991), *Share Incentive Scheme Guidelines* (London: ABI).

Baumol, W. J. (1967), *Business Behaviour, Value and Growth*, rev. edn. (New York: Harcourt Brace).

Benston, G. J. (1985), 'The Self-Serving Management Hypothesis', *Journal of Accounting and Economics*, 7: 67–84.

Black, F., and Scholes, M. (1973), 'The Pricing of Options and Corporate Liabilities', *Journal of Political Economy*, 81: 637–54.

Brickley, J. A., Bhagat, S., and Lease, R. C. (1985), 'The Impact of Long-Range Managerial Compensation Plans of Shareholder Wealth', *Journal of Accounting and Economics*, 7: 115–29.

Conyon, M., and Gregg, P. (1994), 'Pay at the Top: A Study of the Sensitivity of Chief Executive Remuneration to Company Specific Shocks', *National Institute Economic Review*, 3: 88–92.

—— and Leech, D. (1994), 'Top Pay, Company Performance and Corporate Governance', *Oxford Bulletin of Economics and Statistics*, 56: 229–47.

—— Gregg, P., and Machin, S. (1995), 'Taking Care of Business: Executive Compensation in the United Kingdom', *Economic Journal*, 105: 704–14.

Cosh, A. (1975), 'The Remuneration of Chief Executives in the United Kingdom', *Economic Journal*, 85: 75–94.

—— and Hughes, A. (1987), 'The Anatomy of Corporate Control: Directors, Shareholders and Executive Renumeration in Giant US and UK Corporations', *Cambridge Journal of Economics*, 11: 285–313.

Coughlan, A., and Schmidt, R. (1985), 'Executive Compensation, Management Turnover, and Firm Performance: An Empirical Investigation', *Journal of Accounting and Economics*, 7: 43–66.

Davis, E., and Kay, J. (1993), 'Corporate Governance, Take-Overs, and the Role of the Non-Executive Director', in M. Bishop and J. Kay (eds.), *European Mergers and Merger Policy* (Oxford: Oxford University Press).

Deckop, J. R. (1988), 'Determinants of Chief Executive Officer Compensation', *Industrial and Labor Relations Review* (special issue), 41: 215–26.

Egginton, D. A., Forker, J. J., and Tippett, M. J. (1989), 'Share Option Rewards and Managerial Performance: An Abnormal Performance Index Model', *Accounting and Business Research*, 19: 255–66.

—— —— and Grout, P. (1993), 'Executive and Employee Share Options: Taxation Dilution and Disclosure', *Accounting and Business Research*, 23/91A: 363–72.

Forbes, W., and Watson, R. (1993), 'Managerial Remuneration and Corporate Governance: A Review of the Issues, Evidence and Cadbury Committee Proposals', *Accounting and Business Research*, 23: 331–8.

Foster, T. W., Koogler, P. R., and Vickery, D. (1991), 'Valuation of Executive Stock Options and the FASB Proposal', *Accounting Review*, 66: 595–610.

Garen, J. E. (1994), 'Executive Compensation and Principal–Agent Theory', *Journal of Political Economy*, 102: 1175–99.

Gregg, P., Machin, S., and Szymanski, S. (1993), 'The Disappearing Relationship between Directors' Pay and Corporate Performance', *British Journal of Industrial Relations*, 31: 1–9.

Grossman, S. J., and Hart, O. D. (1983), 'An Analysis of the Principal Agent problem', *Econometrica*, 51: 7–45.

Guesnerie, R. (1992), 'The Arrow–Debreu Paradigm Faced with Modern Theories of Contracting: A Discussion of Selected Issues involving Information and Time', in L. Werin and H. Wijkander (eds.), *Contract Economics* (Oxford: Blackwell).

Hull, J. C. (1993), *Options, Futures and Other Derivative Securities* (Englewood Cliffs, NJ: Prentice-Hall).

Jensen, M. (1993), 'The Modern Industrial Revolution, Exit, and the Failure of Internal Control Systems', *Journal of Finance*, 48: 831–80.

—— and Murphy, K. J. (1990), 'Performance Pay and Top-Management Incentives', *Journal of Political Economy*, 98: 225–64.

Kaplan, R. S. (1982), *Advanced Management Accounting* (Englewood Cliffs, NJ: Prentice-Hall).

Lambert, R. A., Lanen, W. N., and Larcker, D. F. (1989), 'Executive Stock Option Plans and Corporate Dividend Policy', *Journal of Financial and Quantitative Analysis*, 24: 409–25.

Leonard, Jonathan S. (1990), 'Executive Pay and Firm Performance', *Industrial and Labour Relations Review*, 43 (special issue), S13–S29.

Lewellen, Wilbur G. (1968), *Executive Compensation in Large Industrial Corporations* (New York: National Bureau of Economic Research).

—— and Huntsman, Blaine (1970), 'Managerial Pay and Corporate Performance', *American Economic Review*, 60: 710–20.

—— Loderer, C., and Martin, K. (1987), 'Executive Compensation and Executive Incentive Problems: An Empirical Analysis', *Journal of Accounting and Economics*, 9: 287–310.

Main, B. G. M., and Johnston, James (1992), *The Remuneration Committee as an Instrument of Corporate Governance*, Hume Occasional Paper No. 35 (Edinburgh: David Hume Institute).

—— —— (1993), 'Remuneration Committees and Corporate Governance', *Accounting and Business Research*, 23: 351–62.

—— O'Reilly, Charles, A., III, and Wade, James (1993), 'Top Executive Pay: Tournament or Team Work?', *Journal of Labor Economics*, 11: 606–28.

—— Bruce, A., and Buck, T. (1996), 'Total Board Renumeration and Company Performance', *Economic Journal*, 106/439, 1627–1644.

Mangel, Robert, and Singh, Harbir (1993), 'Ownership Structure, Board Relationships and CEO Compensation in Large US Corporations', *Accounting and Business Research*, 23: 339–50.

Meeks, Geoffrey, and Whittington, Geoffrey (1975), 'Directors' Pay, Growth and Profitability', *Journal of Industrial Economics*, 24: 1–14.

Merton, R. C. (1973), 'Theory of Rational Option Pricing', *Bell Journal of Economics and Management Science*, 4: 141–83.

Milgrom, Paul, and Roberts, John (1992), *Organization and Management* (Englewood Cliffs, NJ: Prentice-Hall).

Monks, R. A. G., and Minow, N. (1995), *Corporate Governance* (Oxford: Blackwell).

Murphy, Kevin J. (1985), 'Corporate Performance and Managerial Remuneration: An Empirical Analysis', *Journal of Accounting and Economics*, 7: 11–42.

Reitman, D. (1993), 'Stock Options and the Strategic Use of Managerial Incentives', *American Economic Review*, 83: 513–24.

Rosen, S. (1992), 'Contracts and the Market for Executives', in L. Werin and H. Wijkander (eds.), *Contract Economics* (Oxford: Blackwell).

Ross, Stephen A. (1973), 'The Economic Theory of Agency: The Principal's Problem', *American Economic Review*, 63: 134–9.

Szymanski, S. (1992), 'Directors' Pay Incentives in the 1980s: The UK Experience', London Business School Centre for Business Strategy Working Paper.

Tehranian, Hassan, and Waegelein, James F. (1985), 'Market Reaction to Short-Term Executive Compensation Plan Adoption', *Journal of Accounting and Economics*, 7: 131–44.

Warner, Jerold B. (1985), 'Stock Market Reaction to Management Incentive Plan Adoption', *Journal of Accounting and Economics*, 7: 145–9.

5

INSTITUTIONAL ARRANGEMENTS FOR SETTING DIRECTORS' COMPENSATION IN UK COMPANIES

Martin J. Conyon

1. Introduction

The compensation received by top directors has recently attracted much media attention. Many commentators have been critical of the large increases in compensation received by some directors of leading UK companies. It is important in the circumstances to provide a detailed review of the issues involved, based on our existing knowledge of company policy in the United Kingdom. In particular, we aim to document some of the existing institutional arrangements for setting directors' compensation in the light of the policy recommendations by, *inter alia*, the Cadbury (1992) and Greenbury (1995) committees.

Much of the existing empirical evidence on the determination of senior management compensation has found that there is only a weak link between direct compensation (i.e. that which excludes long-term incentive pay including share options) and measures of company performance such as shareholder return. Moreover, the estimated link between top pay and corporate performance has sometimes been found to be quite small; especially in relation to the effect of company size in shaping top pay (see Conyon *et al.* 1995 and Chapter 4 in this volume, by Bruce and Buck).

The supposed weak link between pay and performance has sometimes been interpreted in the literature as reflecting the incorrect alignment of incentives between shareholders and executive management. Accordingly, such evidence does not sit comfortably with standard economic models which view shareholders as company owners and senior management as their agents.

It is not surprising, in the light of such evidence, that attention has recently focused on the institutional arrangements by which top directors' pay is actually set in leading UK companies. There have now been many proposals advanced in the UK for the reform of the top pay setting process.

The best-known examples which have contributed to the public debate about executive pay setting are contained in the Cadbury Committee recommendations (Cadbury 1992) and, more recently, the Greenbury Report (1995). Both documents prescribe recommendations for the appropriate governance of boardroom pay, for example by the establishment of remuneration or emoluments committees.

However, apart from knowing that directors' compensation is set by a remuneration committee, there is very little further evidence about the way remuneration committees actually operate. For example, little is known about the committees' membership composition, the mix between executive and nonexecutive directors, the frequency of meetings, or even who else typically attends such meetings. The objective of this chapter, then, is to cast some light on the structure of remuneration committees in UK companies and to detail some of the procedures that they follow when determining directors' compensation.

The rest of the chapter is organized as follows. In the next section we consider the determination of senior management compensation. This will highlight the recent UK empirical literature which has tended to conclude that there is only a weak link between pay and company performance. In Section 3 we focus on the institutional mechanisms for setting directors' compensation, highlighting the role of the non-executive directors and the importance of remuneration committees. In Section 4 we present some new evidence on the institutional arrangements for setting directors' pay in UK firms. In particular, we highlight company adoption of remuneration committees and their membership structure. We also consider some of the sources of information used by remuneration committees in determining directors' pay (e.g. the use of expert compensation consultants) and the frequency with which they meet, and examine who else participates in remuneration committee proceedings.

2. The Determination of Directors' Compensation

The usual way in which economists consider the setting of directors' compensation packages is within the context of the principal–agent framework (see e.g. Tirole 1988; Milgrom and Roberts 1992). These models assume that there is a divergence of interests between the owners of companies and senior management so that one can think of introducing incentive-based contracts to eliminate this potential conflict of interests.[1] A standard way in which these models are formed is to posit a risk neutral principal (the owners of the firm) who attempts to design the optimal contract for the risk-averse agent (the senior management of a company) which best aligns their mutual interests. It is often argued that one way in which the potentially non-congruent goals of owners and managers can be

---

[1] For instance, shareholders cannot perfectly monitor the actions undertaken by senior management and verify that they are in the long-term interests of the shareholders (i.e. a moral hazard problem exists).

brought into line is to make executive compensation depend on measures of corporate value added such as stock market return (see Holmstrom 1979; Jensen and Murphy 1990; Milgrom and Roberts 1992).

With this underlying structure in mind, many authors have tried to estimate how sensitive to measures of company performance executive compensation actually is. The typical way in which such empirical models proceed is to estimate a simple reduced-form equation rather than the parameters of a structural model informed by a specific principal–agent model (see Conyon *et al.* 1995). So, a standard regression equation would model the compensation of an individual director *i* at time *t* as:

$$\Delta\log(\text{Compensation})_{it} = \alpha + \beta\text{Performance}_t + \varepsilon_{it} \qquad (1)$$

where the term β is the reaction coefficient reflecting the sensitivity of director compensation to corporate performance. The magnitude of the coefficient is often interpreted as reflecting the operation of principal–agent type mechanisms with higher values of β suggesting closer alignment of owner and management interests. There has now been a considerable amount of research estimating such models (see Chapter 4 in this volume, by Bruce and Buck). However, before briefly reviewing the evidence on the magnitude of the estimated βs so far produced in the literature, it is worth noting some of the unresolved issues in estimating equations such as (1).

The first issue, as far as UK data is concerned, is the relevant unit of analysis. Most research has not been able to identify individual executives but instead models a company-level time series on the highest-paid director. So, when the individual who is the highest-paid director changes, this can cause problems for the estimated relationship between pay and performance. For instance, a large annual increase in the salary and bonus of the highest-paid director may reflect a recruitment payment for a new chief executive officer and not be a pay rise for a given individual director. Under the Greenbury recommendations this problem can easily be overcome since paragraph B4 of the Report argues that full details of all elements in the remuneration package of each director should be given by name. In the future we would expect, therefore, to see more complete company disclosure of individual directors so that a relevant time series on individual director pay can be constructed. Second, there is the controversial area of how to measure the director compensation variable. Until comparatively recently most UK studies have used only the direct emoluments of the highest-paid director which are available from the company accounts. This measures only current compensation and excludes long-term compensation such as the estimated value of share options, equity holdings, and other forms of deferred compensation. In Chapter 4, Bruce and Buck argue that, by excluding these extra components of the directors' overall compensation, the estimated relationship between compensation and performance may be biased (see also Conyon *et al.* 1995). However, the primary reason why the wider compensation measures are typically not used in the UK context is the lack of available and consistent data (see again Conyon *et al.* 1995). Again, if companies adhere to the principles contained within the Greenbury Report (para. B5), then it should become much easier, in the future, to compute total director compensation measures based on, for example, the Black and Scholes (1973) method.[2] Finally, there is the question how to measure company performance. Some empirical models use market-based measures of corporate performance such as shareholder returns or shareholder wealth, whereas others use accounting-based measures such as earnings per share or return on capital employed. It is not immediately apparent which is the correct performance measure to use, and these potentially problematic issues should be considered when interpreting the existing literature on director compensation.

Estimates of the relationship between director compensation and company performance have revealed a remarkably consistent picture (the evidence is reviewed in detail by Bruce and Buck in Chapter 4). Much of the work emanating from the United States, and increasingly the evidence pertaining to the United Kingdom, has concluded that the compensation–performance sensitivity parameter is quite small (see e.g. Conyon *et al.* 1995). Such relatively small estimates of β for the United Kingdom are typically based on the direct emoluments (i.e. excluding long-term components such as share options) of highest-paid director compensation and suggest that incentives facing senior management may be weak. Also, evidence from Gregg *et al.* (1993) further suggests that this already weak link between measures of direct compensation and company performance has become weaker in the post-1988 period. Indeed, in their study of 288 UK companies between 1983 and 1991 the authors find that after 1988 it was not possible to detect any significant relationship between the direct emoluments of the highest-paid director and the stock market value of their companies.

However, as noted by Conyon *et al.* (1995), and stressed further by Bruce and Buck (Chapter 4), the estimated weak link between director compensation and company performance may simply reflect the changing composition of director emoluments in UK companies. This might be especially important if stock options are becoming more important, as is widely believed, in the directors' compensation packages. But incorporating stock options, and other forms of deferred pay, into the director compensation variable is only a new area of research in the UK literature on top pay determination. A detailed analysis by Main *et al.* (1996) studied fifty-nine large UK companies over the period from 1982 to 1989 and included explicitly a role for share options in the boardroom compensation variable. They find that when such executive share options are accounted for, the sensitivity of director compensation to company performance increases considerably (see Chapter 4 of this volume for more details). Overall, then much of the UK evidence finds (bearing in mind some of the caveats already raised) that the relationship between director compensation and corporate performance is perhaps

---

[2] It will be possible to compute such measures since the disclosure of the option exercise price, market price on the date of exercise, and the number of options for each director will be revealed. The Greenbury model closely follows the recommendations of the Urgent Issues Task Force, Abstract 10, 'Disclosure of Directors' Share Options'.

weak. It is this, coupled with public unease about the growth in director compensation generally, which has heightened the focus on matters of corporate governance. We therefore consider the current institutional arrangements that exist for setting boardroom compensation in the next section.

3. Setting Directors' Compensation: The Board and Remuneration Committees

Clearly, shareholders do not write contracts and set director compensation in the mechanistic way suggested by the previous section (indeed, there is typically very little involvement by shareholders in setting boardroom compensation). This function is delegated to the board of directors. The role of the board, and in particular the non-executive director, is central for a complete understanding of how director compensation is set (see Jensen 1993; and, in the UK policy context, Greenbury 1995). The board of directors, as representatives of shareholders, has its roots in agency theory (see Fama and Jensen 1983; and Jensen 1993). As Jensen (1993: 862) comments: 'The board, at the apex of the internal control system, has the final responsibility for the functioning of the firm. Most importantly, it sets the rules of the game for the CEO. The job of the board is to hire, fire and compensate the CEO and to provide high-level council. Few boards in the past decades have done this job well in the absence of external crises.'

The board of directors, acting as the agents of the owners, can be split into two groups, each with quite separate functions: an executive and a non-executive element.[3] A primary function of the executive directors is the administrative management of the company's affairs. By convention there is typically a senior executive director who can be referred to as the chief executive officer. Non-executive directors, on the other hand, are responsible, *inter alia*, for monitoring the performance of the executive directors (see Chapter 4). They may be thought of, then, as more directly representing shareholder interests on the board (e.g. by monitoring performance and commenting on corporate strategy) since there are less potential conflicts of interest between them and shareholders. The agency problem associated with setting executive compensation is one area of potential conflict. A self-serving executive management unchecked by a strong non-executive independent element on the board and with little effective monitoring by outside investors has a potential opportunity to self-award excessive pay increases.

However, the role of the non-executive director, as the boardroom guardian of

---

[3] Since there is no legal distinction between executive and non-executive director in the UK, some prefer to distinguish between full-time and part-time directors (corresponding to inside and outside directors in the USA). The importance of distinguishing between the two types is that they have different functions and roles to perform in the company. See Pettigrew and McNulty (1995).

shareholder interests, has been questioned. We shall simply highlight three areas of potential concern (a much more complete analysis of the role of boardroom directors is contained in Lorsh and MacIver 1989; see also Hart 1995).

First, there are the potential asymmetries of information between the non-executive directors and the senior executive management. Non-executive directors may not have complete access to all the relevant information when performing their monitoring function, perhaps due to the dominance of the CEO position. As Jensen (1993: 864) remarks: 'Serious information problems limit the effectiveness of board members in the typical large corporation. For example, the CEO almost always determines the agenda and the information given to the board. This limitation on information severely hinders the ability of even highly talented board members to contribute effectively to the monitoring and evaluation of the CEO and the company's strategy.' In consequence, the monitoring function of non-executive directors, and their influence, may be considerably diminished (see Jensen 1993; Crystal 1992; Chapter 4 in this volume). Empirical work by Main and Johnston (1993) considered the relationship between the highest-paid director compensation and non-executive presence on the boardroom for a sample of 220 UK companies in 1990. They found that the compensation received by the highest-paid director, after controlling for company size, was higher in companies with a greater ratio of non-executive to executive directors. This empirical evidence questions the potential ability of non-executives to hold director top pay in check (should such a situation be deemed necessary).

Second, there is the potential problem produced by interlocking directorships. An interlocking directorship occurs when a director of one company serves as a non-executive director at another company. The evidence and extent of interlocks and, more importantly, what actual effect they have on economic variables such as corporate performance or executive compensation is limited. Evidence from PIRC (1993), for example, indicates that in the ten highest-paying FTSE 100 companies over half the members of each company's remuneration committee currently serve, or have done so recently, as executive directors at other companies. A KPMG survey of 235 non-executives, from a total of 430 directors at companies in the *Times* 1000, found that 43.8 per cent of non-executive directors also hold at least one *executive* directorship (KPMG 1994). Such arrangements, where directors of one company serve as non-executive directors at another, can foster a mutuality of interests and cloud the distinction between executive and non-executive directors (see Conyon and Machin 1995*a*). In such circumstances there is a danger that such commonality of interests may result in a spiralling upward pay round (see Conyon *et al.* 1995).

Finally, the process by which non-executive directors are selected is important if they are to carry out their monitoring function effectively. If the selection and appointment of directors comes merely within the patronage of the chairman, then the ability of non-executive Directors to perform their monitoring tasks effectively may be diminished. The Cadbury Report discusses the use and adoption of nomination committees as a means to select directors. It points out that the adoption of a nomination committee makes it clear how director appointments are made and therefore assists the main board (see Cadbury 1992: 27). However, the existing evidence suggests that companies do not appear to be adopting such nomination committees in great numbers. Main (1993) carried out twenty-four interviews with top executives from some of the largest UK companies. Only nine of these twenty-four companies had adopted a nomination committee. From the remaining fifteen companies there were diverse views on whether they would actually set up such committees, ranging from those who definitely would not to those who probably would move to setting up a nomination committee. Main (1993) notes that 'the nominations process rests firmly in the hands of the chairman. Finding suitable non-executives is universally regarded as the chairman's job.' This view is supported by the results of KPMG's (1994) survey, which found that more than half of all non-executive appointments of directors surveyed were made by the chairman alone.

The role of the non-executive director in the explicit area of setting executive compensation is formalized through the institutional mechanism of a remuneration committee. The function of the remuneration committee is to determine the appropriate reward structure for executive directors, taking into consideration shareholders as well as other stakeholder interests. The Cadbury Committee recommended that 'boards should appoint remuneration committees, consisting wholly or mainly of non-executive directors and chaired by a non-executive director, to recommend to the board the remuneration of the executive directors in all its forms, drawing on outside advice as necessary. Executive directors should play no part in decisions on their own remuneration' (Cadbury 1992, para. 4.42, p. 31).

It is perhaps important to stress some aspects concerning the status of the Cadbury Report. First, it does not confer a statutory obligation on companies to comply with its recommendations. This may be important since, as Hart (1995: 686) comments, 'There is in fact a strong argument that a market economy can achieve efficient corporate governance without government intervention.' The argument, which has its roots in the Chicago tradition, is that the founders of companies have an incentive to choose corporate governance structures that maximize the total surplus they receive and will not, therefore, choose governance structures that are suboptimal (see Hart 1995: 686–9 for more detail and qualifications). Second, the Cadbury Code may be viewed as trying to persuade companies about what is regarded as best practice in boardroom structures, and corporate governance more generally. As Hart (1995: 688) concludes, 'the case for statutory rules is weak and so the Cadbury approach of trying to educate and persuade companies to make changes in corporate governance is probably the best one'.

It would also be wrong to suggest that the Cadbury Committee is the only body to offer guidance on what constitutes good practice in the arena of top pay setting. The Institute of Directors (1995), the Association of British Insurers (1994), the Institutional Shareholders' Committee (1993), ProNed (1992), and PIRC (1993) all offer recommendations about the procedures and processes by which top director pay should be set in UK companies. All make pronouncements about the appropriate structure of remuneration committees and issues relating to disclosure requirements for executive pay. In the main most of these bodies endorse the Cadbury principle that executive directors should not be involved in matters relating to their own compensation and that remuneration committees should be made up (primarily) of non-executive directors.

Most recently, the Greenbury Report recommended that 'Boards of Directors should set up remuneration committees of Non-Executive directors to determine on their behalf, and on the behalf of shareholders, within agreed terms of reference, the company's policy on executive remuneration' (Greenbury 1995, para. A1). In addition, the Report urged that 'Remuneration committees should consist exclusively of Non-Executive Directors' (para. A4).

The importance of remuneration committees for top pay setting cannot be understated. They are the principal mechanism by which senior compensation awards are determined in UK companies. Oliver Williamson (1985) once remarked that the absence of an independent remuneration committee for the setting of top directors' compensation was akin to an executive writing his pay contract with one hand and then signing it with the other. For instance, where executive directors form part of the pay-setting procedure, there may be an opportunity (or incentive) to write compensation contracts that are in the interests of senior management and not necessarily in those of the shareholders.

In theory, then, remuneration committees comprised of non-executive directors represent a potential check on the alleged abuses of a self-serving executive management. In practice, however, remuneration committees may share many of the potential disadvantages that affect non-executive directors when monitoring board performance. For example, in companies which do not have a nominations committee, an important forum whereby directors are proposed and selected, the effectiveness of the remuneration committee may be impaired. This may arise if non-executive directors who are assigned to the compensation committee owe their position to management. Clearly, such a situation may result in either partial or ineffective decisions that are not necessarily in the long-term interests of shareholders or other stakeholders of the company.

4. Setting Boardroom Compensation in UK Companies: Some New Evidence

To examine the institutional arrangements for the setting of boardroom compensation I make use of a survey questionnaire on corporate governance carried out in January 1995. The postal survey was administered to the 1,000 largest UK quoted companies ranked by market value. After excluding investment trusts from this population of companies, I achieved a sample of 298 usable responses. The respondents, who were typically the company secretary, were asked various retrospective questions relating to aspects of boardroom corporate governance. These

included: when the company first adopted a remuneration and nominations committee; the membership composition of the committees; how frequently the meetings occur and who chairs them; what sources of information the remuneration
committee makes use of when deciding the structure of boardroom pay; and who
else typically participates in these meetings.

In Table 5.1 I document the adoption of remuneration and nomination committees by these UK quoted companies. Of the 298 respondents only six companies did not have a remuneration committee for the purposes of top pay setting
by 1995. This picture is consistent with other recent evidence. For instance,
Conyon (1995) illustrates that all of the current FTSE 100 companies have now
adopted remuneration committees for the purposes of top pay setting.
Furthermore, the evidence produced by Cadbury (1995) indicates that the overwhelming majority of the Top 500 companies report the existence of remuneration committees in 1993/4. The situation is markedly different from only a few
years ago. Main and Johnston (1992) analysed the existence (and structure) of
remuneration committees in a sample of 220 large UK companies using company
accounts data from 1990. They found that only sixty-seven of these companies
(i.e. less than one-third) reported the existence of a remuneration or emoluments committee. Clearly, since the publication of the Cadbury Report (1992),
companies have been keen to establish remuneration committees or report their
existence.

The situation concerning the adoption of nomination committees is quite different, though. The evidence in Table 5.1 indicates that only about half of the companies in the sample had adopted nominations committees by 1995. This is also
consistent with the findings of the Cadbury (1995) investigations on compliance
with the Code of Best Practice which illustrated a significant increase in companies of all sizes disclosing a nomination committee, the percentage of companies
in the Top 500 disclosing the existence of a nomination committee rising from 5
per cent in 1991/2 to 50 per cent in 1993/4. The current situation in the United
Kingdom contrasts with evidence from the United States. Lorsh and MacIver
(1989: 20) reported that 84 per cent of the directors which they surveyed revealed

Table 5.1. The adoption of key board committees

Year of adoption	Remuneration committee		Nominations committee	
	No.	%	No.	%
Not established by 1995	6	2.01	146	49.16
Established:				
before 1990	136	45.64	32	10.77
in 1991	37	12.42	14	4.71
in 1992	45	15.10	23	7.74
in 1993	61	20.47	62	20.88
in 1994	13	4.36	20	6.73
TOTAL	298	100.00	297	100.00

that the boards on which they served have nominations committees. More recently Monks and Minow (1995: 193) reported the results of a Korn Ferry study that showed that in 95 per cent of large US companies, potential boardroom candidates are recommended to the board by a nominating committee.

The UK situation is clearly different. There are far fewer companies with formal nomination committees. Conyon and Mallin (1995) are critical of this current low adoption rate of nomination committees by UK listed companies. They argue that one way in which boardroom independence may be potentially enhanced is by having procedures for selecting and appointing directors that are transparent. The current paucity of such committees in 1995 represents a failure in contemporary governance arrangements.

The structure of boardroom committees is also important since those which are dominated by executive directors may take actions that are in management rather than shareholder interests. This is not to suggest that executive management will take such actions, but only to suggest that pressure or incentives may exist in these circumstances. In Table 5.2 I probe how far remuneration committees are free from executive director presence. The evidence indicates that remuneration committees are indeed made up primarily of non-executive directors with the median number of non-executives being three. This result is broadly consistent with the Cadbury guide-lines, which recommend that such committees be dominated by non-executives.

However, it is perhaps important to note that there is still a significant executive presence on these important committees. The data clearly indicates that for those companies with remuneration committees approximately half have at least one executive director on the committee. This is consistent with the analysis contained in Main and Johnston (1992). In their 1990 sample of sixty-seven remuneration committees, they found that, 'In terms of executive participation in the

Table 5.2. The membership of board committees in 1995

No.	Remuneration committee		Nominations committee	
	No.	%	No.	%
Non-executive directors				
2 or less	70	24.48	53	37.06
3	109	38.11	46	32.17
4	58	20.28	23	16.08
5 or more	49	17.13	21	14.69
TOTAL	286	100.00	143	100.00
Executive directors				
0	147	51.22	44	30.77
1	124	43.21	71	49.65
2 or more	16	5.57	28	19.58
TOTAL	287	100.00	143	100.00

Remuneration Committee, although not the rule (32 of the 67 committee examined have no executive members), it is quite common to have one or two executive members.' Such evidence is also consistent with the more recent and comprehensive study by Conyon (1995), who finds that the average number of non-executives on the remuneration committees of the FTSE 350 companies in 1995 was 3.82. This compared to the average size of such emoluments committees, including the executive directors, which was 4.23. The UK evidence, then, is consistent with the notion that non-executive directors form the overwhelming membership of remuneration committees. However, there is still some way to go before companies are complying fully with the Greenbury Report, which states that there should be no executive presence on company remuneration committees. In circumstances where there are such executive directors involved in directors' pay setting, it opens up the possibility of executive pay awards, and pay structures, that may be self-serving.[4]

Main and Johnston's (1993) study, which addressed the empirical relationship between directors' pay and remuneration committees in 220 large UK companies in 1990, found that there was a positive correlation between highest-paid director compensation and whether the company revealed the existence of a remuneration committee in its annual report. This suggests that companies with remuneration committees actually pay their top directors more than those without such institutional structures. At first glance this might appear to suggest that adopting remuneration committees does little to check directors' pay (if, indeed, this is the objective). However, a number of points should be borne in mind when interpreting this statistical result. First, the data used by Main and Johnston apply to a cross-section of companies in a given year and so cannot account for important firm-specific effects in the particular estimating strategy. This may result in a statistically biased estimate to be isolated for the remuneration committee variable. Second, there is the associated problem of endogeneity and reverse causation. Innovative companies, which may be highly performing, may pay their top directors more but are also more likely to adopt remuneration committees. A recent study by Benito and Conyon (1995) tries to overcome some of these issues by examining the relationship between remuneration committee adoption and highest-paid director emoluments in a panel of over 200 companies between 1986 and 1994. They find that there is a negative association between highest-paid director emoluments and companies which had previously adopted a remuneration committee. Whilst the latter study controls for company fixed effects, these contrasting results do point to a need for more research into the precise mechanisms by which remuneration committees (and their structure) influence boardroom compensation.

In Table 5.2 the evidence also indicates that there is more executive involvement in the nominations committee than is the case for the remuneration committee.

[4] It is noteworthy that the evidence contained in Main and Johnston (1993) also indicates that the presence of executive directors on the remuneration committee is not associated with high levels of CEO pay. The result controls for company size and firm performance.

Table 5.3. Chair of the board committees in 1995

Chair	Remuneration committee		Nominations committee	
	No.	%	No.	%
Non-executive chair	266	93.66	114	77.55
Executive chair	18	6.34	33	22.45
TOTAL	284	100.00	147	100.00

In those companies which have a nominations committee, approximately 70 per cent of the sample have at least one executive director as a committee member. Although we do not have direct evidence on exactly how the selection of directors is made, the non-reporting of such committees by companies, and the relatively high number of executive directors on nominations committees where they do exist, is consistent with the notion that director selection is firmly controlled by the chairman of the board. As the KPMG report (1994) notes, 'Over half the respondents in our survey had been selected personally by the chairman with relatively few having been recommended either through a nominations committee or by an investment institution. Clearly it will take time for the Cadbury recommendations to work through.'

In Table 5.3 I examine further the issue of executive involvement in remuneration and nomination committee procedure by documenting who actually chairs these committees. In almost all cases the remuneration committee is chaired by a non-executive director. Only about 6 per cent of the sample have remuneration committees in which the chairman is an executive director. This is consistent with the Cadbury prescript that if there are executive directors on the remuneration committee, then it should be chaired by a non-executive director. In contrast, there is a more significant involvement by executive directors on the nominations committee since about one-fifth of all committees are chaired by an executive director.

The data illustrate, then, that there is considerable structural compliance with the Cadbury (and also Greenbury) Code in the area of remuneration and nomination committee adoption as compared with the situation only five years ago. Indeed, the data in Table 5.1 shows a marked jump in the adoption of these committees immediately after the publication of the Cadbury Report in 1992. However, the data here, which is consistent with other recent evidence, suggests that companies seem much more reluctant to adopt nominations committees as a formal mechanism for the selection of directors.

One potential implication of the slow adoption rate of nomination committees is that the selection of non-executive directors may be heavily influenced by the executive directors and, what is perhaps also likely, the CEO. As Lorsch and MacIver (1989) comment in relation to the changing US situation, 'The CEO's role in selecting directors, while still a factor in stacking the power deck in his favour, is less predominant as more nominating committees allow directors to participate in the process.[5]

From Structure to Behaviour

Although the existence and membership composition of remuneration committees, as well as evidence on the selection of non-executive directors, can give an indication of the degree to which alleged executive excess in the compensation arena can be ameliorated, it is only part of the overall story. It simply allows us to isolate, at a particular point in time, the key institutional or structural features that exist, in a given company or group of companies, for the setting of directors' pay. However, the actual and potential behaviour of members of the remuneration committee, and the practices that they adopt for setting directors' compensation, is also of considerable importance. For instance, in the wider context of corporate governance theory and practice, Pettigrew and McNulty (1995) comment that

Traditionally discussions of corporate governance in the U.K. context are preoccupied with rules, regulations, institutional practices and structures which provide a framework for managerial accountability. Such discussions of accountability do not always take place informed by the realities of boardroom power and influence. Behavioural dynamics in and around the boardroom represent one of the keys to the effectiveness of NEDs (non-executive directors) and this is a crucial ingredient in shaping the conditions for board and managerial accountability.

According to these authors the legitimate focus of corporate governance research resides not only in documenting structural changes that have occurred, for example, in the mix between executive and non-executive directors on the remuneration committee, but also in identifying power and influence exercised by such directors. Future research in corporate governance policy is, therefore, likely to focus on this issue.

However, it is still important to understand the institutional practices adopted by remuneration committees in the compensation-setting process. One issue to address is the information that is available to committee members. It seems intuitively clear that access to detailed information and expert advice by the remuneration committee, as well as knowledge about who else participates in the executive compensation-setting process, is germane to a more complete understanding of the compensation-setting process (see Crystal 1992; Jensen 1993). In Table 5.4 the evidence shows that the majority of remuneration committees meet only once a year, although a significant percentage meet at least twice a year. One might suppose that the more times a specialist committee meets, the more able they become in scrutinizing the details of a given compensation strategy.

The Greenbury Report, too, stressed the role of adequate support structures for

---

[5] See also the report by KPMG (1994) detailing the considerable role and influence of the chairman in personally selecting non-executive directors.

the remuneration committee (see Greenbury 1995, paras. 4.14–4.17). For instance, Greenbury (1995, para. 4.17) argues that 'The committee may need to draw on outside advice. This should combine quality and judgement with independence. The company's management will normally hire outside consultants, if any, but the committee should be consulted about such appointments and should be free to retain its own consultants in case of need.' In Table 5.5 some information on where the remuneration committee seeks advice about boardroom pay issues is presented. The most important areas of expert advice it seeks are, indeed, from outside compensation consultants and internal company research. For instance, almost 80 per cent of the 250 companies who responded to this question said that remuneration consultants were an important source of advice and information used by the remuneration committee. The use of the company's own accounting firm was much less common, since only about one-fifth of respondents said that they used this route for gaining information about top pay determination.

In Table 5.6 we detail who actually hires and/or briefs the advisers to the remuneration committee. In two-thirds of cases the chairman of the remuneration committee, who is typically a non-executive director, is involved in the hiring or

Table 5.4. Frequency of remuneration committee meetings

No. of times per year	No.	%
1	150	54.15
2	86	31.05
3	25	9.03
4	16	5.78
TOTAL	277	100.00

Table 5.5. Sources of advice and information for the remuneration committee in setting boardroom pay

Source	Use the source	No.	%
Company's accounting firm	No	161	77.03
	Yes	48	22.97
	Total	209	100.00
Outside remuneration consultants	No	51	20.48
	Yes	198	79.52
	Total	249	100.00
Internal company research (e.g. from the personnel department)	No	68	29.82
	Yes	160	70.18
	Total	228	100.00

Table 5.6. Individuals or institutions who hire and/or brief the advisers to the remuneration committee

Individual or institution	Do hire or brief advisers	No.	%
Chairman of the remuneration committee (delegated authority)	No	57	34.13
	Yes	110	65.87
	Total	167	100.00
Remuneration committee	No	72	50.00
	Yes	72	50.00
	Total	144	100.00
Chief executive officer	No	66	48.53
	Yes	70	51.47
	Total	136	100.00

briefing of the advisers to the compensation committee. However, perhaps a striking feature of the data is that about half of the 144 companies who responded to the question also indicated that the CEO was involved in briefing (or hiring) the advisers.

Although this practice is in line with the Greenbury Report (1995, para. 4.17), which suggests that management will normally hire the compensation consultants, it is not regarded as best practice by Crystal (1992). He is sceptical about the independence of compensation consultants who are hired by executive management since this practice may create a conflict of interest between the consultants' effective employer (executive management) and the advice they provide (to the remuneration committee, non-executives, and shareholders). His position is that remuneration consultants hired by management may be unduly influenced by the CEO and hence may not be objective.[6] Because of such concerns, Crystal (1992: 242) recommends that the compensation committee hire its own compensation consultant and that, in the interests of fostering objectivity, the committee's consultant should not be permitted any ties with the executive management.

In Table 5.7 we present some evidence regarding who else participates at remuneration committee meetings. The most interesting feature of the data is that, of the 229 respondents to this question, three-quarters indicated that the CEO is present at remuneration committee meetings. Such a practice, at first sight, seems to be extremely peculiar. Here is a situation where the CEO attends meetings where his own pay, and other executive directors' pay, is determined. One potential reason for CEO attendance at remuneration committee meetings is to provide expert advice. For example, Main and Johnston (1992: 16) comment on executive

[6] Crystal (1992: 242) rhetorically comments, 'what do you think is likely to happen to an outside compensation consultant who bucks the CEO? He, too, can be summarily fired.'

Table 5.7. Other participants at remuneration committee meetings

Other participants	Do participate	No.	%
Company secretary	No	96	38.55
	Yes	153	61.45
	Total	249	100.00
Outside remuneration consultants	No	160	82.90
	Yes	33	17.10
	Total	193	100.00
Chief executive officer	No	51	22.27
	Yes	178	77.73
	Total	229	100.00

involvement in remuneration committees: 'But it is possible that the information they provide can prove useful in determining the appropriate pay level and pay structure of more junior executives.' Similarly, the Greenbury Report (1995, para. 4.14) states that 'Although Executive Directors should not be members of the remuneration committee, the company's chairman and/or Chief Executive should normally be invited to attend meetings to discuss the performance of the other Executive Directors and make proposals as necessary.'

This situation, though, still may cause a conflict of interest where individuals' own pay is being discussed. However, evidence from Main (1993: 5), based on twenty-four interviews, suggests that the CEO absents himself from proceedings when his own pay is being directly discussed. Despite this, such a practice does question the potential ability for a remuneration committee to engage in frank and open discussion when the most senior board member is present—especially if there is a possibility that they are about to be critical of the CEO (see Jensen 1993; Conyon and Machin 1995*a*).

Previous research has typically focused on the incidence of remuneration committees, and sometimes their membership composition (as in Conyon 1995). However, the results in this chapter also try to isolate other institutional arrangements for setting directors' compensation (for instance, by exploring how the remuneration committee seeks advice on compensation issues and who else is present at its meetings). Some interesting results emerge from the analysis. Whilst, there is a low incidence of executive directors in the formal membership composition of the remuneration committee, there is, in fact, CEO involvement in the compensation procedure by hiring and/or briefing the advisers to the remuneration committee and by being present at committee meetings. Whether, these arrangements have any overall effects on director compensation levels or growth rates is another matter. What is clear is that merely documenting the establishment of a remuneration committee in the company accounts (along with its membership structure) might give a misleading impression of the degree of executive involvement in the compensation-setting procedure.

5. Concluding Remarks

This chapter has considered the institutional mechanisms for setting directors' compensation in large UK companies. Against a background of concern about the perceived growth in executive compensation and the apparent difficulty in isolating a strong quantitative link between directors' pay and company performance, attention has recently switched to the mechanisms by which top pay is actually set.

The Cadbury Report is influential in this area as it has become a standard by which to judge good corporate governance practice. The more recent Greenbury Committee Report, supported by the CBI, addressed directly the issue of directors' pay. It remains to be seen whether the disclosure recommendations and institutional arrangements for setting pay advocated by this committee will materialize in practice. In the area of top pay setting, Cadbury (1992) argued for the establishment of remuneration committees comprised wholly or mainly of non-executive directors and chaired by a non-executive director. Greenbury (1995) went a step further by suggesting that compensation committees should contain only non-executive directors. In this sense, the Cadbury and Greenbury reports focus on the structural features of the compensation committee. The evidence presented in this chapter has illustrated that the majority of companies have now come into line on the establishment of remuneration committees.

However, with such an emphasis placed on the role to be played by non-executive directors in the setting of directors' pay, it is important to ascertain how directors are selected in practice. The review of the evidence contained in this chapter shows that companies are now more likely to have adopted nominations committees as a formal mechanism for selecting directors than they were a few years ago. It turns out that about 50 per cent of companies in 1995 had a nominations committee. Moreover, for those companies which do have nominations committees there is a considerable executive presence as compared with remuneration committees. This may be an unwelcome feature of contemporary boardroom governance arrangements.

Moving beyond the structure of the remuneration committee, captured by its membership composition and chairmanship, we examined some of the procedures involved in setting director compensation. We found that remuneration committees in about half the responding companies met at least twice a year and that companies made considerable use of internal company research and outside remuneration consultants. However, when it came to hiring or briefing these consultants, about 50 per cent of the responding companies indicated that the CEO played some role in this procedure. Moreover, the data revealed that in three-quarters of cases the CEO was a participant at remuneration committee meetings (although not necessarily a formal member of the remuneration committee).

An overall assessment of whether the boardroom governance innovations that have been taking place recently in the UK will assuage the public controversy over directors' pay is perhaps premature. The evidence on the institutional mechanisms by which director compensation is set suggests considerable compliance with the Cadbury Code. The primary structural evidence (i.e. adoption, committee membership, and chairmanship) illustrates clearly that companies are moving towards what is generally considered to be best practice governance structures. However, whether this will be enough to tie management rewards to performance effectively and to reassure shareholders and stockholders about the transparency of top pay setting remains to be seen. In addition, the selection procedure of non-executive directors in a large number of companies is far from clear, and this implicitly questions the ability of non-executive directors to perform their monitoring function adequately. Other evidence on the procedure of director compensation setting similarly reveals a partly ambiguous picture. Although, directors are making use of expert advice (such as remuneration consultants and internal company research) there is evidence of CEO involvement in the hiring and briefing these advisers.

The results contained in this chapter provide a snapshot of the institutional arrangements for setting directors' compensation in large UK companies. However, the generality obtained through such survey evidence potentially conceals a richer analysis which may be obtained through individual case-studies. Having documented these institutional arrangements for setting directors' compensation in UK companies, future research should aim also at understanding why individual firms adopt these particular procedures, the behavioural dynamics between individual board members, and the consequent effect on both directors' pay and company performance.

REFERENCES

Association of British Insurers (1994), *Long Term Remuneration for Senior Executives* (London: ABI).

Benito, Andrew, and Conyon, Martin (1995), 'Top Directors' Pay, Product Market Influences and Internal Control Systems', University of Warwick mimeo.

Black, F., and Scholes, M. (1973), 'The Pricing of Options and Corporate Liabilities', *Journal of Political Economy*, 81: 637–54.

Cadbury, A. (1992), *Report of the Committee on the Financial Aspects of Corporate Governance* (London: Gee).

—— (1995), *Report of the Committee on the Financial Aspects of Corporate Governance: Compliance with the Code of Best Practice* (London: Gee).

Conyon, Martin (1995), *Cadbury in the Boardroom* (London: Hemmington-Scott, June).

—— and Machin, Stephen (1995a), 'Decoding the Greenbury Code', *Parliamentary Brief* (Summer), 14–16.

—— —— (1995b), 'Investors' Watchdogs', *Parliamentary Brief* (Summer), 12–14.

—— and Mallin, Chris (1995), 'A Review of Compliance with Cadbury', University of Warwick mimeo.

—— Gregg, Paul, and Machin, Stephen (1995), 'Taking Care of Business: Executive Compensation in the United Kingdom', *Economic Journal*, 105: 704–14.

Crystal, Graef (1992), *In Search of Excess: The Overcompensation of American Executives* (New York: Norton).

Fama, Eugene, and Jensen, Michael (1983), 'Separation of Ownership and Control', *Journal of Law and Economics*, 26: 301–25.

Greenbury, R. (1995), *Directors' Remuneration: Report of a Study Group Chaired by Sir Richard Greenbury* (London: Gee).

Gregg, Paul, Machin, Stephen, and Szymanski, Stephan (1993), 'The Disappearing Relationship between Directors' Pay and Corporate Performance', *British Journal of Industrial Relations*, 31: 1–10.

Hart, Oliver (1995), 'Corporate Governance: Some Theory and Implications', *Economic Journal*, 105: 678–89.

Holmstrom, Bengt (1979), 'Moral Hazard and Observability', *Bell Journal of Economics*, 10: 74–91.

Institute of Directors (1995), *The Remuneration of Directors: A Framework for Remuneration Committees* (London: Institute of Directors).

Institutional Shareholders' Committee (1993), *The Role and Duties of Directors: A Statement of Best Practice* (London: ISC).

Jensen, Michael C. (1993), 'The Modern Industrial Revolution, Exit, and the Failure of Internal Control Systems', *Journal of Finance*, 48: 831–80.

—— and Murphy, Kevin (1990), 'Performance Pay and Top Management Incentives', *Journal of Political Economy*, 98: 225–64.

KPMG (1994), *Survey of Non-Executive Directors* (London: KPMG).

Lorsch, Jay, and MacIver, Elizabeth (1989), *Pawns or Potentates: The Reality of America's Corporate Boards* (Boston: Harvard Business School).

Main, Brian (1993), 'Pay in the Boardroom: Practices and Procedures', *Personnel Review*, 22: 3–14.

—— and Johnston, James (1992), *The Remuneration Committee and Instrument of Corporate Governance*, Hume Occasional Paper No. 35 (Edinburgh: David Hume Institute).

—— —— (1993), 'Remuneration Committees and Corporate Governance', *Accounting and Business Research*, 23: 351–62.

Main, Brian, Bruce, Alistair, and Buck, Trevor (1996), Total Board Remuneration and Company Performance, *Economic Journal*, 106/439, 1627–1644.

Milgrom, Paul, and Roberts, John (1992), *Economics, Organization and Management* (Englewood Cliffs, NJ: Prentice-Hall).

Monks, Robert, and Minow, Nell (1995), *Corporate Governance* (Oxford: Blackwell).

Pettigrew, Andrew, and McNulty, Terry (1995), 'Power and Influence in and around the Boardroom', *Human Relations*, 48/8: 845–73.

ProNed (1992), *Remuneration Committees* (London: ProNed).

Tirole, Jean (1988), *The Theory of Industrial Organization* (Cambridge, Mass.: MIT Press).

Williamson, O. (1985), *The Economic Institutions of Capitalism* (New York: Free Press).

6

GOVERNANCE BY EXIT: AN ANALYSIS OF THE MARKET FOR CORPORATE CONTROL

Pauline O'Sullivan

1. Introduction

The market for corporate control is frequently advocated as an important mechanism of governance in public companies. Takeovers may contribute to governance in a number of ways. The threat of takeover provides an incentive for managers to administer the company in the interests of shareholders. The occurrence of a takeover provides an opportunity for a potential acquiror to scrutinize the performance of the incumbent management team, and replace them if appropriate. In addition, the takeover market may function as an external governance of last resort, utilized only when internal control mechanisms have failed. However, the disciplinary effects of the takeover market may be circumvented when target managers adopt defence tactics to thwart an unwanted bid. Moreover, the available empirical evidence concerning takeover gains is unclear, and at the very least only provides equivocal support for the governance role of corporate takeovers.

The objective of this chapter is to provide a critical assessment of the role of takeovers in the corporate governance process. The chapter reviews the principal theoretical and empirical literature on the role of takeovers in corporate governance, drawing from the financial economics, industrial organization, management, and legal literatures. The chapter is structured as follows. Section 2 discusses the case for and against takeovers as a method of exercising corporate governance. Section 3 examines the issue of defensive strategies and illustrates how these devices, undertaken for managerial entrenchment purposes or shareholders' interest, may hinder the takeover process. Section 4 analyses the empirical evidence on takeover gains and losses. This section is segregated according to the research methodology used, distinguishing between results based on event study techniques and studies utilizing accounting data. Section 5 reviews the evidence on the post-takeover displacement of target management. Such research may provide more direct insights into the disciplinary role of takeovers. Section 6 examines the governance role of takeover threat, specifically focusing on the consequences of abandoned takeovers. Some concluding comments are presented in Section 7.

2. The Role of Takeovers in the Governance Process

The functions of ownership and management in public companies are typically held by separate entities, ownership being in the hands of a large number of dispersed shareholders, while management is vested in a small number of professional managers. Such a corporate structure, though yielding the benefits of specialization and risk spreading, gives rise to potential agency problems since the objectives of shareholders and managers may not concur (Berle and Means 1932; Jensen and Meckling 1976). For example, managers may choose to shirk, indulge in excessive consumption of perquisites (Williamson 1963), pursue an empire-building strategy (Mueller 1969), or adopt an unduly risk-averse attitude with respect to corporate investment decisions (Coffee 1988). Agency problems are compounded by the inability or unwillingness of diversified shareholders to monitor managerial behaviour adequately, thereby leaving managers free to pursue their own objectives at shareholders' expense.

Despite the obvious weaknesses which are apparent in this form of organizational structure, the public corporation continues as a popular form of business entity. Fama (1980) and Fama and Jensen (1983) justify the apparent success of the public corporation based on the utilization of a set of governance mechanisms to mitigate the adverse consequences of the separation of ownership and control. Within the company, a number of mechanisms exist which are capable of facilitating shareholder monitoring of management activities. The board of directors, for example, is the principal internal mechanism through which shareholders can monitor and evaluate managerial performance (Fama and Jensen 1983). In addition, executive compensation contracts may be utilized to encourage management to administer the company in the interests of shareholders (Jensen and Murphy 1990). Alternatively, variations in internal organizational structure may also serve to restrain managerial self-interest (Ezzamel and Watson 1993). However, should these mechanisms of internal governance fail to reconcile the interests of shareholders and managers, the market for corporate control is frequently advocated as a control mechanism of last resort (Jensen 1986; Hart 1995).

Takeovers can contribute to the corporate governance process in two ways. The possibility of a takeover, with the inherent threat of displacement, encourages managers to act in the interest of shareholders. In addition, the occurrence of a takeover may correct for managerial failure by replacing underperforming or opportunistic managers. This disciplinary view of takeovers is rooted in Manne's (1965) thesis that the stock market is the only objective measure of managerial performance. Essentially, Manne hypothesizes that actual and potential competition between would-be management teams drives up asset values and reduces the discretion for company managers to pursue non-profit goals. The likely consequence of any non-profit-maximizing behaviour is a reduction in the company's share price and the creation of an incentive for a competing team to acquire ownership of the assets and redirect their use, replacing the incumbent management team in the process. Obviously, the greater the management team's departure from value-maximizing objectives, the larger the potential gain for an acquiror and the more vulnerable the company is to a takeover bid. It is in this context that the market for corporate control is heralded as being one of the most effective governance mechanisms available to shareholders (Rappaport 1990).

Despite such widespread belief in the effectiveness of takeovers as a governance mechanism, takeover efficiency has been questioned on a number of grounds. Grossman and Hart (1980), for example, argue that the takeover process may be hampered by the free rider problem caused by widely dispersed shareholdings in large companies. Small target shareholders who believe that an individual decision will have a negligible impact on the successful outcome of a bid may refrain from tendering their shares in the expectation of obtaining post-merger gains. As a consequence, socially desirable takeovers will fail or not occur if acquisition costs are raised to a high level and bidders have to surrender all potential gains to the existing shareholders. The free rider problem may be resolved if bidders are allowed to acquire 'toe-hold' interests (Shleifer and Vishny 1986), or to adopt 'exclusionary' devices, such as dilution and two-tier offers (Grossman and Hart 1980). In the UK, Yarrow (1985) suggests that the free rider problem may be attenuated by the compulsory acquisition rights required under the City Code on Mergers and Takeovers, thereby preserving the credibility of the takeover threat.

A second criticism of takeover governance is the possibility that an active market for corporate control can lead to a number of socially inefficient consequences. It is argued that the existence of a takeover threat may encourage managers to concentrate on maximizing short-term performance at the expense of long-term investment decisions. Stein (1988) provides a formal model in support of this hypothesis. Shareholder value may be damaged as corporate resources are diverted from beneficial projects with long-term pay-offs, such as investment in capital and research and development, to projects which are less profitable but yield immediate returns. The implication of this may be that firms which concentrate on long-term investment are undervalued *vis-à-vis* their short-term counterparts and accordingly become more attractive acquisition targets (Shleifer and Vishny 1990).

A third source of criticism is based on how the takeover market realigns contractual relationships that exist prior to a takeover. Implicit in the contractual view of the firm is the reliance on a series of long-term contracts which promote the company's investment in firm-specific assets (Williamson 1985) and ensure additional effort from employees (Lazear 1979). However, in an active takeover market such long-term arrangements are unstable since new owners are not obliged to honour existing implicit contracts. As a consequence, the displacement of existing managers allows shareholders to appropriate rents from other stakeholders via an unilateral default on any unwanted implicit contracts. Shleifer and Summers' (1988) analysis of the TWA takeover by Icahn in the USA suggests that at least one and a half times the takeover premium was accounted for by way of wage losses by the members of three TWA unions. In the authors' view, wealth is not created but merely redistributed by the takeover process.

A fourth criticism of the takeover process is its ability to be manipulated by managers of bidding firms who themselves are pursuing managerial objectives (Malatesta 1983). Several arguments based on the managerialist theory of the firm have been put forward to explain the desire of company management to expand corporate assets under their control (Baumol 1959; Marris 1964). Given that growth by takeover is likely to be more rapid than internal growth, a direct relationship is expected between takeover activity and size-maximizing behaviour of the managers in bidding firms (Reid 1968). In addition, managers may embark on a strategy of conglomerate takeovers in an attempt to reduce the variability of the firm's earnings (Amihud and Lev 1981). Unlike shareholders, managers are likely to be over-invested in their firms as a result of specialized human capital or holdings of stock options. By pursuing a diversifying takeover, managers can utilize the takeover mechanism to diversify the risk to their human capital, even though such a strategy offers little benefit to shareholders.

Alternatively, managers may undertake takeovers for entrenchment purposes. By investing excessively in assets which complement their skills and knowledge, corporate managers may seek to make themselves indispensable and costly to replace. Of course, such a strategy may also enable managers to demand higher compensation and other forms of perquisites from shareholders (Shleifer and Vishny 1989). Hence, critics argue that takeovers which transfer wealth from bidding shareholders to bidding managers and target shareholders are merely manifestations of, not solutions, to the agency problem.

A final criticism of the efficiency of takeover governance relates to the costs involved in executing a successful takeover. The transaction costs associated with professional fees (Law 1986), post-acquisition integration (Schweiger and Walsh 1990), and regulation (Jarrell and Bradley 1980) can be substantial. Disruption costs are also non-trivial when managers become unduly occupied by coping with the pressure of takeovers, and as a consequence diverting attention from carrying out the management duties of the business in a diligent manner (Jenkinson and Mayer 1992). The incurrence of large transaction costs stipulates that takeovers may provide efficient governance only in extreme instances of managerial discretion. The implication seems to be that, because of the costs involved, takeovers may indeed be a governance mechanism of last resort.

The objective of this section has been to analyse the role of takeovers in the corporate governance process. In theory, takeovers provide an obvious mechanism by which shareholders can seek to control managerial discretion. However, this method of corporate governance can lead to several socially dysfunctional consequences involving managerial short-termism, contractual realignment, and wealth redistribution. Moreover, the effectiveness of takeover governance may be compromised by problems of free-riding. An additional problem arises when incumbent managers adopt a number of defensive strategies designed to hinder effective takeover activity and subsequent displacement. Such defensive strategies are examined in the following section.

3. The Adoption of Defensive Tactics

The interests of target shareholders and managers may deviate significantly during a corporate control contest. Whilst shareholders may earn substantial wealth gains from accepting a takeover bid, managers may suffer loss of security, salary, and reputation and a significant investment in human capital if displacement subsequently occurs. This potential conflict of interest has led to two differing theories on the use of defensive tactics. The managerial entrenchment hypothesis posits that takeover defences are adopted by managers to protect their own self-interest and position (Cary 1969). Attempts to increase deliberately the costs, and correspondingly reduce the profitability of corporate control changes, will erode a potential acquiror's incentive to launch a bid. As the likelihood of a bid reduces, the disciplinary (governance) effect of the takeover market may be weakened considerably. In addition to the loss of corporate value, shareholders will also suffer a direct loss of wealth if the managerial resistance results in the defeat of a particular bid.

An interesting aspect of the use of managerial entrenchment tactics is the likelihood that such tactics require shareholder approval. In view of the negative impact on shareholder wealth which entrenchment implies, why do shareholders permit managers to utilize such tactics? Essentially, three reasons have been suggested in the literature (DeAngelo and Rice 1983). First, shareholders may simply be irrational. Second, large shareholders may vote with management rather than risk jeopardizing existing and future relations with the company. Third, 'uninformed' shareholders may have to incur substantial costs before the effects of proposed defensive tactics can be evaluated. Since these costs are likely to outweigh any potential benefits, 'uninformed' shareholders have a tendency to sanction proposals of takeover defences even though it may be in their own interests to oppose them.

Unlike the managerial entrenchment hypothesis, the shareholder interest hypothesis assumes that alternative mechanisms for monitoring managers are sufficient to protect shareholder welfare and hence the utilization of defensive tactics will not result in a material increase in managerial inefficiency. Several arguments have been suggested supporting the contention that resistance actually benefits shareholders (DeAngelo and Rice 1983). First, it is argued that defensive tactics overcome the communal resource problem associated with corporate control by allowing a cartelized response to tender offers. As a result, higher premiums can be extracted as the bargaining power of managers is strengthened.

Higher premiums may also result if incumbent managers can employ defensive measures to delay the acquisition and generate an auction in the process. Second, the adoption of defensive tactics may discourage management from becoming overly concerned with short-termism and encourage the adoption of a longer-term perspective when it comes to making corporate decisions. Third, advantages should also accrue to shareholders when there is greater stability and continuity of management (Linn and McConnell 1983). For example, Knoeber (1986) argues that shark repellents, that is anti-takeover amendments to the corporate charter, benefit shareholders by enabling more efficient contracting between managers and shareholders. An efficient compensation scheme usually dictates the inclusion of a deferred element to prevent any manipulation of the share price or accounting figures and to allow better evaluation as more information becomes available at a later date (Lambert and Larcker 1985). However, managers may not view this form of contracting favourably because a hostile takeover creates the opportunity for bidders to capture this element of deferred payment. Hence, the adoption of takeover defences may prevent such exploitation and encourage the use of better compensation methods.

Finally, according to Hirschey (1986), fakeouts—a term denoting a variety of takeover defences—also allow managers to obtain a greater share of rents accruing to their firm-specific human capital. This encourages additional investments in firm-specific human capital which may increase the value of the firm and is beneficial to shareholders especially in industries where such additional investments are desired.

The Takeover Code in the UK is governed by the underlying principle that the decision to accept or reject a bid should rest in the hands of the shareholders in target companies. Hence, target management are not permitted to undertake any activity which impedes a takeover without the approval of shareholders. However, this does not mean that target management in the UK are devoid of weapons to protect themselves against unwanted takeovers. Surveys undertaken by Jenkinson and Mayer (1991) and Sudarsanam (1994) reveal that target firms in the UK can utilize a wide range of non-mutually exclusive defence strategies to resist their bidders. These broadly include attacking the offer terms and ability of bidders, revised financial forecasts, asset restructuring, management changes, seeking white knights, antitrust lobbying, and legal appeal. In particular, Sudarsanam (1994), using a survey of 238 UK hostile bids between 1984 and 1989, finds that soliciting the support of friendly shareholders and unions and white knights may be effective in quelling a hostile bidder but did not necessarily help to maintain independence. The following is a review of the structures and empirical evidence regarding the methods of defensive strategies commonly utilized by companies.

Dual-Class Recapitalization

In a dual-class recapitalization, shares with limited voting rights are exchanged for common equity shares. Since managers are not participants in the exchange, a dual-class recapitalization leads to an increase in the voting power of insiders—allowing managers with relatively small equity holdings to increase its voting power in the firm without increasing its equity investment. The impact of dual-class recapitalization on shareholder wealth is conflicting. DeAngelo and DeAngelo (1985), Partch (1987), and Cornett and Vetsuypens (1989) report evidence of shareholder gains on the announcement of dual-class recapitalization schemes. However, Jarrell and Poulsen (1988) produce evidence of negative returns around the announcement period. In particular, the authors found the largest negative returns for companies with insider holdings in the region of 30 to 55 per cent—evidence which is consistent with the managerial entrenchment hypothesis.

Elimination of Cumulative Voting

Cumulative voting entitles a shareholder to cast all votes for a single director instead of having to distribute the votes among several candidates and is often considered an important mechanism which allows corporate raiders to facilitate changes in control. Hence, attempts to eliminate cumulative voting rights from the company charter may be used by managers in the face of a takeover threat. Bhagat and Brickley (1984) examine the shareholder wealth effects of a sample of 126 changes to cumulative voting rights proposed by managers. Significant negative returns are reported for the eighty-four firms who eliminated cumulative voting rights, as opposed to the absence of any noticeable stock price reaction for those firms who sought to enhance cumulative voting. The authors argue that these results support the notion that a reduction in cumulative voting rights is inconsistent with the pursuit of shareholder wealth maximization.

Anti-takeover Amendments

Anti-takeover amendments, commonly referred to as shark repellents, can be broadly categorized into three groups. The first is supermajority voting provisions, which require that shareholder approval, ranging from say two-thirds to 96 per cent, must be obtained before any change in corporate control can be effected. The second variation is the staggered board of directors, which classifies directors into three classes of equal size and provides a minimum tenure of three years. Since only a fraction of the whole board is elected annually, it is longer and harder for a bidder to achieve control of the board—even though it may own a majority of the equity. The third type of anti-takeover amendment is the fair price amendment which specifies a minimum offer price in the event of a takeover proposal.

DeAngelo and Rice (1983) fail to find any significant wealth effects accruing from anti-takeover amendments in a sample of companies which adopted such provisions between 1974 and 1979. In contrast, Linn and McConnell (1983) report a weak positive stock price reaction in a sample of 388 firms between 1960 and 1980. Jarrell and Poulsen (1987) distinguish their analysis between those firms adopting fair price as opposed to other forms of anti-takeover amendments. They report little effect in response to fair price amendments but a significant negative impact in response to supermajority voting and staggered boards techniques. In addition, they report that non-fair price amendments are more likely to be utilized in firms with a significant insider shareholding—a finding which is consistent with similar work by McWilliams (1990) and Mahoney and Mahoney (1993).

Pound (1987) examines the direct effects of anti-takeover amendments on the level of takeover activity. By comparing a sample of firms adopting such amendments with a control sample without amendments, Pound (1987) finds that the frequency of takeover is significantly higher in the control sample. This evidence suggests that anti-takeover amendments are utilized as managerial entrenchment devices. A recent study by Pugh *et al.* (1992), however, finds that anti-takeover amendments encourage managers to undertake longer-term investments, such as capital expenditure and expenditure on research and development.

Targeted Share Repurchases and Standstill Agreements

Targeted share repurchases, popularly known as greenmail, occurs when a target firm buys back a block of shares from a potential bidder by offering an attractive premium over the prevailing market price. These repurchases are often accompanied by standstill agreements which prohibit a potential bidder from owning more than a specified percentage of the firm's equity for a specified period of time. Empirical studies by Dann and DeAngelo (1983) and Bradley and Wakeman (1983) found that non-participating shareholders experience a significant wealth decline during the period surrounding the announcement of defensive share repurchases. However, contrasting evidence is provided in studies by Mikkelson and Ruback (1985), Holderness and Sheehan (1985), and Klein and Rosenfield (1988).

Litigation

Litigation, where charges against bidding firms are filed on the grounds of fraud, antitrust, or securities violation, can be used as a post-offer tactic to frustrate takeover bids. In the UK, for example, this method of defence can take the form of lobbying for a reference to the Monopolies and Mergers Commission (MMC) or to the European Commission. Litigation imposes significant delay and costs on the bidder. Franks and Harris (1986) suggest that the possibility of MMC referral may discourage bidders from seeking to acquire inefficiently run companies. Alternatively, shareholders may benefit from higher premiums if the delay arising from litigation allows target management to generate an auction. Jarrell (1985) examines the wealth effects of eighty-nine control contests which involved the use of litigation. The study found that 75 per cent of targets which were subsequently acquired did reap higher premiums and that auctions were initiated in 80 per cent of the targets. Moreover, Jarrell (1985) reports that these auctions gave target shareholders an additional 17 per cent excess return on the original premiums.

Poison Pills

Poison pills confer special rights and privileges to target shareholders in the event of a possible control change. There are five variants of the poison pill: preferred stock rights, flip-over plans, flip-in plans, back-end rights plans, and voting plans. When discharged, these rights impose significant financial penalties on bidders. The use of poison pills is usually justified on the grounds that they protect target shareholders against the coercive nature of two-tier and tender offers (*Harvard Business Review* 1984).

The available empirical evidence shows that the adoption of poison pills has a detrimental effect on shareholders' wealth. In an analysis of 380 firms, Ryngaert (1988) finds significant negative returns during the adoption period. Similar findings are reported by Malatesta and Walking (1988) in their study of 113 firms adopting poison pills between 1982 and 1986. An interesting finding of Malatesta and Walking's study is the greater likelihood of poison pill use in those firms where managers own a relatively small proportion of total equity. Brickley *et al.* (1994) report that the market actually reacts favourably to poison pill announcements when the board comprises a majority of outside directors. This finding, when contrasted with the negative reaction reported in previous studies, suggests that the market distinguishes between poison pills which are adopted to safeguard managers from those which are adopted to benefit shareholders.

Golden Parachutes

Golden parachutes are provisions in an employment contract which pays a specified amount of monetary compensation to senior executives in the event of displacement following a corporate control contest. Supporters argue that golden parachutes can help align the interests of shareholders and managers during a takeover contest. Opponents view such payments, which can increase takeover costs substantially, as devices which are designed to deter potential bidders (Coffee 1988; Eisenberg 1989). Lambert and Larcker's (1985) analysis of ninety firms adopting golden parachutes between 1975 and 1982 provides some support for the shareholder interest arguments. Their study finds that announcements of golden parachutes are associated with an increase in share price. There is some ambiguity on the precise interpretation of these results since the positive reaction could also be interpreted as the stock market's anticipation of a future takeover bid.

Defensive Corporate Restructuring

Corporate restructuring may be undertaken as a defensive response to hostile takeover bids. Leveraged cash-outs or ESOPs may be used to consolidate owner-ship in parties who are perceived to be affiliated to the existing management (Scholes and Wolfson 1990). Similarly, takeovers may be resisted by changing the capital structure through the issue of new equity to dilute the bidder's percentage of shares and voting rights or by using proceeds of the issuance of new debt to purchase equity from non-aligned parties. An increase in the debt equity ratio of the target may also frustrate the plans of cash-constrained bidders to use the target's cash flow or assets for securing the finance necessary to effect the takeover (Stulz 1988; Harris and Raviv 1988).

Target management may also engage in asset restructuring via sell-offs, demergers, or acquisitions as a defensive strategy. Assets which are not required by the bidder or ones which will create antitrust or regulatory problems are delib-erately acquired. Alternatively 'crown jewels' may be divested to diminish the target's attractiveness. Empirical studies of defensive restructuring generally support the entrenchment view (Dann and DeAngelo 1988; Denis 1990). A significant average wealth loss during announcements of defensive restructuring is recorded in Dann and DeAngelo's (1988) study of thirty-three targets between 1962 and 1983.

The objective of this section has been to illustrate the ability of target compa-nies to hinder the pure operation of the governance role of takeovers. The section explains the variety of defensive strategies available and has attempted to identify the effect of adopting such defensive strategies on managerial and shareholder objectives. Overall, the evidence appears to favour the managerial entrenchment hypothesis with the majority of studies suggesting either none or negative share price reactions. However, it should be appreciated that a number of studies have reported a positive reaction to the adoption of defensive tactics. This is particu-larly noticeable in instances where either shareholders or a properly balanced board of directors have sanctioned the proposals.

4. Evidence of Takeover Gains

Central to the governance role of takeovers is the belief that takeovers seek to correct for inadequate corporate performance and thereby reconcile the interests of managers and shareholders. This interpretation of the takeover process pro-vides a number of testable hypotheses. First, in order to justify takeover activity from a governance perspective, we would expect target firms to exhibit inferior performance prior to the bid announcement. Second, if the objective of a takeover is to correct for managerial failure, we would expect the post-takeover performance of companies to improve. In addition to the possibility of enhancing governance through completed takeovers, we would also expect failed takeover attempts to improve corporate efficiency since abandoned takeovers allow us to gain a deeper insight into the governance role of the takeover threat. Not surprisingly, a large amount of empirical research has sought to test the validity of each of these hypotheses.

Two distinct approaches have emerged in the analysis of corporate performance in respect of takeover activity. One approach argues that the appropriate measure of corporate gains or losses should reflect the primary interests of company shareholders. This is based on the view that shareholders 'are the ultimate holders of the rights to organisational control and therefore must be the focal point of any discussion concerning it' (Jensen 1984). Supporters of this view have utilized stock market data in the analysis of takeover activity—measuring the economic impact of takeovers by focusing on abnormal share price movements during the pre-announcement, announcement, and post-acquisition periods.

Critics of event study analysis typically argue that shareholder gains are not an adequate measure of future takeover benefits. This is based on the belief that such gains are a measure of anticipated performance which can be compromised by an asymmetry of information between managers and corporate outsiders (Porter 1987; Morck *et al.* 1990). In addition, it is often suggested that share price movement surrounding takeover activity may merely reflect shareholders' anticipation of wealth transfers from existing bondholders or wealth benefits arising from taxation readjustments—and thereby serves as an inappropriate measure of improvements in efficiency (Shleifer and Vishny 1988).

An alternative method of analysing the efficiency gains from takeovers is to utilize accounting data to examine the financial health of companies prior to becoming takeover targets and to ascertain how performance changes over a substantial period following the takeover. This approach uses traditional historic accounting measures such as returns on sales, assets, and capital employed, as well as profit and sales growth measures. In the following sections the empirical evidence on using event studies and accounting measures of performance are presented separately.

Event Studies

If the principal motive of a takeover is to correct for managerial failure, the pre-bid performance is expected to be significantly negative before the bid announcement. Studies in the USA by Dodd and Ruback (1977), Kummer and Hoffmeister (1978), and Asquith (1983) report large negative abnormal returns in the pre-merger period. Asquith (1983), for example, found consistent negative cumulative returns for his sample of 302 target firms for a period spanning 480 days to twenty days before the bid announcement date. Similar results are also reported for the UK by Franks *et al.* (1977) and Firth (1979, 1980). These studies, however, do not distinguish between friendly and hostile targets.

To examine whether there is an association between the mood and motive of a takeover, Franks and Mayer (1991) undertake a comparison of the pre-bid performances of hostile and friendly targets. There are, however, no significant pre-acquisition share price performance differences between the two groups. While hostile targets did show worse share price performance in the year preceding the bid, the differences between the two groups were not significant. The lack of clear performance differences based on the nature of bid casts some doubt on the wisdom of interpreting pre-bid negative returns as being indicative of inefficient management. Franks and Mayer (1996) suggest that their findings indicate that takeovers are motivated not by *ex post* managerial failures but by *ex ante* valuation differences amongst firms. This interpretation has received some support from other researchers (Malatesta and Thompson 1985; Caves 1989).

Unlike findings on pre-bid performance, there is unequivocal evidence that shareholders in target firms earn sizeable positive returns during takeover announcements. Studies of completed mergers in the US by Dodd (1980), Asquith (1983), and Eckbo (1983) report two-day abnormal returns ranging from 6.24 per cent to 13.4 per cent around the bid announcement date. Over a one month period, the positive returns are estimated at between 13.3 per cent and 21.78 per cent (Asquith *et al.* 1983; Malatesta 1983). Total abnormal returns from the announcement of an offer through to bid outcome range from 15.5 per cent to 33.9 per cent (Dodd 1980; Asquith 1983; Weir 1983). Similarly, studies of completed tender offers document positive abnormal returns to shareholders of between 16.85 per cent and 34.1 per cent for one or two months surrounding the bid announcement (Dodd and Ruback 1977; Kummer and Hoffmeister 1978; Bradley 1980). A more complete measure of the total gains to shareholders, however, should also take into account stock price reactions to initial purchases. Mikkelson and Ruback (1985), for example, find positive stock market reactions to Schedule 13D filings. In cases where the initial purchases are perceived to be associated with a future bid, an increase of 7.74 per cent is recorded. When purchases are likely to be for investment purposes only, an increase of 3.24 per cent occurs. Similarly, stock price reactions to 13D filings by corporate raiders are significantly higher compared to a sample of other filers (Holderness and Sheehan 1985).

Jarrell *et al.* (1988) provide an interesting insight on the time dimension on the gains to target shareholders over the past three decades. Their study examines the returns to shareholders of 663 completed takeovers between 1962 and 1985. The average shareholder gain was 19 per cent in the 1960s, 35 per cent in the 1970s, and 30 per cent in the 1980s. Bradley *et al.* (1988) report similar results in their study of 236 completed takeovers for the periods 1963–8 and 1981–5.

The gains to target shareholders are replicated in studies of takeovers in the UK. Franks *et al.* (1977), in a study of seventy-four mergers in brewing and distilling between 1955 and 1972, report abnormal gains of around 26 per cent. Firth (1979,

1980) reports gains of 37 per cent between months −4 and +1, and gains of 29 per cent in the announcement month itself. In a study of 1,900 takeovers between 1955 and 1985, Franks and Harris (1989) find gains of 23 per cent in the announcement month alone, with overall gains between months −4 and +1 of 29 per cent. Limmack (1991) reports overall gains of 37 per cent in a study of 462 completed bids between 1977 and 1986.

These gains, however, do not appear to be sustained in the long run. In a survey of six US studies, Jensen and Ruback (1983) find systematic declines in bidder share price of approximately 5.5 per cent in the year following the takeover. In a later study by Magenheim and Mueller (1988), the abnormal returns to bidders are estimated to be around −16 per cent over a three-year period. These results, however, appear to be sensitive to the choice of event window and benchmarks. Indeed, in the UK, Franks and Harris (1989) and Limmack (1991) emphasize the importance of choice of methodology in measuring post-acquisition performance. In a recent study of 1,164 US acquisitions between 1955 and 1987, Agrawal (1992) reports losses of 10 per cent to bidders over a period of five years after the takeover announcement. However, Franks *et al.* (1991) fail to find evidence of abnormal performance post-acquisition. Hence, the debate on long-run performance of takeovers remains unresolved.

Accounting Studies

Accounting-based studies which seek to compare the performance of target and non-target firms generally fail to provide conclusive evidence that target firms underperform their non-target counterparts. In the USA, for example, Mueller (1980) analyses the performance of 287 acquisitions between 1962 and 1972. Controlling for size and industry, he finds target firms produced greater pre-acquisition return on assets than non-target firms. These results are echoed in other studies by Boyle (1970), Harris *et al.* (1982), and Herman and Lowenstein (1988).

More recent research has sought to examine whether the nature of takeover may be an important consideration when analysing the pre-acquisition performance of targets. The principal objective of this research has been to test the proposition that hostile takeovers, in particular, may be motivated by governance shortcomings, whilst friendly acquisitions are more likely to be motivated by synergistic benefits (Morck *et al.* 1988). The implication is that hostile takeovers are more likely to be associated with inferior levels of performance than their friendly counterparts.

Ravenscraft and Scherer (1987) compare the performance of ninety-five target firms segregating the sample on the basis of bid type. They report evidence that targets acquired in hostile acquisitions exhibit inferior pre-acquisition performance compared to firms acquired in friendly takeovers or via 'white knight' rescues. However, the difference is not significant. Morck *et al.* (1988) compare the pre-acquisition performance of hostile and friendly target firms between 1981 and

1985. They find that hostile targets are associated with a significantly lower Tobin's Q. In addition, those hostile targets located in low-Q industries, exhibited lower Q-values than the industry average. The authors conclude that hostile takeovers are therefore more likely to be associated with disciplinary (governance) reasons.

The ambiguity with respect to the pre-acquisition performance of takeover targets is replicated in a number of UK studies. For example, Meeks (1977) finds that targets may be more profitable than their non-target counterparts in similar industries. Similarly, studies by Levine and Aaronovitch (1981) and Franks and Mayer (1996) fail to find distinguishable performance between the two groups of firms. In contrast, a number of studies find that target firms may indeed exhibit inferior performance. Kuehn (1975), Cosh *et al.* (1980), Tzoannos and Samuels (1972), and Buckley (1972) report evidence that UK companies may have inferior performance returns prior to becoming acquisition targets.

The inconsistent evidence on pre-bid performance of targets provides no strong support for the notion that the primary motive of a takeover is to redress managerial inefficiency or opportunism. Moreover, the empirical analysis of post-acquisition performance fails to produce conclusive evidence that the acquisition process enhances corporate performance. In the USA, Ravenscraft and Scherer (1987) undertake a comprehensive assessment of post-acquisition performance. Their results provide clear evidence that accounting profitability declines after an acquisition. In attempting to understand this evidence the authors suggest that their results are consistent with the evidence of acquired firms being divested in later years. This is a view shared by Porter (1987), who notices that more than half of related acquisitions and three-quarters of unrelated acquisitions made in the 1970s were subsequently divested.

An interesting time dimension on post-acquisition performance is provided by Herman and Lowenstein (1988). The authors identify differences in post-acquisition performance between firms acquired between 1975–8 and 1981–3. The former exhibit a significant increase in return on equity between the year prior to acquisition and subsequent years. The sample from the 1980s, however, shows a sharp decline in post-acquisition return on equity compared to the returns achieved in the year immediately prior to takeover. In a recent study, Healy *et al.* (1992) provide evidence of improved post-merger operating cash flow returns for a sample of acquired firms between 1979 and 1984. The evidence suggests that this improvement is evenly distributed amongst all targets, with no evidence that return rates vary in respect of size, method of financing, or nature of bid.

The UK studies of post-acquisition performance appear to mirror the US evidence, most studies failing to find any evidence of positive post-acquisition returns. Singh (1971), for example, compares the pre- and post-acquisition performance of seventy-seven companies involved in acquisitions between 1955 and 1960. He finds that two-thirds of companies in the sample had lower profit levels in the year of acquisition, with three-quarters experiencing lower returns in the third post-acquisition year. Meeks (1977) reports very similar results—rates of return were significantly negative for all seven years after the acquisition. Cosh *et al.* (1980), on the other hand, find small but significant increases in their study of post-merger profitability. In another study, Cosh *et al.* (1989) record small, albeit insignificant, post-merger improvements for sample of acquirors with large institutional holdings.

In summary, *ex ante* evaluations of takeover gains, using the event study approach, appear to provide some support that takeovers generate economic gains. However, a major disadvantage of this methodology is its inability to identify precisely the source of gains which may stem from improved efficiency through either the displacement of poorly performing managers, the benefits of tax savings, monopoly power, or wealth redistributions. Moreover, the poor long-run performance of bidders appears to suggest that the market may have been over-optimistic in its estimation of takeover gains during the announcement period. The governance ability of the takeover market is also challenged by the disappointing performance shown by *ex post* accounting studies. In particular, the subsequent divestments and the dismantling characteristics of the takeover wave in the 1980s appear to suggest that takeovers, motivated by the diversification objectives of management, have been unsuccessful (Shleifer and Vishny 1991).

5. Post-Acquisition Managerial Turnover

An important motivation for takeovers may arise because the bidding firm perceives the existing management team as failing to maximize the target's potential. Therefore, in addition to analysing the performance consequences of takeovers, it is necessary to examine whether a relationship exists between takeovers and managerial displacement. In many respects, analysing post-acquisition management turnover provides an important insight into the role of takeovers in disciplining inefficient managers since successful bidders are expected to introduce new policies and strategies using a new management team rather than seeking to change the behaviour of incumbent managers (Manne 1965). This is particularly expected in the case of hostile takeovers since incumbent managers of targets are usually the most active opponents to a takeover bid.

Empirical work on post-acquisition managerial change is still in its infancy. However, a number of researchers in both the USA and the UK have sought to provide some initial insights to this aspect of the takeover debate. Walsh (1988) compares managerial turnover in a sample of fifty-five target firms and a corresponding sample of independent firms. The turnover rate is significantly higher for the sample of acquired firms in the five years immediately following the takeover. In a subsequent study of a larger sample, Walsh (1989) reports that managerial turnover is indeed higher in the case of hostile bids compared to friendly acquisitions. However, the departures of top management following a takeover may not necessarily be associated with the pruning of managerial deadwood.

Instead, managers may leave voluntarily owing to culture clashes or better career opportunities elsewhere.

In order to provide a more comprehensive understanding of the association between corporate inefficiency and managerial displacement, some recent studies have attempted to incorporate both pre-acquisition performance measures and post-acquisition managerial turnover measures. Walsh and Ellwood (1991) find no evidence that takeovers occur to replace inefficient or entrenched managers. Although 39 per cent of managers leave within two years of an acquisition compared to 15 per cent in a control sample of non-acquired firms, no correlation between turnover and performance is identified. Similar results are reported by Walsh and Kosnik (1993) based on a study of firms pursued by corporate raiders.

However, some dissenting evidence is presented by Martin and McConnell (1991). Using a sample of 253 successful takeovers between 1958 and 1984, the authors report that top management turnover in the year immediately after the takeover is 41.9 per cent. More than half the managers are replaced by persons appointed from outside the target firm itself. Moreover, a significant negative association is found between pre-acquisition performance and post-acquisition turnover. These results are particularly true for targets whose pre-acquisition performance lagged behind the performance of the average firm in that industrial sector. In the UK, Franks and Mayer (1996) provide evidence that 65 per cent of executives are displaced as a result of a hostile takeover, whilst the corresponding displacement rate for managers of friendly targets is only 47 per cent.

6. The Potency of a Takeover Threat

It is frequently argued that the mere threat of a takeover serves to discourage managers from seeking to pursue non-value-maximizing objectives (Chiplin and Wright 1987). This is particularly so in instances where takeovers are launched but not eventually consummated due to successful defences or insufficient acceptances. Hence, an empirical analysis of abandoned takeovers may provide a useful avenue in which to measure the potency of the takeover threat.

Financial economists using event study techniques have attempted to measure the shareholder wealth effects of takeover terminations. One method of measuring such an effect is to examine the share price reaction to termination announcements. An alternative method is to trace the targets' share price performance for a period after the abandonment. In the UK, significant negative stock returns to target shareholders are recorded during the announcements of bid terminations. However, the losses recorded during the announcement of terminations do not appear to obliterate completely gains realized during the initial bid announcement. Such revaluation often persists for as long as two years after the abandonment (Firth 1980; Limmack 1991; Parkinson and Dobbins 1993). Similar to UK evidence, a number of studies in the USA observe that the cumulative residuals of failed targets do not revert to pre-bid levels for up to two years after termination (Dodd and Ruback 1977; Kummer and Hoffmeister 1978; Bradley *et al.* 1983). The findings of positive revaluation of targets and positive post-abandonment returns to bidding firms (Firth 1980; Parkinson and Dobbins 1993) suggest that takeover defeat may not necessarily harm shareholders' interests. However, there is also evidence of significant negative post-abandonment losses to target shareholders (Easterbrook and Jarrell 1984; Pound 1986; Ryngaert 1988). Ruback (1988), for example, reports negative abnormal returns of 36 per cent over a three-year period for a sample of twenty-four failed targets.

The consequences of abandoned takeovers using accounting data is equally mixed. According to Pickering's (1983) qualitative study, the post-abandonment performance of targets did not improve. Interestingly, many of the firms launching unsuccessful bids themselves experienced financial problems—with many becoming takeover targets. Obviously, failure to execute a takeover attempt successfully exposes weaknesses in the bidding firm and these bidders are subsequently chastised by the market for corporate control. An additional implication of the Pickering study is the possibility that failed bidders may be seeking a profitable target to camouflage weaknesses in its own performance. In a subsequent quantitative analysis of this sample of abandonments, Holl and Pickering (1988) report that unsuccessful targets exhibit improved growth rates, return on equity, and return on capital employed in the three years immediately following the failed bid. Denis (1990), examining a sample of abandoned targets in the USA, finds evidence of significant restructuring in the post-abandonment period. For example, the study reports changes in capital, asset, and ownership structure, as well as a significant amount of managerial turnover. The evidence produced by the Holl and Pickering (1988) and Denis (1990) studies is consistent with the governance role of the takeover threat.

However, some dissenting evidence is provided by Taffler and Holl (1991). Studying a sample of abandoned bids in the UK, the authors report that targets exhibit worse post-bid performance, irrespective of whether one- or three-year benchmarks are used. The study also finds significantly worse post-bid performance by unsuccessful bidders. The authors argue that takeovers are used to satisfy the pursuits of managers, and the market for corporate control has little contribution to make to the corporate governance process, regardless of bid outcomes.

7. Conclusion

This chapter provides an assessment of the governance role of the market for corporate control. The theoretical justification for takeover governance is rooted in the belief that the possibility of ownership change encourages corporate management to run their companies in the interest of shareholders. The failure to achieve this provides an opportunity for potential bidders to acquire undervalued companies and replace ineffective managers in the process. However, the disciplinary ability of the takeover market may be hindered by a variety of defensive strategies designed either to safeguard shareholders' interests or to assist incumbent managers to resist unwelcome predators.

In addition to outlining the theoretical justification for the governance role of takeovers, the chapter reviews those studies which provide some empirical insights into the effects of takeovers. The available evidence on the adoption of defence strategies suggests that the majority are designed to benefit the entrenchment objectives of incumbent managers, with positive wealth benefits to shareholders only in the few instances where such defences have either shareholder or outside director approval. In respect of takeover gains, a distinction is made between event study and accounting methodologies. In general, the share price performance of target companies is positively affected by a bid announcement, but the long-run performance deteriorates post-acquisition. Accounting studies, on the other hand, fail to report a positive relationship between takeovers and corporate efficiency.

An interesting insight into the governance role of takeovers is also provided by studies which examine the extent of managerial turnover surrounding acquisition activity. Though still in its infancy, this research suggests a positive relationship between takeover activity and managerial displacement, particularly in the case of hostile takeovers. Finally, the examination of the wealth effects of abandoned takeovers is capable of providing a useful insight into the potency of the takeover threat. However, the evidence on post-abandonment performance remains ambiguous.

The empirical evidence does not suggest that governance by exit, via takeovers, confers clear benefits to shareholders. Apart from potential liabilities such as managerial short-termism and infringement of contractual relations, the ability to adopt defensive tactics often makes takeover an expensive mechanism to execute. As a consequence, several reforms to the takeover market have been proposed. To discourage managers from focusing too excessively on the short term, Lipton and Rosenbaum (1991) suggest the adoption of a quinquennial system of corporate governance which involves granting managers a five-year moratorium from takeovers, in exchange for a periodic review of performance and control. The primary goal of such a quinquennial system is not to entrench managers but to grant them the scope to concentrate on the long-term business success of the corporation. The managerialist view of takeovers and the overall negative share returns to bidders have also prompted a critique of the way in which takeover bids are launched. Davis and Kay (1993) argue that bidding shareholders should be fully informed, and their approval obtained, before managers are allowed to embark on the takeover trail. A review of the existing competition policy, according to Plender (1990), may also help to curb the incidence of non-value-maximizing hostile bids. These include lowering the threshold at which it becomes obligatory for a bid to be launched, from 30 per cent to 15 per cent and making it the bidders' responsibility to rationalize referred takeovers on economic grounds.

Severe impediments to the operation of the takeover mechanism may, however,

140   *Pauline O'Sullivan*

have a detrimental effect on the process of corporate governance (Hart 1995). Governance by exit exercised through a free market in takeovers remains important in the UK, where shareholdings are diffused. Moreover, takeovers play a vital role in compelling reluctant managers to exit from industries with excess capacity arising from changing technological or market conditions (Jensen 1993). Hence, an interesting aspect of the future role of the takeover market is likely to be its interaction with the adoption of improved internal governance, as suggested by the Cadbury Report. Although recent discussions have emphasized the importance of improving internal governance mechanisms, governance via voice and governance via exit are not necessarily substitutes but complementary devices in reconciling the interests of stakeholders involved in the firm.

REFERENCES

Agrawal, A., Jaffe, J., and Mandelker, G. N. (1992), 'The Post-Merger Performance of Acquiring Firms: A Re-Examination of an Anomaly', *Journal of Finance*, 47/4 (Sept.), 1605–21.

Amihud, Y., and Lev, B. (1981), 'Risk Reduction as a Managerial Motive for Conglomerate Mergers', *Bell Journal of Economics*, 12: 605–17.

Asquith, P. (1983), 'Merger Bids, Uncertainty and Shareholder Returns', *Journal of Financial Economics*, 11: 51–83.

—— Bruner, R., and Mullins, D. (1983), 'The Gains to Bidding Firms from Merger', *Journal of Financial Economics*, 11: 121–40.

Baumol, W. J. (1959), *Business Behaviour, Value and Growth* (New York: Macmillan).

Berle, A. A., and Means, G. C. (1932), *The Modern Corporation and Private Property* (New York: Macmillan).

Bhagat, S., and Brickley, J. A. (1984), 'Cumulative Voting: The Value of Minority Shareholder Voting Rights', *Journal of Law and Economics*, 27/2 (Oct.), 339–65.

Boyle, S. E. (1970), 'Pre-Merger Growth and Profit Characteristics of Large Conglomerate Mergers in the United States 1948–1968', *St John's Law Review*, 44 (Spring), 152–70.

Bradley, M. (1980), 'Interfirm Tender Offers and the Market for Corporate Control', *Journal of Business*, 53: 345–76.

—— and Wakeman, L. M. (1983), 'The Wealth Effects of Targeted Share Repurchases', *Journal of Financial Economics*, 11: 301–28.

—— Desai, A., and Kim, E. H. (1983), 'The Rationale Behind Interfirm Tender Offers: Information or Synergy', *Journal of Financial Economics*, 11: 183–206.

—— —— —— (1988), 'Synergistic Gains from Corporate Acquisitions and their Division between the Stockholders of Target and Acquiring Firms', *Journal of Financial Economics*, 17: 3–40.

Brickley, J. A., Lease, R., and Smith, C. (1988), 'Ownership Structure and Voting on Antitakeover Amendments', *Journal of Financial Economics*, 21: 267–92.

—— Coles, J., and Terry, R. (1994), 'Outside Directors and the Adoption of Poison Pills', *Journal of Financial Economics*, 35: 371–90.

Buckley, A. (1972), 'A Profile of Industrial Acquisition in 1971', *Accounting and Business Research*, 2: 243–52.

Cary, W. (1969), 'Corporate Devices Used to Insulate Management from Attack', *Antitrust Law Journal*, 39: 318–33.

Caves, R. (1989), 'Mergers, Takeovers and Economic Efficiency Foresight and Hindsight', *International Journal of Industrial Organisation*, 7: 151–74.

Chiplin, B., and Wright, M. (1987), 'The Logic of Mergers: The Competitive Market for Corporate Control in Theory and Practice', IEA Hobart Paper No. 107 (London: Institute of Economic Affairs).

Coffee, J. C., Jr. (1988), 'Shareholders versus Managers: The Strain in the Corporate Web', in J. C. Coffee, Jr., Louis Lowenstein, and Susan Rose Ackerman (eds.), *Knights, Raiders and Targets: The Impact of Hostile Takeovers* (Oxford: Oxford University Press).

Cornett, M. M., and Vetsuypens, M. R. (1989), 'Voting Rights and Shareholder Wealth: The Issuance of Limited Voting Common Stock', *Managerial and Decision Economics*, 10: 175–88.

Cosh, A. D., Hughes, A., and Singh, A. (1980), 'The Causes and Effects of Takeovers in the UK: An Empirical Investigation for the Late 1960s at the Micro-Economic Level', in D. C. Mueller (ed.), *The Determinants and Effects of Mergers* (Cambridge, Mass.: Oelschlager, Gunn & Hain).

——— ——— Lee, K., and Singh, A. (1989), 'Institutional Investment, Mergers and the Market for Corporate Control', *International Journal of Industrial Organisation*, 7: 73–100.

Dann, L. Y., and DeAngelo, H. (1983), 'Standstill Agreements, Privately Negotiated Stock Repurchases and the Market for Corporate Control', *Journal of Financial Economics*, 11/1–4: 275–300.

——— ——— (1988), 'Corporate Financial Policy and Corporate Control: A Study of Defensive Adjustments in Asset and Ownership Structure', *Journal of Financial Economics*, 20: 87–127.

Davis, E., and Kay, J. (1993), 'Corporate Governance, Take-Overs and the Role of the Non-Executive Director', in M. Bishop and J. Kay (eds.), *European Mergers and Merger Policy* (Oxford: Oxford University Press).

DeAngelo, H., and DeAngelo, L. (1985), 'Managerial Ownership of Voting Rights: A Study of Public Corporations with Dual Classes of Common Stock', *Journal of Finance*, 14: 33–70.

——— and Rice, E. M. (1983), 'Antitakeover Charter Amendments and Stockholder Wealth', *Journal of Financial Economics*, 11: 329–60.

Denis, D. J. (1990), 'Defensive Changes in Corporate Payout Policy: Share Repurchases and Special Dividends', *Journal of Finance*, 45/5 (Dec.), 1433–56.

Dodd, P. (1980), 'Merger Proposals, Managerial Discretion and Stockholder Wealth', *Journal of Financial Economics*, 8/2: 105–37.

——— and Ruback, R. (1977), 'Tender Offers and Stockholder Returns: An Empirical Analysis', *Journal of Financial Economics*, 5: 351–73.

Easterbrook, F. H., and Jarrell, G. A. (1984), 'Do Targets Gain from Defeating Tender Offers', *New York University Law Review*, 59 (May), 277–92.

Eckbo, B. E. (1983), 'Horizontal Mergers, Collusion and Stockholder Wealth', *Journal of Financial Economics*, 11: 241–74.

Eisenberg, M. A. (1989), 'The Structure of Corporation Law', *Columbia Law Review*, 89/7 (Nov.), 1461–525.

Ezzamel, M., and Watson, R. (1993), 'Organisational Form, Ownership Structure and Corporate Performance: A Contextual Empirical Analysis of UK Companies', *British Journal of Management*, 4: 161–76.

Fama, E. F. (1980), 'Agency Problems and the Theory of the Firm', *Journal of Political Economy*, 88: 288–307.

—— and Jensen, M. C. (1983), 'Separation of Ownership and Control', *Journal of Law and Economics*, 26/2 (June), 301–25.

Firth, M. (1979), 'The Profitability of Takeovers and Mergers', *Economic Journal*, 89: 316–28.

—— (1980), 'Takeovers, Shareholder Returns and the Theory of the Firm', *Quarterly Journal of Economics*, 94: 235–60.

Franks, J. R., and Harris, R. S. (1986), 'The Role of the Mergers and Monopolies Commission in Merger Policy: Costs and Alternatives', *Oxford Review of Economic Policy*, 2/4: 58–78.

—— —— (1989), 'Shareholder Wealth Effects of Corporate Takeovers: The UK Experience 1955–1985', *Journal of Financial Economics*, 23/2 (Aug.), 225–49.

—— and Mayer, C. (1996), 'Hostile Takeovers and the Correction of Managerial Failure', *Journal of Financial Economics*, 40: 163–81.

—— Broyles, J. E., and Hecht, M. J. (1977), 'An Industry Study of the Profitability of Mergers in the UK', *Journal of Finance*, 32: 1513–25.

—— Harris, R., and Titman, S. (1991), 'The Postmerger Share-Price Performance of Acquiring Firms', *Journal of Financial Economics*, 29: 81–96.

Grossman, S. J., and Hart, O. D. (1980), 'Takeover Bids, the Free Rider Problem and the Theory of the Firm', *Bell Journal of Economics*, 11/1 (Spring), 42–64.

Harris, M., and Raviv, A. (1988), 'Corporate Control Contests and Capital Structure', *Journal of Financial Economics*, 20: 55–86.

Harris, R. S., Stewart, F. S., and Carleton, W. T. (1982), 'Financial Characteristics of Acquired Firms', in M. Keenan and L. J. White (eds.), *Mergers and Acquisitions: Current Problems in Perspective* (Lexington, Mass.: Lexington Books).

Hart, O. (1995), 'Corporate Governance: Some Theory and Implications', *Economic Journal*, 105 (May), 678–89.

Harvard Law Review (1984), 'Protecting Shareholders against Partial and Two-Tiered Takeovers: The "Poison Pill" Preferred', 97/5 (Mar.), 1064–83.

Healy, P. M., Palepu, K. G., and Ruback, R. S. (1992), 'Does Corporate Performance Improve after Mergers?', *Journal of Financial Economics*, 31: 135–75.

Herman, E., and Lowenstein, L. (1988), 'The Efficiency Effects of Hostile Takeovers', in J. C. Coffee, Jr., Louis Lowenstein, and Susan Rose Ackerman (eds.), *Knights, Raiders and Targets: The Impact of Hostile Takeovers* (Oxford: Oxford University Press).

Hirschey, M. (1986), 'Mergers, Buyouts and Fakeouts', *American Economic Review*, 76/2 (May), 317–22.

Holderness, C. G., and Sheehan, D. P. (1985), 'Raiders or Saviours? The Evidence of Six Controversial Investors', *Journal of Financial Economics*, 14 (Dec.), 555–79.

Holl, P., and Pickering, J. E. (1988), 'The Determinants and Effects of Actual Abandoned and Contested Mergers', *Managerial and Decision Economics*, 9: 1–19.

Hughes, A. (1993), 'Mergers and Economic Performance in the UK: A Survey of the Empirical Evidence 1950–1990', in M. Bishop and J. Kay (eds.), *European Mergers and Merger Policy* (Oxford: Oxford University Press).

Jarrell, G. A. (1985), 'The Wealth Effects of Litigation by Targets: Do Interests Diverge in a Merger?', *Journal of Law and Economics*, 28/1 (Apr.), 151–77.

—— and Bradley, M. (1980), 'The Economic Effects of Federal and State Regulation of Cash Tender Offers', *Journal of Law and Economics*, 23/2 (Oct.), 371–407.

—— and Poulsen, A. B. (1987), 'Shark Repellents and Stock Prices: The Effects of Antitakeover Amendments since 1980', *Journal of Financial Economics*, 19: 127–68.

—— —— (1988), 'Dual Class Recapitalisations as Antitakeover Mechanisms: The Recent Evidence', *Journal of Financial Economics*, 20/1–2 (Mar.), 129–52.

—— Brickley, J. A., and Netter, J. M. (1988), 'The Market for Corporate Control: The Evidence since 1980', *Journal of Economic Perspectives*, 2/1 (Winter), 49–68.

Jenkinson, T., and Mayer, C. (1991), *Takeover Defence Strategies* (Oxford: Oxford Economic Research Associates).

—— —— (1992), 'The Assessment: Corporate Governance and Corporate Control', *Oxford Review of Economic Policy*, 8/3: 1–10.

Jensen, M. C. (1984), 'Takeovers: Folklore and Science', *Harvard Business Review*, 62 (Nov.–Dec.), 109–21.

—— (1986), 'Agency Costs of Free Cash Flow, Corporate Finance and Takeovers', *American Economic Review*, 76/2 (May), 323–9.

—— (1993), 'The Modern Iudustrial Revolution, Exit, and the Failure of Internal Control Systems', *Journal of Finance*, 48/3: 831–80.

—— and Meckling, W. H. (1976), 'Theory of the Firm: Managerial Behaviour, Agency Costs and Ownership Structure', *Journal of Financial Economics*, 3: 305–60.

—— and Murphy, K. J. (1990), 'Performance Pay and Top Management Incentives', *Journal of Political Economy*, 98: 225–64.

—— and Ruback, R. (1983), 'The Market for Corporate Control: The Scientific Evidence', *Journal of Financial Economics*, 11 (Apr.), 5–50.

Klein, A., and Rosenfield, J. (1988), 'Targeted Share Repurchases and Top Management Changes', *Journal of Financial Economics*, 20: 493–506.

Knoeber, C. R. (1986), 'Golden Parachutes, Shark Repellents and Hostile Tender Offers', *American Economic Review*, 155–67.

Kuehn, D. A. (1975), *Takeovers and the Theory of the Firm* (London: Macmillan).

Kummer, D. R., and Hoffmeister, J. R. (1978), 'Valuation Consequences of Cash Tender Offers', *Journal of Finance*, 33 (May), 305–516.

Lambert, R., and Larcker, D. (1985), 'Executive Compensation, Corporate Decision-Making and Shareholder Wealth', *Journal of Accounting and Economics*, 7: 179–203.

Law, W. A. (1986), 'A Corporation is more than its Stock', *Harvard Business Review*, 64: 80–3.

Lazear, E. P. (1979), 'Why is there Mandatory Retirement', *Journal of Political Economy*, 87: 1261–84.

Levine, P., and Aaronovitch, S. (1981), 'The Financial Characteristics of Firms and Theories of Mergers', *Journal of Industrial Economics*, 30: 149–72.

Limmack, R. J. (1991), 'Corporate Mergers and Shareholder Wealth Effects 1977–1986', *Accounting and Business Research*, 21/83: 239–51.

Linn, S., and McConnell, J. (1983), 'An Empirical Investigation of the Impact of "Antitakeover" Amendments on Common Stock Prices', *Journal of Financial Economics*, 11: 361–99.

Lipton, M., and Rosenbaum, S. (1991), 'Corporate Governance: An End to Hostile Takeovers and Short Termism', *University of Chicago Law Review*, 58/187 (Winter), 1–253.

McWilliams, V. B. (1990), 'Managerial Share Ownership and the Stock Price Effects of Antitakeover Amendments', *Journal of Finance*, 45: 1627–40.

Magenheim, E. B., and Mueller, D. (1988), 'Are Acquiring Shareholders Better Off after an

Acquisition?', in J. C. Coffee, Jr., Louis Lowenstein, and Susan Rose Ackerman (eds.), *Knights, Raiders and Targets: The Impact of Hostile Takeovers* (Oxford: Oxford University Press).

Mahoney, J. M., and Mahoney, J. T. (1993), 'An Empirical Investigation of the Effect of Corporate Charter Antitakeover Amendments on Stockholder Wealth', *Strategic Management Journal*, 14: 17–31.

Malatesta, P. (1983), 'The Wealth Effects of Merger Activity and the Objective Functions of Merging Firms', *Journal of Financial Economics*, 11: 155–81.

—— and Thompson, R. (1985), 'Partially Anticipated Events: A Model of Stock Price Reactions with an Application to Corporate Acquisitions', *Journal of Financial Economics*, 14: 237–50.

—— and Walkling, R. A. (1988), 'Poison Pill Securities, Stockholder Wealth, Profitability and Ownership Structure', *Journal of Financial Economics*, 20/1–2: 247–376.

Manne, H. G. (1965), 'Mergers and the Market for Corporate Control', *Journal of Political Economy*, 73: 110–20.

Marris, R. (1964), *Theory of Managerial Capitalism* (London: Macmillan).

Martin, K. J., and McConnell, J. J. (1991), 'Corporate Performance, Corporate Takeovers and Management Turnover', *Journal of Finance*, 46/2 (June), 671–87.

Meeks, G. (1977), *Disappointing Marriage: A Study of the Gains from Merger* (Cambridge: Cambridge University Press).

Mikkelson, W. H., and Ruback, R. S. (1985), 'An Empirical Analysis of the Interfirm Equity Investment Process', *Journal of Financial Economics*, 14: 523–53.

Morck, R., Shleifer, A., and Vishny, R. W. (1988), 'Characteristics of Targets of Hostile and Friendly Takeovers', in A. Auerbach (ed.), *Corporate Takeovers: Causes and Consequences* (Chicago: National Bureau of Economic Research).

—— —— —— (1990), 'Do Managerial Objectives Drive Bad Acquisitions?', *Journal of Finance*, 45: 31–48.

Mueller, D. C. (1969), 'A Theory of Conglomerate Mergers', *Quarterly Journal of Economics*, 83: 643–59.

—— (1980), *The Determinants and Effects of Mergers: An International Comparison* (Cambridge: Oelgeschlager, Gunn and Hain).

Parkinson, C., and Dobbins, R. (1993), 'Returns to Shareholders in Successfully Defended Takeover Bids: UK Evidence 1975–1984', *Journal of Business Finance and Accounting*, 20/4 (June), 501–20.

Partch, M. M. (1987), 'The Creation of a Class of Limited Voting Common Stock and Shareholder Wealth', *Journal of Financial Economics*, 18/2: 313–39.

Pickering, J. E. (1983), 'The Causes and Consequences of Abandoned Mergers', *Journal of Industrial Economics*, 31/3 (Mar.), 267–81.

Plender, J. (1990), 'Some Policy Options', in A. Cosh, A. Hughes, A. Singh, J. Carty, and J. Plender, *Takeovers and Short Termism in the UK*, Industrial Policy Paper No. 3 (London: Institute for Public Policy Research).

Porter, M. E. (1987), 'From Competitive Advantage to Corporate Strategy', *Harvard Business Review* (May–June), 43–59.

Pound, J. (1986), 'Takeover Defeats Hurt Shareholders: A Reply to the Kidder Peabody Study', *Midland Corporate Finance Journal*, 4 (Summer), 33–8.

—— (1987), 'The Effects of Antitakeover Amendments on Takeover Activity: Some Direct Evidence', *Journal of Law and Economics*, 30/2 (Oct.), 353–67.

—— (1988), 'Proxy Contests and the Efficiency of Shareholder Oversight', *Journal of Financial Economics*, 20/1–2: 237–65.

Pugh, W. N., Page, D. E., and Jahera, J. S., Jr. (1992), 'Antitakeover Charter Amendments: Effects on Corporate Decisions', *Journal of Financial Research*, 15/1 (Spring), 57–67.

Rappaport, A. (1990), 'The Staying Power of the Public Corporation', *Harvard Business Review*, 1 (Jan.–Feb.), 96–104.

Ravenscraft, D. J., and Scherer, F. M. (1987), *Mergers, Sell-Offs and Economic Efficiency* (Washington: Brookings Institution).

Reid, S. R. (1968), *Mergers, Managers and the Economy* (New York: McGraw-Hill).

Ruback, R. S. (1988), 'Do Target Shareholders Lose in Unsuccessful Control Contests?', in A. Auerbach (ed.), *Corporate Takeovers: Causes and Consequences* (Chicago: National Bureau of Economic Research).

Ryngaert, M. (1988), 'The Effects of Posion Pill Securities on Shareholder Wealth', *Journal of Financial Economics*, 20: 377–417.

Scherer, F. M. (1988), 'Corporate Takeovers: The Efficiency Arguments', *Journal of Economic Perspectives*, 2/1 (Winter), 69–82.

Scholes, M., and Wolfson, M. (1990), 'Employee Stock Ownership Plans and Corporate Restructuring: Myths and Realities', *Financial Management*, 19: 12–28.

Schweiger, D. M., and Walsh, J. P. (1990), 'Mergers and Acquisitions: An Interdisciplinary View', in K. M. Rowland and J. R. Ferris (eds.), *Research in Personnel and Human Resources Management* (Greenwich, Conn.: JAI Press).

Shleifer, A., and Summers, L. H. (1988), 'Breach of Trust in Hostile Takeovers', in A. Auerbach (ed.), *Corporate Takeovers: Causes and Consequences* (Chicago: National Bureau of Economic Research).

—— and Vishny, R. (1986), 'Large Shareholders and Corporate Control', *Journal of Political Economy*, 94: 461–88.

—— —— (1988), 'Value Maximisation and the Acquisition Process', *Journal of Economic Perspectives*, 2/1 (Winter), 7–20.

—— —— (1989), 'Management Entrenchment: The Case of Manager-Specific Investments', *Journal of Financial Economics*, 25: 123–39.

—— —— (1990), 'Equilibrium Short Horizons of Investors and Firms', *American Economic Review*, 80/2 (May), 148–53.

—— —— (1991), 'Takeovers in the 60s and 80s: Evidence and Implications', *Strategic Management Journal*, 12: 51–9.

Singh, A. (1971), *Takeovers: Their Relevance to the Stock Market and Theory of the Firm* (Cambridge: Cambridge University Press).

Stein, J. C. (1988), 'Takeover Threats and Managerial Myopia', *Journal of Political Economy*, 96: 61–80.

Stulz, R. M. (1988), 'Managerial Control of Voting Rights, Financing Policies and the Market for Corporate Control', *Journal of Financial Economics*, 20/1–2: 25–54.

—— Walkling, R., and Song, M. H. (1990), 'The Distribution of Target Ownership and the Division of Gains in Successful Takeovers', *Journal of Finance*, 45/3 (July), 817–33.

Sudarsanam, P. S. (1991), 'Defensive Strategies of Target Firms in UK Contested Takeovers', *Managerial Fianance*, 17/6: 47–56.

—— (1994), 'Defensive Strategies of Target Firms in UK Contested Takeovers: A Survey', Working Paper No. 94/1, City University Business School.

Taffler, R. J., and Holl, P. (1991), 'Abandoned Mergers and the Market for Corporate Control', *Managerial and Decision Economics*, 12: 271–80.

Tzoannos, J., and Samuels, J. M. (1972), 'Takeovers and Mergers: The Financial Characteristics of Firms Involved', *Journal of Business Finance*, 4/3: 5–16.

Walsh, J. P. (1988), 'Top Management Turnover following Mergers and Acquisitions', *Strategic Management Journal*, 9: 173–83.

—— (1989), 'Doing a Deal: Merger and Acquisition Negotiations and their Impact upon Top Management Turnover', *Strategic Management Journal*, 10: 307–22.

—— and Ellwood, J. W. (1991), 'Mergers, Acquisitions and the Pruning of Managerial Deadwood', *Strategic Management Journal*, 12: 201–17.

—— and Kosnik, R. D. (1993), 'Corporate Raiders and their Disciplinary Role in the Market for Corporate Control', *Academy of Management Journal*, 36/4: 671–700.

—— and Seward, J. K. (1990), 'On the Efficiency of Internal and External Corporate Control Mechanisms', *Academy of Management Review*, 15: 421–58.

Weir, P. (1983), 'The Costs of Antimerger Lawsuits: Evidence from the Stock Market', *Journal of Financial Economics*, 11: 207–24.

Williamson, O. E. (1963), 'Managerial Discretion and Business Behaviour', *American Economic Review*, 53/5: 1032–57.

—— (1985), *The Economic Institutions of Capitalism* (New York: Free Press).

Yarrow, G. K. (1985), 'Shareholder Protection, Compulsory Acquisition and the Efficiency of the Takeover Process', *Journal of Industrial Economics*, 34/1 (Sept.), 3–16.

7

VENTURE CAPITALISTS, BUY-OUTS, AND CORPORATE GOVERNANCE

Mike Wright, Steve Thompson, and Ken Robbie

1. Introduction

The purpose of this chapter is to examine and evaluate the contribution of the mechanisms involved in venture capital investments and leveraged management buy-outs to dealing with corporate governance problems in a wide variety of enterprise types. In the current debate on governance issues there is a widely articulated view (e.g. Charkham 1994) that the Anglo-American-style capital market, with its emphasis on liquidity and the separation of institutional shareholders from the firms they invest in, too often results in poor managerial accountability and substantial departures from shareholder value maximization.[1] It is further suggested that neither of the principal *market* restraints on managerial behaviour—namely, the managerial labour market and the corporate acquisitions market—is particularly effective. The former, which might be expected to reward success and penalize failure (Fama 1980) shows, at best, a very weak average relationship between top executive remuneration and performance (see e.g. Conyon *et al.* 1995; Chapters 4 and 5 in this volume); whilst the market for corporate control hypothesis is flawed if managers can deploy effective costly defences, including size, or if errant managers use their discretion to pursue takeover targets.[2] Concerns such as these were among those leading to the Cadbury Report (1992), whose Code of Practice has received widespread adoption in the UK, and have encouraged others to call for more far-reaching institutional changes.

Both venture capitalists and leveraged and management buy-outs represent developments in Anglo-American capital markets in particular which address the

---

[1] Some critics appear to argue that Anglo-American corporate governance applies *too much* pressure to maximize (short-term) shareholder value—e.g. Charkham (1994: 312–14).

[2] For a review of the literature, see the special issue of the *Journal of Economic Perspectives* (Winter 1988).

governance problems encountered therein. Leveraged and management buy-outs are a major subset of a range of corporate restructuring transactions which also includes leveraged recapitalizations and cash-outs, employee stock ownership plans, etc., and involve simultaneous changes in the ownership, financial structure, and incentive systems of firms. Such changes typically have the effect of securing, first, a substantial reunification of share ownership and manager control; second, the partial substitution of various debt instruments for equity in the firm's financial structure; third, the introduction of increased incentives for investors and/or lenders to monitor senior managers; and fourth, the introduction of greater incentives at the peak tier of the managerial hierarchy and often at subordinate levels as well.[3] These changes to existing corporate governance systems may be expected to enhance performance but may also introduce other governance problems and related issues, concerning in particular adverse selection and post-transaction monitoring.

Buy-outs and buy-ins taken together are a significant element of the UK market for corporate control, accounting for 45 per cent of the number of ownership transfers in 1994 and 30 per cent of their value (Chiplin *et al.* 1995).[4] Having developed primarily from the early 1980s,[5] they have remained important in both volume and value terms into the 1990s, though there have been marked shifts in their nature over time (Table 7.1). Divestments are the most important single source of buy-outs, though in recessionary conditions significant numbers of transactions involve parts of failed firms. Privately owned (family) firms also account for an important part of the buy-out market, but are the most notable single source of buy-ins. Privatizations from the public sector are also a contributory source of buy-outs. In contrast to the USA, relatively few buy-outs and buy-ins in the UK involve the privatization of companies quoted on a stock market.

There is some considerable degree of overlap between specialist providers of funds to buy-outs (leveraged buy-out (LBO) associations) (Jensen 1989) and venture capitalists (Sahlman 1990). Both invest funds on behalf of other institutions and although there is a degree of heterogeneity in the forms they take, both are often, especially in the USA, organized as limited partnerships.[6] Both cases involve relationship investment with management; managerial compensation is

---

[3] Restructuring transactions are here distinguished from traditional acquisitions, although it is recognized that the underlying motivation may be similar. They are also distinguished from certain other recent phenomena affecting the corporate sector, especially voluntary divestment (including 'refocusing') and so-called 'downsizing'—although it is clear that these and other retrenchment activities may be strongly associated with restructuring organizational forms (see e.g. Liebeskind *et al.* 1992).

[4] These shares have fluctuated over the last decade, with buy-outs and buy-ins accounting for 28 per cent and 22 per cent of volume and value at the end of the last takeover boom in 1989, and 57 per cent and 35 per cent of volume and value in the recessionary period of 1992.

[5] See Wright *et al.* (1992) for discussion of their development in the UK and elsewhere.

[6] Investors in buy-outs and venture capital projects may, of course, take other structural forms, such as being subsidiaries of clearing banks, and have differing investment stage preferences as well as differing approaches to monitoring, depending on whether they closely monitor their investments or are more hands-off (see below for further discussion).

Table 7.1. Buy-out and buy-in sources (% based on number of deals in each category)

Source	Buy-outs						Buy-ins					
	1989	1990	1991	1992	1993	1994	1989	1990	1991	1992	1993	1994
Receivership	0.8	13.2	19.2	19.1	15.8	3.7	1.4	5.5	17.8	11.2	14.3	9.0
UK and foreign parent	61.4	52.4	53.8	54.3	52.8	55.0	28.6	33.6	31.4	31.2	27.5	34.6
Family	30.9	27.8	23.5	23.3	27.5	34.9	49.7	48.2	44.1	51.2	45.9	51.1
Privatization	4.5	4.7	2.2	2.4	3.4	5.7	—	—	0.8	—	—	0.8
Quoted	2.4	1.9	1.3	0.9	0.5	0.7	20.3	12.7	5.9	6.4	12.3	4.5
TOTAL	100.0	100.0	100.0	100.0	100.0	100.0	100.0	100.0	100.0	100.0	100.0	100.0

Source: Centre for Management Buy-out Research (1995).

oriented towards equity and there are likely to be severe penalties for underperformance. The principal differences concern the nature of the relationship between investor and investee and that in investments by LBO associations most of the funding required to finance an acquisition is through debt. Investments by venture capitalists, which may also involve buy-outs as well as start-ups and development capital, make greater use of equity and quasi-equity. As will be seen below, these differing relationships and financing instruments may be used to perform similar functions in different types of enterprise, so widening the applicability of the active investor concept within the Anglo-American system of corporate governance.

Venture capitalists have an important role to play in providing equity and quasi-equity funding for buy-outs and buy-ins, especially in the UK. In the UK, for example, some 84 per cent of larger buy-outs and buy-ins, those with a transaction value above £10 million, involve equity finance provided by venture capitalists, whilst around half of smaller buy-outs make use of finance from this source (Chiplin *et al.* 1995). Although buy-outs and buy-ins represent an important share of the investments made by venture capitalists (Table 7.2), these institutions will also be involved in the provision of funding and relational investor skills to early and development stage projects.

This chapter examines the corporate governance issues involved in buy-outs and venture capital investments. The following section discusses theoretical issues, firstly relating to corporate governance problems in large organizations with diffuse ownership and the role played by the governance mechanisms involved in buy-outs. It then analyses the governance problems which may arise in privately held firms following the introduction of a buy-out or venture capitalist.

The second major section examines the empirical evidence relating to the effects of buy-outs and venture capitalists on various dimensions of firm performance as well as the effectiveness of the governance mechanisms which are involved. In the first instance, if buy-outs and venture capital investments represent, in principle, an enhancement on previous governance mechanisms, then post-transaction improvements in performance may be expected. Alternatively, it may be the case that apparent improvements are merely a redistribution from

Table 7.2. Venture capital investment in the UK by stage

Year	Early stage		Expansion		Buy-out/buy-in		Total	
	n%	£%	n%	£%	n%	£%	No.	£m.
1989	38	15	37	24	25	61	1,351	1,420
1990	26	12	48	36	26	52	1,316	1,106
1991	22	6	55	39	23	55	1,262	989
1992	17	6	57	29	26	65	1,319	1,251
1993	19	6	62	32	19	62	1,215	1,231
1994	14	5	68	28	18	67	1,253	1,668

Note: n% = percentage of the number of investments in each year in a particular investment stage. £% = percentage of the total value of investments in each year in a particular investment stage.

Source: British Venture Capital Association (1995).

other stakeholders in the firm. In terms of the effectiveness of new governance mechanisms, in the context of the general corporate governance debate, particular attention focuses upon the voice exercised by active investors.

2. Theoretical Issues

This section first outlines the nature of governance problems which may be expected to give rise to conditions where buy-outs and venture capitalists may be appropriate. In particular, these problems concern the absence of voice-related—that is active—monitoring by investors and weaknesses in internal control mechanisms. Second, the nature of buy-outs and their expected contribution to enhancing performance are outlined. However, after a buy-out or venture capital investment has taken place, new governance problems may be introduced and the third section discusses their potential nature.

Governance Problems in Large Organizations with Diffuse Ownership

It has long been recognized, certainly since Berle and Means (1932), that a widely dispersed share ownership generates a monitoring problem, with individual shareholders having the incentive to free ride rather than participate in decision-making. The evolution of equity markets in the USA and UK—although not necessarily in Japan or continental Europe—has intensified this problem by arrangements which have tended to lower the costs of *exit*, in the sense of Hirschman (1970), whilst further discouraging *voice*. Bhide (1993) has demonstrated that stock market policy in the USA—and somewhat similar arguments apply in the UK—has favoured maximum *liquidity*, i.e. the ease of making trades without more than a marginal disturbance on price, and *breadth*.[7] He shows that the effect of regulations designed to protect outside investors from being disadvantaged in trading with insiders or financial institutions is to promote liquidity at the expense of penalizing active investors. In the context of capital markets dominated by fund managers, this has had the effect of confining institutional investors to a passive role in governance, a position facilitated by the ease of partial or complete exit in a liquid market.

Outside the Anglo-American context, capital markets may place a much lower premium on liquidity and typically permit much more investor voice in corporate decision-making. For example, in Germany and Japan very much smaller proportions of companies' shares are traded on open markets, whilst long-term cross-shareholding between firms and their trading partners and bankers are commonplace with consequent cross-representation on boards of directors (Kester 1992). In Germany, banks also exercise considerable voting power as delegated proxies for their shareowning customers[8] (Cable 1985; Edwards and Fischer 1994), and some European capital markets favour the separation of voting and non-voting equity claims, facilitating the operation of controlling blocks. In general, a more tolerant view of insider trading is taken in Japan and many European nations, some of which only introduced prohibitive regulation as part of the harmonization of the European Community prior to 1992 (Bhide 1993). Weaker restrictions on insider behaviour, or less rigorous enforcement of such restrictions, encourages active investors rather than passive portfolio managers. France is an interesting case since large shareholders may exchange exit for voice by accepting board membership, on condition they cease short-term dealings in their firm's shares (Charkham 1994: 152–3).

Thus critics of Anglo-American corporate governance contrast its reliance on exit, backed by the sanction of hostile acquisitions, with the role played by investor and banker voice in Japanese and European firms. In the latter the concentration of equity ownership and especially equity voting power, the active participation of large investors, and the important position of banks provide a continuing incentive for the monitoring of senior management.

Failure of Internal Control Mechanisms

Restructuring transactions which developed in the 1980s pointed to a failure of firms' internal control mechanisms. In particular, it appears that the multi-divisional (M-form) firm, which had become the dominant form of corporate organization in the USA and UK (Caves 1980), was failing to deliver the shareholder benefits that its proponents, Williamson (1975) included, had anticipated. The M-form is characterized by a separation of operational decision-making,

---

[7] 'Breadth' meaning the number of stocks in the liquid market; see Bhide (1993).
[8] The extent to which this is used by the banks to achieve substantial voice in monitoring managers is a matter of debate. Edwards and Fischer (1994) give bank involvement a much more passive interpretation than Cable (1985).

located in profit-accountable divisions, from strategic planning and capital allocation, which are the responsibility of corporate headquarters. Williamson hypothesized that such a structure enjoyed both corporate governance and informational efficiency advantages over its typical predecessors, the functionally organized firm and the holding company. As a governance device, the M-form was hypothesized to reduce managerial discretion by placing the *direct* control of most corporate resources in the hands of divisional managements who were themselves remunerated by performance. The structure did not directly improve the peak tier agency problem, but Williamson (1985) suggested that since the M-form facilitated the absorption of acquisitions, an M-form population would intensity the threat of the takeover sanction on poor performance.

It was, however, via its informational advantages that Williamson saw the M-form contributing most to shareholder value. He argued that the internal capital market, created where profit-generating divisions remit cash to corporate headquarters which then reallocates investment funds back to finance divisional projects, enjoys substantial information transmission and monitoring advantages over its external counterpart. This generates the synergy for diversified M-forms.

Although the early empirical work was generally supportive of the M-form hypothesis (e.g. Steer and Cable 1978), several caveats emerged: first, at least some of the apparent gains for introducing M-forms reflected abnormally poor performance *prior* to M-form adoption (Thompson 1981); second, researchers continued to find significant coefficients for agency cost variables in regressions of performance on organizational form, suggesting that the M-form is at best an incomplete governance device (Cable 1988); third, many M-forms lacked the control and/or incentive mechanisms described by Williamson (Hill 1985); and fourth, whilst the M-form was clearly associated with conglomerate mergers in the 1970s the latter have increasingly become viewed as detrimental to firm performance (Hoskisson and Turk 1990). Bhide (1990) argues that the comparative advantage of the internal capital market declined with improvements in the efficiency of external markets, weakening the case for diversified firms.

The Nature of Buy-Outs

Buy-outs may be considered as devices which restore active governance and help resolve internal control problems by re-creating many of the ownership, financial, and incentive characteristics associated with newly emergent and/or bankrupt firms.[9] In an LBO a publicly quoted corporation is acquired by a specially established private company. The latter's equity is usually subscribed by a specialist LBO association; some institutional investors, often with continuing dealings with the

[9] Detailed descriptions of the characteristics of corporate restructuring transactions, which also include leveraged recapitalizations and cash-outs, are available elsewhere; for example, in Jensen (1989) for US LBOs; Thompson *et al.* (1992*a*) for UK MBOs; Denis and Denis (1993) for leveraged recapitalizations; Chen and Kensinger (1988) for ESOPs; and Robbie *et al.* (1992) for UK management buy-ins. The main emphasis here is upon buy-outs and buy-ins, as these form the most common type of transaction.

LBO association; and the management of the bought-out corporation. The principal equity subscribers are able to obtain substantial percentages of ownership because the bulk of the deal price—perhaps between two-thirds and seven-eighths—is met by borrowings. The same institutions may be involved as debt and equity subscribers under a so-called 'strip financing' arrangement; or specialist institutions may be involved with debt instruments ranging from bank loans to 'junk bonds' (Jensen 1989). The resulting private company is typically controlled by a small board of directors representing the LBO association and other major equity holders, with the CEO usually as the only insider on the board (Jensen 1989, 1993).

The LBO, as described above, is a device for taking private an entire public corporation. The management buy-out (MBO), the dominant restructuring transactions in the UK, by contrast, usually involves the acquisition of a divested division or subsidiary by a new company in which the existing management takes a substantial proportion of the equity. In place of the LBO association, (MBOs) usually require the support of a venture capitalist.[10] Since the transaction involves divisional divestment, the former parent may retain an equity stake, perhaps to support a continuing trading relationship. A management buy-in (Robbie *et al.* 1992) is simply an MBO in which the leading members of the management team are outsiders. Such buy-outs as a generic concept have strong implications for corporate governance. First, there is a substantial reconcentration of equity in the hands of insiders or with institutions with a close association with the new firm. Second, not merely do institutions (inluding venture capitalists) become motivated to act as monitors, normally by providing non-executive directors, but the process of going through the initial buy-out transaction ensures that the individuals concerned have a thorough knowledge of the affairs of the new company (Jensen 1993) and thus the capacity to monitor. Third, the large-scale substitution of debt for equity in the financial structure of the new company substantially reduces managerial discretion and commits the management team to a repayment timetable. Together with the now significant management equity stake, vulnerable in the event of failure, this 'bonds' management to deliver on the performance plan agreed at the time of the buy-out. Fourth, most buy-out transactions are accompanied by a variety of incentive schemes. For example, in the UK many MBO deals allow the management's final equity stake to reflect performance, according to a ratchet mechanism (Thompson *et al.* 1992*b*), whilst employee shareholding schemes are not uncommon.

Expected Effects of Buy-Outs

It has been widely suggested (Jensen 1986, 1989, 1993; DeAngelo *et al.* 1984; Hoskisson and Turk 1990; Thompson *et al.* 1992*b*; etc.) that, taken together, these characteristics imply that the governance mechanisms in buy-outs coerce business

---

[10] The venture capitalist, like the LBO association, is likely to be involved as a supplier of debt—perhaps as lead lender in a syndicate—as well as a subscriber of equity funds, Wright *et al.* (1992).

units into a closer approximation to profit-maximization than occurs within a comfortably resourced quoted company. Apart from reducing direct expense preference behaviour by senior managers, which whilst it might be flagrant is rarely quantitatively important, the corporate restructuring present in buy-outs is likely to improve performance in four interrelated ways.

The first concerns increased management efforts towards cost minimization. Buy-out activity is particularly concentrated in profitable but mature, low-growth industries. Enterprises therein, where the opportunities for growth in the core business are strictly limited, may find it particularly difficult to motivate managers with conventional reward systems.[11] An LBO, or a leveraged recapitalization for the entire firm, or an MBO for any cash flow division represent methods of injecting new incentives into potentially sclerotic businesses. The second relates to the reversal of *unprofitable diversifications*. Jensen (1986, 1989) has argued that mature businesses which generate *free cash flows*—i.e. funds in excess of those required for reinvestment in the core business—will tend to engage in unprofitable diversification rather than disgorge the cash in abnormally large dividends. Such diversifications may have agreeable consequences for managers—including increased firm size and therefore remuneration (see Conyon *et al.* 1995) and lower earnings fluctuations—but not for shareholders. A debt-financed buy-out may be used to commit the firm to raise the (pre-interest) cash flow and hence reduce unprofitable investments and even to divest past diversifications to meet the terms of a debt repayment plan. The third concerns a reduction in *the response time for adaptation to market conditions*. A multi-product firm with a satisfactory overall cash flow and a weak governance mechanism may experience considerable inertia in taking decisions to reorganize its activities in line with changing market conditions. For example, Jensen (1993) has argued that the largest US corporations have demonstrated a marked reluctance to disinvest in domestic manufacturing, in line with trends in productivity growth and world trade, provided that overall cash flows have been acceptable. A debt-laden entity with active industry and strong incentives is likely to accelerate the process of adapting to changes in underlying economic conditions. Fourth, where there is a trading relationship with a former parent, a divestment buy-out may have an increased incentive to perform where it is heavily dependent on its former parent and where the former parent retains an equity interest (cross-holding) (Wright 1986). In such cases, the buy-out may mimic some of the relational investment characteristics of the Japanese keiretsu.[12]

---

[11] Stock options are not particularly appropriate for *divisional* manager motivation, whilst performance bonuses may be problematic where different divisions within a firm possess widely different growth prospects.

[12] Critics of buy-outs have suggested that it is misleading to compare LBO Associations to the main board of Japanese keiretsu (Gilson and Roe, 1993) as argued by Jensen (1993). Though financial institutions play a large role in both buy-outs and keiretsu, the Japanese bank's role is embedded in a system of relational cross-holdings which includes industrial companies. The contractual governance structure among factors of production and its dependence on product market competition is critical to the keiretsu. In the absence of trading relationships described here such arrangements are absent from LBO associations.

Critics of buy-outs have argued that the apparent short- and/or medium-term gains for equity holders at least in part transfers from other categories of economic agent. The suggested losers include: *long-term equity owners* as such a transfer would be consistent with a 'short-termist' reduction in avoidable expenditures, such as R & D or advertising, to boost the apparent profitability after a buy-out; *other stakeholders within the firm*, including the holders of senior debt in an LBO, who experience an increase in risk with no concomitant reward, and employees— at any level within the firm—who may find that their required performance breaches the expectations held on joining the firms (Shleifer and Summers 1988); *and the tax authorities* as, in general, debt interest is allowable against tax and hence restructuring transactions tend to reduce the firms obligations.

Governance in Privately Held Firms

In young and privately held firms the problems of diffuse ownership are absent as there is typically still a major ownership interest of the founders or their family (Hart 1995). As such, corporate governance problems do not drive the need for change. Rather, these firms may experience an increased need for external finance, either to fund growth and or to enable ownership succession to occur whilst maintaining the firm as an independent entity, which may introduce governance problems. These problems may arise in the absence of the accompanying introduction of control devices either where former full owners remain as managers or former managers become part owner-managers but with a less than full ownership stake since they may have an incentive to engage in some degree of opportunistic behaviour (Jensen and Meckling 1976). As with buy-outs, control devices can be introduced which give voice for venture capitalist investors (Sahlman 1990) and an important monitoring role for bankers and other debtholders.

Governance in Buy-Outs and Venture Capital Investments

In both buy-outs and venture capital investments, the governance problems which may arise are sufficiently severe to warrant further discussion. These issues relate to both pre- and post-transaction monitoring, both of which may influence the effectiveness of the newly introduced governance structures.

Pre-Contracting Problems   At the time that a buy-out or venture capital investment is being considered, institutions are faced with a potential adverse selection problem in that they are unable to gauge the managers' performance in the enterprise prior to deal completion (Amit *et al.* 1993). Adverse selection issues also raise crucial problems in the potential effectiveness of post-transaction monitoring by institutional investors (Stiglitz and Weiss 1981). To the extent that these problems lead investors to misjudge the situation, a deal and accompanying financial structure may be agreed which is inappropriate and possibly unviable. As a result, the control mechanism introduced by the commitment to meet the cost of servicing external finance may lead to suboptimal decisions. In addition, even if active investors are efficient in carrying out their governance role, they may be faced with severe problems in effecting marked increases in performance.

In appraising potential investments, venture capitalists are faced with both uncertainty and an adverse selection problem. Uncertainty arises in relation to problems in forecasting future performance, and the venture capitalist may attempt to address this problem by reference to available information on the sector and more general environmental data. Adverse selection arises as venture capitalists have to rely greatly on information about the state of affairs of the enterprise which is supplied by the entrepreneur. Whilst the entrepreneur generally possesses an accurate understanding of the enterprise, there is no guarantee that this is conveyed in an unbiased and complete manner to the venture capitalist, giving the entrepreneur an asymmetric information advantage.

Amit *et al.* (1993) point out that, while the entrepreneur's familiarity with the industry, personal characteristics, and track record can provide some insight for the venture capitalist, these criteria are at best partial predictors of future success. These problems may vary between types of investment. In the case of a management buy-out proposal, financiers need to take funding decisions on the basis of observed managerial performance in post, expectations about whether improving managerial incentives will improve performance, and management's willingness to take on the risk of a buy-out in order to secure the fruits of their human capital. Management buy-ins typically focus on enterprises which require turn-round and restructuring, but as the buy-in entrepreneur comes from outside there are problems of asymmetric information, both in relation to their true skills and because it has not been possible to observe the manager in post. In replacement and development capital situations it may be difficult to judge whether the entrepreneur's apparent previous performance will continue in the future where his or her equity stake is diluted by the introduction of venture capital. Amit *et al.* (1993) show that where venture capitalists are unable to access private information about an entrepreneur's capabilities, low-ability entrepreneurs will accept the venture capitalist's price offer while high-ability entrepreneurs will not. Moral hazard problems are also raised, since after the entrepreneur has been funded it may be difficult to distinguish between the effects of low entrepreneurial ability and adverse environmental conditions.

In a management buy-out, investing institutions may be guided by incumbent management's deep knowledge of the business. This is not to say that management will necessarily have clear incentives to reveal truthful information, since they may either wish to underplay problems in their anxiety to make the deal appear viable or overplay problems in order to reduce the transaction price. However, detailed probing may enable the venture capitalist to uncover major difficulties and approach an accurate assessment of the true state of affairs. In a buy-in, incoming management face similar problems to the venture capitalist. Management buy-in entrepreneurs may be able to reduce some of the problems of asymmetric information where they have detailed knowledge about the industry sector. In such cases they may be able to use personal networks to carry out informal verification about the state of the target enterprise.

Post-Contracting Governance Problems

In order for investors to engage in effective post-transaction monitoring in order to reduce moral hazard problems a key requirement is access to reliable information about the firm's activities. Whilst active investors may be faced with less severe moral hazard problems than arm's length shareholders, significant asymmetric information problems may remain. Sahlman (1990) indicates that venture capitalists and LBO associations use various mechanisms to encourage entrepreneurs both to perform and to reveal accurate information. These mechanisms include staging of the commitment of investment funds, using convertible financial instruments ('equity ratchets') which may give financiers control under certain conditions, basing compensation on value created, preserving mechanisms to force agents to distribute capital and profits, and having powers written into articles of association which require approval for certain actions (e.g. acquisitions, certain types of investment and divestment, etc.) to be sought from the investor(s).[13] In addition, to such structural mechanisms, the process of the relationship with the investee company is also an important aspect of the corporate governance framework. It has been pointed out that staging of investments can lead to myopia and over-investment where initially entrepreneurs and subsequently first-round venture capitalists as insiders present misleading information to outsiders in an attempt to persuade them to invest. Admati and Pfleiderer (1994) show that a contract in which venture capitalists continue to maintain the same fraction of equity in the various rounds of financing a venture capital project can neutralize a venture capitalist's incentive to mislead. As will be seen below, the degree to which institutions may become involved directly in the process of corporate governance may vary both between LBO associations and venture capitalists and between different types of venture capitalist.

In sum, the discussion in this section suggests that buy-outs and venture capital investments can involve mechanisms which make a contribution to dealing with governance problems associated with diffuse ownership and control. However, new governance problems may be introduced which result from adverse selection at the time of a transaction and post-transaction moral hazard.

3. Empirical Evidence

The evidence presented in this section covers two broad themes. The first addresses the effects of buy-outs and venture capital investments. If these forms

---

[13] For a detailed case example of the use of such mechanisms see the case of Maccess in Robbie and Wright (1990).

of organization in principle involve enhanced governance mechanisms, then improvements in various aspects of performance may be expected to be observed. The second reviews evidence on the apparent efficacy of the differing elements of the corporate governance framework introduced in buy-outs, with particular attention focused on the role of active investors in exercising governance through voice.

The Effects of Buy-Outs

In reviewing the available empirical evidence it is necessary to note the scarcity of large-sample longitudinal studies. Most published work takes a relatively short-term measure of performance, an approach which is partly explained by the recent nature of most restructuring transactions. Furthermore, because the majority of such transactions involve the creation of a *private* company, at least in the first instance, and private companies tend to generate limited information, there may be particular sampling difficulties with research in this area.[14] In what follows, the results of an extensive set of studies relating to the impact of buy-outs on various dimensions of performance are reviewed. Apparent performance improvements may be the result of improved corporate governance mechanisms or they may simply be redistributions from other stakeholders or may follow from apparent underperformance prior to buy-out as a result of the manipulation of accounting information by management. An issue is also raised about the time dimension of the role of corporate governance mechanisms in buy-outs and buy-ins. Although there is an argument that they pose a long-term challenge to the widely held company quoted on a stock market (Jensen 1989), this is highly debatable. Accordingly, evidence on the longevity of buy-outs and buy-ins is also reviewed.

This review of the empirical evidence first addresses performance effects in terms of effects on share prices, operating performance, and reductions in deferable expenditures. The second set of empirical results cover evidence relating to the notion that in addition to or instead of performance improvements, buy-outs may involve transfers from other stakeholders, previous owners, and taxation. Third, evidence relating to the longevity of buy-outs is briefly reviewed.

Stock Market Responses and Operating Performance

A series of studies (DeAngelo *et al.* 1984; Kaplan 1989*a*; Lehn and Poulsen 1989; Marais *et al.* 1989) have examined the share price response to 'going private' LBO deals and each finds, as expected, a large abnormal gain for the target's share-

---

[14] Private LBOs with publicly quoted debt generate performance data for the public domain, but these tend to give an upward size bias. LBOs which return to the stock market via an IPO generate data, but here there is a success bias. It is difficult to get information on failed buy-outs.

holders. The implied bid premium appears even larger than that found in conventional acquisitions: Kaplan (1989*a*) reports a median abnormal gain of 42 per cent for seventy-six US buy-outs in the period 1980–6. Furthermore, since the assets pass to a new private owner, there is no partially offsetting price movement for the acquiror. In part, the bid premium may reflect anticipated gains for divestment. Similar stock market studies of voluntary divestments by diversified companies (e.g. Hite and Vetsuypens 1989; Markides 1992) reveal small but significant positive announcement effects.

Research on US LBOs indicates substantial mean improvements in profitability and cash flow measures over the interval between one year *prior* to the transaction and two or three years *subsequent* to it. A series of studies of early 1980s LBOs (Kaplan 1989*a*; Kaplan and Stein 1993; Smith 1990; Muscarella and Vetsuypens 1990) reports mean gains in the operating cash flow–sales ratio of between 11.9 and 55 per cent. A subsequent study (Opler 1992), using deals completed in the later 1980s, reports a 16.5 per cent gain in that ratio over a similar three-year period. Smart and Waldfogel (1994) suggest these pre- and post-restructuring comparisons fail to control for firm-specific trends in performance. To isolate the shock effect of the buy-out they use a series of estimators which are adjusted for forecast performance. Their best estimates imply a median shock improvement in the operating income–sales ratio of 30 per cent between the pre-LBO year and the second post-LBO year. A survey of 182 mid-1980s MBOs in the UK indicated that 68 per cent showed clear improvements in profitability, compared with 17 per cent that showed a clear profitability fall (Wright *et al.* 1992). In this study and the American work (Kaplan 1989*a*; Smith 1990) improvements in working capital management, particularly credit management, appear to be an important identified source of improved performance. Asset sales also appear important in the US context (Liebeskind *et al.* 1992).

The productivity impact of LBOs was examined by Lichtenberg and Siegel (1990) using a longitudinal database of 12,000 US manufacturing plants. They found that total factor productivity for plants involved in LBOs between 1981 and 1986 rose from 2 per cent above its industry control to 8.3 per cent above over the first three years of post-LBO operation. However, the mean changes conceal considerable differences between yearly cohorts, the significant productivity gains occurring in the later years of their sample period. Wright *et al.* (1992) also found a variable productivity impact in their study of UK MBOs—the proportion of respondents citing productivity gains as the principal source of performance improvement halved (to 9 per cent) between the early and mid-1980s. UK evidence shows that cross-holdings and monitoring occur in around three-tenths of buy-outs arising on divestment where trading relationships continue with the former parent, in many cases involving a high degree of interdependence (Thompson and Wright 1987).

Increased leverage may be expected to put pressure on managements to reduce deferable expenditures. If the effect is to curb some negative net present value projects, as Jensen (1986, 1989) suggests, the result will be value-enhancing. However, if managers are forced to abandon profitable opportunities, the reverse holds. The

US evidence strongly supports the view that capital investment falls immediately following the LBO (Kaplan 1989*a*; Smith 1990). Palepu (1990) notes that since this appears to hold for LBOs which subsequently return to a public listing, with large positive returns for investors, it is difficult to view the reduction in capital investment as damaging. The evidence on UK MBOs is rather different. Wright *et al.* (1992) report that asset sales are offset by new capital investment, particularly in plant and equipment.[15]

Several studies (Long and Ravenscraft 1993; Lichtenberg and Siegel 1991; Smith 1990) report that LBO firms reduce R & D spending, but that LBOs are very largely in low R & D industries, such that the overall effect is unsubstantial.

Transfers from Other Stakeholders, Previous Owners, and Taxation

Following Shleifer and Summers (1988), it may be that restructuring transactions create opportunity to revise implicit labour contracts and so transfer value from employees to equity owners. However, evidence on the measurable dimensions of *employment* and *employee compensation* does not indicate any major transfers. Opler (1992), Kaplan (1989*a*), and Smith (1990)—but not Muscarella and Vetsuypens (1990)—report small increases in total firm employment following LBOs. Kaplan (1989*a*) and Smith (1990), however, report rather larger falls after an adjustment for industry effects—i.e. LBO firms failed to expand their employment in line with industry averages. Lichtenberg and Siegel (1990) report an 8.5 per cent fall in non-production workers over a three-year period, with production employment unchanged. (Their database excludes head offices, so that the total impact on non-production workers is probably even greater.) Lichtenberg and Siegel also report a decline in the relative compensation of non-production workers.

UK studies suggest that job losses occur most substantially at the time of the change in ownership. Wright *et al.* (1992) report an average 6.3 per cent fall in total employment with an MBO, but note that the firms surveyed indicated a subsequent 1.9 per cent improvement by the time of the authors' survey. In both US and UK *firm*-level studies the aggregate employment losses may be inflated somewhat by voluntary divestments.

The wealth of existing bondholders will be adversely affected if new debt, issued at the time of the restructuring, impacts adversely on the perceived riskiness of the original debt. Marais *et al.* (1989) fail to detect any such wealth transfer. However, a more detailed study by Asquith and Wizman (1990) reports a small average loss of 2.8 per cent of market value. Those original bonds which had protective covenants actually showed a positive effect, whilst bonds without covenants experienced a significant negative reaction.

Purchasers of corporate assets, like buyers on any other market, may overpay

---

[15] The evidence from *divisional* buy-outs is consistent with restructuring creating opportunities for expansion as well as stimulating cost economies; see Wright *et al.* (1992).

or underpay on occasions. However, in MBOs and LBOs with significant insider participation, there is the possibility of systematic underpricing. This could be passive, where managers simply exploit asset prices which appear (to them) to be too low, or it could be the result of some deliberate misrepresentation or conceal-ment by them. Evidence of the former has been obtained from abnormal stock market returns for announced and then withdrawn LBOs. DeAngelo *et al.* (1984) report on substantial (25 per cent) net cumulative prediction error and Marais *et al.* (1989) a much smaller one (7 per cent). Smith (1990) argues that abandoned hidden information buy-outs should show the same subsequent performance gains as completed ones and hence the same market response, assuming the buy-out is solely motivated by insider information. She finds no such evidence and hence concludes against the hidden information view. However, the stock market response appears to depend substantially on whether or not a subsequent bid occurs (Lee 1992); whilst existing owners' returns are greater when competitive bids are received (Easterwood *et al.* 1994).

Evidence of 'earnings management' prior to a management bid is somewhat contradictory. DeAngelo (1986) reports none, whilst Perry and Williams (1994) find evidence of consistent falls in the last complete financial year prior to an announcement. Kaplan and Stein (1993) analyse the structure of MBO pricing across the whole 1980s. They suggest that deal prices rose with the level of lever-age, leading to over-heating and a sharp rise in the failure rate at the end of the decade. Thus if there were initial transfers from the pre-MBO owners, this trend was reversed across the period.

Since restructuring transactions typically substitute debt for equity, they tend to reduce corporate tax liabilities. Kaplan (1989*b*) and Schipper and Smith (1988) suggest that tax savings do account for a small fraction of the value gains from LBOs—a finding underpinned by a significant correlation between estimated tax savings and the observed buy-out bid premium. Jensen *et al.* (1989) suggest that the overall impact of LBOs on tax receipts is likely to be positive, with increased tax receipts for capital gains, operating income increases, and interest income received.

Longevity

If the new organizational forms created in buy-outs and buy-ins remedy corpo-rate agency problems, they might be expected to pose a long-term challenge to the widely held public limited company (Jensen 1989). However, recent work (Kaplan 1991; Wright *et al.* 1994) in both the USA and the UK indicates that the longevity of buy-outs is heterogeneous. Though the majority of buy-outs may be relatively long-lived, a substantial proportion, particularly larger firms,[16] either return to

---

[16] There may be size bias effects in the samples of firms which show a very rapid return to public listing. Easterwood and Seth (1993) find a wide range of variation. They suggest that the speed of return via a flotation is negatively related to the complexity of the task of reorganization required at the time of buy-out.

quoted status or are sold to third parties within a relatively short period. A significant proportion have also failed, the governance aspects of which are returned to below.

The Effects of Corporate Governance Mechanisms

What is so far unclear from the evidence is the *relative* importance of the different elements in the corporate governance mechanisms present in buy-outs and venture capital transactions. It was noted above that typically these transactions had the effect of increasing managerial equity interest in the firm, increasing monitoring incentives in institutions, raising leverage, and introducing performance-related contracts at different levels in the organization. The first subsection briefly reviews the general effects of the corporate governance changes in buy-outs and venture capital investments compared to other forms of corporate restructuring. The second subsection discusses in turn the implications for corporate governance of evidence relating to adverse selection problems and post-transaction monitoring.

General Some indications of the effects of corporate governance mechanisms introduced in buy-outs and venture capital investments are given by comparing alternative organizational forms. For example, leveraged recapitalizations, which simply substitute debt for equity in quoted companies, have been shown to raise shareholder value (Denis and Denis 1993), but they do not appear to have the same performance impact as LBOs, which also involve managerial ownership and institutional involvement (Denis 1994). Similarly, defensive ESOPs, in which leveraged employee share purchases are used to forestall takeovers, do not appear to perform as well as LBOs (Chen and Kensinger 1988). Thompson *et al.* (1992*b*) regressed equity returns to investors on a number of governance devices, including leverage, ratchet contracts, etc., and found that the management team shareholding size had by far the larger impact on relative performance in UK MBOs.

Investors' Monitoring In the light of the previous discussion, the effectiveness of corporate governance mechanisms needs to be viewed both before and after the buy-out or venture capital transaction. Pre-transaction issues concern the ability of investors to deal with adverse selection problems during their screening and appraisal process. Post-transaction concerns involve the efficacy of monitoring devices in general, but also the more problematical cases of restructuring and failure. The ability of corporate governance mechanisms in buy-outs and venture capital investments to intervene in a more timely manner than in firms with non-active investors has been argued to be an especially important attribute. Monitoring also has a time dimension because of the objectives of both management and financial investors. This section considers these issues in turn.

Screening and Adverse Selection Several studies examine the relative importance of a wide range of factors taken into account by venture capitalists in the screening process for new venture investment (e.g. Bruno and Tyebjee 1985; MacMillan *et al.* 1985, 1987). MacMillan *et al.* (1987) show that the most important criteria used by venture capitalists in screening investment proposals were entrepreneurial personality and experience, with lesser dependence being placed on market, product, and strategy. Sweeting (1991) addresses the use of accounting information in the venture capital monitoring process. A more recent study by Wright and Robbie (1995) of UK venture capitalists showed that venture capitalists place considerable emphasis on the specific attributes of a potential investee company in relation to both assessment of its value and the rate of return to be expected from it. While accounting information is an important element in deal screening and in arriving at a valuation and a target rate of return, it appears neither to be taken at face value nor to be the only kind of information used. Venture capitalists are found to place most emphasis on very detailed scrutiny of all aspects of a business, typically including discussions with personnel and accessing considerably more information of an unpublished and subjective kind, especially unaudited management projections.

Evidence from a survey of buy-ins (Robbie *et al.* 1992) indicates that institutions themselves play a minor role in initiating buy-ins, with management playing the most important role, and with their frequent special knowledge of the target company being key to reducing asymmetric information problems. Case-study evidence also relating to buy-ins (Robbie and Wright 1995) identified a major problem related to the ability to obtain adequate up-to-date information concerning the target company, especially in relation to management accounts, indications of current trading positions, and the status of major contracts. Indeed, after the cost of finance, the second most important area of difficulty identified by managers in the buy-in survey was the discovery of a variety of problems not identified during the due diligence procedures and which may be expected to arise because of asymmetric information. While due diligence is expected to be undertaken in a thorough manner, its cost in relation to transaction value in smaller buy-ins and time constraints in negotiations meant that this ideal was difficult to achieve. However, in the light of the consequences of the problems which subsequently did emerge, there was a general view expressed that insufficient thoroughness had been exercised in the due diligence process. Recent developments involving hybrid inside and outside management (so-called buy-ins/management buy-outs—BIMBOs) in principle enable greater access to information for due diligence purposes and may make a significant contribution to overcoming these problems. Similarly, the more recent growth of institutional buy-outs, with there being direct negotiations between vendors and venture capitalists, provides a means of enhancing target identification as well as due diligence.

Post-Transaction Governance Mechanisms Post-transaction governance problems can be considered in relation to the nature and effectiveness, first, of venture capitalists and, second, in respect of the mechanisms involved in buy-outs and buy-ins. In other words, although active investors may be in place, it is not clear how they may operate in order to be effective.

In respect of venture capitalists, Sapienza *et al.* (1992) provide evidence that there is less involvement in monitoring activities which are more developed and presumably less risky, such as buy-outs, buy-ins, and development capital cases. MacMillan *et al.* (1989) show that differing levels of involvement in venture capital investments (e.g. hands-on/close trackers versus hands-off/*laissez-faire* approaches) were related not to the nature of the operating business but to the choice exercised by the venture capital firm itself of the general style it wished to adopt. There were, however, no significant differences in the performance of businesses subject to differing levels of involvement. Similarly, Elango *et al.* (1995) identify three levels of assistance by venture capitalists in their investees, inactives, active advice-givers, and hands-on, but point out that these are not primarily related to the stage of investment. However, there were major variations in the amount of time different venture capitalists spent on problem investees. Some venture capitalists tended to fire managers quickly in such circumstances, whilst others became closely involved in working with existing management. Barry (1994) cites evidence that venture capitalists intensify their monitoring activities as the need dictates.

Rosenstein *et al.* (1993) find that the value added by venture capitalists was not rated significantly higher by CEOs than that of other board members. There was some evidence that larger venture capitalists provided significantly more value added, but that in such cases the venture capitalist frequently controlled the board. Entrepreneurs were found to value venture capitalists on their board with operating experience more than those with purely financial expertise. Indications are that the general types of skill possessed by venture capital executives varies between types of venture capitalist, with those employed by captive funds (e.g. development capital subsidiaries of clearing banks) tending to be more financial-skills-oriented whilst those employed by independents tend to have greater industrial skills (Beecroft 1994).

The study by Sweeting (1991) suggests that relationships need to be such that problems are revealed to the venture capitalist at an early stage rather than being left to fester and emerge as a surprise at a later stage. Fried and Hisrich (1995) also provide evidence of the importance of personal relationships in the governance of venture capital investments in the USA and that formal power needs to be used sparingly to be effective. Sweeting (1991) finds that venture capitalists 'tend to leave well alone when there is confidence in what is going on and the people in charge, and, alternatively, they are concerned and proactive to put matters right when this is not so' (p. 18). While venture capitalists may take control when things go seriously wrong, such action has to be exercised with care since, as Sweeting points out, to act precipitously may destroy carefully nurtured relationships and commit the venture capitalists to unknown amounts of time to put matters right.

Similarities, but also differences, emerge in the operation of active investor governance in buy-outs and buy-ins. Sahlman (1990), comparing LBO associations with venture capitalists, notes that executives in the former may typically assume control of the board of directors but are generally less likely than venture capitalists to assume operational control. UK evidence in buy-outs and buy-ins shows that board representation is the most popular method of monitoring investee companies, with venture capitalists also requiring regular provision of accounts (Robbie *et al.* 1992). However, evidence shows that there appears to be a greater degree of control exercised by institutions over management buy-ins than for buy-outs or other forms of investment. A much higher requirement for regular financial reports than for venture capital investments generally is indicated (Robbie *et al.* 1992). Equity ratchets are also found to be more frequently used in buy-ins, reflecting the greater uncertainty about their future performance, but there is little difference between buy-outs and buy-ins in the extent to which institutions require board representation.

As for venture capital investments generally, evidence from buy-outs and buy-ins emphasizes the importance of keeping the venture capitalists informed of developments through regular contact. Hatherly *et al.* (1994) show that on balance the relationships between financial institutions and management buy-outs involve partnership and mutual interest, with devices to control agency problems generally being used in a flexible manner. However, there is case-study evidence that, in smaller buy-ins in particular, institutions do not appear to have been as active in responding to signals about adverse performance as might have been expected (Robbie and Wright 1995) and that relationships between entrepreneurs and investors have not developed to the extent that potential crises could be identified and understood by the venture capitalist. These problems reflect the high cost of monitoring and control in relation to the value of investments. Monitoring via non-executive directors who were not full-time employees of the venture capitalists frequently appear to be inefficient, particularly in problem cases requiring close supervision.

In larger buy-ins there is evidence of extensive and repeated active monitoring, as for example in the case of Isosceles–Gateway, the largest buy-in to date in the UK (see Wright *et al.* 1994 for detailed case-study). This difference illustrates the comparative cost–effort–reward trade-offs involved in the active monitoring of large and small investments. Interviews with buy-out investors indicate that larger deals, partly with a view to eventual exit through stock market flotation, are increasingly following the Cadbury Committee recommendations concerning board committees and the roles of non-executive directors (Chiplin *et al.* 1995). Typically, it may be expected that a larger deal would include two independent non-executive directors, one of whom would be chairman, together with one director representing financing institutions.

Restructuring Particular importance has been attached to the governance role of active investors in cases where buy-outs and other venture capital investments require restructuring. The extent and nature of action by institutions may depend crucially upon their judgement concerning the causes of poor performance, the prospects for the success of restructuring action, and the costs–reward relationship involved in such actions. The authors' interviews with venture capitalists suggest that it is possible to identify two general types of problem cases: 'Living Dead' and 'Good Rump'. Living Dead investments essentially involve enterprises where the business collapses with little prospect of turn-round. Such investments risk involving a disproportionate amount of monitoring and control, especially if the enterprises concerned are small. Moreover, it may be difficult for the venture capitalist to implement change in such companies where management typically have a majority of the equity, until a pressure point arises which cannot be relieved by other funding sources.

The second category, 'Good Rump', is distinguishable from the first in that these firms are viewed as capable of being turned round, but the effects of restructuring have yet to be seen. Such cases may be underperforming because of general sectoral problems. In both cases the ability of active investors to effect change may be heavily influenced by whether they are controlling shareholders or not. A problem of enforcing restructuring is that it may be difficult to agree with other parties what form it should take. In smaller investments, since management are usually important majority shareholders great care is needed in taking action, with the principal strategy typically being to produce a consensus on necessary action. If institutions are a controlling shareholder, as is usually the case in larger buy-outs and buy-ins, making changes is theoretically straightforward. However, in cases with large syndicates of financiers, restructuring may be delayed or take a particular direction because of differences in the attitudes of syndicate members.[17]

Larger management buy-ins may be able to bear extensive restructuring, and it may be economical for institutions to invest the effort to undertake it, whereas the possibilities may be very limited for smaller cases. In small buy-outs and buy-ins, management may own the vast majority of the equity and a very small group of managers may carry out the major functions, thus making it difficult to remove underperforming management or enforce a trade sale. In larger buy-outs and buy-ins, no single manager may be indispensable and it may thus be easier for institutions to exert pressure to remove underperforming senior managers.

Failure   In the limit, problems with governance structures in buy-outs may be expected to be closely associated with business failure. Following Jensen (1991), the governance role of higher leverage may mean that financial distress is signalled earlier than if an enterprise were funded substantially by equity. As a result, a firm which defaults on loan payments may still retain greater value, including going-concern value, and stand a better chance of being reorganized than one which is finally forced to waive a dividend. However, where buy-outs are funded with excessive levels of debt, they may not realistically be able to service it, leading to a greater probability of failure (Bruner and Eades 1992). Kaplan and Stein (1993), in a study of larger US buy-outs, provide strong evidence that excessive prices paid for buy-

---

[17]   See Lerner (1994) for discussion of syndication of venture capital investments.

outs in the late 1980s meant that buy-outs took on higher amounts of debt and had an increased probability of failure or need to be restructured, particularly if planned asset sales were not forthcoming, than buy-outs funded earlier in the 1980s. As in the USA, larger UK buy-outs which entered receivership or were refinanced in the early 1990s also had markedly higher proportions of senior debt than those which did not experience such problems (Wright *et al*. 1994).

The influence of governance factors on likelihood of failure, after controlling for firm-specific factors, was examined using logit analysis by Wright *et al*. (1996). Using a sample of failed and non-failed buy-outs and a set of financial and non-financial variables, a 92 per cent correct classification rate was produced. Initial and start-up characteristics of MBOs, reflected in a number of key non-financial variables, demonstrate a strong ability to explain failure up to five years later. Thus, *ceteris paribus*, greater levels of restructuring undertaken expeditiously at buy-out are associated with survival, whilst the need to deal with problems some time after buy-out is associated with failure. The shedding of labour in buy-outs is well documented (Palepu 1990) and a significant positive association with delay in reducing employment and failure may reflect the superior performance of those buy-outs that are able to restructure and shed labour early in the life cycle and have underlying strength in their product base. Direct investor monitoring was found not to be significant. Positive managerial motives for buy-out were associated with reducing the probability of subsequent failure. Buy-outs which raise funds from the wider body of employees had a lower probability of failure. Variables relating to the proportion of equity held by management and initiative being taken by management were weakly significant. However, it was found that leverage and size *per se* do not increase the risks of failure if the appropriate incentives and restructuring actions can be implemented and the enterprise is able to generate sufficient cash flow to service its debt. In an agency theory context, these findings are consistent with the control function of high levels of debt which place pressure on management to restructure, and that variables which measure the taking of restructuring action at the time of the buy-out reduce the probability of failure.

Longevity   Examination of the buy-out process suggests that for each transaction the interests of the three parties involved so that a buy-out can be completed—management, institutions, and the company itself—influence the longevity of the buy-out form (Wright *et al*. 1994). Institutions' desire for realization in order to achieve their returns may influence the nature of corporate governance to achieve a timely exit. Buy-outs funded through closed-end funds may especially seek exit within a given time period. For example, some 30 per cent of buy-outs completed in 1988 funded through closed-end funds had either floated or been sold by March 1995 compared with only 13.2 per cent of buy-outs funded through other sources of finance (Chiplin *et al*. 1995). In order to achieve timely exit, institutions are more likely to engage in closer (hands-on) monitoring of their buy-out investments and to use exit-related equity ratchets on management's equity stakes (Wright *et al*. 1995).

Successful managers' desires for wealth diversification and career enhancement, and the enterprise's ability to compete successfully in changing markets in the longer term, also raise the potential for conflicts of interest and emphasize the life cycle of the buy-out form. Meeting the interests of these parties also has implications for the appropriate governance structure in a particular buy-out. Both quantitative and case-study evidence suggests that the greater the degree of environmental dynamism and the greater the conflicts in the objectives of the parties which had to be suppressed at the time of the transaction to enable it to be completed, the more the governance structure has to be able to respond and be flexible (Wright *et al.* 1994).

In the context of venture capital investments generally, Barry (1994) cites evidence that venture capitalists' governance may be biased where they have incentives to offer bad advice to their investees in the matter of premature initial public offering (stock market flotation) timing. Such a potential reverse principal–agent conflict may arise where venture capitalists seek a premature IPO in order to gain profile and report prior performance in the raising of new funds.[18] Megginson and Weiss (1991), however, do show that there is less underpricing in venture-backed IPOs than in those with such finance, a finding consistent with a recognized role for venture capitalists as monitors.

4. Conclusions

The theoretical and empirical discussion in this chapter indicates that buy-outs and venture capital investments can make a considerable contribution to dealing with governance problems both in firms with diffuse ownership and control and in cases where previously entirely closely held firms sell at least part of their equity. The evidence reviewed indicates that such changes in the ownership and financial structure may yield large gains in shareholder value and operating performance, but that both pre- and post-transactional governance problems also need to be addressed.

It is also necessary to recognize that buy-outs and venture capital investments are heterogeneous phenomena, with apparently similar forms having differing governance implications, as evidenced by the insider–outsider distinction between an MBO and an MBI, where the latter involves an outside management team. Incoming managers (and their investors) in a buy-in are faced with potentially severe asymmetric information problems. To the extent that these problems lead managers and/or investors to misjudge the situation, the restructuring contract effected may be inappropriate and possibly unviable.

The evidence presented in this chapter also has more general implications for the corporate governance debate. First, it suggests the need for a flexible approach

---

[18]   This issue also raises further governance problems in relation to conflicts between venture capitalists and their investors.

to governance under which the forms adopted take account of such specific factors as the firm's product market and life cycle circumstances. The governance debate can be said to have focused on the relative merits of *exit* and *voice* in reducing the agency costs of control. The innovations involved in the restructuring transaction would appear to recognize a role for enhanced voice, even in the context of exit-dominated capital markets. Second, the discussion of the monitoring problems of active investors suggests that, even in cases where they have a major incentive to exercise voice, their ability to do so may be constrained by access to information, the nature of the relationship with the management of the firm being monitored, and the effort–cost–reward trade-off involved in close involvement. Third, the evidence on the longevity of buy-outs and buy-ins suggests that governance structures are not necessarily fixed over time. As enterprises develop, they may need to change their governance structure if value for shareholders is to be optimized.

REFERENCES

Admati, A., and Pfleiderer, P. (1994), 'Robust Financial Contracting and the Role of Venture Capitalists', *Journal of Finance*, 49: 371–402.

Amit, R., Glosten, L., and Muller, E. (1993), 'Challenges to Theory Development in Entrepreneurship Research', *Journal of Management Studies*, 30: 815–34.

Asquith, P., and Wizman, T. (1990), 'Event Risk, Wealth Redistribution, and its Return to Existing Bondholders in Corporate Buyouts', *Journal of Financial Economics*, 27: 195–213.

Barry, C. (1994), 'New Directions in Research on Venture Capital Finance', *Financial Management*, 23/3: 3–15.

Beecroft, A. (1994), 'The Role of the Venture Capital Industry in the UK', in Dimsdale and Prevezer (1994).

Berle, A. A., and Means, G. C. (1932), *The Modern Corporation and Private Property* (New York: MacMillan).

Bhide, A. (1990), 'Reversing Corporate Diversification', *Journal of Applied Corporate Finance*, 3: 70–81.

—— (1993), 'The Hidden Costs of Stock Market Liquidity', *Journal of Financial Economics*, 34: 31–51.

British Venture Capital Association (1995), *Report on Investment Activity* (London, BVCA).

Bruner, R., and Eades, K. (1992), 'The Crash of the Revco LBO: The Hypothesis of Inadequate Capital', *Financial Management*, 21: 35–49.

Bruno, A., and Tyebjee, T. (1985), 'The Entrepreneur's Search for Capital', *Journal of Business Venturing*, 1: 61–74.

Cable, J. R. (1985), 'Capital Market Information and Industrial Performance: The Role of West German Banks', *Economic Journal*, 95: 118–32.

—— (1988), Organizational Form and Economic Performance', in S. Thompson and M. Wright (eds.), *Internal Organisation, Efficiency and Performance* (Oxford: Philip Allan).

Cadbury, A. (1992), *Report of the Committee on the Financial Aspects of Corporate Governance* (London: Gee).

Caves, R. E. (1980), 'Corporate Strategy and Structure', *Journal of Economic Literature*, 18: 64–92.

Centre for Management Buy-out Research (1995), *Management Buy-outs: Quarterly Review from CMBOR* (Nottingham: CMBOR, University of Nottingham, Autumn).

Charkham, J. (1994), *Keeping Good Company: A Study of Corporate Governance in Five Countries* (Oxford: Oxford University Press).

Chen, A. H., and Kensinger, J. W. (1988), 'Beyond the Tax Benefits of ESOPs', *Journal of Applied Corporate Finance*, 1: 67–75.

Chiplin, B., Wright, M., and Robbie, K. (1995), 'UK Management Buy-Outs in 1994', *Management Buy-Out Quarterly Review* (Spring).

Conyon, M., Gregg, P., and Machin, S. (1995), 'Taking Care of Business: Executive Corporation in the UK', *Economic Journal* (May), 704–14.

DeAngelo, L. (1986), 'Accounting Numbers as Market Valuation Substitutes: A Study of the Management Buyouts of Public Stockholders', *Accounting Review*, 61: 400–20.

DeAngelo, M., DeAngelo, L., and Rice, E. (1984), 'Shareholder Wealth and Going Private', *Journal of Law and Economics*, 27: 367–402.

Denis, D. J. (1994), 'Organizational Form and the Consequences of Highly Leveraged Transactions: Kroger's Recapitalization and Safeway's LBO', *Journal of Financial Economics*, 36: 193–224.

—— and Denis, D. (1993), 'Managerial Discretion, Organizational Structure and Corporate Performance', *Journal of Accounting and Economics*, 16: 209–36.

Dimsdale, N., and Prevezer, M. (eds.) (1994), *Capital Markets and Corporate Governance* (Oxford: Oxford University Press).

Donaldson, G. (1994). 'Corporate Restructuring in the 1980s and its Impact for the 1990s', *Journal of Applied Corporate Finance*, 6: 55–69.

Easterwood, J. C., and Seth, A. (1993), 'Strategic Restructuring in Large Management Buyouts', *Journal of Applied Corporate Finance*, 6: 25–37.

—— Singer, R. F., Seth, A., and Lang, D. F. (1994), 'Controlling the Conflict of Interest in Management Buyouts', *Review of Economics and Statistics*, 76: 512–22.

Edwards, J., and Fischer, K. (1994), *Banks, Finance and Investment in Germany* (Cambridge: Cambridge University Press).

Elango, B., Fried, V., Hisrich, R., and Polonchek, A. (1995), 'How Venture Capital Firms Differ', *Journal of Business Venturing*, 10/2: 157–79.

Fama, E. (1980), 'Agency Problems and the Theory of the Firm', *Journal of Political Economy*, 88: 288–307.

Fried, V., and Hisrich, R. (1995), 'The Venture Capitalist: A Relationship Investor', *California Management Review*, 37/2: 101–13.

Gilson, R., and Roe, M. (1993), 'Understanding the Japanese Keiretsu: Overlaps between Corporate Governance and Industrial Organization', *Yale Law Journal*, 102: 871–906.

Hart, O. (1995), 'Corporate Governance: Some Theory and Implications', *Economic Journal* (May), 678–89.

Hatherly, D., Innes, J., MacAndrew, J., and Mitchell, F. (1994), 'An Exploration of the MBO–Financier Relationship', *Corporate Governance*, 2/1: 20–9.

Hill, C. W. L. (1985), 'Internal Organization and Enterprise Performance: Some UK Evidence', *Managerial and Decision Economics*, 6: 210–16.

Hirschman, A. O. (1970), *Exit Voice and Loyalty* (Boston: Harvard University Press).

Hite, G. L., and Vetsuypens, M. R. (1989), 'Management Buyouts of Divisions and

Shareholder Wealth', *Journal of Finance*, 44: 953–70.

Hoskisson, R. E., and Turk, T. A. (1990), 'Corporate Restructuring: Governance and Control in the Internal Capital Market', *Academy of Management Review*, 15: 455–75.

Jensen, M. C. (1986), 'Agency Costs of Free Cash Flow, Corporate Finance and Takeovers', *American Economic Review*, 76: 323–9.

—— (1989), 'The Eclipse of the Modern Corporation', *Harvard Business Review*, 89/5: 61–74.

—— (1991), 'Corporate Control and the Politics of Finance', *Journal of Applied Corporate Finance*, 4/2: 13–33.

—— (1993), 'The Modern Industrial Revolution: Exit, and the Failure of Internal Control Systems', *Journal of Finance*, 48: 831–80.

—— and Meckling, W. (1976), 'The Theory of the Firm: Managerial Behavior, Agency Costs and Ownership Structure', *Journal of Financial Economics*, 3: 305–60.

—— Kaplan, S., and Stiglin, L. (1989), 'Effects of LBOs on Tax Revenues of the US Treasury', *Tax Notes*, 42: 727–33.

Kaplan, S. N. (1989*a*), 'The Effects of Management Buyouts on Operations and Value', *Journal of Financial Economics*, 24: 217–54.

—— (1989*b*), 'Management Buyouts: Evidence on Taxes as a Source of Value', *Journal of Finance*, 44: 611–32.

—— (1991), 'The Staying Power of Leveraged Buyouts', *Journal of Financial Economics*, 29: 287–313.

—— and Stein, J. C. (1993), 'The Evolution of Buyout Pricing in the 1980s', *Quarterly Journal of Economics*, 108: 313–57.

Kester, W. C. (1992), 'Governance, Contracting and Investment Horizons: A Look at Japan and Germany', *Journal of Applied Corporate Finance*, 5: 83–98.

Lee, D. S. (1992), 'Management Buyout Proposals and Inside Information', *Journal of Finance*, 47: 1061–79.

Lehn, K., and Poulsen, A. (1989), 'Free Cash Flow and Stockholder Gains in Going Private Transactions', *Journal of Finance*, 44: 771–88.

Lerner, J. (1994), 'The Syndication of Venture Capital Investments', *Financial Management*, 23/3: 16–27.

Lichtenberg, F. R., and Siegel, D. (1990), 'The Effects of Leveraged Buyouts on Productivity and Related Aspects of Firm Behaviour', *Journal of Financial Economics*, 27: 165–94.

Liebeskind, J., Wiersema, M., and Hansen, G. (1992), 'LBOs, Corporate Restructuring and the Incentive-Intensity Hypothesis', *Financial Management*, 21 (Spring), 73–86.

Long, W. F., and Ravenscraft, D. J. (1993), 'LBOs, Debt and R & D Intensity', *Strategic Management Journal*, 14: 119–35.

MacMillan, I., Kulow, D., and Khoylian, R. (1989), 'Venture Capitalists' Involvement in their Investments: Extent and Performance', *Journal of Business Venturing*, 4: 27–47.

—— Siegel, R., and Subbanarasimha, P. N. S. (1985), 'Criteria Used by Venture Capitalists to Evaluate New Venture Proposals', *Journal of Business Venturing*, 1/1: 119–28.

—— Zemann, L., and Subbanarasimha, P. N. S. (1987), 'Criteria Distinguishing Successful from Unsuccessful Ventures in the Venture Screening Process', *Journal of Business Venturing*, 3: 123–37.

Marais, L., Schipper, K., and Smith, A. (1989), 'Wealth Effects of Going Private on Senior Securities', *Journal of Financial Economics*, 23: 155–91.

Markides, C. C. (1992), 'Consequences of Corporate Refocusing: Ex ante Evidence', *Academy of Management Journal*, 35: 398–412.

Megginson, W., and Weiss, K. (1991), 'Venture Capitalist Certification in Initial Public

Offerings', *Journal of Finance*, 46: 879–903.

Muscarella, C., and Vetsuypens, M. (1990), 'Efficiency and Organizational Structure: A Study of Reverse LBOs', *Journal of Finance*, 45: 1389–413.

Ofek, E. (1994), 'Efficiency Gains in Unsuccessful Management Buyouts', *Journal of Finance*, 49: 637–54.

Opler, T. C. (1992), 'Operating Performance in Leveraged Buyouts', *Financial Management*, 21: 27–34.

Palepu, K. G. (1990), 'Consequences of Leveraged Buyouts', *Journal of Financial Economics*, 27: 247–62.

Perry, S. E., and Williams, T. M. (1994), 'Earnings Management Preceding Management Buyout Offers', *Journal of Accounting and Economics*, 18: 152–79.

Robbie, K., and Wright, M. (1990), 'The Maccess Buy-Outs', in S. Turley and P. Taylor (eds.), *Case Studies in Financial Management* (Oxford: Philip Allan).

—— —— (1995), 'Managerial and Ownership Succession and Corporate Restructuring: The Case of Management Buy-Ins', *Journal of Management Studies*, 32/4: 527–50.

—— —— and Thompson, S. (1992), 'Management Buy-Ins in the UK', *Omega*, 20: 445–56.

Rosenstein, J., Bruno, A., Bygrave, W., and Taylor, N. (1993), 'The CEO, Venture Capitalists and the Board', *Journal of Business Venturing*, 8: 99–113.

Sahlman, W. A. (1990), 'The Structure and Governance of Venture-Capital Organizations', *Journal of Financial Economics*, 27: 473–521.

Sapienza, H., Manigart, S., and Herron, L. (1992), 'Venture Capitalists' Involvement in Portfolio Companies: A Study of 221 Portfolio Companies in Four Countries', in N. Churchill, S. Birley, W. Bygrave, D. Muzyka, C. Wahlbin, and W. Wetzel (eds.), *Frontiers of Entrepreneurship Research* (Wellesley, Mass., Babson College).

Schipper, C., and Smith, A. (1988), 'Corporate Income Tax Effects of Management Buy-Outs', Working Paper, University of Chicago.

Shleifer, A., and Summers, L. (1988), 'Breach of Trust in Hostile Takeovers', in A. Auerbach (ed.), *Corporate Takeovers: Causes and Consequences* (Chicago: University of Chicago Press).

Smart, S. B., and Waldfogel, J. (1994), 'Measuring the Effect of Restructuring on Corporate Performance: The Case of Management Buyouts', *Review of Economics and Statistics*, 76: 503–11.

Smith, A. (1990), 'Corporate Ownership Structure and Performance: The Case of Management Buy-Outs', *Journal of Financial Economics*, 27: 143–64.

Steer, P., and Cable, J. R. (1978), 'Internal Organization and Profit: An Empirical Analysis of Large UK Companies', *Journal of Industrial Economics*, 27: 13–30.

Stiglitz, J., and Weiss, A. (1981), 'Credit Rationing in Markets with Imperfect Information', *American Economic Review*, 71 (June), 393–410.

Sweeting, R. (1991), 'Early-Stage New Technology-Based Businesses: Interactions with Venture Capitalists and the Development of Accounting Techniques and Procedures', *British Accounting Review*, 23: 3–21.

Thompson, R. S. (1981), 'Internal Organization and Profit: A Note', *Journal of Industrial Economics*, 30: 201–11.

—— and Wright, M. (1987), 'Markets to Hierarchies and Back Again: The Implications of MBOs for Factor Supply', *Journal of Economic Studies*, 14: 5–22.

—— —— (1995), 'Corporate Governance: The Role of Restructuring Transactions', *Economic Journal* (May), 690–703.

—— —— and Robbie, K. (1992*a*), 'Buy-Outs, Divestment and Leverage: Restructuring

Transactions and Corporate Governance', *Oxford Review of Economic Policy*, 8: 58–69.

—— —— —— (1992*b*), 'Management Equity Ownership, Debt and Performance: Some Evidence from UK Management Buy-Outs', *Scottish Journal of Political Economy*, 39/4: 413–30.

Williamson, O. E. (1975), *Markets and Hierarchies: Analysis and Antitrust Implications* (New York: Free Press).

—— (1985), *The Economic Institutions of Capitalism: Firms, Markets and Relational Contracting* (New York: Free Press).

Wright, M. (1994), 'Management Buy-Outs: Issues and Evidence', in M. Wright (ed.), *Management Buy-Outs* (Aldershot: Dartmouth).

—— (1986), 'The Make–Buy Decision and Managing Markets: The Case of Management Buy-Outs', *Journal of Management Studies*, 23/4: 434–53.

—— Thompson, S., and Robbie, K. (1992), 'Venture Capital and Management-Led Leveraged Buy-Outs: A European Perspective', *Journal of Business Venturing*, 7: 47–71.

—— Robbie, K., Thompson, S., and Starkey, K. (1994), 'Longevity and the Life Cycle of MBOs', *Strategic Management Journal*, 15: 215–27.

—— —— —— and Wong, P. (1995), 'Management Buy-Outs in the Short and Long Term', *Journal of Business Finance and Accounting*, 22/4 (June), 461–82.

—— Wilson, N., Robbie, K., and Ennew, C. (1996), 'An Analysis of Failure in UK Buy-Outs and Buy-Ins', *Managerial and Decision Economics*, 17: 55–70.

8

MARKET (UNITED STATES) VERSUS MANAGED (JAPANESE) GOVERNANCE

Hicheon Kim and Robert E. Hoskisson

1. Introduction

In extending Chandler's (1962) work, Williamson (1985: 279) hails the multi-divisional (M-form) structure as 'the most significant organizational innovation of the twentieth century'. Chandler described how the M-form structure was first adopted by early diversified firms such as Du Pont and General Motors in the 1920s. According to Williamson, the M-form structure was implemented to manage and allocate resources better among various lines of business through the creation of an internal capital market. Put differently, the M-form replaced the functional form (U-form) as a structure for large diversified firms because the former was more efficient at allocating resources. Although Williamson's theoretical arguments are compelling, scholars who have examined this issue have not fully corroborated his assertion (see Hoskisson *et al.* 1993 for a review). Some research finds a positive association between M-form adoption (e.g. Teece 1981), while others find a contingency effect with diversification strategy (e.g. Hoskisson 1987). M-form adoption facilitates performance for highly diversified firms but has less effect for firms that have interdependence between divisions (Hoskisson *et al.* 1991). Still other scholars point out unintended negative effects of shortened time horizons (Hill 1985) and lower R & D expenses (Hoskisson and Hitt 1988) associated with the M-form adoption. Another significant criticism is that the M-form can facilitate over-diversified firms (Hoskisson and Turk 1990; Hoskisson *et al.* 1994) when internal governance is lacking. Diversification can improve firm performance if it is expanded up to a certain level in a discriminatory manner, but excessive diversification creates performance problems. In fact, during the 1960s and 1970s, many M-form firms actively pursued diversification, but its result were disappointing, as Shleifer and Vishny (1991) indicate. Accordingly, Markides (1992) finds that breaking up highly diversified M-form firms creates wealth for shareholders.

However, most of the previous work on the M-form has not been done on an international comparative basis. As such, this chapter is oriented to foster more comparative research on the M-form structure. We suggest, therefore, that the effects of M-form adoption may be context-specific. Boyacigiller and Adler (1991) argue that organizational scientists have not paid adequate attention to the differences in cultural values and economic systems across countries in theory development. They also argue that organizational scientists have inappropriately imbued theories with universalism by neglecting these differences across countries. Research on multi-divisional (M-form) structures may be subject to this criticism in the sense that previous research on M-form structures has focused primarily on the United States (e.g. Armour and Teece 1978; Chandler 1962; Hoskisson 1987) and the United Kingdom (e.g. Channon 1973; Steer and Cable 1978; Hill 1988). However, there are distinct differences in corporate governance contexts across countries. Accordingly, it is conceivable that the relative advantage associated with a certain type of organization structure varies by the governance arrangements that oversee firms. This chapter highlights the significance of comparing M-form structures across Japanese and US firms by examining the differences in two governance tools used to supervise large firms, capital market financial systems, and managerial labour markets.

Through our comparative examination of the differences between these governance systems, we propose that the M-form structure may fare better as an organizational innovation for Japanese than for US firms. Our argument begins by recognizing distinctive differences in institutional arrangements between the USA and Japan in providing financial and managerial resources. These institutional arrangement differences are suggested to have non-trivial impacts on the functioning of M-form firms.

First, Japanese financial systems are likely to be more efficient in governing large M-form firms than US counterparts. Williamson (1975) indicates that the M-form structure innovation has two components: improving control and information processing for diversified firms and facilitating governance of potential stand-alone U-form firms as they become M-form divisions and therefore subject to the scrutiny of the M-form corporate office. That the M-form is an innovation that facilitates management of diversified firms from a control or information processing point of view is consistent with Williamson's argument. However, Hoskisson and Turk (1990) point out that unless the M-form system is accompanied by efficient governance checks on the corporate office and its overall diversification strategy, it can also be used as a vehicle whereby managers pursue over-diversification. Governance systems are a set of mechanisms (ownership monitoring, boards of directors, executive compensation) that induce managers to run firms in the best interests of shareholders. Without effective governance, the positive relationship hypothesized by Williamson (1975) between the M-form structure and performance is unlikely to materialize (Hoskisson *et al.* 1993). Thus, in so far as Japanese financial governance systems more efficiently govern M-form firms than their US counterparts, Japanese M-form firms not only improve the efficiency in managing their diversified lines of business, but also pursue diversification in more profit-maximizing ways. However, in studying this issue

Cable and Yasuki (1985) failed to find support for improved performance among Japanese firms adopting the M-form. This may be due to the fact that large Japanese firms already have governance mechanisms that foster good stewardship and M-form implementation and therefore would not improve performance based on a governance effect.

Managerial labour market differences also have significant implications for M-form performance. Career systems of US firms are open to external labour markets at all levels and, while there is some movement across firms, there is significantly less managerial labour market openness in Japan, except at the entry level (Kanemoto and MacLeod 1991; Quinn and Rivoli 1991). As such, US M-form firms may have deficiencies among middle-level managers because high-performing middle managers are better off moving into smaller U-forms unless they have a reasonable chance of being promoted to corporate levels. In contrast, most Japanese high-potential managers develop their career within a firm and therefore prefer to work for firms with abundant opportunities of intra-firm mobility and less bankruptcy risk. As such, Japanese M-form firms are likely to attract more competent managers than Japanese U-form firms to the extent that M-form organizations provide more career opportunities and entail less bankruptcy risk. Although this may be true for US firms, high-potential Japanese managers have less opportunity to move across firms. In sum, our comparative analysis suggests that Japanese financial systems and managerial labour markets are more supportive of the M-form structure than those in the USA.

The next section starts with a brief review of the prior research on M-form structures. Then, financial governance and managerial labour markets are examined for differences between the USA and Japan and the potential effect these differences have for the M-form system. Finally, implications for theory development and comparative research on M-form structures are discussed. Also, because our arguments may be misconstrued such that the Japanese system is seen as 'superior', governance trade-offs between the two systems are examined in the discussion section of the chapter.

2. M-Form Structures

In his 'M-form hypothesis', Williamson (1975, 1985) hypothesizes that M-form structures are more efficient in managing large firms operating in diverse businesses than U-form structures. Williamson suggests that U-form structures inevitably encounter two problems as they grow in size and diversification: cumulative control loss and the confounding of strategic and operating decision-making. Because U-form firms are organized around functions, not businesses, it is difficult for top officers to identify the profit contribution of each business. This leads to control loss and makes it extremely difficult to achieve optimal allocation of financial resources. Strategic considerations are de-emphasized by top officers, whose time is focused on short-run administrative problems occurring within the firm. Therefore, performance of U-form firms declines with increases in size and diversity. On the other hand, M-form structures, which entail divisionalization and separation between strategic and operating decision-makings, are an appropriate organizational arrangement to resolve these two problems. Corporate managers can focus on strategic decision-making such as long-range planning, control and co-ordination of divisions, and resource allocation among divisions while delegating operating decision-making to division managers. Moreover, corporate managers can properly control division managers through evaluation and reward systems, promotion systems, and hierarchical power. In short, Williamson argues for the superiority of M-form structures in managing diversified firms over U-form structures.

Numerous studies have empirically examined the M-form hypothesis, but they appear to offer only qualified support for the M-form hypothesis (see Hoskisson *et al.* 1993 for a comprehensive review). Aside from methodological difficulties in measuring firm performance and controlling for extraneous variables, some studies assume that M-form structures are a homogeneous organizational arrangement. However, there exist substantial differences in internal arrangements and diversification strategies among M-form firms (Hill and Hoskisson 1987; Hill *et al.* 1992; Jones and Hill 1988). Thus, M-form structures *per se* may not improve performance of diversified firms. Instead, achieving fit between diversification strategies and M-form structures is crucial to the performance of diversified firms (Hill 1988; Hill and Hoskisson 1987; Hill *et al.* 1992; Hoskisson 1987; Hoskisson *et al.* 1991).

Diversification Strategy, Economic Benefits, and M-Form Structures

In reviewing the research on the M-form and performance, Hoskisson *et al.* (1993) suggest that two different types of M-form structures have evolved: one focusing on related businesses and having co-operative business unit structures; the other focusing on unrelated businesses and having competitive resource allocation. Co-operative M-form firms focusing on related divisions can achieve synergistic economies by transferring skills and sharing resources among divisions (Porter 1987). Skill transfer and resource sharing can help diversified firms enhance their competitiveness, but create interdependence among division at the same time (Gupta and Govindarajan 1986; Govindarajan and Fisher 1990). Although this system compromises accountability, which is an advantage of the M-form, the potential to realize gains from synergy is a strong incentive to move to the co-operative form. As such, gains come when a company realizes co-ordination of activities of interdependent divisions with an M-form structure where co-operative processes and incentives between divisions are emphasized.

On the other hand, competitive M-form firms pursuing unrelated diversification can achieve financial economies through competitive allocation of resources. The realization of financial economies involves the creation of internal capital markets that have advantages in controlling managers and allocating resources over external capital markets (Dundas and Richardson 1982; Williamson 1975, 1985). The competitive M-form structure has the following characteristics: division managers should have a high degree of autonomy so that they can be accountable for division performance; division managers are evaluated primarily by financial budgets (*ex ante*) and financial outcomes (*ex post*); and the corporate office seeks to allocate financial resources in high-yield uses among divisions on a competitive basis. Indeed, the competitive M-form structure is closer to Williamson's theoretical description of the M-form structure (Hoskisson 1987).

The above discussion points out two very different variants of the M-form structure: co-operative and competitive ones. Because of different organizational schemes, it is difficult to achieve synergistic and financial economies simultaneously. In fact, Hoskisson and Johnson (1992) found that firms pursuing both synergistic and financial economies were more likely targets of corporate restructuring and that these hybrid strategy firms tended to become more purely co-operative or competitive types in the post-restructuring period.

Note that the classification of co-operative and competitive M-form structures is based upon the observation of US and UK firms. It is not clear that the same classification holds in Japan because Japan has quite different governance arrangements than in the USA or UK. In fact, we argue in the next section that financial governance systems in Japan generally nullify the need for the competitive M-form system. The competitive M-form may exist in the USA because it is needed as an additional governance device. However, because of the internal governance systems in Japan, there would be less need for competitive M-form firms in Japan than in the USA.

3. Comparative Financial System Governance: Relationship to Strategy and Structure

In this section, we propose a conceptual framework that illustrates different types of financial governance systems along two dimensions of governance, financial institution involvement and governance orientation (individual or collective), and discuss how they influence M-form structures and diversification strategy. Financial institution involvement refers to the role of financial institution (e.g. banks, insurance companies, and pension funds) in corporate governance. This dimension is useful in that Japanese financial institutions play a significant role in financing and governing large firms to a greater extent than US counterparts do, although this difference has been decreasing somewhat recently (e.g. Prowse 1990). The other dimension is governance orientation, individual versus collective. The individual orientation indicates that individual shareholders act independently in governing firms; the collective orientation indicates that individual

Governance Orientation

	Individual	Collective
Low	• Typical US firms	• Collective strategy firms with low institutional involvement (employee owned firms, farm cooperatives, cooperative research firms)
	1	2
High	3 • Japanese independent firms • US firms with a high level of institutional involvement	4 • Japanese keiretsu firms

Financial Institution Involvement

Fig. 8.1. Four types of financial governance systems based on two dimensions: financial institution involvement and governance orientation

shareholders co-ordinate their governance activities. While US shareholders hold individual orientations, Japanese shareholders, particularly those of keiretsu firms, hold collective orientations (Hoshi *et al.* 1990*b*, 1991; Prowse 1992).

Figure 8.1 illustrates four quadrants or governance types suggested by these two dimensions. Of these four, three represent significant governance types existing in the USA and Japan: quadrant 1 is typical of US firms; quadrant 4 is typical of Japanese keiretsu firms; and quadrant 3 typical of Japanese independent firms and US firms with high levels of institutional ownership. Quadrant 2 firms are found in the USA and Japan, but are not likely to impact the M-form arrangement. Although this quadrant could represent employee buy-out firms which have a collective reason for existence such as that of the United Airlines employee buy-out, this is an atypical organizational arrangement. Other examples may be farm co-operatives and credit unions. Each quadrant will be discussed in detail below.

Quadrant 1

Quadrant 1 is typical of the US governance system where capital markets for corporate stocks and bonds, rather than financial institutions, play a major role in financing and governing firms (Prowse 1992; Zysman 1983). US financial institutions such as banks are subject to numerous legal and political restrictions that discourage them from holding firm stocks (see Roe 1990 for a review): commercial banks cannot hold firm stocks because of the Glass-Steagall Act; other financial institutions (insurance companies, mutual funds, and pension funds), owing to various legal constraints, tend to own only small portions of firm stocks, except for large fund managers. Because of the passive role of financial institutions, US stock ownership is typically diffused among individuals. Prowse (1992) reports that individuals in the USA hold 58.1 per cent while corporations hold 37.7 per cent of firm equities.

Diffused ownership structure is usually equated with inefficient corporate governance. Individual shareholders with small positions do not have sufficient incentives to collect information and discipline managers because they bear all the costs of doing so, but share benefits with other shareholders (Baysinger *et al.* 1991; Williamson 1975, 1985). This incentive problem can be overcome if individual shareholders co-ordinate actions in gaining information and disciplining managers. However, US shareholders tend to act independently in governance activities. First, in so far as ownership is diffused, it is difficult or at least very costly for individual shareholders to co-ordinate actions (Hill and Snell 1988, 1989). Moreover, there are legal restrictions in doing so. Although the new Security and Exchange Commition (SEC) rules in the USA allow more communications among shareholders, these rules clearly reject the idea of shareholders taking action in concert (Pozen 1994). Diffused ownership structure, along with the lack of collective co-ordination among shareholders, tend to result in less powerful governance mechanisms.

It is in this governance context that Williamson (1975, 1985) proposes the competitive M-form structure as an alternative governance device. He argues that the external capital market fails as a governance device in two ways. First, because of substantial information asymmetries between management and shareholders, management can misrepresent the position of the firm to shareholders. Second, because it is expensive for the external capital market to discipline underperforming management, it usually corrects non-marginal performance problems, but is not able to fine tune management. He further argues that the corporate office of the M-form, as an asset allocator in the internal capital market, can overcome these information and control disadvantages. The corporate office can attenuate information asymmetries by auditing operations of divisions and can more easily influence operations of divisions by manipulating reward and incentives through hierarchical power.

Although the M-form structure can be an efficient governance device in controlling division managers, it cannot be an efficient governance device in controlling corporate managers (Hoskisson and Turk 1990). Corporate managers of U-form and M-form firms are governed by shareholders who have information and control disadvantages, as Williamson argues. Moreover, shareholders of M-form firms may experience informational disadvantages to a greater extent than those of U-form firms because M-form firms have the potential to be larger in size and more complex in product scope than U-form firms. Thus, corporate managers of M-form firms might have more latitude for pursuing strategies for their own benefits that are inconsistent with maximizing firm performance.

In fact, Shleifer and Vishny (1991) among others suggest that the M-form is partially responsible for unprofitable diversification move among US firms. The M-form is appropriate not only for managing diversification, but also for increasing diversification. The M-form can reduce potential disruptive effects of starting a new business on the entire company by assigning a semi-autonomous status to the new business (Russo 1991). Diversification beyond the point where firm performance is maximized can still be beneficial to corporate managers because it reduces managerial employment risk and increases managerial compensation and status in society (Hoskisson and Turk 1990).

In sum, the M-form structure may serve as an efficient governance device for division managers, not for corporate managers, although, as Wright (1988) points out, internalization, even for division managers, needs to be continually assessed. Thus, M-form implementation may improve management of divisions, but when coupled with an inefficient governance system, as is likely in this quadrant, it can be a mechanism whereby corporate managers diversify the firm to non-optimal levels. Although the market for corporate control can help to correct this problem through external analysis, outside corporate raiders are subject to the information asymmetry problem. Furthermore, a study by Walsh and Kosnik (1993) of the most active corporate raiders in the USA showed that 50 per cent of their takeover attempts were targeted at firms with above average performance in their industries. In these cases, the firms were neither undervalued nor poorly managed. This caused some effective managers to undertake expensive defensive strategies to justify their positions. Thus, external market governance controls do not always create effective change.

Quadrant 4

Quadrant 4 is typical of Japanese keiretsu systems, where financial institutions play an important role in financing and governing large firms (Aoki 1990; Sheard 1989; Zysman 1983). A bank can hold up to 5 per cent of the total equity in a firm and a group of financial institutions can hold up to 40 per cent of the total equity in the firm. In addition, Japanese keiretsu systems promote a collective orientation among major partner shareholders and debtholders through main bank systems.

The keiretsu is an industrial group which involves a group of firms around a major commercial bank.[1] There are six major industrial keiretsus in Japan: Mitsui, Mitsubishi, Sumitomo, Fuyo, Sanwa, and Dai-Ichi Kangyo. These six industrial groups include one or more firms in almost all important industrial sectors, accounting for a significant portion of the Japanese economy. About half of the 200 leading industrial firms and almost all the leading financial institutions maintain clear affiliations with these six keiretsu (Gerlach 1992).

---

[1] Two types of keiretsu exist in Japan: horizontal and vertical. In order to be brief, the industrial groupings referred to as 'keiretsu' in this chapter refer to the horizontal variety. The vertical keiretsu consists of a main manufacturer such as Toyota and its affiliated subcontractors (Gerlach 1992). However, we would argue that governance of vertical and horizontal keiretsus in terms of financial institutional involvement and collectivistic orientation is similar.

Keiretsu firms obtain a significant portion of debt and equity from group financial institutions and firms, and from banks outside the keiretsu to a lesser extent. Gerlach (1992) reports that proportions of debt borrowed from group financial institutions ranged from 23.3 per cent for Dai-Ichi Kangyo to 42.4 per cent for Sumitomo and 42.8 per cent for Mitsubishi in 1986. Equity owned by group financial institutions and firms ranged from 31.6 per cent for Dai-Ichi Kangyo to 63.9 per cent for Sumitomo and 63.4 per cent for Mitsubishi in 1986.

In particular, the large commercial bank in the keiretsu plays a key role in arranging financial resources for group firms and, as such, it is known as the main bank. Among the major financial resource providers, there is an implicit agreement that the main bank is responsible for monitoring group firms and helping them in times of trouble (Aoki 1990; Sheard 1989). As such, the main bank may be regarded as a delegated monitor for group firms (Horiuchi *et al.* 1988). In fact, main banks often bear a disproportionally large burden in providing financial assistance to turn around firms in trouble (see Pascale and Rohlen 1983; Sheard 1989 for cases). Main banks are willing to do so because maintaining reputations as responsible monitors is important to maintaining their relations with the keiretsu and with other banks who will contribute to future business opportunities (Aoki 1990).

Indeed, main banks have strong incentives to monitor group firms. Because of equity and debt positions, main banks can safeguard their investment and gain from firm profit by monitoring firms. In addition, main banks can avoid bearing excessive burden of restructuring firms in financial trouble, and maintain their reputation as responsible monitors (Aoki 1990; Hoshi *et al.* 1990*b*; Sheard 1991).

Main banks are relatively well positioned to get access to information about firm management and strategy. It is not uncommon for main banks to arrange for some of their employees to have an additional role as a board member in group firms. Of course, interpersonal connections created by employee transfer among keiretsu firms stimulate information flow and co-ordination between main banks and group firms. In addition, the keiretsu typically has many councils for various levels of managers. Of these councils, the most prominent are presidents' councils, in which CEOs of core firms and financial institutions including main banks participate. Although having no formal decision-making authority, these councils are mechanisms whereby main banks and group firms can share information, discuss mutual concerns, and co-ordinate decision-making. In short, main banks have not only the incentives but also the processes to monitor group firms.

The above discussion indicates that main banks are likely to monitor keiretsu firms efficiently, but corporate governance in keiretsu systems extends beyond this main bank monitoring. Keiretsu firms are also governed by cultural norms of the keiretsu system (Gerlach 1992). The keiretsus have established a sense of coherence among group members in various ways: debt, equity, trade, and employee exchange networks; group-wide councils, industrial projects, public relations, and social activities; and even sharing names and logos. In addition, the keiretsus present themselves as a whole and compete with each other for higher standings in the business community, which has facilitated the sense of cohesion among group members even more. This sense of cohesion certainly induces group members to behave in ways consistent with expectations of other network members (Hakansson and Johanson 1993). For instance, one common rule among keiretsus is known as the 'one set principle'. This rule dictates that each industrial group tries to have only one firm in each product area (Gerlach 1992). This means that keiretsu members firms are less likely to diversify into the businesses of other member firms, thus reducing diversification within keiretsu member firms based on collective norms of behaviour.

This discussion suggests that the M-form is an organizational structure to manage diversified lines of business, but also can be utilized to take further diversification. It is a good governance device for division managers, but not for corporate managers. As a result, in the absence of efficient governance devices for corporate managers, M-form adoption could result in unprofitable diversification. The main bank monitoring and strong culture in the keiretsu constitute an efficient monitor of corporate managers, at least compared to diffuse shareholders in quadrant 1. Thus, in keiretsu systems, M-form implementation improves the management of diversified businesses without the risk of creating excessively diversified firms over time. It is also likely that competitive M-form firms as a governance device will not be likely to exist to the same extent as it would in quadrant 1.

Quadrant 3

Quadrant 3 represents the governance system for Japanese independent firms (firms unaffiliated with keiretsu) and US firms with a high level of institutional ownership. Because financial institutions are major shareholders, ownership is, on average, more concentrated than in quadrants 1 and 2. Also, unlike quadrant 4, major shareholders act independently without much effort to co-ordinate their monitoring activities.

Prowse (1992) suggests that there is a difference between the way independent and keiretsu firms are governed in Japan, although both have financial institutions as major shareholders. As discussed before, main banks in the keiretsu are responsible for monitoring keiretsu firms on behalf of other major shareholders and debtholders. In contrast, major shareholders need to monitor and influence management of independent firms individually as a shareholder, as in the USA. For instance, if a bank holds a 4 per cent equity position of an independent firm, the bank can exert influence based upon 4 per cent ownership. However, if a bank holds a 4 per cent equity position of a keiretsu firm as the main bank, the main bank actually represents far more than 4 per cent, which at least equals the positions held by financial institutions and other firms in the same keiretsu. As such, independent firms have more arm's length relations with financial institutions and a less collective set of behavioural norms.

Independent firms in Japan would be similar to firms with significant financial institutional ownership in the USA. However, there may be less collective action among institutional investors in the USA because, as current rules illustrate, co-ordinated action among shareholders is discouraged (Black 1992). Furthermore, to avoid collective action by shareholders managers can manipulate the agenda on proxy votes. For instance, a vote agenda may contain a number of proposals favoured by institutional investors surrounding one that they are against. In essence, the voting forces institutions to vote against themselves. Also, institutions have to pay the full cost of a proxy vote fight, while firms and their managers can spend firm resources to fund the proxy battle. Even with the recent SEC changes allowing more co-operative discussion (Pozen 1994), the rules still prohibit collective action. Until institutions can create changes on boards of directors, including having board member representation as well as providing better monitoring incentives for board members, institutional voice in the USA is likely to remain relatively passive. This is reinforced by the fact that some institutions (mutual funds) with high ownership positions may not want to exercise their voice option for fear of offending important customers (managers of corporate pension funds who look unfavourably on any anti-managerial proposals). The success of fund managers exercising voice is indirect at best. As Black (1992) puts it:

> Corporate and money managers often talk about the need for dialogue between shareholders and managers. The money managers, who are outside the walled citadel and want in, recognize the limited value of shooting arrows over the walls. The managers want the infidels to go away, but when pushed, often prefer compromise to a public fight. To date, many shareholder successes come through negotiations with managers, in which the managers 'voluntarily' adopt all or part of a shareholder proposal. (pp. 847–8)

Although the rules governing the voice option for financial institutions favours managers, there is yet another reason for institutions to be relatively passive in most firms. Given the level of diversification and large number of firms in an institutional investor's portfolio and the limit amounts that institutional investors can hold in one firm, it is unlikely that institutions can devote much attention to a single portfolio company. Even with high levels of institutional positions in large visible firms, the limits on the size of positions which may be held to create the need for collective action only in a few cases. Therefore, in the USA the major approach to governance is still largely the market (or exit) option.

As such, the main bank system in Japan, even among independent firms, is likely to be more effective in curtailing inefficient diversification and overly large M-form structures relative to US M-forms with high levels of institutional ownership. Given that the level of ownership in a Japanese and US M-form firm is the same, it is likely that the Japanese M-form would pursue more efficient diversification because the delegated main bank monitor would be more effective in exercising voice in the Japanese firm than the indirect voice possible in the US firm.

Quadrant 2

Quadrant 2 represents firms that have a collective orientation without significant financial institution involvement. These firms are on the periphery of public enterprises. In Japan and increasingly in the USA, they may be the research consortia between firms supported by the government. In the USA they may also represent farm co-operatives, credit unions, and other ventures that have a co-operative form, but which lack significant financial institution involvement. Although these forms may be important contributors to the economic development of the parties involved, they relate little to diversified firms and M-form implementation. However, if a firm lacks capital and does not want the involvement of financial institutions, it may use collective strategy (joint equity ventures or strategic alliances) as a means to raise the capital necessary. But this assumes that the individual parties in the venture have excess retained earnings and that they do not need to go to the market or to financial institutions for the necessary capital to initiate the venture. Thus, this approach is likely to have limited effect on diversification strategy or M-form structures unless it becomes a dominant strategic alternative. As Hoskisson *et al.* (1993) argue, the M-form is still the dominant form for diversified businesses.

  Besides governance differences, managerial labour market differences also affect the functioning of M-form structures. These labour market differences are addressed next.

4. Effects of Managerial Labour Market Differences Between the USA and Japan

United States Managerial Labour Markets

Comparatively, there is much more managerial inter-firm mobility in the USA than in Japan (Lincoln 1990; Quinn and Rivoli 1991). Indeed, Cannella and Best (1993) examined turnover of top management team members (excluding presidents, CEOs, chief operating officers, chairpersons, and vice-chairpersons) of large firms and found that almost 30 per cent of them joined their present firm within five years before promotion to the top management team. The USA has active external labour markets which allow managers the possibility to develop their careers across different firms. Therefore, understanding how the external labour market values managers may help predict the pattern of managerial mobility between U-form and M-form firms.

  In his theory on signalling, Spence (1973) argues that because firms cannot accurately assess abilities of managers to hire, firms rely on observable characteristics and attributes of managers to assess their abilities. Top managers in smaller U-form firms might be in a better position to send clear individual signals than division managers in M-form firms. Unlike divisions of M-form firms, smaller U-form firms have publicly available market-based and accounting-based performance indicators if they are publicly held. In addition, these performance indicators can be attributed to top managers in smaller U-form firms in the sense that top managers of U-form firms make major strategic decisions primarily on their own. On the other hand, division managers of M-form firms make major strategic decisions in consultation with corporate managers, making it more difficult for the external market to ascertain contributions that division managers make (Alchian and Demsetz 1972). Research by Baker *et al.* (1994) suggests that this may be a way for firms to retain high-quality managers because they possess asymmetric information relative to external labour market buyers of managerial talent. As a consequence, top managers in smaller U-form firms can send clearer individual market signals than division managers in M-form firms.

The best career path of managers in M-form firms, of course, might be in becoming corporate managers through internal promotion. In general, top corporate managers in M-form firms have higher wages than top managers in smaller U-form firms to the extent that the size of firms is positively related to executive compensation (Finkelstein and Hambrick 1989). However, given that only a comparatively few managers are promoted to be top corporate-level executives in M-form firms, only a small portion of managers might perceive a reasonable chance of being promoted to such positions. Managers who do not perceive a reasonable chance of being promoted to the top corporate position might consider moving into a smaller U-form firm as an alternative career path. By moving into a small U-form firms, managers can send clearer individual signals to the external labour market than by continuing as a division-level manager in an M-form firm. Alternatively, they may consider moving to another M-form firm as a division or corporate executive. However, the possibility of moving to the top position in another M-form firm is remote, unless they have had CEO experience in a smaller (e.g. U-form) firm.

Sending clear individual signals does not necessarily mean sending favourable individual signals to the external labour market. For instance, managers run the risk of sending clear unfavourable as well as favourable individual signals when moving into smaller U-form firms. Therefore, two types of managers may tend to move into smaller U-form firms from M-form firms as their careers proceed. First, above-average-performing managers may tend to move into smaller U-form firms to the extent that they, as compared to low-performing managers, would have higher confidence in their capabilities of sending favourable individual signals. They may see that those with outstanding (compared to above average) performance ratings are likely to be promoted to the top corporate M-form positions in their current firm. This comparison of ratings is likely to provide above average performance employees with an incentive to leave because they realize that, compared to individuals rated outstanding, they are unlikely to receive an opportunity to achieve a higher executive office than they currently occupy. Moreover, given their above average performance rating, they are likely to receive equivalent or better opportunities from other companies (Zenger 1992). If M-form firms are more efficient than U-form firms, they may simply outbid them. However, Baker *et al.* (1994) suggest that 'administrative constraints may keep the firm from giving the best performers raises large enough to retain them' (p. 916).

Second, managers with a high propensity of risk-taking tend to move into smaller U-form firms to the extent that this entails the risk of more clearly sending unfavourable as well as favourable individual signals. This is supported indirectly by Chaganti and Sambharya (1987), who found that firms which hired an outside top executive were associated with prospector (high-risk) rather than defender (low-risk) strategy types. Taken together, managers with a high propensity for risk-taking and high average (not outstanding) performance would be likely to move from M-form firms to smaller U-form firms as their careers proceed.

In the long run, because there are many more U-form firms than M-form firms, good managers may move from M-form firms to smaller U-form firms in order to send positive market signals. Furthermore, it may be difficult to move into another M-form firm because there is significant internal promotion among M-form firms. Cannella and Lubatkin (1993) demonstrate that there are significant socio-political processes at work within large firms that allow for internal promotion, even when performance is poor. Of course, this may also be true at smaller U-form firms, but many more smaller U-form firms are at early stages of development and require the transition to professional management. For instance, there is often an heir apparent to the presidency of a large public firm because this method of selection signals stability to stakeholders. If an inside manager who has a good performance record does not become the heir apparent, movement to a smaller U-form firm is likely because of the potential market signal. Although not being the heir apparent could provide a negative signal, moving from an M-form firm to the top position in a smaller U-form firm provides a positive, although not optimal, signal. For instance, although Lee Iacoca lost his bid to become the heir apparent at Ford, his move to Chrysler Corporation provided a positive signal for his career even though the move was risky because of the poor position of Chrysler at the time.

The above discussion does not imply that US M-form firms have an advantage in top-level managerial resources over smaller U-form firms, due to an active external labour market. However, US M-form firms may create deficiencies among middle managers because high risk-taking and above-average-performing managers in M-form firms may tend to move into smaller U-form firms as their careers proceed. The tendency may be reinforced by the individual versus collective orientation of US managers. The literature on corporate entrepreneurship has recognized middle managers as important contributors to radical innovations in large firms (e.g. Burgelman 1983, 1991; Maidique 1980). Middle managers not only generate new initiatives for radical innovations, but also serve as product champions who actively and enthusiastically promote new initiatives generated by other individuals throughout innovation processes (Burgelman 1983, 1991). Therefore, the potential incentive for above average managers of the US M-form firms to move to smaller U-form firms may have a bearing on corporate entrepreneurship in the US M-form firms. M-form firms would produce less innovation over time and entrepreneurial managers moving to smaller U-form firms would help foster innovation. They may also contribute to new start-ups that eventually become successful independent ventures. There are many new ventures, such as the Compaq Computer Corporation, which was initiated by managers who worked for Texas Instruments, that had their origins in larger M-form firms.

Japanese Managerial Labour Markets

Except for entry-level positions, Japanese firms rely on internal labour markets for selecting managers to a much greater extent than US firms (Dore 1987; McMillan 1985; Lincoln 1990; Quinn and Rivoli 1991). Once in the firm, employees develop skills and knowledge specific to the firm through job rotation and internal training, and compete with each other for promotion (Doeringer and Piore 1971). In addition, the internal labour market of Japanese firms has been characterized by the practice of lifetime employment, which provides employees with job security until retirement (see e.g. Ouchi and Jaeger 1978).

However, recent studies have indicated that permanent employment is not a guaranteed benefit provided by all Japanese firms (Koike 1988). The use of permanent employment and internal labour markets for human resources is, on the whole, a characteristic of large firms rather than smaller firms (Dore 1987; McMillan 1985; Lincoln 1990). Moreover, managers in large firms, as in the USA, receive higher salaries than those in small firms. Therefore, Japanese managers may want to work for large rather than small firms.

Because large Japanese firms rely primarily on internal labour markets for filling managerial positions, Japanese managers might want to work for firms whose internal labour markets provide more opportunities for horizontal and vertical intra-firm mobility. Japanese managers in large firms benefit from intra-firm mobility, not from inter-firm mobility, as in US firms. Also, Japanese managers, because of firm-specific investment, might want to work for firms whose bankruptcy risks are as small as possible. It is unlikely that managers in large firms can move into other large firms to the extent that large firms rely on internal labour markets for managerial resources. Accordingly, Japanese managers in a large firm would be more likely to have to move into small firms when a firm fails. Also, managers would receive lower salaries by moving from large into small firms. Therefore, it is likely that managers want to work for firms whose bankruptcy risks are as small as possible. Taken together, it appears that Japanese managers would prefer to work for firms whose internal labour markets provide more opportunities for horizontal and vertical intra-firm mobility and whose bankruptcy risks are as small as possible. Although to a degree this may also be the case for the US managers in large firms, US managers have comparatively more opportunities to work for another large firm.

Given that M-form firms, on average, are bigger and are more complex in scope than smaller U-form firms (Hoskisson and Hitt 1988), M-form firms provide opportunities for horizontal and vertical intra-firm mobility to a greater extent than smaller U-form firms. Additionally, M-form firms can stabilize cash flow and reduce bankruptcy risks by creating a portfolio of divisions to the extent that correlations among divisional returns are less than one (Lewellen 1971; Amit and Livnat 1988). Hoskisson (1987) reported that M-form implementation decreased risk measured by variability in the accounting rates of return. Also, Suzuki and Wright (1985) found that, among firms in financial distress, firm size rather than accounting performance was a better predictor of actual bankruptcy and that firm size was negatively associated with actual bankruptcy. Therefore, to the extent that the M-form firm is bigger than the typical U-form firm, the M-form firm would have less bankruptcy risk. Taken together, high-potential Japanese managers might prefer M-form firms to smaller U-form firms as employers. As a consequence, Japanese M-form firms might have advantages over Japanese U-form firms in terms of managerial resources. Smaller U-form firms in the USA, on the other hand, might have a managerial resource advantage compared to smaller U-form firms in Japan.

5. Discussion

Williamson (1975, 1985) argues that M-form structures are more efficient in managing large firms operating in diverse businesses than U-form structures. However, our analysis suggests that Japanese financial systems and managerial labour markets are more supportive for M-form firms than their US counterparts. This conclusion comes to light as a comparison is made between quadrant 1 and quadrant 4 of Figure 8.1. Managed governance as found in Japan provides a better framework for M-form governance; such governance obviates the necessity of the M-form as a governance device and, as such, M-form implementation in Japan is likely to be more naturally associated with information processing needs. US M-forms may serve as a governance device to division managers, but market governance of the M-form creates asymmetries in favour of M-form top executives. Therefore, Japanese M-form firms would be likely to pursue diversification strategy in a more profit-maximizing way than the US M-form firms. Also, we suggest that M-form firms have advantages in managerial resources in Japan, while the US market provides at least equal managerial resource advantages for smaller U-form firms.

Therefore, in the US, M-form implementation may increase efficiency in managing diverse businesses due to governance advantage of division managers, but may lead to over-diversification (Markides 1992). Also, M-form implementation in the US may put firms in a less advantageous position in regard to managerial resources over time. Therefore, consistent with Baysinger and Hoskisson (1989) and Hoskisson and Hitt (1988), M-form implementation may increase short-term efficiency while sacrificing long-term efficiency in the USA. Also, managers of US M-form firms are concerned about developing skills that generalize to more than one firm, given the comparative increased possibility of employment gain at another firm or avoiding downside risk through employment separation in the current firm. On the other hand, our analysis suggests that in Japan M-form implementation may enable firms to hold competent managers who pursue asset-specific investment that contributes to competitive advantage. Furthermore, Japanese M-forms are likely to pursue more profitable diversification over time because of close governance by those who have stronger incentives for optimal monitoring. Therefore, it appears that in Japan M-form implementation enables firms to increase long-term as well as short-term efficiency. This is not to say that the Japanese system is without flaw. The following between-system comparison illustrates trade-offs associated with governance systems and managerial labour markets.

Financial System Comparisons

Japanese financial systems are much more centralized than their US counterparts. Comparatively speaking, in Japan, financial institutions such as banks play a dominant role in funding large firms, whereas in the USA individual investors play a dominant role in funding large firms. In Japan, Prowse (1992) reports that individuals hold 26.7 per cent of firm equity, while corporations hold 67.3 per cent. The reverse is the case in the USA: individuals hold 58.1 per cent and corporations hold 37.7 per cent. The implication is that large Japanese firms obtain financial resources from a much smaller number of sources than the US large firms. This centralization of sources of financial resources provides strong incentives in governing large firms. Therefore, as is suggested above, Japanese banks are more efficient in governing large firms than US shareholders.

Centralized financial systems like the Japanese systems, however, are not without limitations. A project is evaluated by a smaller number of sources of financial resources in centralized financial systems than in decentralized financial systems. Accordingly, a project has a lower chance of getting funded in a centralized than in a decentralized financial system because the project will be evaluated by more analysts in the decentralized system. In particular, an innovation-oriented project, which entails a high level of uncertainty by nature, would have a much lower chance of getting funded in centralized financial compared to decentralized financial systems (Sah 1991).

This problem, however, may be moderated by the longer time horizons facilitated by the Japanese financial system. Furthermore, this may not have posed a serious problem to date because the central issue regards the type of project that may receive funding in a more centralized system. Japanese firms, for instance, have emphasized the adaptation and improvement of existing technology rather than creation of new technology (Mansfield 1988). Also, Japanese firms have focused on process R & D, which tends to be less risky, than product R & D (Mansfield 1988). Therefore, Japanese innovation-oriented projects may entail a much lower level of uncertainty than the US innovation-oriented projects. However, as Japanese firms more frequently engage in projects for creation of new technology, the Japanese financial systems may become a hindrance. These kinds of systems represent over-governance in that activities which may create value are restricted as they appear (Kim and Hoskisson 1996) too risky to conservative controllers of capital.

Also, during the 1980s Japanese firms enjoyed an economic boom and thus corporate earnings were quite high. This success has created the opportunity for large diversified firms to attract capital in global capital markets. As such, many keiretsu firms have been lowering their borrowings from main bank firms (Kester 1991). This has reduced their dependence on main banks. Interestingly, the Japanese government has also been loosening its regulations on corporate bond markets (see Hoshi *et al.* 1990*a*: 108–14 for a review). Accordingly, large firms can loosen their ties to banks and more easily borrow from open markets. These recent developments may have significant implications for the functioning of Japanese firms. On the one hand, loosening main bank relations might decrease governance efficiency of main banks, and therefore allow managers to pursue strategies which are inconsistent with maximizing firm and other stakeholder efficiency. On the other hand, the emergence of corporate bond markets might help firms fund risky projects which banks are not willing to fund. Furthermore, because of banking deregulation Japanese banks have had to seek business in more diversified areas and from other (usually smaller) firms outside the keiretsus. Thus, in regard to short-term borrowing, main banks have been distanced somewhat from keiretsu partner firms. However, ownership patterns have been fairly stable over time and insurance companies that have been growing more strongly than banks have taken up the financial slack among keiretsu partners (Kester 1991). The trend towards a decrease in emphasis of bank relations has been reversed, however, with the recession. Banks are playing a stronger role in helping to restructure partner firms during the downturn. Furthermore, outside directors, usually bank officers, do not play a large role in firm affairs unless the firm encounters financial difficulty. Thus, banks are now playing their traditional role. However, banks appear to have significant problems of non-performing loans during the downturn in the economy. It is unclear, therefore, whether they will be able to handle crises at other troubled keiretsu firms. Future research should be directed at addressing the outcomes of these changes and the implications for corporate governance, M-form implementation, corporate diversification, and R & D activities.

Another difference between US and Japanese publicly traded firms is that there is more formal regulation of security markets in the US compared to Japan. Although the Japanese have regulatory bodies that mirror those in the US (e.g. the Security and Exchange Commission), the formal constraints are not strongly enforced except through informal constraints as indicated by the 1992 Japanese stock market scandal. Because the Japanese emphasize the informal constraints described above (Hill 1995), large shareholders within the industrial group may have asymmetric information relative to outside shareholders. If stock trades are made on this information, industrial group members have an advantage over outside shareholders. This type of 'insider trading' would tend to create a crisis of confidence and lead to excessive market volatility.

Furthermore, the co-operation within industrial groups may dampen product market competition. For instance, each industrial group follows a 'one-set principle' where the industrial group tries to have only one firm in each product area (Gerlach 1992). This means that other firms are less likely to diversify into the businesses of group member firms. Even though member firms are encouraged to compete with firms from different industrial groups in the same product market, the number of possible new entrants is restricted. Therefore, these informal governance constraints of industrial groups may have the same result as product market collusion. For instance, it is often cheaper to buy Japanese-made products in the USA than in Japan. Although these informal structures reduce monitoring failure relative to US firms, they are not without trade-offs. There is a need for comparative research to examine advantages and disadvantages of financial system differences.

Managerial Labour Markets Comparison

There are some US firms (e.g. Exxon), like large Japanese firms, which rely primarily on internal labour markets (e.g. internal promotion) for managerial resources. However, it would be difficult to establish internal labour markets which are not disrupted by external labour markets, as IBM and other large 'lifetime' employment firms which have had significant lay-offs are discovering. In the presence of active external labour markets, a high-performing US manager is more likely to find a better opportunity in another firm than a low-performing manager. Therefore, if a firm relies exclusively on the internal labour market for its managerial resources while other firms rely on external as well as internal labour markets, the firm would lose some above-average-performing managers but retain lower-performing managers. Although these disadvantages may, to a certain extent, be overcome by a positive organizational culture and higher pay, establishing a positive organizational culture is difficult and costly, especially where an external labour market bids up competitive salaries for high-performance individuals.

Furthermore, excessive reliance on internal labour markets in the USA is likely to result in increased managerial risk-aversion. As above-average managers move up in the hierarchy, such managers are likely to bid on positions in large, but low-business-risk divisions. Large and low-risk divisions reduce employment risk and increase compensation for the division manager. These businesses are usually the most prominent and may lead to the very top executive positions in the corporation. Thus, firm-specific investment would lead to implementation of a more conservative strategy as managers move up the career ladder. This may suggest that US firms that pursue internal labour markets become more risk-averse and, as such, innovation projects may be adversely affected. This line of argument is supported by research by Baysinger and Hoskisson (1989), Hoskisson and Hitt (1988), and Hoskisson and Johnson (1992), who found a negative relationship between diversification and R & D intensity. Wright (1988) also discusses alternative situations when less internalization (less diversification) becomes the more efficient strategy.

Although this same argument may apply to large Japanese firms, high-performing managers have less opportunity to leave. Large Japanese firms typically rely on internal labour markets for their managerial resources, although this is said to be changing in recent years. But because inter-firm mobility is discouraged, intra-firm mobility may encourage the development of firm-specific knowledge by Japanese managers (Hill 1995). In the presence of a strong external labour market, US managers may be more encouraged than Japanese managers to develop generalizable skills. Firm-specific knowledge enables managers not only to conceive of strategies exploiting firm heterogeneity (Barney 1986), but also to generate new applications from knowledge existing within the firm (Kodama 1992; Kogut and Zander 1992). However, excessive reliance on internal labour markets might reduce the firm's ability to learn from the environment (March 1991). Thus, although the Japanese system may allow for more within-system competitive advantage through firm-specific investments (Hill 1994), it is more closed to external ideas (Chaganti and Sambharya 1987).

Recently, large Japanese firms have hired non-entry-level managers from outside, although it is still the exception. Furthermore, as Japanese multinational corporations extend their reach into other countries, they are forced to hire local nationals to run foreign divisions. Even though the Japanese have emphasized centralized export strategies rather than direct foreign investment, global regionalization (trading blocks in Europe, North America, and Asia) may force more direct foreign investment and, therefore, more hiring of foreign nationals. Ultimately, this will require more openness to external labour markets because foreign nationals are unlikely to follow Japanese norms of lifetime employment within the same firm. Although the US may be the outlier on its emphasis on external labour markets, the trends towards international entry may change the Japanese system over time, making it more open to outside hiring. However, for now, Japanese M-form firms may have a distinct managerial resource advantage relative to US M-form firms because managers are encouraged to make firm-specific investments and it is difficult for high-performing managers to leave.

This is not to say that internal labour markets of Japanese firms are not without their problems. External labour markets in the USA exist for efficiency reasons. Internal labour markets may not be good at eliminating selection of poor-performing managers, especially under conditions of lifetime employment practices. Japanese firms depend on peer pressure to discourage shirking, while the external market for talent in the USA works to reallocate managerial talent. This, of course, encourages more development of generalizable skills as opposed to firm-specific skills among US managers. Thus, this still gives Japanese firms an advantage among M-form firms, especially co-operative M-forms, where firm-specific skills are more likely to be an asset.

6. Conclusion

In general, the M-form structure may be an organizational innovation that creates advantage for Japanese rather than US firms. Hoskisson *et al.* (1993) have recently suggested that governance is likely to have an impact on the relationship between structure and performance. Not only are some structures more efficient than others, but this relationship may be affected by governance devices. The scheme proposed above examines two critical areas where competition between alternative approaches to governance are proposed: financial systems and managerial labour markets. The central point is that governance may be a contributor to effective competition between firms. Thus, systems of governance that evolve in one country setting may provide a source of competitive advantage in comparison to governance in another country. Thus, this chapter is a call for more research which examines the comparative effects of governance on firms between countries. For example, this line of research may also be extended to making comparisons not only between US and Japanese firms, but also between these countries and large firms in Germany or Sweden and other firms in the European setting.

Such research may contribute significantly to understanding not only the restructuring that has been undertaken to revise strategies and structures in the USA (Hoskisson and Johnson 1992; Hoskisson and Turk 1990; Markides 1992) and elsewhere, but also restructuring of governance devices such as new ownership and capital structure arrangements. For instance, Jensen (1989) proposed that LBO associations may replace current governance arrangements in the USA. Furthermore, board reforms such as those proposed by Porter (1992) and participation on boards by institutional managers (pension and mutual funds) (Roe 1993) need serious consideration. These suggestions are often due to the increased concentration of ownership shares at pension and mutual fund institutions. Thus, the Japanese system may foreshadow increased management of governance devices among large US firms. This is not to suggest that the US can duplicate the Japanese governance system, but that the comparison will, at least, spark the search for new and better governance systems that facilitate comparative governance efficiency.

Managerial labour market differences may also have implications for success of organization structure. The relative attractiveness of an organizational structure in providing opportunities for career development may vary across different types of labour market. Therefore, it is conceivable that, given a type of labour market, a certain structure can attract and retain more competent managers, thereby creating a source of advantage attributable to human resources (Castinais and Helfat 1991). Following this logic, this chapter suggests the relative advantage and disadvantage of M-form structures against smaller U-form structures as a function of labour market types. In Japan, a high-potential manager would be likely to choose to work for an M-form firm rather than the comparable smaller U-form alternative. M-form firms provide more opportunities for experience and advancement because M-form structures in Japan have more fully developed internal labour markets. In the USA, like Japan, large M-form firms may be able to attract high-potential entry-level managers. However, because of the emphasis in the USA on external labour markets, top executives in smaller U-form firms may be able to send a stronger market signal than the comparable division executive in an M-form firm. In other words, over time M-form firms may lose competent managers to smaller U-form firms, while this is not likely in Japan.

These conclusions, however, must be subjected to empirical research. Whether or not the M-form innovation has created an advantage for Japanese firms and whether the M-form in the USA is an alternative governance device or a way to create wealth for US managers are important questions for future research.

REFERENCES

Alchian, A. A., and Demsetz, H. (1972), 'Production, Information Costs, and Economic Organization', *American Economic Review*, 62: 777–95.

Amit, R., and Livnat, J. (1988), 'Diversification Strategies, Business Cycles and Economic Performance', *Strategic Management Journal*, 9: 99–110.

Aoki, M. (1990), 'Toward an Economic Model of the Japanese Firm', *Journal of Economic Literature*, 28: 1–27.

Armour, H. O., and Teece, D. J. (1978), 'Organizational Structure and Economic Performance: A Test of the Multidivisional Hypothesis', *Bell Journal of Economics*, 9: 106–22.

Baker, G., Gibbs, M., and Holmstrom, B. (1994), 'The Internal Economics of the Firm: Evidence from Personnel Data', *Quarterly Journal of Economics*, 109: 881–919.

Barney, J. B. (1986), 'Strategic Factor Markets: Expectations, Luck, and Business Strategy', *Management Science*, 32: 1230–41.

Baysinger, B. D., and Hoskisson, R. E. (1989), 'Diversification Strategy and R & D Intensity in Large Multiproduct Firms', *Academy of Management Journal*, 32: 310–32.

—— Kosnik, R. D., and Turk, T. A. (1991), 'Effects of Board and Ownership Structure on Corporate R & D Strategy', *Academy of Management Journal*, 34: 205–14.

Black, B. S. (1992), 'Agents Watching Agents: The Promise of Institutional Investor Voice', *UCLA Law Review*, 39: 812–939.

Boyacigiller, N., and Adler, N. J. (1991), 'The Parochial Dinosaur: Organizational Science in a Global Context', *Academy of Management Review*, 16: 262–90.

Burgelman, R. A. (1983), 'A Model of the Interaction of Strategic Behavior, Corporate Context, and the Concept of Strategy', *Academy of Management Review*, 8: 61–70.

—— (1991), 'Intraorganizational Ecology of Strategy Making and Organizational Adaptation: Theory and Field Research', *Organization Science*, 2: 239–62.

Cable, J., and Yasuki, H. (1985), 'Internal Organisation, Business Groups and Corporate Performance: An Empirical Test of the Multidivisional Hypothesis in Japan', *International Journal of Industrial Organization*, 3: 401–20.

Cannella, A. A., and Best, A. (1993), *Executive Origin and Executive Turnover: An Examination of Officer-Director Tenure*, Working Paper, Texas A & M University, College Station.

Cannella, A. A., and Lubatkin, M. (1993), 'Succession as a Sociopolitical Process: Internal Impediments to Outsider Selection', *Academy of Management Journal*, forthcoming.

Castinais, R., and Helfat, C. (1991), 'Managerial Resources and Rents', *Journal of Management*, 17: 155–71.

Chaganti, R., and Sambharya, R. (1987), 'Strategic Orientation and Characteristics of Upper Management', *Strategic Management Journal*, 8: 393–401.

Chandler, A. D. (1962), *Strategy and Structure* (Cambridge, Mass.: MIT Press).

Channon, D. F. (1973), *The Strategy and Structure in British Enterprise* (New York: Macmillan).

Doeringer, P. B., and Piore, M. J. (1971), *Internal Labor Markets and Manpower Analysis* (Lexington, Mass.: Heath).

Dore, R. P. (1987), *Taking Japan Seriously* (Stanford, Calif.: Stanford University Press).

Dundas, K. N. M., and Richardson, P. R. (1982), 'Implementing the Unrelated Product Strategy', *Strategic Management Journal*, 3: 287–301.

Fama, E. F. (1980), 'Agency Problems and the Theory of the Firm', *Journal of Political Economy*, 88: 288–307.

—— and Jensen, M. C. (1983), 'Separation of Ownership and Control', *Journal of Law and Economics*, 26: 301–25.

Finkelstein, S., and Hambrick, D. C. (1989), 'Chief Executive Compensation: A Study of the Intersection of Markets and Political Processes', *Strategic Managment Journal*, 10: 121–34.

Gerlach, M. L. (1992), *Alliance Capitalism: The Social Organization of Japanese Business* (Berkeley: University of California Press).

Govindarajan, V., and Fisher, J. (1990), 'Strategy, Control Systems, and Resource Sharing: Effects on Business-Unit Performance', *Academy of Management Journal*, 33: 259–85.

Gupta, A. K., and Govindarajan, V. (1986), 'Resource Sharing among SBUs: Strategic Antecedents and Administrative Implications', *Academy of Management Journal*, 29: 695–714.

Hakansson, H., Johanson, J. (1993), 'The Network as a Governance Structure: Interfirm Cooperation beyond Markets and Hierarchies', in F. Grabher (ed.), *The Embedded Firm* (London: Routledge), 35–51.

Hill, C. W. L. (1985), 'Oliver Williamson and the M-Form Firm: A Critical Review', *Journal of Economic Issues*, 19 (Sept.), 731–51.

—— (1988), 'Internal Capital Market Controls and Financial Performance in Multidivisional Firms', *Journal of Industrial Economics*, 32: 197–212.

—— (1995), 'National Institutional Structures, Transaction Cost Economizing and Competitive Advantage: The Case of Japan', *Organization Science*, 6: 119–31.

—— and Hoskisson, R. E. (1987), 'Strategy and Structure in the Multiproduct Firm', *Academy of Management Review*, 12: 331–41.

—— and Snell, S. A. (1988), 'External Control, Corporate Strategy, and Firm Performance in Research-Intensive Industries', *Strategic Management Journal*, 9: 577–90.

—— —— (1989), 'Effects of Ownership and Control on Corporate Productivity', *Academy of Management Journal*, 32: 25–46.

—— Hitt, M. A., and Hoskisson, R. E. (1992), 'Cooperative versus Competitive Structures in Related and Unrelated Diversified Firms', *Organization Science*, 3: 501–21.

Horiuchi, A., Packer, F., and Fukuda, S. (1988), 'What Role has the "Main Bank" Played in Japan?', *Journal of the Japanese and International Economies*, 2: 159–80.

Hoshi, T., Kashyap, A., and Scharfstein, D. (1990a), 'Bank Monitoring and Investment: Evidence from the Changing Structure of Japanese Corporate Banking Relationships', in R. G. Hubbard (ed.), *Asymmetric Information, Corporate Finance, and Investment* (Chicago: University of Chicago Press), 105–26.

—— —— —— (1990*b*), 'The Role of Banks in Reducing the Costs of Financial Distress in Japan', *Journal of Financial Economics*, 27: 67–88.

—— —— —— (1991), 'Corporate Structure, Liquidity, and Investment: Evidence from Japanese Industrial Groups', *Quarterly Journal of Economics*, 106: 33–60.

Hoskisson, R. E. (1987), 'Multidivisional Structure and Performance: The Contingency of Diversification Strategy', *Academy of Management Journal*, 30: 625–44.

—— and Hitt, M. A. (1988), 'Strategic Control Systems and Relative R & D Investment in Large Multiproduct Firms', *Strategic Management Journal*, 9: 605–21.

—— and Johnson, R. A. (1992), 'Corporate Restructuring and Strategic Change: The Effect on Diversification Strategy and R & D Intensity', *Strategic Management Journal*, 13: 625–34.

—— and Turk, T. A. (1990), 'Corporate Restructuring: Governance and Control Limits of the Internal Market', *Academy of Management Review*, 15: 459–77.

—— Harrison, J. S., and Dubofsky, D. A. (1991), 'Capital Market Evaluation of M-Form Implementation and Diversification Strategy', *Strategic Management Journal*, 12: 271–9.

—— Hill, C. W. L., and Kim, H. (1993), 'The Multidivisional Structure: Organizational Fossil or Source of Value?', *Journal of Management*, 19: 269–98.

—— Johnson, R. A., and Moesel, D. D. (1994), 'Corporate Divestiture Intensity in Restructuring Firms: The Effects of Governance, Strategy and Performance', *Academy of Management Journal*, 37: 332–52.

Jensen, M. C. (1989), 'Eclipse of the Public Corporation', *Harvard Business Review*, 67/5: 61–74.

Jones, G. R., and Hill, C. W. L. (1988), 'Transaction Cost Analysis of Strategy-Structure Choice', *Strategic Management Journal*, 9: 159–72.

Kanemoto, Y., and MacLeod, W. B. (1991), 'The Theory of Contracts and Labor Practices in Japan and the United States', *Managerial and Decision Economics*, 12: 159–70.

Kester, W. C. (1991), *Japanese Takeovers: The Global Contest for Corporate Control* (Cambridge, Mass.: Harvard Business School).

Kim, H., and Hoskisson, R. E. (1996), 'Japanese Governance Systems: A Critical Review', in Benjamin Prasad (ed.), *Advances in International Comparative Management* (Greenwich, Conn., JAI Press), 165–89.

Kodama, F. (1992), 'Technology Fusion and the New R & D', *Harvard Business Review*, 70/4: 70–8.

Kogut, B., and Zander, U. (1992), 'Knowledge of the Firm, Combinative Capabilities, and the Replication of Technology', *Organization Science*, 3: 383–97.

Koike, K. (1988), *Understanding Industrial Relations in Modern Japan* (New York: St Martin's Press).

Lewellen, W. (1971), 'A Pure Financial Rationale for the Conglomerate Merger', *Journal of Finance*, 26: 521–37.

Lincoln, J. R. (1990), 'Japanese Organization and Organization Theory', in B. M. Staw and L. L. Cummings (eds.), *Research in Organizational Behavior* (Greenwich, Conn.: JAI Press), 255–94.

McMillan, C. J. (1985), *The Japanese Industrial System* (New York: Walter de Gruyter).

Maidique, M. A. (1980), 'Entrepreneurs, Champions, and Technological Innovation', *Sloan Management Review*, 21/2: 59–96.

Mansfield, E. (1988), 'Industrial R & D in Japan and the United States: A Comparative Study', *America Economic Review*, 78/2: 223–8.

March, J. G. (1991), 'Exploration and Exploitation in Organizational Learning', *Organization Science*, 2: 71–87.

Markides, C. C. (1992), 'Consequences of Corporate Refocusing: Ex ante Evidence', *Academy of Management Journal*, 35: 398–412.

Ouchi, W. G., and Jaeger, A. M. (1978), 'Type Z Organization: Stability in the Midst of Mobility', *Academy of Management Review*, 2: 305–14.

Pascale, R., and Rohlen, T. P. (1983), 'The Mazda Turnaround', *Journal of Japanese Studies*, 9: 219–63.

Porter, M. E. (1987), 'From Competitive Advantage to Corporate Strategy', *Harvard Business Review*, 65/3: 43–59.

—— (1992), 'Capital Disadvantages: America's Failing Capital Investment System', *Harvard Business Review*, 70/5: 65–82.

Pozen, R. C. (1994), 'Institutional Investors: The Reluctant Activists', *Harvard Business Review*, 72/1: 140–9.

Prowse, S. D. (1990), 'Institutional Investment Patterns and Corporate Financial Behavior in the United States and Japan', *Journal of Financial Economics*, 27: 43–66.

—— (1992), 'The Structure of Ownership in Japan', *Journal of Finance*, 47: 1121–40.

Quinn, D. P., and Rivoli, P. (1991), 'The Effects of American- and Japanese-Style Employment and Compensation Practices on Innovation', *Organization Science*, 2: 323–41.

Roe, M. J. (1990), 'Political and Legal Restraints on Ownership and Control of Public Companies', *Journal of Financial Economics*, 27: 7–41.

—— (1993), 'Mutual Funds in the Board Room', *Journal of Applied Corporate Finance*, 5/4: 56–61.

Russo, M. V. (1991), 'The Multidivisional Structure as an Enabling Device: A Longitudinal Study of Discretionary Cash as a Strategic Resource', *Academy of Management Journal*, 34: 718–33.

Sah, R. K. (1991), 'Fallibility in Human Organizations and Political Systems', *Journal of Economic Perspectives*, 5/2: 67–88.

Sheard, P. (1989), 'The Main Bank System and Corporate Monitoring and Control in Japan', *Journal of Economic Behavior and Organization*, 11: 399–422.

—— (1991), 'The Role of Firm Organization in the Adjustment of a Declining Industry in Japan: The Case of Aluminum', *Journal of the Japanese and International Economies*, 5: 14–40.

Shleifer, A., and Vishny, R. W. (1991), 'Takeovers in the 1960s and the 1980s: Evidence and Implications', *Strategic Management Journal*, 12: 51–9.

Spence, M. (1973), 'Job Market Signaling', *Quarterly Journal of Economics*, 83: 355–74.

Steer, P., and Cable, J. (1978), 'Internal Organization and Profit: An Empirical Analysis of Large UK Companies', *Journal of Industrial Economies*, 27: 13–30.

Suzuki, S., and Wright, R. W. (1985), 'Financial Structure and Bankruptcy Risk in Japanese Companies', *Journal of International Business Studies*, 16/1: 97–110.

Teece, D. J. (1981), 'Internal Organization and Economic Performance: An Empirical Analysis of the Profitability of Principal Firms', *Journal of Industrial Economies*, 30: 173–99.

Walsh, J. P., and Kosnik, R. (1993), 'Corporate Raiders and their Disciplinary Role in the Market for Corporate Control', *Academy of Management Journal*, 36: 671–700.

Williamson, O. E. (1975), *Markets and Hierarchies* (New York: Free Press).

—— (1985), *The Economic Institutions of Capitalism* (New York: Free Press).

Wright, M. (1988), 'Redrawing the Boundaries of the Firm', in S. Thompson and M. Wright (eds.), *Internal Organization, Efficiency and Profit* (Oxford: Philip Allan), 183–210.

Zenger, T. (1992), 'Why do Employers only Reward Extreme Performance? Examining the Relationships among Performance, Pay, and Turnover', *Administrative Science Quarterly*, 37: 198–219.

Zysman, J. (1983), *Governments, Markets, and Growth: Financial Systems and the Politics of Industrial Change* (Ithaca, NY: Cornell University Press).

9

CROSS-BORDER GOVERNANCE IN MULTINATIONAL ENTERPRISES

Peter J. Buckley

1. Introduction

The primary meaning of governance in the literature and in common parlance is that decision-takers (in the firm) must be accountable to someone for their actions. The problem arises from the separation of ownership from control in the modern (multinational) company. The structures which constrain managers' pursuit of self-interest at the expense of the true owners' (shareholders') interests are nowadays termed the 'governance structure' of the company. The accountability of managers to shareholders can be accomplished by a number of such means and the choices between these means are grist to the mill of those who study corporate governance.

Structures of governance are largely national. There are immense differences in the structures of governance between countries—even within economic blocs such as the European Union. Multinational firms, by definition, operate across these national governance structures and are, therefore, faced with problems of cross-border governance as a major consequence of international expansion.

This chapter analyses cross-border governance by examining the two meanings which analysts have given the term. The first meaning of governance is the conventional one outlined above, which concerns the control of managers by owners and which has been analysed by variants of principal–agent theory (following Jensen and Meckling 1976). The second meaning, more often utilized by international business theory, concerns the governance of economic transactions. This mode of analysis follows Williamson (1975, 1979, 1985) and Teece (1983) and relates closely to the internalization approach to the explanation of multinational enterprise (Buckley and Casson 1976, 1985; Buckley 1983, 1988, 1990) which builds on the pioneering work of Ronald Coase (1937) (see Blaine 1994 for an exposition). This chapter attempts to combine these approaches, and to point out the complementarities between them in a fuller explanation of cross-border governance.

There are, of course, many extra dimensions of governance when we consider cross-border issues. Overlapping regimes is only one additional issue. Multinational firms straddle all forms of system but also have internal governance issues—in particular the relationship between subsidiary managers and parent companies.

2. Governance Costs

If we begin with the notion of the firm as a set of relationships or a portfolio of contracts, it is easy to see that the particular configuration of contracts (the architecture of the firm, as Kay 1994 puts it) will be a major determinant of its success and of the nature of the firm (to echo the key sentiment of Coase's seminal 1937 article). The boundary of the firm is set by the point at which further internal relationship is more expensive than an external market-based relationship (Buckley and Casson 1976), thus the 'make or buy' decision is the determinant of the boundary of the firm. This feature, the internalization decision, has been well analysed in the analysis of the growth of the (multinational) firm. What has not been so well analysed is the precise configuration of the internal architecture of the firm, i.e. its governance structure (Buckley and Carter 1996a,b).

An attempt to show the power of these ideas was made by Teece (1983), who investigated technological and organizational factors as determining the scope of the firm through production costs. Teece's analysis of horizontal integration envisages governance costs and production costs as both being a function of an 'index of the complexity of know how' in the firm. Governance costs of different forms of doing business abroad (licensing versus foreign direct investment, FDI), are a function of the complexity of technology. The FDI mode is invariant to increasing complexity of knowledge because of the ease with which tacit knowledge can be transferred by internal markets. But the governance costs of licensing increase with the complexity of knowledge because of increasing costs of firm-to-firm transfer. A similar evaluation is made of the production costs in each mode, and then production costs and governance costs are summed to give total costs of the modes of doing business abroad so that an optimal scope of horizontal integration is given for each level of complexity of know-how. A similar exercise is conducted for vertical integration. Market-based relations are contrasted with vertically integrated relations by making their governance costs of market relations and vertical integration functions of an index of asset specificity where vertical integration has both a set-up cost (higher than setting up market relationships) and a lower variable cost of operation. As asset specificity increases, so does the possibility of integration.

In Teece's model (which has much in common with Buckley and Casson 1981), governance costs are a function of complexity of knowledge and asset specificity. There is also a (minor) international determinant of governance costs of integration—the risk of expropriation. The greater these risks, the more international governance costs will rise, favouring arm's length relationships (licensing, pur-chasing) rather than internal ones (FDI, integration).

Teece's analysis is interesting from our point of view in attempting to put gov-ernance costs centre-stage in the analysis of multinationals, but it does so only as an intermediate variable (the real drivers are complexity of (tacit) knowledge and asset specificity) and it has a weak international dimension. That governance costs and production costs are separable and additive also requires justification, at the least.

If we step back from Teece's exposition to Williamson's basic framework, we can first agree with Williamson's most recent work that markets and hierarchies are not a simple opposition, but may be more like extreme points on a continuum. Richardson (1972) made this point most cogently, arguing that firms are sur-rounded by a sea of co-operative relationships.

Williamson himself argues that 'governance structures—the institutional matrix within which transactions are negotiated and executed—vary with the nature of the transaction' (1979: 103). All transactions are not equal. Some may be endowed with social characteristics which others lack. Moreover, repeated trans-actions may take on a different character than one-off deals. This opens the pos-sibilities for a more rounded discussion of governance costs.

3. Governance and Internal Transaction Costs

Theoretical arguments on the internal organization of the firm suggest two polar extremes: the purist view of internalization expounded by Buckley and Casson (1976, 1985), in which the firm functions as an approximation to a perfect market, which can be contrasted with the 'markets and hierarchies' approach of Williamson (1975, 1979), which considers that integration (internalization) is accompanied by suspension of the price mechanism and the allocation of inter-nal resources by management fiat.

In the first of these approaches, the firm's internal organization is designed so as to transmit shadow prices to managers between decentralized cost centres and profit centres, so that the overall profits are maximized (Buckley 1983). Hennart (1986) has drawn parallels between this view and approaches to economic plan-ning (Heal 1973). Each decision-maker within the firm maximizes profits, given the internal prices; in effect the firm includes in these prices an optimal tax, leaving members with an income which is just enough to keep them in their present employment (Hirshleifer 1986).

In contrast, the markets and hierarchies approach takes the view that 'bounded rationality' and 'opportunism' mean either that it is impossible to find the 'correct' prices, even in an internalized market, or that individuals' response to price would result in damaging externalities for the rest of the organization. Hierarchy over-comes these problems by constraining actions through management directive rather than price signals, replacing the market by another mechanism and not merely internalizing it.

In practice, internal organization often lies between these two extremes. The actual internal organization of the firm is a response to three problems of organizational design: the *motivation problem* arising from decentralized information, the *co-ordination problem* arising from the complementarity between the actions of separate individuals, and the *maturation problem* arising from the pursuit of individual rather than shared goals. Buckley and Carter (1996*a,b*) use these problems to construct a classification of internal transaction costs.

These internal transaction costs are the result of derogation from the optimal set of actions, which only arise if:

1. all participants have access to the best decision-relevant knowledge (*perfect information*),
2. all complementary actions are chosen jointly (*perfect co-ordination*), and
3. all members of the firm share the firm's objective function (*perfect motivation*).

The following cost measures arise from departures from the optimal pay-off for the firm:

Information loss: the reduction in pay-off to the firm caused by members (managers) not having the best available information
Information cost: the cost of acquiring and transmitting information
Co-ordination loss: the reduction in pay-off to the firm arising when complementary actions are not chosen jointly
Co-ordination cost: the cost of communication about complementary actions or of providing for them to be combined
Motivation loss: the reduction in pay-off to the firm caused by members pursuing their own objectives
Motivation cost: the cost of incentive measures taken by the firm.

Motivation costs might include the cost of incentive schemes to align the actions of managers with the objectives of the firm, i.e. eliminating 'agency costs' through shadow pricing (Jensen and Meckling 1976), or the cost of supervision and monitoring of employees' actions or the cost of training and socializing designed to induce employees to adopt the firm's goods.

Information, co-ordination, and motivation losses are, in effect, internal 'externalities' arising from the division of managerial labour within the firm, and the associated costs measure the resources deployed in correcting the externalities. The goal of the firm's governance structure is to minimize the sum of these internal transaction costs.

4. Governance and Internal Transaction Costs in Multinational Firms

There are grounds for believing that organizational externalities and costs (information, co-ordination, and motivation), and therefore problems of governance, will be more severe in multinational firms than in uninational ones (Buckley and Carter 1996*a*,*b*). The simplest set of factors which increase the costs of communication and the exchange of ideas and knowledge is the spatial separation of individuals who hold complementary knowledge and who could gain from co-ordinating the actions. In a multinational firm, it is likely that spatially separated individuals have different first languages. Advances in technology and in education have played a large part in reducing these costs in recent years. The growth of electronic mail and video conferencing, together with the adoption of English as the world's business language, make it likely that international intra-office communications costs will converge with local costs. For example, English is the official language of the ABB group, even though only a third of its employees speak it as their mother language (*Economist* 1996).

Language may, however, be obscuring more fundamental differences between national outlooks and routines, which fundamentally influence communication and co-ordination. Hedlund and Nonaka (1993) examine the way in which information and knowledge are constructed in different cultures. They summarize common perceptions about the differences between Japanese and Western firms in terms of differences in the extent to which the firm's knowledge is 'tacit' or 'articulated' and the degree to which knowledge is held by individuals or groups. Western firms are characterized by individually held, articulated knowledge and Japanese firms by tacit knowledge held at the level of the group. More generally, there are numerous differences in the everyday assumptions (norms) which individuals make about the actions of others in a given situation, about the standards of acceptable behaviour and the interpretation of tacit signals, such as body language, which play a major part in the successful co-ordination of the actions of groups. These differences in routines may in themselves imply differences in performance of some kinds of task (cf. Buckley and Casson 1992: 228–31), but where related tasks are to be carried out by individuals who hold different social and cultural assumptions, the dangers of misunderstanding and misinformation may detract significantly from the joint effectiveness of the collaboration, unless considerable time is spent in developing mutual understanding.

It may be particularly difficult to motivate individuals in different countries diligently to pursue the interests of the organization as a whole. In the conventional economic arguments on moral hazard and adverse selection in organizations, the monitoring problem is exacerbated by the geographic and cultural distance involved in multinational operations. The risks of opportunism may therefore be higher and the costs of counter-measures may be higher, too. In cultures which do not conform to the individualist stereotype, individuals may identify with a group or community, within which they behave altruistically, or with the shared interest of the community in mind. Thus, it may be expected (or suspected) that individuals will favour the perceived interests of their national subsidiary rather than the overall interests of the firm.

5. Governance in International Business Theory

A large part of micro- (firm-) level international business theory has concerned the foreign market servicing decisions of multinational firms. Crudely put, this concerns the choices which firms make between exporting, foreign licensing of technology (or rights), and foreign direct investment. The key elements determining this decision can be resolved into two: the location decision and the internalization (or externalization) decision. Thus exporting is foreign-located, internally controlled, licensing is foreign-located, market-determined (externally controlled), and FDI is foreign-located, internally controlled. The governance decision (represented crudely by internal versus market transfer) is a key element in this analysis.

However, this crude picture becomes more complex—and more interesting—when we move to a consideration of intermediate forms: alliances and joint ventures. It is in the analysis of alliances and joint ventures where issues of governance are central. Alliances (usually meaning an alliance between two established multinational firms to do business globally, in third countries or within one 'trading bloc') and joint ventures (most often used to denote a venture between a foreign multinational and a host country entity to do business, initially at least, in the host country or in its trading bloc) involve some notion of shared governance. Shared internationally, moreover, key issues then become the nature of co-operation and the cultural influences on governance.

Buckley and Casson (1988) define co-operation as 'coordination effected through mutual forbearance' (p. 32). This leads to the notion that the operation of a joint venture is a repeated game in which the partners move towards a *modus operandi* where each forbears from damaging the interests of the other. Over time, mutual goals can be achieved by the operation of this mechanism and a second-order condition comes into being where co-operation becomes an end in itself. The partners can then begin to build a reputation for co-operative behaviour and, as with any other asset, this reputation can yield returns of its own.

Mutual forbearance generates trust between the partners and trust has an economic value in that it substitutes for monitoring costs making governance less expensive. Thus a link is established between the social concept of trust and the economic concept transaction costs. Governance costs in the presence of trust will be lower. Thus we have an alternative scenario to the principal–agent model. Rather than engineering incentives to engender action in accord with the wishes of the principal, trust between the two can be a (less costly) substitute.

6. The Cultural Dimension

Hofstede's studies (1980) have shown that even in a multinational with a strong company culture (IBM was the key example), national differences between (workers and) managers can have strong manifestations. This can potentially give an extra dimension to the principal–agent problems where the principal (the headquarters company) and the agent (the subsidiary management) have a very different cultural orientation. This can entail extra costs of global governance.

As well as this internal dimension, the external societal and institutional structures which multinational firms encounter differ greatly across nations and continents. These two issues are not additive, however. The use of local subsidiary management can help to offset 'costs of foreignness' because of their understanding of local institutions and markets.

Of particular importance in this context are lesser forms of association between companies (and other local institutions) including networks such as kieretsu structures in Japan and throughout Asia in different guises. Such associations have a social as well as an economic dimension. They may be regarded as alternative forms of governance (Blaine 1994; Johanson and Mattson 1987; Hakansson and Johanson 1993) or as major variations on the theme of co-operative relationships between companies.

The legal system reflects and supports the institutional culture at national level. This has ramifications from determining the mode of entry of multinationals (preventing wholly owned subsidiaries in favour of joint ventures, excluding imports (except of technology), etc.) through to setting standards of corporate behaviour which may differ from those of the host country. Codes of corporate governance, such as those set by the Cadbury Committee in the UK, are invariably national codes, even within the European Union, and awareness and compliance with these codes have non-trivial costs.

Wider notions than legal regulations need to be invoked. Norms of behaviour—expectation, public opinion, unwritten rules—need to be respected by multinational firms even more so than local ones that do not have the stigma of foreignness. An important example of this issue can be seen in the contrasting attitudes to exchanges of personnel between government (political) service and business. In Britain, a set of rules is being enacted, following the Nolan Committee's recommendations, to inhibit (if not prevent) the transfer of recently retired government ministers to private sector boardrooms. In Japan, the transfer of ex-politicians and particularly civil servants to the private sector is known as *amukadari* (descent from heaven) and is often held by commentators to account, at least in part, for the unity of view and of purpose between government policy and business strategy.

Many commentators have divided systems of corporate governance between market-based systems and bank-based systems (e.g. numerous chapters in Dimsdale and Prevezer 1994). The market-based systems of Britain and the USA are often contrasted with the bank-based systems of Germany and Japan. Frequently, the bank-based system is held to be superior because of the superior recent economic performance of its representative country cases. In a market-dominated system, titles can be traded without the ownership right being exercised. It is argued that the bank-based system enforces the accountability of managers to shareholders on long-term basis because of the closer co-operation between the suppliers of capital (the banks) and the users of capital. This caricature has been clouded recently by recent Japanese bank crises, which have caused doubts to emerge about the efficacy of the system. In theory at least, stock markets allow managerial failure to be corrected through markets for corporate control.

Multinational firms straddle both 'systems'. To some degree this is an opportunity because it enables them to access a wide variety of (local) financing. It also imposes adjustment costs. In a sense, multinational firms operate both systems as a matter of course.

7. Governance in Multinational Firms

Adam Smith felt that there was serious doubt about the ability of managers of joint stock companies to behave efficiently and reliably . . . particularly managing foreign ventures! Smith puts the principal–agent problems firmly at the forefront of the difficulties of managing a joint-stock company.

The trade of a joint stock company is always managed by a court of directors. This court, indeed, is frequently subject, in many respects, to the control of a general count of proprietors. But the greater part of those proprietors seldom pretend to understand anything of the business of the company, and when the spirit of faction happens not to prevail among them, give themselves contentedly such half yearly or yearly dividend, as the directors think proper to make to them. This total exemption from trouble and from risk, beyond a limited sum, encourages many people to become adventurers in joint stock companies, who would, upon no account, hazard their fortunes in any private copartnery! (Smith 1776/1976: ii. 264).

This problem is compounded when large joint-stock companies venture into foreign lands.

The directors of such companies, however, being the managers rather of other people's money than of their own, it cannot well be expected, that they should watch over it with the same anxious vigilance with which the partners in a private copartnery frequently watch over their own. Like the stewards of a rich man, they are apt to consider attention to small matters as not for their master's honour, and very easily give themselves a dispensation from having it. Negligence and profusion, therefore, must always prevail, more or less, in the management of the affairs of such a company. It is upon this account that joint stock companies for foreign trade have seldom been able to maintain the competition against private adventurers. They have, accordingly, very seldom succeeded without an exclusive privilege, and frequently have not succeeded with one. Without an exclusive privilege they have commonly mismanaged the trade. With an exclusive privilege they have both mismanaged and confined it. (Smith 1776/1976: ii. 264–5)[1]

---

[1] Part of this section is quoted by Leslie Hannah (1976: 19–20), whose book on the rise of the corporate economy can be read as a business history of corporate governance.

Far from regarding multinationality as a problem for the governance of firms, many modern commentators see it as an advantage. Kogut (1983) sees sequential internationalization as conferring dynamic benefits on multinational firms. Whilst it is true that experience in international operations lowers governance costs relative to an inexperienced foreign investor, it is not self-evident that governance costs will be lower than a purely local (or uninational) firm. Indeed, this is in opposition to the Hymer postulate (1976) that the costs of doing business abroad are positive and that firms require a compensating advantage in order to be able to compete with locals. It seems reasonable to conclude that the extra costs of cross-border governance will be positive but will be a declining function of time and geographical spread. There will be exceptions to this, however, particularly for idiosyncratic markets, unusually large foreign markets, and ones with large cultural entry and operational barriers.

8. Organizational Responses of Multinational Firms to Problems of Governance

There has been no shortage of organizational prescriptions for solving the problems of governance in multinational firms. Buckley and Casson (1992) discuss several responses: divisionalization, matrix structures, and strategic business units and joint ventures.

The divisional (M-form) organization makes use of local information in decision-making by devolving operating decisions to specialist divisions, co-ordinates the application of shared assets via the head office, and motivates divisional managers through their profit contributions in the firm's internal capital market (see Williamson 1975, ch. 8). The process of internationalization often results either in national divisions, where divisions duplicate marketing and sometimes production, or in product division, where several divisions operate within the same territory. Both forms of divisionalization leave residual opportunities for sharing common resources and knowledge, and the matrix approach is an attempt to provide cross-cutting channels of information exchange and co-ordination of activities. However, these channels are often a cumbersome way of dealing with information, for they can be bureaucratic and excessively hierarchical in character, and they complicate managerial motivation, for 'no man can serve two masters'. Divided loyalties can result in losses of motivation, and the cost of information and co-ordination can result in the heavy overheads of a large head office.

The strategic business unit can be seen as a development of the full matrix structure and it has been termed the 'weak matrix' (Lorange 1993). Selected linkages (e.g. country and product) are combined into identified 'business element' teams charged with achieving specified targets where an opportunity has been identified for capitalizing or improving the combination of knowledge and co-ordinating action. Team performance targets can provide clear motivation for team members. However, competition between groups can reduce the beneficial sharing of complementary knowledge and resources, particularly as the business unit leaders are often engaged on a 'managerial' promotion track which encourages them to focus on group performance rather than the fullest possible exploitation of technology (Buckley and Casson 1988).

Networks of joint ventures and alliances are often claimed to have advantages of increased flexibility and decentralization of authority, but these are not always evident in practice. A key advantage of joint venture networks is that individual elements of the firm can be free to choose appropriate collaborations and can, if they wish, participate in several joint ventures (Buckley and Casson 1995). Knowledge can be exploited in the way that its holders choose, and the motivation for success comes from the holders' returns on their portfolio of joint ventures. However, the value of joint ventures is contingent upon the circumstances of the partners, and the risk that they will prove short-lived has often resulted in reduced trust between the partners and less than complete disclosure of the information that the venture is established to share (Buckley and Casson 1988, 1992).

9. Conclusion

The problems of cross-border governance are the analogue of the costs of internalizing a market across national boundaries. There are four categories of such costs: the resource costs of managing internal markets, the extra communication costs involved, the higher management costs, and the specifically international element stemming from (potential) discrimination against foreign owned firms (Buckley and Casson 1976). Although only the final cost is specifically international, differences in culture and language and problems of distance are likely to mean that the internalization of markets across international boundaries (costs of cross-border governance) are likely to be greater than purely domestic internalization.

There are undoubtedly learning effects which reduce the cost of cross-border governance both over time and in repeated international ventures. It is not, however, possible to claim that cross-border governance costs ever fall to zero (or below zero).

REFERENCES

Blaine, Michael (1994), *Cooperation in International Business: The Use of Limited Equity Arrangements* (Aldershot: Avebury).

Buckley, Peter J. (1983), 'New Theories of International Business: Some Unresolved Issues', in Mark Casein (ed.), *The Growth of International Business* (London: George Allen & Unwin).

—— (1988), 'The Limits of Explanation: Testing the Internalisation Theory of the Multinational Enterprise', *Journal of International Business Studies*, 19: 181–93.

—— (1990), 'Problems and Developments in the Core Theory of International Business', *Journal of International Business Studies*, 21: 657–65.

—— and Carter, Martin J. (1996a), 'The Economics of Business Process Design: Maturation, Information and Co-ordination within the Firm', *International Journal of the Economics of Business* (forthcoming).

—— —— (1996b), 'The Economics of Business Process Design in Multinational Firms', in Ram Mudambi and Martin Ricketts (eds.), *The Organisation of the Firm: International Business Perspectives* (London: Routledge, forthcoming).

—— and Casson, Mark (1976), *The Future of the Multinational Enterprise* (London: Macmillan).

—— —— (1981), 'The Optimal Timing of a Foreign Direct Investment', *Economic Journal*, 92: 75–87.

—— —— (1985), *The Economic Theory of the Multinational Enterprise* (London: Macmillan).

—— —— (1988), 'A Theory of Cooperation in International Business', in Farok J. Contractos and Peter Lorange (eds.), *Cooperative Strategies in International Business* (Lexington, Mass.: Lexington Books).

—— —— (1992), 'Organising for Innovation: The Multinational Enterprise in the Twenty-First Century', in Peter J. Buckley and Mark Casson (eds.), *The Multinational Enterprise in the World Economy: Essays in Honour of John H. Dunning* (Cheltenham: Edward Elgar).

—— —— (1995), 'An Economic Model of International Joint Ventures', Centre for International Business, University of Leeds (CIBUL), mimeo.

Chandler, Alfred D., Jr. (1962), *Strategy and Structure: Chapters in the History of the American Industrial Enterprise* (Cambridge, Mass.: MIT Press).

—— (1977), *The Visible Hand: The Managerial Revolution in American Business* (Cambridge, Mass.: Belknap Press).

—— and Herman Daems (eds.) (1980), *Managerial Hierarchies: Comparative Perspectives on the Rise of the Modern Industrial Enterprise* (Cambridge, Mass.: Harvard University Press).

Coase, Ronald H. (1937), 'The Nature of the Firm', *Economica*, 4: 386–405.

Dimsdale, Nicholas, and Prevezer, Martha (eds.) (1994), *Capital Markets and Corporate Governance* (Oxford: Oxford University Press).

Economist (1996), 'The ABB of Management', 6 Jan. 1996, 64.

Hakanson, Hakan, and Johanson, Jan (1993), 'The Network as a Governance Structure: Interform Cooperation beyond Markets and Hierarchies', in G. Brabher (ed.), *The Embedded Firm: On the Socioeconomics of Industrial Networks* (London: Routledge).

Hannah, Leslie (1976), *The Rise of the Corporate Economy* (London: Methuen).

Heal, Geoffrey M. (1973), *The Theory of Economic Planning* (Amsterdam: North-Holland).

Hedlund, Gunnar, and Nonaka, Ikujiro (1993), 'Models of Knowledge Management in the West and Japan', in Peter Lorange, Bela Chakravarthy, Johan Roos, and Andrew Van der Ven (eds.), *Implementing Strategic Processes: Change Learning and Cooperation* (Oxford: Blackwell).

Hennart, Jean-François (1986), 'What is Internalisation?', *Weltwirtschaftliches Archiv*, 122: 791–804.

Hirshleifer, Jack (1986), 'On the Economics of Transfer Pricing', *Journal of Business*, 29: 172–84.

Hofstede, Geert (1980), *Culture's Consequences: International Differences in Work Related Values* (London: Sage).

Hymer, Stephen H. (1976), *The International Operations of National Firms* (Cambridge, Mass.: MIT Press).

Jensen, Michael, and Meckling, William (1976), 'Theory of the Firm, Managerial Behavior, Agency Costs, and Ownership Structure', *Journal of Financial Economics*, 3: 305–60.

Johanson, Jan, and Mattson, Lars-Gunnar (1987), 'Interorganizational Relations in Industrial Systems: A Network Approach Compared with the Transactions-Cost Approach', *International Studies of Management and Organization*, 17: 34–48.

Kay, John (1994), 'Corporate Strategy and Corporate Accountability', in Dimsdale and Prevezer (1994).

Kogut, Bruce (1983), 'Foreign Direct Investment as a Sequential Process', in C. P. Kindleberger and D. Audretsch (eds.), *The Multinational Cooperation in the 1980s* (Cambridge, Mass.: MIT Press).

Lorange, Peter (1993), *Strategic Planning and Control: Issues in the Strategy Process* (Oxford: Blackwell).

Richardson, G. B. (1972), 'The Organisation of Industry', *Economic Journal* (Sept.), 883–96.

Smith, Adam (1776), *An Inquiry into the Nature and Causes of the Wealth of Nations*, ed. Edwin Cannan (Chicago: University of Chicago Press, 1976).

Teece, David (1983), 'Technological and Organisational Factors in the Theory of the Multinational Enterprise', in Mark Casson (ed.), *The Growth of International Business* (London: George Allen & Unwin).

Williamson, Oliver E. (1975), *Markets and Hierarchies* (New York: Free Press).

—— (1979), 'Transaction Cost Economics: The Governance of Contractual Relations', *Journal of Law and Economics*, 22: 223–61.

—— (1985), *The Economic Institution of Capitalism* (New York: Free Press).

10

CORPORATE GOVERNANCE IN CENTRAL AND EASTERN EUROPE

Mike Wright, Igor Filatotchev, and Trevor Buck

1. Introduction

Extensive privatization has now been undertaken across many countries of Central and Eastern Europe (CEE). Political factors have often played a major role in both the pace and the form of privatization adopted in a particular country. These political influences have meant that the importance attached to the establishment of corporate governance mechanisms in privatized enterprises has varied considerably. The need for political acceptability of privatization has often meant that greater emphasis has been placed on the need for accountability and/or speed in the sale process. In Hungary, for example, the so-called self-privatization process was introduced as a means of achieving rapid but regulated privatization after the political problems raised by abuses seen in earlier programmes (Karsai and Wright 1994). In Russia, the voucher privatization programme was introduced as a means of effecting rapid privatization which would involve widely based individual ownership of firms (Boycko *et al.* 1993).

As the process of transformation has become more advanced, the emphasis of policy is beginning to shift. In particular, increasing attention begins to focus on the issue of ensuring enhanced enterprise efficiency, though of course political factors may still place severe constraints on actions designed to deal with this problem. This changing emphasis brings consideration of corporate governance issues to the fore.

The development of appropriate corporate governance mechanisms in CEE is distinguished from the economies of the West by the initial complete absence of the necessary prerequisites of an appropriate legal infrastructure and financial institutions in an environment where incumbent management and employees have entrenched rights within enterprises. Legislation has had to be enacted which for the first time introduces Western-style property rights, financial reporting requirements, and bankruptcy laws. While this legislation is now generally in place throughout much of CEE, the effectiveness of its enforcement varies between countries and the associated institutions remain to be developed. For example, in countries of CEE where privatization has relied heavily on the establishment of investment funds, there have been problems in making these operational and effective. At the same time, social justice arguments have frequently meant that incumbents generally have acquired substantial equity stakes on privatization in the enterprises in which they are employed. Given these conditions and the changing emphasis towards seeking efficiency improvements in enterprises, the governance problem in CEE becomes one of identifying how one might move towards a structure which will better enable efficiency benefits to be delivered.

The aim of this chapter is to discuss the nature of governance problems in CEE and to analyse the potential for the various elements of a corporate governance framework to resolve these difficulties. Given the heterogeneity of countries and governance problems in CEE, the approach adopted is based on the issues involved with examples of experience in particular countries being introduced as appropriate. The following section discusses the nature of privatization objectives in CEE which has generally meant that governance mechanisms geared to generating efficiency benefits have not been introduced at the time of transfer to the private sector. Section 3 outlines the nature of corporate governance in the various types of approach to privatization adopted in CEE. The fourth section discusses in turn the role of the various parties available in principle to undertake corporate governance. The fifth section presents some conclusions.

2. Corporate Governance and Privatization Objectives

Differing approaches to privatization across CEE have major implications for the nature of governance structures introduced on privatization. Essentially, the three principal objectives of privatization in CEE concern the speed with which it takes place, the need for acceptability and accountability in the process (which includes political acceptability and impact on the state budget), and the impact on efficiency. These objectives may be partly complementary in that privatized enterprises which generate efficiency gains will make greater contributions to the state budget in the long run. However, there may also be conflicts where the objective of rapid privatization necessitates disposals at minimal prices and involves governance structures which yield low-efficiency gains. For privatization policy to be implemented successfully, there is a need to balance the three objectives of accountability, speed, and efficiency (Fig. 10.1). These conflicts, which have been addressed in the West (e.g. Kay and Thompson 1986), are writ large in the context of the privatization of state enterprises in CEE.

Early experience of unregulated ('spontaneous') privatization by several countries in the region raised arguments concerning the need for some form of regulation to deal with abuses arising from incumbent management obtaining state-owned assets under highly advantageous conditions. In a number of countries privatization programmes became strictly regulated, aiming for high levels

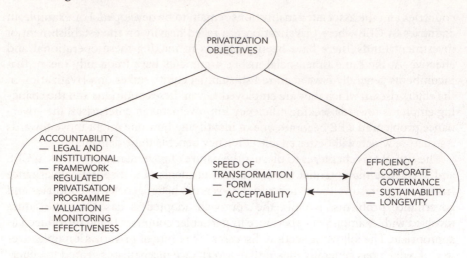

Fig. 10.1. Interaction of privatization objectives

of perceived fairness. The result was that the formal privatization process was effectively brought to a halt, although managers still had scope to dissipate state assets. The nature of the abuses which may arise is illustrated in an early stage in transformation in the case of Apisz in Hungary (Pasztor 1991), and continues to be illustrated as other countries begin to undergo the transition process (see e.g. the case of Ukraine as discussed by Kushnirsky 1994).

This need for accountability is linked to ethical issues of justice and fairness. In CEE this entails perceived fairness in the distribution of initial ownership not only within the enterprise but also between enterprises and the wider society. Otherwise, employees who happen to be in profitable enterprises will receive windfall gains whilst those in loss-making enterprises will receive losses, which in turn may have adverse consequences for the acceptability and eventual speed of privatization programmes (Filatotchev *et al.* 1994).

These issues suggest that a system of accountability may need to make trade-offs between ethical and wider efficiency issues. In general, a system of accountability requires there to be clearly defined objectives, a body to whom enterprise managers and privatization officials are accountable, and an appropriate legal and regulatory framework. In CEE this framework may be incomplete, raising issues concerning the extent to which some element of accountability is to be achieved whilst allowing privatization to proceed in order to meet other objectives (see Wright *et al.* 1994*b* for a discussion of approaches to centralized and decentralized regulation of the privatization process).

As countries move beyond the problems involved in actually transferring assets to the private sector, efficiency issues become more important. The following sections examine the role of corporate governance in meeting post-privatization attempts to increase efficiency.

Table 10.1. Alternative privatization approaches and governance I: governance elements

Type of privatization	Governance by individual shareholders	Governance by financial institutions and industrial partners	Indirect governance (through share sales)
Absentee Shareholders:			
trade sale	Medium	Medium	Quite high
flotation	Low to medium	Low to medium	High
Mass voucher schemes (without mutual funds or institutional shareholders)	Insignificant	Insignificant	High if shares immediately tradable
Holding company/ mutual fund voucher schemes	Low	High, if capable institutional managers available	Low in long term

3. Corporate Governance and Differing Privatization Approaches in Central and Eastern Europe

The important elements of a governance framework are discussed in detail in Chapter 1. An important issue concerns the comparative strength of voice and exit in the governance process. In CEE governance problems in privatized firms may be widespread, given the general absence of financial institutions with sufficient expertise to undertake close monitoring, the importance of wider employee share ownership, and the importance of buy-outs with a 'give-away' element which means reduced pressure to meet financing commitments, greater likelihood of managerial entrenchment behaviour, problems of diffuse ownership, and actions to meet the short-term objectives of employees.

The relative strengths of corporate governance in the various types of privatization observed in CEE are summarized in Tables 10.1 and 10.2, which highlight the importance of voice and exit governance mechanisms. Given the general absence of external monitoring, of the ability to exit through share sales in a situation of weak stock markets and markets for corporate control, of weak product market competition and bankruptcy laws,[1] corporate governance is likely at least in the short term to rely heavily on the voice of insiders. This means that the employee and management buy-outs listed in Table 10.2 have often been used in CEE privatizations in contrast with the more conventional Western privatization vehicles considered in Table 10.1. Nevertheless, the governance characteristics of management and employee buy-outs in Table 10.2 can be expected to vary with the circumstances. It may be expected that corporate governance will be weaker the more privatizations are of the 'give-away' type and the wider is employee

[1] While in theory it may be preferable to introduce and implement a full panoply of market-oriented institutional and regulatory frameworks which promote product market competition and enforce hard budget constraints through bankruptcy, in practice there are likely to be political constraints which make this unfeasible until a later stage in the transformation process has been reached (see Filatotchev *et al.* 1995*b* for discussion).

Table 10.2. Alternative privatization approaches and governance II: incumbents (buy-outs)

	Governance by individual shareholders	Governance by financial institutions or industrial partners
'CONVENTIONAL' buy-outs (shares bought out of individual savings or 'hard' credit)		
MBO	High. Managers motivated by job preservation, share of profits, and fear of losses to 'voice' effective control, *but* • free riding within management teams? • little opportunity to sell shares, except through internal market?	High in principle where financial institutions impose vertical control. Individual managers must repay 'hard' credit. In the region such control may be absent because of undeveloped financial system
EBO	Quite high. Employees voice effective control, *but* • free riding throughtout work-force? • little opportunity to sell shares	As above
'GIVE-AWAY' privatizations (shares acquired through privatization vouchers and, where appropriate, enterprise funds and personal savings)		
MBO	Quite low. Managers gain from job preservation and enterprise profits, but no personal financial sacrifice through ownership of shares if enterprise makes losses	Quite low as absence of commitment to meet loans taken on to finance the acquisition, except where incumbents have undertaken personal borrowings to acquire shares for cash. Though external investors may be present, their governance role is generally weak, at least in the earlier post-privatization environment
EBO	Quite low. Free rider issues will exacerbate the problems with 'give-away' MBOs; see above	Low, as above

Note: MBO = management buy-out; EBO = employee buy-out.

ownership. The rationale for this view is developed further below. However, before analysing the potential contribution of the various elements of corporate governance mechanisms to contribute voice to the monitoring process, the following section presents some evidence on the extent and nature of governance in privatized enterprises in CEE.

It is important to be aware that the nature of privatization in CEE varies considerably between and in some cases within countries, reflecting the relative importance of the privatization objectives identified earlier, which in turn are conditioned by political and economic contexts (see e.g. Frydman *et al.* 1993 and Estrin 1994 for outlines of varying privatization programmes). This section and the next provide a flavour of the variety of types and the governance issues they raise, but with an emphasis on the issues which may be raised in attempting to enhance governance in companies which are privatized as independent entities, and especially the widespread cases in CEE where insiders hold significant equity stakes.

In Hungary, there are indications that management- and employee-owned groups chiefly had to share ownership with the State Property Agency (the Hungarian state holding company), local governments, commercial banks, and, on occasion, with outside investors who retained a very small ownership proportion generally left over from the period of transformation. In most cases, the only significant minority shareholder was the SPA, mainly due to the requirement that a proportion of shares be set aside for holders of compensation certificates. A survey by the SPA of sixty-four buy-outs effected using employee share ownership plans (ESOPs) shows that the average holding by the ESOP being 56.1 per cent (SPA 1994). The remaining ownership stakes comprised the SPA (24.5 per cent on average), municipalities (6.7 per cent), companies (5.5 per cent), and other Hungarian owners (7.3 per cent). In contrast the average ownership proportion held by employees within all firms privatized by the SPA up to August 1993 was 3.4 per cent, although the introduction of ESOPs meant that more recent transactions had much higher employee stakes. Banks providing finance have typically rarely taken equity stakes, and when they have, their shareholdings have generally been modest. Ownership involvement by a foreign firm has often concerned cases where the foreign partner had taken part in the initial transformation of the company. Whilst there has been wider employee ownership, shareholdings have tended to be concentrated amongst management, since the rules for share subscriptions tend to weight ownership towards managers and long-serving employees through a system of points reflecting the number of years at the company, position, and salary, or simply the amount of money that management is willing and able to invest. Evidence also indicates that the ability of employee shareholders in buy-outs involving ESOPs to engage directly in governance was constrained since supervisory and ESOP management bodies were typically dominated by the firm's managers. Evidence from detailed case-studies of seventeen Hungarian buy-outs (Karsai and Wright 1994) shows that, though employees as a group often had significant equity stakes, management played the dominant role. A relatively small group of between fifteen and twenty-five managers frequently acquired a majority stake or one in excess of 25 per cent, ensuring a power of veto, sometimes reinforced by special regulations on voting rights. Employee-owners were typically, because of their low and diffuse equity stakes together with lack of expertise, unable to exercise an effective supervisory role. The banks, which provided finance to most of these companies, also preferred management to occupy a dominant position as a condition of extending the loan. Employment was known to have increased in only one enterprise. In the seven cases where redundancies occurred, the reduction in employment varied between 10 per cent and 31 per cent.

The focus of employees' attention was on receiving higher wages and keeping their jobs, but as the firms generally had substantial debts, employees generally accepted relatively low wage increases. Recognizing the role of employees at the time of privatization, management tended to refrain as long as possible from taking reorganization steps which would result in resistance from employees. There was little evidence of significant capital investment. In only four of the seventeen cases could investment expenditure be classified as significant.

In respect of post-privatization governance in Poland, there is evidence that the ownership structure of leased firms becomes more concentrated with time, mainly in the hands of outsiders but also in the hands of managers, who often buy shares from employees. However, the tradability of shares is usually limited. In eighteen enterprises monitored by Dabrowski *et al.* (1993), the founders and employees had priority in buying shares and the sale to outsiders had to be accepted by management, supervisory boards, etc. Nevertheless, this monitoring of a group of enterprises observed some increase in the extent of share trading over time, primarily because of the termination of employment, with outside investors becoming more involved. According to another survey of 142 enterprises (cited in Filatotchev *et al.* 1996*a*) up to December 1992, 13.5 per cent of all shares changed owner. Generally, the increasing share of outside investors and that of managers indicate that constraints on the tradability of shares are being progressively eased.

Interesting evidence on post-privatization changes in Poland is available from a survey completed in June 1993 of 110 of the 200 enterprises established prior to the end of 1991 which had subsequently leased the assets of previously state owned enterprises (see Jarosz 1994*a,b* for full details). This evidence shows that, as compared with the period before privatization (i.e. beginning of 1990), employment by June 1993 had been reduced significantly. In 21 per cent of companies employment was more than halved, in 40 per cent of companies it fell by more than 31 per cent and less than 50 per cent, and in only 9 per cent of companies it increased. Moreover, reductions in employment in lease buy-outs exceeded that for the economy as a whole. Between January 1992 and June 1993 employment in the Polish economy fell by 6.93 per cent, whereas in lease buy-outs it fell by 10.91 per cent (Jarosz 1994*a,b*). The study also shows that from the end of 1991 real wages in leased enterprises first rose by 4.6 per cent and then fell to 10 per cent below the starting level by the first half of 1993. In contrast, the enterprise sector as a whole saw real wages initially increase by 18.1 per cent before falling to finish the period an eighth below the level seen at the end of 1991. The same survey shows that wages increased more in those companies where the reduction of employment was greater. The main weakness of the Polish leased enterprises seems to be lack of capital and low investment, and their main strength the strong support from their employees.

The results of 171 face-to-face interviews of privatized firms in Russia provides evidence of the nature of corporate governance in such enterprises (Filatotchev *et al.* 1996*b*). Evidence on changes in the distribution of managerial and employee share ownership is beginning to emerge.[2] The survey shows that between privatization and one year afterwards, the average share of the equity held by non-senior managerial employees had on average fallen from 47.4 per cent to 46 per cent. The average stake held by the State Property Agency fell sharply from 22.8 per cent to

---

[2] Other surveys of ownership, which include some post-privatization trading of shares, show that managers and employers own on average between 60 and 70 per cent of the shares, of which about 17 per cent is owned by the management team (see discussion in Boycko *et al.* 1993). Outsiders own on average about 14 per cent and the property fund the remaining 16 per cent.

14.1 per cent, though it remained one of the most significant shareholders. Corresponding increases occurred in respect of management's stake (from 19.4 per cent to 21.3 per cent), private and institutional external investors (from 6.2 per cent to 10.8 per cent), industrial groups (6.3 per cent to 10.4 per cent), and banks (0.2 per cent to 0.7 per cent). Despite managements' attempts to frustrate share sales by workers to outsiders, it is also becoming clear that this is happening but that managers are also acquiring shares from employees. Indeed, in 27.6 per cent of enterprises, managers claimed that they had already purchased shares from employees. Some 62.1 per cent of enterprises said that they still intended to purchase shares from employees.

Employees as a body are reported to have relatively little involvement in decision-monitoring but their influence appears to be increasing slightly. Formal consultation on strategic issues rose slightly after privatization and informal consultations on these issues also showed a modest rise. In a detailed analysis of twenty-seven privatized Russian firms, Gurkov and Asselbergs (1995) also show that employees, even where they are shareholders, perceive managers to be the real owners of the firm. Their study also supports the view that employees have little role in the decision-making process and indeed that their role has been reduced since privatization whilst that of management has increased.

Despite their low levels of equity holdings, the evidence (Filatotchev *et al.* 1996*b*) suggests that outsiders are represented on boards or otherwise present as active investors to a greater extent than their shareholdings would indicate (Table 10.3). In most of the sample there are no active or passive outside investors, but in three-tenths of cases, private individuals are involved in control, and in almost a quarter of cases other firms. Banks and the state property fund also fulfil an active role, notably as directors and to a lesser extent as chairmen of the privatized enterprises. Representation by investment funds, whilst present in some cases, is not as evident as these other stakeholders.

Gurkov and Asselbergs (1995) find that acquisitions of controlling interests by financial institutions was viewed more acceptably than acquisitions by strategic partners. They adduce the reason for this difference to be that it is more feasible to obtain agreements to long-term financial investment from financial institutions, whereas foreign strategic partners are likely to introduce massive corporate

Table 10.3. Post-privatization outside shareholdings and channels of control (% of sample)

OUTSIDE investor	Chairman	Director	Otherwise active	Passive	None
Private individual	5.9	11.2	5.3	14.2	70.6
Investment fund	2.4	9.5	2.4	7.7	80.5
Another firm	2.4	11.2	8.9	7.7	76.9
State property fund	3.5	21.3	5.3	13.5	65.9
Bank	1.2	4.7	5.9	11.2	79.4

Note: Many firms responded positively to more than one category, so that percentages in the rows sum to more than 100 per cent. Base of percentages is 171.

restructuring and major shifts in product mixes to meet Western requirements. Freinkman (1995) argues that large financial-industrial groups are emerging in Russia which may be able to contribute to both the rate of enterprise restructuring and patterns of corporate governance for privatized firms through investment in them.

Earle *et al.* (1995), comparing the performance of privatized firms in Russia, find little difference between those which are employee-owned and those which are classed as managerially owned. They find similar objectives, similar importance attached to marketing and finance, no significant differences in restructuring of inventories and costs, and no indication that employee-owned firms under-invested. However, employee-owned firms were less likely to restructure their products whilst managerially owned firms were significantly more likely to engage in reorganization. Such insider-owned firms were, however, less likely than outsider-owned firms to reduce employment levels.

Evidence from the Ukraine (Filatotchev *et al.*, 1996c) shows a substantially greater ownership role for employees and lower involvement by outsiders than is the case in Russia. There are indications that in these enterprises employees have much greater formal and informal involvement in the governance process than is the case in Russia and that post-privatization actions, while involving some restructuring and employment reduction, have also seen continued emphasis on the social assets of enterprises and in increasing real wage rates.

The approach to large-scale privatization in the Czech and Slovak republics primarily, but not exclusively, involved a voucher scheme in which individuals could bid directly for companies or indirectly through buying shares in investment privatization funds which in turn bid for shares in companies. Unlike the variants available under the Russian voucher privatization, insiders in the Czech and Slovak programmes were not granted special preferences, although management may propose a privatization project where they perceived it would be possible for incumbents to place sufficient voucher points in their own firm to create effectively a worker buy-out (Takla 1994).

Evidence from Bulgaria on transformation in enterprises which have been converted to joint-stock companies but which remain state-owned shows that governance structures remain largely ineffective, with boards being largely passive and managerial remuneration not creating incentives to restructure, though informal mechanisms may go some way to constrain managers (Peev 1995). However, the competencies of individual managers were found to be very important in determining whether restructuring took place.

4. Post-Privatization Governance

In the light of the previous evidence relating to governance mechanisms in privatized firms in CEE, this section discusses the potential contribution of the various elements to enhancing the governance of such enterprises. The following elements are discussed in turn: insider ownership, banks, domestic and foreign companies, and non-bank financial intermediaries (such as investment funds, wealthy indiviudals, and venture capitalists).

Insider Ownership

It may be argued that employee participation in share ownership in newly privatized enterprises will have strong positive effects on efficiency and innovation. Employees may participate in decision-making, imposing a strong collective monitoring on management's activities together with mutual monitoring (Ben-Ner 1993). Employees and management will be closely united, stimulating efficiency and innovation. However, there may be severe difficulties in persuading employees to act in a manner which maximizes the longer-term shareholder value (Buck *et al.* 1994).

Compared to conventional shareholders, employee-owners who are unable to sell their shares freely may prefer the firm to take decisions which benefit them in the short term, such as through higher pay-outs of profits in the form of higher wages and the maintenance of employment, and corresponding lower levels of investment. Employees can benefit in the short term from higher job security and remuneration while the benefits from investment programmes are only felt in the longer term. With virtually all their human and financial capital tied up in one enterprise, employee shareholders may seek to reduce risks by voting for excessive product diversification by the firm.

Employee-owners of a firm may be tempted to transfer their ownership rights to outside 'core' investors, since dispersed, internal ownership makes it difficult for them to exercise the control component of their rights, given the costs of mutual monitoring and the lure of the free ride. Moreover, employees may wish to exchange their shares for cash in order to purchase consumer goods and may especially want to do so where the company faces difficulties or has ambitious restructuring plans and is unlikely to provide a dividend or significant realizable gain in share price for some time. Hence, employee ownership may slowly be eroded as individual employees find ways of selling their shares.

It also needs to be borne in mind that equity ownership is only one part of the overall governance process. Corporate governance also involves the control of the dominant decision-makers in an enterprise by other stakeholders. A crucial role is thus assigned to the provision of investable funds, direct monitoring by active investors, and the indirect control exerted by creditors. In general, enterprises involved in significant insider ownership in CEE may be expected to differ markedly from those in the West, with consequent implications for their ability to effect efficiency improvements. If employees are majority equity holders but managers own only minority stakes, they may have little incentive to effect enterprise restructuring. In the absence of other forms of governance, managers and employees may form a coalition of entrenched interests resisting reform. Unless managers in a particular enterprise are dominant and market-oriented, and employees are correspondingly compliant, the extent of market-based transformation may be limited.

Banks

Theory in the West places considerable emphasis on the role of the providers of debt and the need to service this form of finance as hard constraints on the behaviour of managers (Jensen 1986). Failure to meet interest payment provides an early warning signal that rectifying action is required. Debt providers are viewed as introducing mechanisms such as debt covenants and requirements for the supply of regular financial information which places pressure on management to perform. Whilst these mechanisms help minimize the risks of default, after meeting debt repayments companies which are excessively leveraged may have little cash flow available to engage in new profitable investment.

Voucher privatizations in CEE do not involve the taking on of borrowings in order to finance the acquisition. In both Poland and Hungary, for example, where privatization may involve the purchase of businesses, there may be considerable commitment either to service external borrowing or to meet instalment payments. Such leveraged privatizations raise a number of problems in the operation of mechanisms introduced which commit management to perform. The first concerns the nature and role of the banks. Banks may, in principle, exercise control not only through examining the accounts of the client firm, but also by stipulating in loan contracts their information and control rights concerning the firm's operation and financial affairs. However, until bank privatization is fully implemented, state-owned banks are heavily involved in the financing of buy-outs in Hungary and Poland, the same party which is the seller and which has been unable to monitor enterprises in the past. In other words, after privatization of enterprises, the banks may still have neither the staff nor the expertise to exert effective corporate governance.

The second problem is that income streams may be considerably less stable than in mature sectors in the West. Third, many enterprises, especially those using leasing approaches to transformation, may have few assets which can be used as collateral. Fourth, the enterprises are likely to have significant investment needs. Banks are unlikely to be keen to extend their credits, and provide fresh cash for investment and restructuring purposes without there being considerable collateral available from, say, real estate. Problems with obtaining reliable financial information on which to base a decision, doubts about the value of assets, and uncertainties concerning whether real estate actually belongs to a particular enterprise may also make banks cautious in their assessment of the amount of collateral available. In Hungary, evidence from the authors' survey of buy-outs (Karsai and Wright 1994), as noted earlier, suggests that the value of the security demanded usually amounted to one and a half times the total value of the loan. The ESOP law regulated collateral requirements, including detailed rules concerning the bank lien over the property of ESOP groups, the compulsory utilization of dividends for loan repayment, and responsibility for the management of the firm's assets.

A fifth difference is that enterprises in CEE are faced by high interest rates and difficulties in obtaining long-term debt beyond that available with subsidies. Banks are highly constrained in their ability to fund long-term investments of companies because of undercapitalization, maturity mismatch arising from the lack of long-term savings, and high levels of bad debts generated both under the former regimes as well as from poor lending decisions during the transition period. A further problem is the crowding-out effect resulting from the difference between the security of company loans and state securities. Even within these generally problematical conditions, pure buy-outs may be viewed by the banks as a greater credit risk than other enterprise lending. Evidence from a survey of the nine main commercial banks in Warsaw shows that management and employee buy-outs with exclusive insider ownership are generally rated as greater credit risks than those enterprises which have been able to attract foreign or strategic investors (Solarz 1994).

There are, however, some mechanisms which provide a limited means of alleviating these problems. In Hungary, for example, the need to provide collateral has been reduced by a change in SPA policy in 1993 which meant that only 50 per cent of the shares plus one could be sold to incumbents in a buy-out. With the passage of the ESOP law, collateral requirements also became more regulated as it contained detailed rules concerning the bank lien over the property of ESOP groups. In early 1993 a new institution was established to offer guarantees for ventures which, though promising, could not provide the necessary guarantees. The Credit Guarantee Co. Ltd. was authorized to assume risk up to HUF 100 million and up to 80 per cent of the required collateral. Since this institution became involved, the level of collateral has dropped from one and a half times the size of the loan to just 70 per cent. Although a generally available scheme, most of this new institution's early clients were employee groups, the introduction of the scheme removing one of the largest obstacles to the granting of finance for buy-outs. There is a danger, however, that this process will reinforce the practice of using personal contacts and political influence in obtaining finance, with less emphasis being placed on an enterprise's income-earning potential or its ability to provide property guarantees (Voszka 1992).

In Poland, the leasing procedure requires that the down-payment cannot be lower than 20 per cent of the capital of the privatized state enterprise. Transfer of ownership occurs after all of the capital and interest has been repaid. As a result, companies are deprived of the possibility of using assets as collateral in taking long-term credits, though attempts are being made to address this issue through earlier transfer of ownership rights.

Russian enterprises, in contrast, are not exposed to any significant additional debt as a result of privatization. Although the voucher auction does not bring any fresh cash into the company, the banking system may fill this gap in the future and provide much-needed finance for restructuring purposes. However, Russian banks are aware of the problems with corporate governance within newly privatized companies. As a result, banks will be reluctant to provide privatized Russian companies with long-term credits as long as corporate governance problems have not been solved, and will focus on short-term lending. The provision of long-term financial resources to industrial organizations with governance structures which are inadequate in the new market environment will inevitably increase the systemic risk within the fragile system of Russian commercial banking.

The above discussion indicates that, whilst highly leveraged privatizations may be appropriate for enterprises with stable cash flows and low investment needs, this may not be the case for those enterprises such as many in CEE where these conditions do not hold. Moreover, in the absence of banking reforms and enforcement of bankruptcy in CEE, the role of banks in enforcing the exit of unprofitable enterprises may also be weakened.[3]

Domestic and Foreign Companies

The presence of an outsider with a significant equity stake provides for direct influence in the direction of the company. In addition, because such parties also tend to have a significant trading relationship with the bought-out company making the bought-out company typically more dependent on the equity partner than vice versa, an extra element of governance is introduced. Such an asymmetry of dependence provides an incentive to improve performance, especially where the equity partner has access to alternative trading relationships where the other party fails to perform satisfactorily. In addition, there is evidence that such relationships are transitory since attempts are likely to be made to broaden customer and supplier bases so as to reduce dependence. Despite the possibilities of such arrangements in CEE, certain major problems remain.

An important pre-condition for a long-term commitment is the existence of mutual trust between the parties involved. Foreign firms may also be reluctant to become involved unless they can obtain majority control, which insiders may be unwilling to cede. Employee-owners may be unwilling to enter such a relationship where they perceive that the other party may want to close capacity, etc. Similarly, the incoming party may be reluctant to become involved where an unacceptable level of uncertainty exists about conditions inside the enterprise. There are also indications, for example from Hungarian experience, of the vulnerability of CEE enterprises to exploitative behaviour by enterprises from outside the region. For example, whilst there may appear to be attractions in a bilateral agreement whereby a foreign firm takes a partial equity stake and agrees to buy a given level of orders at a guaranteed price in return for which the CEE enterprise purchases foreign capital equipment, enforcement of the foreign enterprise's part of the contract may be especially difficult. In Poland, foreign firms and domestic legal

---

[3] For discussion of the role of bankrupcty as a corporate governance device in CEE, see Frydman *et al.* (1993); Wright *et al.* (1993*a*); Aghion *et al.* (1994). Note that the state of development and implementation of bankruptcy legislation varies considerably between countries.

persons have not be allowed to participate in the initial privatization, except in the regions with high unemployment.

It is perhaps not surprising that in the few cases in Russia at the time of writing where employee owners and outside firms have become involved in joint ownership, there had previously been a long-standing relationship between the parties involved (Khaykin *et al.* 1993). Similarly, the buy-outs interviewed by the authors in Hungary where external firms had become involved in equity ownership had frequently had a relationship with the enterprise from at least the time of transformation into a commercial enterprise. A further route to develop trust is provided by the Russian privatization legislation whereby 20 per cent of the shares of an enterprise can be acquired through an investment tender rather than an open auction. Hence it is possible to achieve a joint arrangement whereby a prospective outside investor reaches an agreement with incumbent management and employees on issues concerning job security, salary levels, distribution of ownership and profits, and amount and type of investment to be contributed by the outside investor. Having established a relationship at the privatization stage, the outside investor may subsequently be able to secure agreement to increase its shareholdings either by direct purchases from incumbents or, perhaps less threateningly, through increasing the capital of the company. Over time the proportion of shares acquired in this way may become a controlling one, though the continued importance of incumbents indicates that they are likely to retain a significant equity stake. In order to maintain management incentives and to ensure that new funds are used for investment, it may be appropriate to increase a company's share capital and persuade a new investor to contribute new funds for investment, rather than management selling their shares.

The efficiency of such joint arrangements would depend upon the degree of product market competition. Contrary to Hungary and Poland, in Russia it proved impossible to enact, let alone enforce, a regulatory framework to enhance competition at the start of the privatization process.[4] As a result, governance structures which involve industrial partners may serve to bolster the already inefficient structures rather than to encourage restructuring, with corporate governance structures of this kind becoming more rigid over time and resembling features of the former system. There is also a fear that the creation of such joint arrangements may hide questionable financial interests of the old nomenclature and even criminal connections.

Non-Bank Financial Intermediaries and Individuals

Non-bank financial intermediaries include a number of institutions, such as pension funds, investment funds, and venture capital funds. The way in which

---

[4] Though attempts are being made with the help of foreign antitrust agencies to establish such a working regime.

these institutions become involved in active corporate governance varies considerably, depending upon regulatory frameworks, incentive schemes, and the skills of fund managers (Frydman *et al.* 1993), and ranging from long-term relationships where institutions prefer constructive intervention to disposing of a holding to short-term perspectives.

Private Investment Funds   Control by a private investment fund introduces the opportunity to split up an enterprise or to strip it of its assets, and may be especially attractive where there are substantial city centre land and buildings which can be redeveloped. Such a prospect may become feasible as markets in land and buildings become established and make assets of this kind valuable after a long period in which they have been ignored or undervalued in accounting statements. Such restructuring may perform an important function in reallocating them to more productive uses than previously.

Whether investment funds will be able to exert effective corporate governance is debatable, at least in the short to medium term. Such funds are not homogeneous. Pistor *et al.* (1994) identify four overlapping types in Russia. The 'restructuring' group come closest to effecting voice-oriented corporate governance, and may in principle be able to exert pressure to restructure which may include ejecting insiders from positions of control. They find little evidence that investment funds have been proactive in effecting dismissals. Ejecting insiders may be difficult unless funds can persuade the body of employees to reject incumbent management. Hence, it is possible that by working with management rather than adopting a hostile stance changes can be effected. The problem, however, is that as with 'managerialists', the second group, funds may become more concerned with bolstering managerial entrenchment than effecting independent corporate governance.

The third group, 'traders', can be viewed as effecting corporate governance through exit. By attempting to identify enterprises whose shares can be traded easily, the funds may provide a degree of monitoring and information creation which may be important for future allocation of investment. However, Pistor *et al.* (1994) note that a high degree of trading by investment funds may be the result of undervaluation of Russian enterprises during the early stages of privatization, meaning that large profits could be generated from the windfall gains available by simply selling the stakes acquired on privatization. In turn this raises the opportunity cost of restructuring and reduces the incentive to become an active investor. Given the overlapping nature of 'restructurers' and 'traders', a high level of trading also raises problems for the level of commitment of funds to a hands-on relationship with a newly privatized company. It is also questionable whether such intermediaries have adequate monitoring skills to deal in detail with the vast numbers of privatized enterprises. Moreover, if individual managers running such intermediaries do not have their own wealth exposed to loss, they may not be particularly concerned about value maximization. The fourth group, 'rent seekers', are motivated by the ability of enterprises to continue to obtain credits from the state and may particularly benefit if the government maintains soft budget constraints.

The extent to which investment funds in Russia can contribute finance for investment in the companies in which they have an equity stake is also debatable. The fact that banks may typically be significant shareholders in voucher funds means that they could be important agents for channelling investment funds into Russian firms. Pistor *et al.* (1994), however, show that share sales may be encouraged by severe cash constraints on the funds, raising doubts about their ability to set aside adequate amounts for the follow-on finance which will often be required for post-privatization enterprise restructuring. Hence, at present there appears to be at best little evidence that investment funds are actively contributing to the long-term growth of enterprises.

Parker (1993) draws attention to the governance shortcomings in the Czech and Slovak privatizations. Investment privatization funds, which were initially intended to have a minor role, have emerged in principle as being able to exert an influence over management, though their limitation to holding no more than 20 per cent of the equity of a particular company may restrict their effectiveness. By the end of the early stages of voucher privatization, investment privatization funds controlled some 37 per cent of all voucher points placed, with six such funds being particularly dominant and having the power to demand management and employment changes (Takla 1994).

In Poland, national investment funds are to be established with the purpose of restructuring enterprises in their portfolios. The remuneration schemes for the managers in national investment funds have been designed to give them appropriate incentives to effect profitable restructuring. However, as yet it remains to be seen how effective these organizations will be in practice.

Therefore, it appears that a combination of two problems, unstable governance and an urgent need for investment finance, can only be solved with the introduction of investors who are closely involved in the process of strategic and operational decision-making in newly privatized companies and with a serious financial commitment to the business. Hence, the emphasis of the process of external funding of newly privatized companies in CEE has to be shifted from debt to equity financing with core investors exercising a higher degree of monitoring and control in newly privatized enterprises.

Wealthy Individuals Wealthy individuals initially external to the enterprise may also have a role to play in the governance and finance of privatized companies in the countries of CEE. They may become involved either in a main controlling and ownership capacity (a management buy-in) or in a minority active investor role (so-called informal venture capitalists or 'business angles'). In the West, management buy-ins may also typically involve formal venture capital funding in the purchase of the business. Business angels as informal venture capitalists are often seen as bringing the advantages associated with a longer investment horizon than conventional venture capitalists as well as perhaps being more flexible regarding the degree of involvement in governance that they seek (Freear 1992). There are general problems with both management buy-ins and business angels concerning their identification and matching to individual enterprises, which relates to compatibility and acceptability between the parties involved as well as the wealth and expertise levels of the business angels (Robbie *et al.* 1992). These issues apply both in the West and in CEE but may be particularly severe in the latter.[5]

However, private individuals have an active governance role in a significant minority of Russian buy-outs. In the Uralmash Heavy Engineering Amalgamation in Russia, where the workers' collective acquired 50 per cent of the shares on privatization, a fifth of the shares were unexpectedly acquired by the private company Bioprocessor, owned by one of Russia's wealthiest individuals. It was agreed that Bioprocessor would not interfere in operational decision-making in Uralmash but that its senior managers would take seats on the board of directors of Uralmash.

Venture Capitalists   The role of venture capitalists in the West has been discussed in Chapter 7. Venture capitalists can, in principle, for generally small and medium-sized firms help to solve the dual problem of an inadequate system of corporate governance and a lack of long-term finance for restructuring and investment in CEE. They offer a form and style of financing which is not provided elsewhere in the spectrum of financial services available in CEE so far, in respect of its combination of a certain length of commitment with greater involvement and a degree of influence over the companies in which equity stakes are taken (Beecroft 1994). Unlike existing investment funds in CEE, the venture capitalists' commitment includes help to companies in restructuring during the process of transition, helping to find suitable management, and assisting in rescue packages.

Venture capitalists, as with other investors, may be faced with serious adverse selection problems in investing in CEE since difficulties are posed in screening the capabilities of management who typically have not operated in a market environment before. Venture capitalists, through close monitoring, may be faced with less severe moral hazard problems than arm's length shareholders, but significant asymmetric information problems may remain, particularly in CEE, where information systems are typically underdeveloped. Moreover, it is also important to bear in mind that incumbent management may wish to select an investor who does not want to exert close monitoring. The inability of the typically small numbers of investment executives found in venture capital firms to monitor more than a modest number of investments constrains the degree of involvement in investee companies, and monitoring involves costs which may not make it worth while for institutions to engage in detailed monitoring in smaller companies. In CEE there are, however, as with the banking system, concerns about the availability of appropriate managerial expertise, at least in the short to medium term. In principle, venture capitalists and similar active investors can use various mechanisms to encourage entrepreneurs both to perform and to reveal accurate information, such as staging of the commitment of investment funds, using convertible financial instruments which may give financiers control under certain conditions,

---

[5] In the *Neue Länder* of Germany, for example, the Treuhand introduced a scheme to promote management buy-ins, but despite receiving several thousand enquiries was able to complete very few transactions (Wright *et al.* 1993*a*).

basing management's compensation on value created and developing relationships of trust between venture capitalists and management.

For these reasons and others relating to uncertain economic conditions the few venture capitalists so far present in the region have been reluctant to invest in privatizations involving incumbent management and employees. In Poland evidence indicates that the bottle-neck in financing investment projects may not be lack of capital but the scarcity of good ideas with reasonable prospects for success (Grosfeld 1994). Evidence from Hungary shows that venture capital has been mainly involved in the funding of joint ventures with some level of foreign participation rather than buy-outs where there are concerns about the returns available (Kocsis 1993).

5. Conclusions

This chapter has examined the problems of governance in CEE. A number of options for addressing the problems of governance were analysed. The development of venture capital firms with their associated governance and finance attributes was seen to be a particularly important means of providing a flexible system of monitoring managers.

A common feature of evidence from differing CEE countries is that post-privatization there is a decline in share ownership by employees as a whole with a corresponding increase in managements' and outside investors' stakes, though the change in the comparative holdings of outsiders varied between countries. In Russia in a comparatively short time since privatization, acquisitions of substantial equity stakes by management and by outsiders, especially private and institutional investors and industrial groups, was evident. Investment funds appeared not to be active in monitoring. In Poland the decline in employee ownership and rise in share ownership by external investors was more in evidence than the increase in managerial equity stakes. In Hungary, in contrast, little movement in ownership structures was observed, though there appeared to be a modest increase in the concentration of managerial shareholdings and a corresponding reduction in employee and outsider holdings. Increases in management equity holding may have some positive impact on corporate governance, especially if managers have to borrow to fund the purchase of shares and are constrained to improve performance in order to be able to repay loans. However, they may still face governance problems where widespread diffusion of employee ownership remains. In addition, it needs to be borne in mind that increasing managerial share ownership does not involve the introduction of new finance for investment.

Newly privatized companies are, however, suffering from the combination of three problems: inadequate systems of corporate governance, variable quality of entrepreneurship, and lack of external finance. The longevity of initial forms of privatized firms will largely depend on the particular shape and structure of the evolving financial systems in Central and Eastern Europe and on the economic power of newly emerging institutions (investment funds, venture capitalists, etc.). There remains a need for the state to create an adequate regulatory environment to ensure that the newly established relations between recently privatized companies, financial and non-financial stakeholders, and lending institutions will ensure economic efficiency improvements and promote corporate restructuring and technological modernization. However, as with corporate governance systems generally, there is a need to balance appropriate monitoring of managerial behaviour with the promotion of entrepreneurial actions which will contribute to improving innovation and efficiency. In underdeveloped market systems as in CEE it may be as important to emphasize measures to enhance entrepreneurial skills as it is to develop good governance systems. Given the barriers to developing institutional voice mechanisms discussed earlier in this chapter, this last point assumes major importance.

REFERENCES

Aghion, P., Hart, O., and Moore, J. (1994), 'Improving Bankruptcy Procedure', University of Edinburgh, Discussion Paper No. 91:I.

Beecroft, A. (1994), 'Venture Capital and Corporate Governance', in N. Dimsdale and M. Prevezer (eds.), *Capital Markets and Corporate Governance* (Oxford: Clarendon Press).

Ben-Ner, A. (1993), 'Organisational Reforms in Central and Eastern Europe: A Comparative Perspective', *Annals of Public and Cooperative Economics*, 3: 327–64.

Boycko, M., Shleifer, A., and Vishny, R. (1993), 'Privatising Russia', *Brookings Papers on Economic Activity*, No. 2: 139–92.

Buck, T., Filatotchev, I., and Wright, M. (1994), 'Employee Buy-Outs and the Transformation of Russian Industry', *Comparative Economic Studies*, 36/2: 1–15.

Dabrowski, J. M., Federowicz, M., Kaminski, T., and Szomburg, J. (1993), *Privatisation of Polish State-Owned Enterprises: Progress, Barriers, Initial Effects* (Gdansk: Gdansk Institute for Market Economics).

Earle, J., Estrin, S., and Leshchenko, L. (1995), *The Effects of Ownership on Behaviour: Is Privatisation Working in Russia?*, World Bank Working Paper.

Estrin, S. (ed.) (1994), *Privatization in Central and Eastern Europe* (London: Longmans).

Filatotchev, I., Starkey, K., and Wright, M. (1994), 'The Ethical Challenge of Management and Employee Buy-Outs in Central and Eastern Europe', *Journal of Business Ethics*, 13: 523–32.

Filatotchev, I., Wright, M., and Buck, T. (1995b), 'Corporate Governance and Voucher Buy-Outs in Russia', *Annals of Public and Cooperative Economics*, 66/1: 77–99.

Filatotchev, I., Grosfeld, I., Karsai, J., Wright, M., and Buck, T. (1996a), 'Buy-Outs in Hungary, Poland and Russia: Governance and Finance Issues', *Economics of Transition*, 4/1: 67–88.

Filatotchev, I., Hoskisson, R., Buck, T., and Wright, M. (1996b), 'Corporate Restructuring and Privatisation in Russia', *California Management Review*, 38/2: 87–105.

Filatotchev, I., van Frausum, Y., Wright, M., and Buck, T. (1996c), 'Privatisation and Industrial Restructuring in the Ukraine', *Communist Economies and Economic Transformation*, 8/2, 185–203.

Freear, J., Sohl, J., and Wetzel, W. (1992), 'The Investment Attitudes, Behaviour and Characteristics of High Net Worth Individuals', in N. Churchill *et al.* (eds.), *Frontiers of Entrepreneurship Research* (Wellesley, Mass.: Babson College).

Freinkman, L. (1995), 'Finanical-Industrial Groups in Russia: Emergence of Large Diversified Private Companies', *Communist Economies and Economic Transformation*, 7/1: 51–66.

Frydman, R., Phelps, E., Rapaczynski, A., and Shleifer, A. (1993), 'Needed Mechanisms of Corporate Governance and Finance in Eastern Europe', *Economics of Transition*, 1/2: 171–207.

Grosfeld, I. (1994), *Financial Systems in Transition: Is there a Case for a Bank-Based System?*, CEPR Discussion Paper No. 1062.

Gurkov, I., and Asselbergs, G. (1995), 'Ownership and Control in Russian Privatised Companies: Evidence from a Survey', *Communist Economies and Economic Transformation*, 7/2: 195–211.

Jarosz, M. (1994*a*), *Pracownicze Spolki Leasingujace* (Warsaw: Instytut Studiow Politycznych Polskiej Akademii Nauk).

—— (1994*b*) (ed.), *Spolki pracownicze* (Warsaw: Instytut Studiow Politycznych Polskiej Akademii Nauk).

Jensen, M. (1986), 'Agency Costs of Free Cash Flow, Corporate Finance and Takeovers', *American Economic Review Papers and Proceedings*, 76 (May 1986), 323–9.

—— (1993), 'The Modern Industrial Revolution, Exit, and the Failure of Internal Control Systems', *Journal of Finance*, 48/3: 831–80.

Kaplan, S. (1989), 'The Effects of Management Buy-Outs on Operating Performance and Value', *Journal of Financial Economics*, 24: 217–54.

—— (1991), 'The Staying Power of Leveraged Buy-Outs', *Journal of Financial Economics*, 29: 287–313.

Karsai, J., and Wright, M. (1994), 'Accountability, Governance and Finance in Hungarian Buy-Outs', *Europe–Asia Studies* (formerly *Soviet Studies*), 46/6: 997–1016.

Kay, J., and Thompson, D. (1986), 'Privatisation: A Policy in Search of a Rationale', *Economic Journal*, 96: 18–32.

Khaykin, O., Lindquist, J., and Ackerman, C. (1993), 'Acquirors Come in from the Cold', *Acquisitions Monthly* (Dec.), 44–6.

Kocsis, G. (1993), 'It is Important that the Initiator Bear Risk as Well: Interview with H. Stevenson', *Heti Vilaggazdasag*, 27 Mar., 33–4.

Kushnirsky, F. (1994), 'Ukraine's Industrial Enterprise: Surviving Hard Times', *Comparative Economic Studies*, 36/4: 21–39.

Parker, D. (1993), 'Unravelling the Planned Economy: Privatization in Czecho-Slovakia', *Communist Economies and Economic Transformation*, 5/3: 391–404.

Pasztor, S. (1991), 'Being Hidden: The Privatisation of Apisz', *Acta Oeconomica*, 43/3: 297–314.

Peev, E., (1995), 'Ownership and Control in Bulgaria', *Europe–Asia Studies*, 47/5: 859–75.

Pistor, K., Frydman, R., Rapaczynski, A. (1994), 'Investing in Insider-Dominated Firms: A Study of Russian Voucher Privatization Funds', Transition Economics Division, Policy Research Department, World Bank, Washington, Dec.

Robbie, K., Wright, M., and Thompson, S. (1992), 'Management Buy-Ins', *Omega*, 20/4: 445–6.

Sahlman, W. (1990), 'The Structure and Governance of Venture Capital Organisations', *Journal of Financial Economics*, 27: 473–521.

Smith, A. (1990), 'Corporate Ownership Structure and Performance: The Case of Management Buy-Outs', *Journal of Financial Economics*, 27: 143–64.

Solarz, J. (1994), 'The Financial Sector and Bottom-Up Privatisation', in R. Schliwa (ed.), *Bottom-Up Privatisation, Finance and the Role of Employers' and Workers' Organisations in the Czech Republic, Hungary, Poland and Slovakia* (Geneva: ILO).

SPA (State Property Agency) (1994), 'ESOP as a Successful Privatisation Technique', *Privinfo*, 1: 14–16.

State Property Committee (1993), *Reforma*, No. 49, Dec. 1993, 2, and No. 41, Oct. 1993, 4–5.

Takla, L. (1994), 'The Relationship between Privatisation and the Reform of the Banking Sector: The Case of the Czech Republic and Slovakia', in S. Estrin (ed.), *Privatization in Central and Eastern Europe* (London: Longman).

Voszka, Éva (1992), 'Privatizáció: kockázatos "keresletélénkítés"', (Privatisation: A Risky Way of 'Stimulating Demand'), *Népszabadság*, 8 Dec.

Wright, M., Thompson, S., and Robbie, K. (1992), 'Venture Capital and Management-Led Leveraged Buy-Outs: European Evidence', *Journal of Business Venturing* (Jan.), 7/1: 47–71.

—— Filatotchev, I., Buck, T., and Robbie, K. (eds.) (1993a), *Management and Employee Buy-Outs in Central and Eastern Europe* (London: European Bank/CEEPN).

—— Thompson, S., and Robbie, K. (1993b), 'Finance and Control in Privatisation Buy-Outs', *Financial Accountability and Management* (May), 9/2: 75–99.

—— Robbie, K., Thompson, S., and Starkey, K. (1994a), 'Longevity and the Life-Cycle of Management Buy-Outs', *Strategic Management Journal*, 15/3: 215–27.

—— Filatotchev, I., Buck, T., and Robbie, K. (1994b), 'Accountability and Efficiency in Buy-Outs in Central and Eastern Europe', *Financial Accountability and Management*, 10/3: 195–214.

11

GOVERNANCE IN GERMANY: THE FOUNDATIONS OF CORPORATE STRUCTURE?

Thomas Clarke and Richard Bostock

1. Introduction

The definition of corporate governance is often wrongly confined to the practices of the company boardroom, when the institutions and practices of governance influence fundamentally the structure and operations of companies. It is apparent that approaches to corporate governance affect not only company performance, but also have an important effect upon overall economic performance through their impact *inter alia* upon:

1. enterprise financing costs and structures;
2. planning horizons and investment behaviour;
3. personnel and remuneration policy;
4. investment in firm-specific human capital;
5. information policies of enterprises;
6. the birth, survival, and growth of firms.

There are generally conceived significant differences between the corporate governance structures of Anglo-American companies, and European companies, with the German model of governance often portrayed as the most distinctive of the European types (Tricker 1994; Monks and Minow 1995; Clarke and Bostock 1994). Among the notable features of the German business sector is the relatively strong concentration of ownership of individual enterprises; the importance of small and medium-sized unincorporated companies, with a close correspondence between owners and managers; and the limited role played by the stock market (OECD 1995a). More broadly the dominant characteristic of German commercial enterprises is the inside characteristic of their governance systems through which all interested stakeholders—managers, employees, creditors, suppliers, and customers—are able to monitor company performance:

A stylised version of the German model is that it relies on continuous monitoring of managers by other stakeholders, who have a long-term relationship with the firm and engage permanently in the important aspects of decision-making and in the case of dissatisfaction, take action to correct management decisions through internal channels. In the case of incorporated firms (*Kapitalgesellschaften*) stakeholder influence is exerted through a two-tier company board structure. The importance of the banks, in their double role as both lenders and important shareowners, has often, perhaps too often, been stressed. In contrast the Anglo-American model is typically taken to imply that individual stakeholders have little direct influence on management and that dissatisfied stakeholders 'vote with their feet', e.g. firms shifting sub-contractors or shareholders selling their equity holdings in a firm. Resulting downward pressure on share prices, however, serves as an indirect disciplining device on management. As a result of these differences, the stock market is seen to be much more central to the Anglo-American model than the German model which, in contrast, relies importantly on continuous participation by banks, business partners and employees in the running of companies, creating greater potential for conflict of interest. (OECD 1995*a*: 85–6)

The economic debate concerning corporate governance is often posed in terms of a potential dilemma between strong direction and accountability, there being a tension in the paradox that assets are most efficiently valued when information to shareholders is maximized, whilst operational efficiency suggests that shareholders should delegate surveillance and decision-making to managers. The German model of governance being based on a pattern of institutional relations, unlike the market-based Anglo-American model, it diminishes such tensions by relying much less on market assessment, and by including a wide range of stakeholders in the governance process:

The issues in a German context are then how to ensure that this alignment—as an alternative to a market for corporate control—can ensure the effective allocation of capital, especially to new firms and 'innovations', and related to this, whether the trend towards greater international integration and capital and product market liberalisation will call for a further evolution in existing arrangements . . . The incentives which led to a particular German model of enterprise control seem set to undergo further rapid change. Among the pressures for change are the on-going processes of technical change and internationalisation as well as the financing patterns that are likely to follow from future changes in private saving and its allocation. (OECD 1995*a*: 84–5)

This chapter sets out to examine the changing parameters of the governance system of German enterprise, including:

1. the characteristics of the distribution and concentration of enterprise ownership in Germany;
2. the comparative financing costs for industry;
3. the structure of shareholdings and the influence of banks upon corporate direction;
4. the limits of the market for corporate control in Germany, and the role played by supervisory boards and the wider representation of stakeholder interests.

Finally, the challenges facing the German system are identified and the possible convergence of governance and regulation considered.

2. The Distribution and Concentration of Enterprise Ownership

The proportion of listed firms and their share of total business activity is relatively low in Germany, and therefore conclusions concerning governance structures should not be based on information concerning listed firms only. According to turnover statistics, joint-stock companies (*Aktien-gesellschaften*, AGs) accounted for only about 20 per cent of business turnover in 1992, and of a total of 3,219 joint-stock companies at the end of 1992 only 664 were listed. Over 500,000 other companies with limited liability (*Gesellschaften mit beschränkter Haftung*, GmbHs) between them account for more than 30 per cent of total turnover and have a nominal capital stock which is a third larger than that of joint-stock companies (OECD 1995a: 87). This is in comparison to 6,309 in the USA on NYSE, AMEX, and NASDAQ and 2,343 in London (Charkham 1994: 29). The relative importance of listed companies in different countries is shown in Table 11.1. In Germany there are few large public joint-stock companies with a wide share ownership and extensive share trading: in 1991 a mere fifty companies accounted for more than 85 per cent of all trading in domestic shares (Schneider-Lenne 1992: 12). The stock market is much less important as an instrument for enterprise control in Germany, and the scope for principal–agent conflicts is more limited since ownership is highly concentrated in non-listed firms with a close correspondence between owners and managers. As stock markets are an instrument for risk sharing, it could indicate also a lower capacity for risk taking. 'The average age of newly listed firms in the UK is about 8 years, for the NYSE about 14 years, but on the German stock exchange about 55 years' (OECD 1995a: 117).

The total number of listed companies in Germany fell from the late 1960s until

Table 11.1. The relative importance of listed companies in different countries

	Frankfurt	Germany (8 exchanges)	NYSE	United States[a]	Tokyo	Paris	UK Ireland	Toronto
Number of listed domestic companies, end 1993	409	664	2,203	7,313	1,667	726	1,865	1,124
Turnover of domestic stocks,[b] DM billion, 1993	688[c]	920[c]	3,605	5,929[d]	1,345	281	721[c]	189
Market value of listed domestic shares, DM billion, end 1993	—	800	7,471	9,006	5,019	791	2,056	559
Stock market capitalization, per cent of GDP, average 1991–4	—	29	65	—	125[e]	39[e]	112	54

Notes: NYSE + AMEX + NASDAQ.

[a] Figures shown are the simple sum of data concerning the three markets and may involve some double counting.
[b] Precise comparisons are not possible because of divergent statistical methods, even within countries. Figures are rounded. Some totals are skewed by including various warrants and drawing rights.
[c] Since raw data for Germany and the UK and Ireland include both ends of each trade, they have been halved to bring them on a base roughly comparable with those of the other countries.
[d] Assuming all turnover on AMEX to relate to domestic shares.
[e] All domestic stock exchanges.

Source: Roby (1994); OECD (1995a).

the mid-1980s. Whilst old domestic joint-stock companies disappeared from the stock exchange due to company failures, mergers, and takeovers, they were not replaced by new listed companies despite an available pool. This probably has its origins in German entrepreneurs' deep reluctance to go public because of public disclosure requirements and an aversion to sharing control of the company with outsiders. However, since the mid-1980s companies have been more easily convinced of the benefits of going public. For example, advantageous share prices in the 1980s increased the incentive as shares could be issued at higher prices. This led to an increase in the number of stock exchange listings. Since 1983, 158 domestic companies have gone public on the German stock exchanges, among them many small and medium-sized firms (Schneider-Lenne 1992: 12). The inside nature of corporate control and the limited emphasis on equity finance in Germany 'may also affect and be affected by enterprise accounting and information policies . . . Indeed a feature commonly associated with German accounting practices is that they lead to the build-up of large hidden reserves' (OECD 1995*a*: 106).

3. Financing Costs for Industry

The non-financial enterprise sector is financed predominantly through internal funds in virtually all industrial countries, and to a somewhat greater degree in Germany. The distinctive aspects of the role of banks in German firms can be summarized as follows:

1. The small and medium-sized unincorporated companies are relatively more important in Germany.
2. The main bank *Hausbank* system implies a long-term relationship involving exchange of information and continual surveillance.
3. In the absence of a strong market for venture capital, bank finance is extremely important for smaller firms.
4. Banks are important shareholders, holding 14 per cent of shares in 1993.
5. The widespread practice of proxy voting implies that banks' influence significantly exceeds their direct shareholding (OECD 1995*a*: 95).

The *Hausbank* system of finance and monitoring by banks through long-term implicit contracts between a firm and its main bank connection to some extent performs a role similar to that of venture capital firms in the Anglo-American system of enterprise governance.

Financing costs for German firms have been relatively stable over time, and in recent years when costs have risen in other countries, financing costs for German firms have been relatively low. Research and development investment is above the OECD average as a proportion of value added. There is a comparative advantage in medium technology sectors, though in the majority of sectors classified as high-tech, Germany displays a comparative disadvantage. Enterprise formation is deficient in Germany, but job creation occurs largely through the expansion of existing enterprises. Job losses as a result of enterprises closing are very rare in Germany, and established AGs have virtually no mortality, though there is a higher rate of mortality in small firms and in the service sector (OECD 1995*a*: 100–3).

At present German capital markets do not match Germany's world economic status; for example, at the end of 1991 market capitalization was DM 596.5 billion whereas in the United Kingdom it was DM 1,507.4 billion and in the USA DM 6,222 billion (Charkham 1994: 29). As a proportion of GNP it was only 23 per cent in Germany as opposed to 89 per cent in the United Kingdom (Schneider-Lenne 1992: 13). This is likely to change as capital markets grow in importance (Friedmann 1984) and already banks are making strenuous efforts in this direction (Schneider-Lenne 1994: 302). As early as 1981 the Bundesbank in its annual report urged the development of the external capital market, in particular the equity market. Low reliance on capital markets up to now has resulted in fundamental differences between this system and that of the Anglo-Saxon model: 'With so many differences between the German capital markets and their transatlantic and cross-channel counterparts it is not surprising that corporate governance in Germany is totally different from that in the US or UK in that shareholder activism by large institutions, hostile takeovers and shareholder involvement in management are less prominent in Germany' (Schmalenbach 1990: 110).

4. German Structure of Shareholdings and Bank Influence

The two basic reasons for these differences can be seen in the legal structure of German public companies, with their two-tier boards as opposed to the unitary board of the Anglo-Saxon model, and the structure of shareholdings in Germany, with the banks controlling the majority of shares. The reason for this is that banks own their own shares and also look after and vote private and corporate investors' shares. For example, in 1988 shares with a nominal value of DM 65 billion were deposited with banks (Schmalenbach 1990: 110). Banks can vote vast numbers of shares which they do not own, giving them significant power at general meetings of shareholders. This is shown by the fact that on average banks collectively represent more than four-fifths (82.67 per cent) of all votes present in the meetings (Baums 1992: 8) with the big three banks accounting for 45 per cent of the votes present. The banks represent 36 per cent of the votes of the 100 largest companies according to the 1978 Monopolkommission Report, if their own holdings are added in; for the ten largest companies it rose to 50 per cent—a commanding position (cited in Charkham 1994: 38). They tend to support management, making opposing shareholder activism by other parties futile. Banks tend also to be lenders, which helps to explain their involvement with company management and their interest in the longer term.

The votes of the banks as discretionary proxies is very important in the context

Table 11.2. Ownership of common stock (% of outstanding shares)

	Germany (1993)	United States (1990)	Japan (1990)	France (1993)	Italy (1993)	United Kingdom (1993)
Financial institutions	29.0	30.4	48.0	6.5	11.3	61.8
Banks	14.3	0	18.9	4.3	9.9	0.6
Insurance firms	7.1	4.6	19.6	2.2	0.8	17.3
Pension funds and others	7.7	25.8	9.5	1.9	0.6	43.9
Non-financial institutions	71.0	69.6	52.0	93.5	88.7	38.2
Non-financial enterprises	38.8	14.1	24.9	54.5	23.0	3.1
Households	16.6	50.2	22.4	20.7	33.9	17.7
Public authorities	3.4	0	0.7	4.5	27.0	1.3
Non-residents	12.2	5.4	4.0	11.9	4.8	16.3

Source: Deutsche Bundesbank (1994c); OECD (1995a); Prowse (1994); Central Statistical Office.

of corporate governance. The banks' voting power is much greater than their economic share, they could stifle shareholder activism, and there is always the danger that, although they are supposed to vote in the interest of shareholders, they may not always act accordingly (Baums 1992). Self-interest may prevail; 'from this it may seem that the banks seek to prevent corporate governance being exercised by shareholders in German companies. This is not the case. The decisive factor is that the shareholders are apparently not aware of, nor interested in fully exercising their rights. The banks are simply the beneficiaries of such habit' (Schmalenbach 1990: 117).

Some politicians are intent on curbing the power of Germany's banks, the most radical ideas for reform coming from the left-wing opposition. Hans Martin Bury, a Social Democrat, wants to limit the banks' direct stakes in individual companies to 5 per cent, oblige banks to sell their fund management companies, and require full disclosure of significant shareholdings (currently banks and other firms can hold large, undisclosed stakes through private shell companies). He also has plans to weaken banks' hold over proxy votes and to strengthen the rights of minority shareholders, which are often ignored by bankers. The governing centre-right coalition also wants to curb the banks' powers. The coalition is toying with more direct controls on banks' influence. Some would like to limit banks' stakes in non-financial firms to 10–15 per cent, an idea probably too radical for some. Others in government propose a timid reform of proxy voting. Instead of exercising proxies themselves, bank would have to appoint a member of their staff to vote in shareholders' interests, which might not necessarily be the same as the banks' (*Economist* 1995a: 91–2; Chernoff 1994: 42).

The shareholders can take an active role in the life of a company if they are willing to do so; however, owing to the two-tier board system, their influence on the day-to-day business decisions will be limited. There is nothing to stop them from exercising their right in general meetings and in appointing representatives on the supervisory board. Although German company law may not encourage corporate governance by shareholders, it should not be seen as an obstacle. Indeed, it is argued that the quietness of the market for corporate control is caused by the fact that shareholders are not interested in pursuing their rights. They are seen as happy with the banks exercising their votes on their behalf, usually in accordance with the proposals of the management. There are no legal or economic reasons to prevent a shareholder from rallying other shareholders to support him or her in an attempt to exercise corporate governance actively. To date there are few such cases, but this is not to say that such attempts would be fruitless.

5. Merger and Takeover Activity

Since the Second World War there have been just three cases of hostile takeovers of non-financial corporations in Germany, compared with twenty-five for the UK and forty for the USA in 1986 alone (Franks and Mayer 1995: 1). In general it can be said that it is not the regulatory framework which discourages such practices in Germany (Schneider-Lenne 1992) but rather the structure of shareholdings and, perhaps, the clauses concerning maximum voting rights in the articles of association of certain companies. There are, for example, preference shares with no voting rights, which are gaining popularity, the number of quoted companies with preferred stock rising from twenty-nine in 1980 to seventy-four in 1987. It is also possible, but not usual, to put limitations on voting rights. These limit the maximum number of votes that any single shareholder can cast, irrespective of the size of its shareholding. The voting right restriction limits the control of the large share stake and shifts voting from one share–one vote closer to a one investor–one vote principle. Finally, clients who deposit with banks can give voting instructions, but if they do not, as is usually the case, the banks can vote as they feel fit. However, as Kochan and Syrett (1991) and Franks and Mayer (1990) point out, hostile takeovers look increasingly likely in Germany, a phenomenon confirmed by Schneider-Lenne (1992), partly because of Germany's relatively low share prices and more importantly because of European economic integration.

The share structure of German companies has in the past also inhibited the market in hostile takeovers. This is due, in part, to the existence of concentrated shareholdings in Germany. Franks and Mayer (1990) report that in the 200 largest companies in Germany, nearly 90 per cent have at least one shareholder with a share stake of at least 25 per cent of issued equity (cited in Jenkinson and Mayer 1992: 6). Most of these large shareholders are other industrial firms (industrial investors often have commercial links, as suppliers or customers, to the companies in which they hold shares) and families, as can be seen by the later work of Franks and Mayer (1995). The most striking feature is that for 85 per cent of the companies there is at least one large shareholder owning more than 25 per cent of voting shares, for 57 per cent of companies there is a majority shareholder (i.e. who owns more than 50 per cent) and for 22 per cent the holding is sufficiently large to prevent a blocking minority (i.e. greater than 75 per cent). A second feature is that other German industrial companies account for 27 per cent of dominant shareholdings, and families for a further 20 per cent. German institutional investors, including trusts and insurance companies, account for only 15 per cent. Their role is a relatively minor one compared with that played by institutional investors in the UK and USA. Still more striking is the absence of bank holdings, which account for only 6 per cent of shareholdings in excess of 25 per cent (Franks and Mayer 1995).

Although the small number of hostile takeovers in Germany suggests a virtual absence of a market for corporate control, Franks and Mayer (1995) find substantial evidence of sales of large share stakes. Furthermore, such share stake sales are related to poor performance and therefore point to a substitute for the Anglo-American market for corporate control. The authors examine a sample of 134 companies drawn from their original sample of 171 companies to determine if there was a sale of a major share stake between 1988 and 1991. In eighty-one cases (60 per cent) the major shareholder was not altered, although in ten cases the size of the holding was changed. In eighteen cases (13.4 per cent) the major shareholder sold its entire stake, and in a further eleven cases, where the company was widely held in 1988, a large stakeholder was recorded in 1991. Thus, in twenty-nine cases (21.6 per cent) a new major stakeholder was in place by 1991 and in another ten cases (7.4 per cent) the size of the stake was altered. This shows a less stable market for shares than many previously imagined.

Despite this lack of a market for hostile takeovers in Germany, there is a market for friendly mergers which has grown in recent years. For example, there were 445 in 1975, 635 in 1980, 709 in 1985, and 1,548 in 1990. However, about 1,100 of the companies acquired were quite small, with a turnover of less than DM 50 million, but fifty-five had turnovers in excess of DM 1 billion and four had turnovers in excess of DM 12 billion. The number of mergers of big companies is on the rise. The 1,548 mergers in 1990 were followed by over 2,000 in 1991, partly as a result of reunification (cited in Charkham 1994: 32). These mergers in Germany, unlike foreign takeovers, tend to be friendly and for commercial reasons.

6. The Limits of German Bank Holdings

The Gessler Commission, which was set up to study universal banking in Germany in the light of much criticism, found little evidence of excessive German banking power. During more than four years' work between 1974 and its first deliberations in 1979 the Commission found little evidence of many of the myths surrounding German banks. For example, they found universal banks' total holdings in non-banks measured by nominal values are small relative to the total equity of non-banks. The inquiry into the banks proxy rights also showed that the banks' power from voting of shares (owned by customers and shares of so-called third holders which are not deposited at banks but represented by banks) is on the whole not very great compared with non-banks (joint-stock companies). They found bank control of a fraction of proxy rights between 10 and 25 per cent to be frequent (Krummel 1980: 49). They also found these proxy rights tend to be con-centrated in a few big universal banks. Finally, the Commission found the quan-titative influence of banks on supervisory boards to be small and again, where it occurred, to be concentrated in a few big banks (see Krummel 1980 for further remarks concerning the Gessler Report).

Contrary to popular belief, German banks as a whole own few shareholdings, less than 10 per cent of Germany's quoted sector, compared to nearly 40 per cent for non-financial companies, although in a few companies the three big private sector banks, Deutsche Bank, Dresdner Bank, and Commerzbank, and increas-ingly some state-owned banks, are important shareholders in their own right. On the whole though, banks are not the source of concentrated ownership in Germany. Indeed Harm (1992) describes the limited role played by German banks in the ownership of German companies. Their power comes from their ability to cast other shareholders' votes as custodians of absent shareholders. Even this power has been questioned by some academics (Edwards and Fischer 1994). As early as 1990 Esser questioned this power:

Shareholdings in industry, presence on supervisory boards and proxy-voting rights repre-sent no indicator of the power of the banks in Germany. First, property rights and personal influence factors are quantitatively not as considerable as is always asserted. Second, a pres-ence on a supervisory board has for long not been translated into control of the business policy of the executive board of the firm. Naturally, the banks exercise influence through their presence on supervisory boards; but influence more in the sense that information is exchanged and common strategies are discussed between representatives of the banks and those of the executive board in the forum of the supervisory board. This is, in essence, a form of mutual dependence. In individual, exceptional situations one can point to the strong position of a bank, but one cannot, however, generalise from that to the majority of cases and situations. Finally, it would also be an exaggeration to attribute to the German banks a general planning and economic guidance capability greater than that of the firms in industry . . . For the reality in Germany today cannot be viewed in terms of a dominat-ing 'financial capitalism' that fuses industrial and other forms of capital under its leader-ship. It is more accurate to say that certain industrial firms have long-established and stable relationship with certain big banks; and these connections compete with other bank-industry connections. (Esser 1990: 29–30)

The majority of banks in Germany do not have representatives on firms' super-visory boards or control proxy votes. These functions are exercised chiefly by the big three banks, and to a lesser extent by banks from the commercial bank sector in general (Edwards and Fischer 1994). For example, Bohm noted that in 1986 the big three banks had more than 61 per cent of all bank seats on supervisory boards (Charkham 1994: 41). This casts a doubt over the ability of German banks to monitor and control managements of firms on behalf of shareholders, and thus ensure that firms are run as efficiently as is often suggested. For example, it recently emerged that Klockner-Humboldt-Deutz, an engine-maker in which Deutsche Bank had a 36 per cent stake, needed a DM 719 million ($472 m.) rescue package (*Economist* 1995b: 95). Franks and Mayer (1995), using the examples of two out of the three German hostile takeovers (that of Feldmuhle Nobel and Hoesch) found banks may not have the influence and power that some suggest. In these cases it was one of the big three banks, Deutsche Bank, that had little influence over the outcome.

Schneider-Lenne (1992), while supporting the idea that the banks have considerable influence, questions the idea that they have total power and dominance over companies. The market share in Germany of the three largest private universal banking groups accounted for 14 per cent of the business volume of the entire banking sector: 'a share of only 14 per cent cannot be construed as dominance over the domestic German economy' (Schneider-Lenne 1992: 18). She also questions banks' power on the grounds of supervisory board mandates using 1988 figures: out of a total of 1,496 supervisory board seats for Germany's 100 biggest companies, private banks held only 104 mandates. She goes on to describe these figures as giving German banks quite substantial, but by no means excessive, influence. It must also be borne in mind that most German firms do not have supervisory boards. Only AGs, which are the equivalent of UK joint-stock corporations, and GmbHs (private limited companies) with more than 500 employees are required to have such boards. It seems likely that the German firms which have supervisory boards account for no more than 30 per cent of total turnover in the German economy (Edwards and Fischer 1994: 94). Edwards and Fischer conclude that the available evidence does not support the view that representation on the supervisory boards of firms enables banks to supply more loan finance to these firms. They found that those German firms which have supervisory boards make less use of bank loan finance than do German firms without supervisory boards, which are, on average, smaller in size. They found that their interviews consistently yielded the response that bank representation on a supervisory board did not increase the information available to a bank for lending decisions (Edwards and Fischer 1994: 151).

7. Supervisory Boards

The German system comprises a two-tier management structure, comprising of the *Vorstand*, or management board, which is entrusted with the day-to-day running of the company, and the *Aufsichtsrat*, or supervisory board, whose job is to supervise the management board, when necessary, and to participate in long-term strategic decisions (Lufkin and Gallagher 1990).

The origins of the system go back to the industrialization of Germany in the second half of the nineteenth century. As German industry sought to overcome its backwardness and catch up with Britain, large amounts of capital had to be mobilized. In the absence of well-developed stock markets or wealthy private investors, this task was performed by universal banks, which expanded into all areas of corporate finance, including the creation and subsequent flotation of industrial companies. The banks established a close relationship with their clients and were represented on their boards. The supervisory board was introduced as an option in 1861 and was made mandatory in 1884; further legislation in 1937 clarified and formalized the distinction between the control function of the supervisory board and the executive responsibilities of the managing board (Owen 1995).

This two-tier system has helped, in the past, to prevent the abuses of management-dominated boards that have occurred in the unitary board system of the Anglo-Saxon model. However, its effectiveness has been severely questioned recently and whenever crises erupt in Germany's normally peaceful and prosperous corporate landscape, accusing fingers are pointed at supervisory boards. It is the job of these non-executive bodies to pick management teams able enough to run companies profitably and stay out of trouble; however, they have not always been effective in this, as recent examples have shown. This has helped to highlight one of the major weaknesses in the system, which is that the supervisory board relies on information provided by the management board concerning the current state of affairs and the possible risks. Schneider-Lenne (1992), a strong advocate of the German system of corporate governance, admits the quality of this information varies and that there have been consequent crises before. In the case of the near-total collapse of Metallgesellschaft, it is not clear whether this important information flow took place between the management board and the supervisory board (Fisher 1995*a*).

Another criticism often levelled at supervisory boards is the infrequency with which they meet—on average four times a year and sometimes no more than the legal minimum of once every six months. For example, the supervisory board of Volkswagen only meets four times a year (Henry 1993: 62). In such circumstances it is obviously very difficult to exercise much control over the company. This is in contrast to the often monthly meetings of the unitary board of the Anglo-Saxon system. In addition, in the Anglo-Saxon system subcommittees of the board made up predominately of non-executive directors will frequently meet to discuss such issues as audit, remuneration, and nomination. Thus the supervisory board members of the German system may have less information and less involvement with senior management than British non-executive directors.

Heinrich Weiss, President of the Federation of German Industries, in a speech to the Royal Society of Arts, points to two serious flaws in the German supervisory board which would tend to indicate that it is not superior to that of the Anglo-Saxon unitary board system:

For political reasons, the supervisory board sometimes has no real control over the managing board. If you sit on the supervisory board of a large company and have labour representatives at the same table, you do not dare to put a critical question to members of the management board because you would be blaming them in the presence of the works councillors, when the managers need to keep their full authority. It is not written in any by-laws, but [my] experience of different companies is that it has come to be considered impolite for a member of a supervisory board to ask a question that is critical of management.

This has led to a situation, especially in very large companies, where control over the management board has diminished to the point where management-board members invite their friends and colleagues from other companies to join the supervisory board, rather than have the situation where the supervisory board is set up by the shareholders and then controls the managers. So from time to time we have a reverse hierarchy. (Cited in Binney 1993: 12)

If this description is accurate, then the supervisory board can be seen to be not so different from the UK unitary board, where in the past chairmen and chief executives have chosen their own non-executives, whose job it ostensibly is to monitor them.

As a monitoring instrument the supervisory board appears far from perfect. Edwards and Fischer's (1994) analysis finds no suggestion that the supervisory board is in a position to subject German managers to a high degree of monitoring and control. Some see its ability to restrain management ambitions, or even to influence the company's long-term strategic direction, as more limited than some non-German accounts of the system suggest. Roe (1994a: 195) has suggested that a more suitable title might be 'advisory board', along the lines of the US Senate's power to advise on and consent to treaties and appointments, a power which provides consultation and influence, but not supervisory control. Within this framework the executives have considerable freedom of manœuvre. In many companies the flow of information from managers to supervisors is sparse, as the Metallgesellschaft example would appear to illustrate. Although the supervisory board has the right to demand additional information and to make certain management decisions conditional on its approval, these powers are rarely used except in times of crisis.

Recently the two-tier system, often cited as an important reason for Germany's post-war economic success, has been criticized for being incestuous as the supervisory board system is being accused of having degenerated into a clique of some 200 ageing men perpetuating each other's power and perks (Prodhan 1993: 176). This could be seen as not too dissimilar to that of the Anglo-Saxon system, where the missing link in corporate governance in the UK is the nomination process. This has helped to perpetuate cosy boards of insiders in place of independent non-executive directors whose job it is to monitor executive management much along the lines of the German supervisory board (Bostock 1995a; Main 1994).

8. Stakeholder Representation

Among the strengths of the supervisory board is that there are both shareholder and employee representatives supervising the managing board, increasing accountability to a greater range of stakeholders, reducing institutional pressures upon boards of directors towards short-term decisions, and allowing for longer-term strategic planning (Clarke and Bostock 1994). The involvement of German employees has a long history, beginning with the attempt by the German parliament at the end of the First World War to counter revolutionary pressures and to reconcile the interests of capital and labour. Co-determination was extended in 1951 and again in 1976, when the present legal framework was established. Indeed, as the success of companies is seen to depend increasingly on the contribution of highly skilled employees (Drucker 1993), the case for recognizing their commitment in the way the business is governed has increased. As Woodworth (1986: 57) suggests, 'if union board representatives are a significant enough presence to occasionally sway corporate policy, and if codetermined boards can minimize paternalistic behavior, the evidence suggests that companies may gain from workers having a voice'. A better flow of information from the shop floor to the boardroom, and vice versa, can lead to improved upper-level decision-making. Indeed the importance of co-determination in corporate policy is suggested by some (Alkhafaji 1987).

Fitzroy and Kraft (1993) confirm that there has been very little empirical work to quantify the economic effects of co-determination and what there has been has lacked adequate data and methodology. This is probably due to the complex nature of such a task and as a result, as Hopt (1994: 212) suggests, it is difficult to make an objective assessment. The social benefits in economic terms have been even more difficult to quantify and hence are often discounted, although they are none the less real for those involved. Even more difficult to quantify are the benefits from co-determination in the form of improved labour relations and co-operation, which almost all observers have emphasized. Despite the lack of empirical evidence, the social benefits, which one would rationally expect to see translated into economic advantage, are plainly there to see.

In companies employing more than 2,000 people half the members of the supervisory board are elected by employees, including white-collar staff and junior management, and trade unions (Owen 1995: 11). In firms with less than 2,000 employees the proportion of employee representatives falls to one-third. In the event of a deadlock, however, the shareholders can impose their will as the chairman, always a shareholder representative, has the casting vote. As the German Federation of Trade Unions indicates, it is not the totally egalitarian system that is sometimes suggested (Furstenberg 1977: 52). The role of employees as stakeholders in the business is further enhanced by the fact that two-thirds of their pension contributions are retained within the company (Owen 1995) and represent an important source of internal finance (Friedmann 1984: 369). About DM 300 billion of pension assets are now held within companies as working capital (Charkham 1994: 27). This further explains why the capital market in Germany is less developed.

The German system of corporate governance has the longer-term interests of the company at heart and, like the Japanese system of corporate governance accountability, can be seen to be accountable to a wider range of interests than solely that of shareholders; hence the two-tier board system and labour representation in the form of co-determination on the supervisory boards. The longer-term interests of the company are also demonstrated in greater investment in plant equipment, intangible assets (for example, corporate training), and research and development than occurs in the Anglo-Saxon models (Porter 1992; Hodges and

Woolcock 1993; etc.). For example, DM 67 billion is spent on R & D annually, which works out at 2.5 per cent of GNP to the UK's 1.9 per cent (cited in Hampden-Turner and Trompenaars 1994: 226, 235). The heavy investment in people is shown by the fact that 70 per cent of all German employees are occupationally qualified, compared to 30 per cent in Great Britain, and many German board members also have doctorates (1994: 233–4).

Less emphasis is placed on share dividends, which tend to be lower than in the USA and the UK (Mayer and Alexander 1990), and more on the long-term viability of the corporation. This low return on shareholdings is not seen as a problem by the major shareholders in German industry, the banks, which have other business relationships with the companies they invest in. Apart from their shareholdings, German banks are also creditors and help debt-finance industry. However, this acceptance of a low return on the stock market may be about to change with the rising influence of the international institutional investor (Baladi 1991; Drucker 1991). Such powerful interest groups, which include the large US public pension funds, for example Calpers, the Californian public pension fund, have already started to indicate their disapproval of low returns on capital markets. If German industry wants to attract more foreign capital, it may well have to show more interest in its capital returns. In doing this, German companies will have to try to satisfy the shareholder without jeopardizing the long-term interests of other stakeholders.

The disadvantage of the German system is its rigidity. The long-term relationships with shareholders and the involvement of employees discourage rash decisions and foster stability, but they also make it difficult for companies to change direction quickly. In a declining industry, for example, companies may be reluctant to take painful measures, such as redundancies or closures, because such steps would damage employees; there might also be a reluctance on the part of supervisory board members to incur the wrath of local authorities in the areas where the plants are located (Baums 1993). The decision-making process and speed of response of boards may also be slower (Hopt 1984: 1354) and conflicts of interest may have to be resolved. This is possibly one of the inherent problems of an inclusive approach to business which may result, in the longer term, in a less competitive environment. However, it must be remembered that such a system also has many advantages and will increasingly do so in the knowledge age, as employees' intelligence and skill are recognized as the principal assets of the business.

In the past the small shareholder has largely been ignored by management. However, minority shareholders in Germany are now taking legal action to get a better deal and are becoming more active (*Economist* 1993: 86, 91). For example, they have pushed managers to disclose their main shareholdings, and to lift caps on shareholder voting (*Economist* 1994a: 11). This active minority shareholder movement is probably a result of a more general trend towards shareholder activism coming over from the USA and the resulting new pressure from foreign investors, who now own up to one-quarter of the freely traded shares in big German companies (*Economist* 1992–3: 90) (Table 11.3). This has resulted in some

Table 11.3. Ownership structure of German companies (%)

Type of shareholder	Germany	UK
Foreigners	20	12
Private investors	20	21
Banks	8	—
Corporate	39	—
Investment funds	3	67
Insurance companies	3	—
State and local government	7	—
TOTAL	100	100

Source: Monks and Minow 1995: 289.

examples of changes to Germany's notoriously shareholder-unfriendly corporate structure, but whether this is just window-dressing or the start of an overhaul is yet to be decided and questionable (see e.g. Cooper 1993).

9. Future Challenges

Despite the acknowledged strengths of the German system of governance, it is now encountering a set of challenges which could lead to significant transformation:

1. the increased importance of new, knowledge-based firms which may not fit easily into the usual governance structures, with heavy investments in intangible assets that may be difficult to collateralize within existing lending structures;
2. the needs of the fledgling enterprise sector in the five eastern *Länder*, which by themselves may influence the German system of enterprise governance;
3. the likelihood that institutional forms of saving may become more important, at the same time as firm-specific pension schemes cease to be a net source of funding;
4. the internationalization of business, which implies an increased role for foreign investors in Germany, and increased scope for German firms in securing finance abroad, and which may call for changes to information and accounting policies;
5. the increasing internationalization of regulatory standards within the framework of integrated capital and product markets, which poses the question of the role of existing governance structures in Germany as elsewhere in establishing an equitable competitive environment.

It is likely that the outcome of these pressure will be a further convergence of governance systems across the industrial world. However, there will be increasing diversity within the general trend towards convergence, as the variety and complexity of corporate forms continues to develop (Tricker 1994). And if the German system of corporate governance is moving toward the Anglo-American system, it is also true that there are important influences directing the Anglo-American system to adopt a wider conception of stakeholder interests.

10. Conclusion

German corporate governance, like all systems of corporate governance, has evolved in its own unique way because of distinctive historical, political, social, and economic developments (Roe 1993; etc.). Of particular importance to the German system has been its historical past, which has resulted in a strong bank-based system of finance and a strong association with social issues which has resulted in a 'partnership' system of governance with all stakeholders having representation (Schneider-Lenne 1993). This structure is uniquely demonstrated in Germany's two-tier board system, which allows employee representation on the supervisory board in the form of co-determination.

While the German corporate governance system with its supervisory board, with both shareholder and employee representatives on it, is in many ways a superior governance system to that in the Anglo-Saxon world, it has some inherent problems. Such a system ignores the interests of small shareholders, is over-secretive, and lacks information and transparency (Collier Sy-Quia 1992), and it is ill designed to cope with the pressures of international investment or the global market for companies. The biggest influence will be international forces (Oxford Analytica 1992)—the shaping of corporate governance by the globalization of the financial and corporate markets. Despite these problems, and others which are solvable, the advantages of the German system of corporate governance, like that of the Japanese system, can be seen in its use of industrial groupings, implicit contracting, and extensive cross-shareholding, which are all relationship-oriented, and ultimately in the financial sector's close links with industry.

REFERENCES

Albert, M. (1993), *Capitalism against Capitalism* (London: Whurr); first pub. in French as *Capitalism contre Capitalism* (Paris: Éditions du Seuil, 1991).

Alkhafaji, A. (1987), 'The Importance of Co-Determination in Corporate Policy', *Industrial Management* (May–June), 29, pt. 3: 26–9.

Baladi, A. (1991), 'The Growing Role of Pension Funds in Shaping International Corporate Governance', *Benefits and Compensation International*, 21: 8–12.

Baums, T. (1992), 'Takeovers vs Institutions in Corporate Governance in Germany', Oxford Law Colloquium, 9–11 Sept.

—— (1993), 'Takeovers vs Institutions in Corporate Governance in Germany', in D. Prentice and J. Holland (eds.), *Contemporary Issues in Corporate Governance* (Oxford: Clarendon Press).

Binney, G. (ed.) (1993), 'Debunking the Myths about the German Company', Anglo-German Foundation Report in collaboration with the Royal Society for the Encouragement of Arts, Manufactures, and Commerce (London: RSA, John Adam Street).

Blair, M. (forthcoming), *Ownership and Control: Rethinking Corporate Governance for the Twenty-First Century* (Washington: Brookings Institution).

Bostock, R. (1995*a*), 'Company Responses to Cadbury', *Corporate Governance: An International Review*, 3/2 (Apr.), 72–7.

—— (1995*b*), 'Rethinking Tomorrow's Company for the Twenty-First Century', *Executive Development* (Summer 1995).

Cable, J. (1985), 'Capital Market Information and Industrial Performance: The Role of West German Banks', *Economic Journal*, 95: 118–32.

Carrington, J. C., and Edwards, G. T. (1979), *Financing Industrial Investment* (London: Macmillan).

Charkham, J. (1989), 'Corporate Governance and the Market for Companies: Aspects of the Shareholders' Role', Bank of England Discussion Paper No. 44 (Nov.), London.

—— (1992), 'Corporate Governance: Lessons from Abroad', *European Business Journal*, 4/2: 8–16.

—— (1994), *Keeping Good Company: A Study of Corporate Governance in Five Countries* (Oxford: Clarendon Press).

Chernoff, J. (1994), 'German Banks May Face New Rules', *Pensions and Investments* (2 May 1994), 22/9: 42.

Clarke, T., and Bostock, R. (1994), 'International Corporate Governance: Convergence and Diversity', in T. Clarke and E. Monkhouse (eds.), *Rethinking the Company* (London: Financial Times Pitman).

Collier Sy-Quia, H. (1992), *Corporate Governance in Germany: Whose Company is it Anyway*, EIU European Trends, No. 3 (Economic Intelligence Unit, Business International Ltd), 40–6.

Cooper, W. (1993), 'Discovering the Foreign Investor', *Institutional Investor* (July 1993), 27/7: 81–4.

Deutsche Bundesbank (1994), 'The Trend and Significance of Assets Held in the Form of Investment Fund Certificates', *Monthly Report*, 46/10 (Frankfurt).

Drucker, P. (1991), 'Reckoning with the Pension Fund Revolution', *Harvard Business Review* (Mar.–Apr.), 106–14.

—— (1993), *Post-Capitalist Society* (Oxford: Butterworth-Heinemann).

Economist (1992–3), 'Corporate Governance in Germany: Rattling the *Vorstand*', 26 Dec. 1992–8 Jan. 1993, 90.

—— (1993), 'German Corporate Governance: Stirring Things Up', 18 Dec., 86, 91.

—— (1994*a*), 'Too Stable by Half', *Economist Survey of Corporate Governance*, 29 Jan., 7–11.

—— (1994*b*), 'After Schneider', *Economist* 16 Apr., 22.

—— (1994*c*), 'One of our Tycoons is Missing', *Economist* 16 Apr., 123.

—— (1995*a*), 'Those German Banks and their Industrial Treasures', *Economist* 21 Jan., 91–2.

—— (1995*b*), 'Metallgesellschaft: Germany's Corporate Whodunnit', *Economist* 4 Feb., 95.

Edwards, J., and Fischer, K. (1993), 'Banks and the Finance of Investment: Lessons from

Germany?', *Economic Review* (Feb.), 10–13.

Edwards, J., and Fischer, K., (1994), *Banks, Finance and Investment in Germany* (Cambridge: Cambridge University Press).

Eisenhammer, J. (1994), 'A Supervisory Board That Could See No Evil', *Independent*, 17 Jan. 1994.

Eltis, W., Fraser, D., and Ricketts, M. (1992), 'The Lessons for Britain from the Superior Economic Performance of Germany and Japan', *National Westminster Quarterly Bank Review* (Feb.), 2–22.

Esser, J. (1990), 'Bank Power in West Germany Revised', *West European Politics*, 13/4 (Oct.), 17–32.

Fisher, A. (1995*a*), 'Cracks Around the Edges', *Financial Times*, 27 Feb., 11.

—— (1995*b*), 'The Oil Deals that Crippled a German Metal-Trading Giant', *Financial Times*, 20 Mar., 20.

Fitzroy, F., and Kraft, K. (1993), 'Economic Effects of Codetermination', *Scandinavian Journal of Economics*, 95/3: 365–75.

Franks, J., and Mayer, C. (1990), 'Capital Markets and Corporate Control: A Study of France, Germany and the UK', *Economic Policy*, 11: 191–231.

—— —— (1995), 'The Ownership and Control of German Corporations', Paper presented at an Accounting and Finance Seminar, University of Leeds, 8 Feb.

Friedmann, W. (1984), 'Business Finance in the United Kingdom and Germany', *Bank of England Quarterly Bulletin* (Sept.), 24: 368–75.

Furstenberg, F. (1977), 'West German Experience with Industrial Democracy', *Annals of the American Academy of Political and Social Science* (May), 44–53.

Hallet, G. (1990), 'West Germany', in A. Graham and A. Seldon (eds.), *Government and Economies in the Post-War World* (London: Routledge).

Hampden-Turner, C., and Trompenaars, A. (1994), *The Seven Cultures of Capitalism* (London: Piatkus).

Harm, C. (1992), 'The Relationship between German Banks and Large German Firms', Working Paper No. 900, Country Economics Department, World Bank.

Henry, P. (1993), 'Corporate Governance in the UK and Germany', De Montfort University MBA thesis.

Hodges, M., and Woolcock, S. (1993), 'Atlantic Capitalism versus Rhine Capitalism in the European Community', *West European Politics*, 16/3 (July), 329–44.

Hopt, K. (1984), 'New Ways in Corporate Governance: European Experiments with Labor Representation on Corporate Boards', *Michigan Law Review*, 82 (Apr.–May), 1338–63.

—— (1994), 'Labor Representation on Corporate Boards: Impacts and Problems for Corporate Governance and Economic Integration in Europe', *International Review of Law and Economics* (June), 14/2: 203–14.

Jenkinson, T., and Mayer, C. (1992), 'The Assessment: Corporate Governance and Corporate Control', *Oxford Review of Economic Policy*, 8/3: 1–10.

Kester, C. (1992), 'Industrial Groups as Systems of Contractual Governance', *Oxford Review of Economic Policy*, 8/3: 24–44.

Kochan, N., and Syrett, M. (1991), *New Directions in Corporate Governance*, Business International Ltd. Report, No. 2137 (London: Business International).

Krummel, H. J. (1980), 'German Universal Banking Scrutinized', *Journal of Banking and Finance*, 4: 33–55.

Kubler, F. (1994), 'Institutional Investors and Corporate Governance: A German Perspective', in T. Baums, R. Buxbaum, and K. Hopt (eds.), *Institutional Investors and*

Corporate Governance (Berlin: Walter de Gruyter).

Lufkin, J., and Gallagher, D. (1990), *International Corporate Governance* (London: Euromoney).

Main, B. (1994), 'The Nomination Process and Corporate Governance: A Missing Link?', *Corporate Governance: An International Review*, 2/3 (July), 161–9.

Mayer, C., and Alexander, I. (1990), 'Banks and Securities Markets: Corporate Financing in Germany and the United Kingdom', *Journal of the Japanese and International Economies*, 4: 450–75.

Monks, R., and Minow, N. (1995), *Corporate Governance* (Cambridge, Mass.: Blackwell).

Monopolkommission (1978), *Report* (Bonn).

OECD (1995a), *OECD Economic Surveys: Germany* (Paris: OECD).

OECD (1995b), *OECD Economic Surveys: Italy* (Paris: OECD).

Owen, G. (1995), *The Future of Britain's Boards of Directors: Two Tiers or One?* (London: Institute of Chartered Accountants in England and Wales).

Oxford Analytica (1992), *Board Directors and Corporate Governance: Trends in the G7 Countries over the Next Ten Years*, Executive Report (Oxford: Oxford Analytica).

Porter, M. (1992), 'Capital Disadvantage: America's Failing Capital Investment System', *Harvard Business Review* (Sept.–Oct.), 65–82.

Prodhan, B. (1993), 'Corporate Governance and Long-Term Performance', *Corporate Governance: An International Review* (Guest Editorial), 1/4 (Oct.), 172–7.

Prowse, S. (1994), *Corporate Governance in International Perspective: A Survey of Corporate Control Mechanisms among Large Firms in the United States, the United Kingdom, Japan and Germany*, BIS Economic Papers, No. 41.

Roby, E. F. (1994), 'Securities Markets Moving Ahead', in Landesbank Hessen-Thuringen, *Finanzplatz Frankfurt* (Frankfurt).

Roe, M. (1993), 'Some Differences in Corporate Structure in Germany, Japan, and the United States', *Yale Law Journal*, 102/8: 1927–2003.

—— (1994a), 'German "Populism" and the Large Public Corporation', *International Review of Law and Economics*, 14: 187–202.

—— (1994b), 'Some Differences in Corporate Governance in Germany, Japan and America', in T. Baums, R. Buxbaum, and K. Hopt (eds.), *Institutional Investors and Corporate Governance* (Berlin: Walter de Gruyter).

Schmalenbach, D. (1990), 'Federal Republic of Germany', in Lufkin and Gallagher (1990).

Schneider-Lenne, E. (1992), 'Corporate Control in Germany', *Oxford Review of Economic Policy*, 8/3: 11–23.

—— (1993), 'The Governance of Good Business', *Business Strategy Review* (Spring), 4/1: 75–85.

—— (1994), 'The Role of the German Capital Markets and the Universal Banks, Supervisory Boards, and Interlocking Directorships', in N. Dimsdale and M. Prevezer (eds.), *Capital Markets and Corporate Governance* (Oxford: Clarendon Press).

Sherman, H. D. (1991), 'Governance Lessons from Abroad', *Directors and Boards*, 15, pt. 3: 24–8.

Tricker, R. I. (1994), 'The Board's Role in Strategy Formulation: Some Cross-Cultural Comparisons', *Futures*, 26/4: 403–15.

Woodworth, W. (1986), 'The Blue-Collar Boardroom: Worker Directors and Corporate Governance', *New Manager*, 3, pt. 3: 53–7.

12

CORPORATE GOVERNANCE IN THE PRIVATIZED UTILITIES: THE CASE OF THE WATER INDUSTRY

Stuart Ogden

1. Introduction

There has been much criticism of recent corporate governance practices, particularly in relation to the pay and reward packages awarded to chairmen and executive directors of companies. Nowhere has this been more pronounced than in the case of the privatized utilities. The recent controversy over the salary increase of Cedric Brown, the chief executive of British Gas (e.g. *Observer*, 27 Nov. 1994) has been one of numerous occasions when newspaper headlines have characterized salary increases in the privatized utilities for senior managers in terms of pay bonanzas, and share options as examples of unconstrained greed through which executives 'make personal fortunes at the consumers' expense' (*Observer*, 14 May 1995). Typical of this calibre of condemnation is the *Independent on Sunday*'s (12 December 1995) criticism of share options for the directors and some executives of the privatized regional electricity companies, which appeared under the headline 'Privatised power bosses give themselves £72m in shares'. However, of all the utilities, it is the water industry that has perhaps attracted most criticism. Hutton (1995), for example, commenting on the general extravagance of remuneration packages for senior executives, states:

The privatised utilities are particularly offensive in this regard. The directors of these natural monopolies (for who else can supply water or gas) granted themselves share options at keen prices which have made them millionaires many times over. The rise in profits which has driven up share prices has not been created by risk-taking or by genuine entrepreneurship: it has simply been achieved by massive lay-offs and exploitation of the companies' position through mechanical price rises. The water industry, writing off two-thirds of its initial £1.2 billion investment outside the industry, while its prices rise and executive salaries balloon, is the most noxious example of a general trend. (p. 7)

Such sentiments have been equally strongly proclaimed by leading Labour politicians, attacking what they believe to be 'the offensive excesses' in salary awards (e.g. speech by Tony Blair reported in the *Guardian*, 16 December 1994). Criticisms of the levels of reward in the ten privatized water plcs have also come from senior industrialists, who have questioned whether it was justified for managers running water companies, where, they allege, there is relatively little competition, to claim salaries comparable to executives running businesses of a similar size who face more competitive conditions (see e.g. comments by Sir Richard Greenbury, chairman of Marks & Spencer and head of the recently established CBI Committee on executive remuneration, and Tim Melville-Ross, also a member of the CBI Greenbury Committee and new head of the Institute of Directors, as reported in the *Sunday Times* (22 December 1995) under the headline 'M. and S. Chief slams water bosses' pay'). Concern that the alleged excessive pay increases have been at the expense of shareholders has been accompanied by equally forthright criticisms that they have also been at the expense of customers. For example, an *Observer* (14 May 1995) article stated that 'The men who run the privatised electricity, gas and water companies are using share options to make personal fortunes at the consumer's expense. You pay, they profit.'

Whether or not such criticisms are justified, they do draw attention to the potential for senior managers in the newly privatized utilities to engage in self-interested behaviour which may not be in the best interests of shareholders or customers. In the case of the water plcs, the scope of this potential is accentuated by the limited extent to which they have been subject to the market disciplines that companies in the private sector are traditionally assumed to experience. The water plcs continue to enjoy their previous public sector monopoly status as regional suppliers of water and sewerage services; they have been protected from takeover in the first five years of privatization by golden share arrangements; and they are relatively immune from the threat of bankruptcy.

However, whatever merit there may be in such criticisms, it is simplistic to think of the behaviour of senior executives in the privatized water industry as opportunistic. The change from public to private ownership has entailed new forms of corporate accountability. Confronted by a radically different structure of incentives and sanctions, senior management is now charged with pursuing improvements in corporate performance that will be measured primarily in terms of profitability, subject to the constraint of meeting the required standards specified by a number of regulatory agencies, and the economic regulation of Office of Water Services (Ofwat). This has had major consequences for the ways in which senior managers perceive and approach their role, and more specifically, for the ways in which they control organizational resources. These changes have been accompanied by new reward systems which are underpinned by a different conceptualization of the motivational basis for securing improvements in managerial performance.

This chapter argues that, despite their continued monopoly status as suppliers of water services, there are ways in which senior managers can significantly affect corporate performance, and that therefore deployment of financial incentives designed to motivate senior managers to act in shareholders' interests is consistent with their use elsewhere in the private sector. Whether or not the size of executives' salaries is fully justified by the scale of performance improvements that have been made since privatization, there is little doubt that the water plcs have complied with the recommended best practice in their governance procedures for determining executives' remuneration. Consequently, rather than single out the water industry as some deviant case of more generally prevailing good corporate governance practice, this chapter argues that the experience of the water industry may on the contrary be used to highlight some of the inadequacies of the present corporate governance arrangements generally operating in the UK.

Section 2 considers the changes in corporate governance that the water plcs have experienced as a result of their transfer from public to private ownership through privatization. The next section discusses the extent to which the privatized water plcs are subject to market disciplines and briefly outlines the new regulatory system, operated by Ofwat, which was established in the light of their continued monopoly status as suppliers of water services. Section 4 examines the ways in which the water plcs have responded to the new accountabilities that now confront them, and argues that, despite their monopoly status, there are ways in which senior managers may have a substantial effect on company performance. Sections 5 and 6 detail the extent and scope of change in rewards and remuneration packages for directors since privatization, and the corporate governance procedures that have been introduced. The latter fully comply with the Cadbury Committee's recommendations, and Section 7 argues that it is the inadequacy of present corporate governance arrangements rather than any lack of compliance with best practice that is responsible for alleged excess in the reward of senior management.

2. Corporate Governance Arrangements prior to Privatization

Keasey and Wright (1993) argue that the two key elements of corporate governance concern 'supervising or monitoring management performance, and ensuring accountability of management to shareholders and other stake holders'. Although stewardship issues have tended to dominate discussions of corporate governance, Keasey and Wright believe that equally important is 'the issue of how the structure of governance motivates those in control to increase the wealth of the business. Good corporate governance is as much concerned with correctly motivating managerial behaviour towards improving the business as with directly controlling the behaviour of managers'. In both these respects provisions for corporate governance and accountability in the water industry changed radically with privatization, but had undergone significant change prior to privatization. The ten regional water authorities formed in 1973 were the product of a rationalization of the industry which had consisted of some 1,600 separate water undertakings. The boards of the water authorities originally consisted of members appointed by local authorities, who had previously been responsible for much of the provision of water services, and members appointed by the Secretary of State. The boards, in consequence, were large bodies and reflected a hybrid character, being 'part nationalised industry, part local authority' (Day and Klein 1987: 145). However, doubts about the effectiveness of these arrangements were soon raised. The Monopolies and Mergers Commission (MMC) in their investigation of efficiency in Severn Trent[1] were particularly critical, and advocated a much reduced size of boards of the water authorities which would be more suitable for promoting efficient management (MMC 1981). The government pursued the MMC's advice in its reorganization of the boards in the 1983 Water Act, replacing the existing ones with much smaller ones, with all members being appointed by the Secretary of State. The purpose underlying this change was, as the White Paper on water privatization made clear, to make the boards 'more business-like' (Cmnd. 9734, 1986), an objective which was given considerable encouragement by the appointment of new chairmen and directors, most of whom were from the private sector (Ogden 1995a).

These changes gave added impetus to achieving targets set through a number of new financial controls that had been introduced by government in the early 1980s. A financial target was set for each water authority which was calculated as a percentage rate of return on the current net value of assets, and was intended to specify the surplus to be achieved after charging operating costs and current cost depreciation, but before charging interest. These financial targets were first applied in 1981/2. External financing limits, which specified the amount of finance the water authorities could raise externally by borrowing, were applied from 1979/80. Performance aims were also agreed following initial discussions in 1980 with the Secretary of State for each water authority for the period 1981/2–1983/4, and were reassessed for each subsequent three-year period. These performance aims defined targets for reductions in operating costs in real terms (defined as total costs before depreciation, exceptional items, and interest). The operation of these performance aims had a major impact on the water authorities, both in terms of an efficiency target to be met, and as a stimulus to develop more precise forms of measurement of costs of operational activities (Ogden 1995a).

In addition to these financial controls and performance aims, six of the ten authorities were subject to efficiency investigations by the MMC, which further encouraged management to exploit the scope for cost improvements. Taken together, these changes in the 1980s constituted considerable pressure on management to secure improvements in economic performance. Moreover, these pressures intensified once the government announced its intention to privatize the industry in 1986. As with other privatized enterprises, the water authorities were encouraged to improve further their profitability and efficiency profiles to make their successful flotation more viable (Aylen 1988; Chambers 1988).

[1] Following a broadening of its terms of reference under the 1980 Competition Act, the government used the MMC to inquire into the efficiency of public bodies with a view to ascertaining whether they could improve their efficiency and therefore reduce their costs.

3. Corporate Governance following Privatization

Although policy objectives for privatization have varied in emphasis and developed somewhat pragmatically during the 1980s (Bishop and Kay 1988; Wiltshire 1988; Veljanovski 1987; Vickers and Wright 1989), the main public justification for pursuing privatization has centred on the claim that it will bring greater efficiency in the production of goods and services through more product competition, easier access to capital markets, and better managerial incentives. In its White Paper of 1986 the government argued that the removal of government intervention and political interference in the day-to-day management of enterprises would improve management performance; that access to private capital markets would make it easier for enterprises 'to pursue effective strategies for cutting costs'; and that the financial markets' assessments of performance 'will provide the financial spur to improved performance'. The government concluded that profit would act as a 'more effective incentive than Government controls' and that the 'demands of the market will give management and staff the impetus they need to secure greater efficiency' (Cmnd. 9734, 1986). Such benefits are likely to be achieved, however, only if the privatized enterprise encounters a more competitive market environment than it previously experienced. In the case of the privatized public utilities generally, this has not happened, a fact which has attracted much critical attention (Bishop and Kay 1988; Heald and Steel 1986; Kay and Thompson 1986; Vickers and Yarrow 1988). In some cases, notably that of British Gas, opportunities to break up the old public sector monopoly and create greater competition were not taken up. This was due in part to the influence of the Treasury and senior management within the industries concerned. The Treasury was largely concerned with the revenue-raising aspects of privatization and was aware that 'monopolies are worth more than competitive industries' (Kay and Thompson 1986). Senior management have also been unenthusiastic about any major restructuring of their enterprises. Although in the early phases of privatization policy some chairmen of nationalized industries were openly critical of the government's policy (Thomas 1986), they generally became supportive when concessions from government were forthcoming in terms of competition, debt write-off, and regulation (Hills 1986; Utton 1986; Abromeit 1988; Heald 1989; Vickers and Wright 1989; Mitchell 1990; Wright and Thompson 1994). In the water industry there was, in any case, little prospect of developing market competition, as it was generally acknowledged to be a naturally monopolistic industry (Littlechild 1986; Harper 1988).

As the monopoly character of the water plcs remained unchanged with privatization, a new economic regulatory framework centred on Ofwat was introduced. The main form of economic regulation is, as with other regulated utilities, through price control. Charges are regulated by the Director-General of Ofwat through a pricing formula based on the retail price index plus a 'K' factor. The K factor is assessed separately for each water plc on the basis of investment requirements, operating costs and revenues, and an efficiency target. The pricing formula is expected to promote efficiency in so far as it provides incentives to management to reduce costs as a means of enhancing profitability. However, in contrast with British Telecom and British Gas, pressures on management to be efficient are likely to be emphasized further in the water industry by the opportunity Ofwat has for making comparisons between the water plcs and the twenty-five water-only companies[2] when reviewing K factors. This will enable the regulator to operate 'yardstick' competition, whereby each company's allowed price increase under the K formula is related, not to its own costs, but rather to the costs achieved by the most efficient of the other companies (Littlechild 1986; Cowan 1994). Opportunities for comparative judgement will also assist the scrutiny of management performance by the financial markets.

The assessments of current and expected future performance of the ten companies incorporated in their share prices provide important incentives to managers to ensure organizational resources are used efficiently and profitably. Consequently, failure to maintain efficiency levels comparable to the rest of the industry will have definite adverse consequences, not least in terms of share price. Thus although the monopoly character of the supply of water services has remained intact, the water plcs are, through the new regulatory system and through stock market scrutiny, subject to some of the disciplines of competition.

Some of the other incentives and sanctions traditionally associated with private sector status have, however, been more mitigated in their impact. As the threat of takeover with all its attendant adverse consequences for senior managers varies considerably, particularly in terms of size of enterprise, with large firms having much better chances of survival than small ones, it may be argued that that threat for the four largest water plcs is limited. They are large undertakings by any criteria and are likely to be more immune from takeover threats than the three smallest, Northumbria, Wessex, and South West. In any case, all ten have been protected from takeover for the first five years of their private sector existence by a restriction on the proportion, 15 per cent, of the total shares that could be held by a single shareholder. Although the restriction was lifted on 31 December 1994 for nine of the water plcs, it will remain in place for Welsh Water unless removed by a special resolution of its shareholders (see Prospectus on Water Share Offers, p. 65). A further mitigation of the takeover threat which is still in operation is the duty of the Secretary of State under Section 32 of the 1991 Water Act to refer any proposed merger between water companies with assets of more than £30 million to the MMC in order to help protect the operation of yardstick competition by the Director-General of Ofwat. Ofwat has argued that 'If the number of Water companies is reduced, comparisons of performance may become more difficult' and that consequently, 'Whenever the MMC investigates the reference of a water

---

[2] These are the former statutory water companies which supply water only and were already in private ownership.

industry merger it must have particular regard to the effect of the proposed merger upon the Director General's ability to make those comparisons' (Ofwat 1992*a*: 54).

Unlike the regional electricity companies, where despite their size there has been considerable takeover activity, there has been only one bid for a water plc since restrictions were lifted: that of Lyonnaise des Eaux, the large French water company, for Northumbrian Water in March 1995. The bid was referred to the MMC, who reported in July that it could only go ahead if substantial benefits to customers could be demonstrated by Lyonnaise's proposal to merge Northumbrian with North East Water, a water-supply-only company which it already owns. Discussions to this end are taking place at the time of writing between the Director-General of Ofwat and Lyonnaise des Eaux.

The threat of bankruptcy is also relatively weak. In carrying out his regulatory functions the Director-General's primary duty is 'to secure that the functions of water and sewerage undertakers are properly carried out' and that companies 'are able (in particular by securing reasonable returns on their capital) to finance the proper carrying out of those functions' (Prospectus for Water Share Offers, p. 25). The extent to which the Regulator is obliged to set prices to ensure that companies earn enough revenues to meet their financing and investment obligations has led Bishop *et al.* (1994) to conclude that 'Privatised firms are some of the most highly financially protected firms in the U.K.: they do not face serious threats of financial distress' (p. 8).

While it can be plausibly suggested that arguments in favour of privatization have tended to idealize the effects of incentives and sanctions under conditions of private sector ownership, and have ignored the substantial literature (see e.g. review by Jackson and Price 1994) which expresses varying degrees of scepticism about the general validity of models of how commercial enterprises are expected to operate in the private sector, it is clear that the privatized water plcs have not been exposed to the full range of incentives and sanctions normally associated with private sector status. Nevertheless, it is important to emphasize that privatization has conferred substantial powers on the Director-General of Ofwat to control the activities of the water plcs. As Bishop *et al.* (1994) have commented: 'The activities and powers of regulators are broadly defined. They were granted a high degree of discretion in evaluating the performance of firms, in setting prices, and imposing obligations to supply services on firms. Regulators have been more active monitors and controllers of privatised firms than the capital markets' (p. 12). In the case of water, the opportunity to make comparisons between the ten companies has reinforced the Director-General's capacity to steer companies in directions he would like them to follow. Moreover, Ofwat's publication of performance data on a variety of measures such as capital investment and financial performance (Ofwat 1993*a*), the cost of water delivered and sewage collected (Ofwat 1993*c*), levels of service (Ofwat 1993*d*), charges for water services (Ofwat 1994*b*), and customer complaints (Ofwat 1994*a*), not only facilitates judgements by shareholders, the City, and financial analysts about management's competence, but has also led managers themselves into the mentality of a football league table, whereby they compare how well they are doing relative to the others.

4. Managerial Responses to the New Corporate Governance Arrangements

As the Regulator has substantial powers and extensive discretion in how to evaluate the performance of companies, set prices, establish service requirements, and determine standards of service, it is not surprising to find that senior executives have devoted considerable attention and resources to managing their relations with Ofwat's Director-General. Regulatory intervention has a major impact on company performance, and on occasion can have a dramatic effect on share price, as demonstrated recently by the electricity Regulator's decision to reconsider the determination of the price caps previously set for the regional electricity companies (*Financial Times*, 7 and 9 March 1995). Consequently, minimizing what may be termed regulatory risk and maintaining good relations with the Regulator has become a major priority for management, and constitutes one of the main areas of managerial discretion where management decisions may have a substantial impact on corporate profitability. As Bishop *et al.* (1994) have observed, 'Most privatised companies have established regulatory departments, whose primary objective is to deter interference from the regulator and ensure that best possible outcomes can be negotiated with the regulator.'

In the case of water the scope for negotiation with the Regulator is considerable. The principle underlying the price-setting process is deceptively straightforward: the cost of capital is combined with asset valuations to determine profits which are then used in combination with comparative efficiency exercises to establish minimum costs and therefore revenues and prices (Bishop *et al.* 1995). However, in practice each element in this process is fraught with measurement problems. The valuation of assets and the determination of the appropriate cost of capital has been subject to considerable debate (Grout 1995; Cowan 1994; Vass 1993). Following the publication of consultation papers on the cost of capital (Ofwat 1991) and discussion of responses, including a three-volume response from the Water Services Association (1991), which represent the ten water plcs, the Director-General (Ofwat 1993*e*) indicated that for the periodic review of prices he would use a cost of capital figure 'towards the lower end of the range of 5–6% (after business taxes)', which was lower than the figure of '7% in real terms (before tax)' assumed in the initial K determinations in 1989. However, this continued to be an issue of some controversy in the lead-up to the periodic price review in 1994. Discussion with the Regulator has also been necessary to determine the cost and extent of investment needed to renew the long-neglected water system's infrastructure and to meet statutory required quality standards over issues such as drinking-water quality, bathing-water and river water quality, and urban waste water treatment.

Assessing the extent of efficiency gains that could be made in operating costs has also been problematic. Although the Regulator has sought to operationalize the concept of yardstick competition so that comparisons may be made about efficiency levels each water plc achieves in terms of costs and standards of services provided, and consequently prices determined on the basis of the costs achieved by the most efficient firm and the best standards of services achieved, it has proved difficult in practice. Comparisons over costs and quality of services are influenced by a variety of factors which vary across the water plcs. These include differences in geography and geology, character of the sources of supply, population, density of connections, customer mix, nature and condition of inherited assets, and the operating environment. Although Ofwat has carried out studies of company performance that take into account the factors that can cause costs to vary between firms (e.g. Ofwat 1993*b*), there is still uncertainty over how much of the variation in costs between firms is due to differences in efficiency levels. Scope for discussion over this issue was confirmed when Ofwat announced that for the 1994 period review of K factors 'the onus of proof will be on high-cost companies to explain their costs' (Ofwat 1993*c*), an invitation all of the companies were eager to take up.

The process of the period review itself involved a great deal of discussion, consultation, and negotiation with the Regulator. The companies began by submitting to the Regulator their strategic business plans (SBPs), which set out their detailed investment proposals and what, in their view, would constitute suitable price limits. These SBPs were then subject to intensive review and analysis by Ofwat staff. Each company was then sent a draft determination. The companies prepared written responses and subsequently senior management of each company met with the Regulator to discuss their concerns. In the light of these written representations and oral presentations, the Regulator then made whatever modifications he thought appropriate to his draft proposals in reaching his determinations (Ofwat 1994*b*). Ensuring acceptable, if not best possible, outcomes from the periodic review was clearly of critical importance for the water plcs and had been the major strategic preoccupation of senior managers for the previous three years. Although appeals against the Regulator's determinations may be made to the MMC, this is a costly and time-consuming process, and prolongs uncertainty about decisions critical to a company's future prospects. Indeed amongst the privatized water plcs only one appeal, from South West Water over the periodic review, has occurred.

The regulatory environment has also provided senior managers with incentives to improve internal efficiency, and this represents another major area of managerial discretion which can substantially effect corporate profitability. The incentive to improve internal efficiency and minimize costs is to meet the targets contained in the Regulator's assessment of what costs should be when he sets prices, and if possible to enhance profitability by going beyond them. Although efficiency improvements were pursued prior to privatization, since 1989 the drive to make cost savings and to secure greater efficiency has accelerated. Better management information systems, new methods of budgeting, more rigorous business plan-

ning, more efficient use of chemicals and energy, the introduction of new technology, and reductions in manpower have all been combined in pursuit of
efficiency gains in managing operations and the large investment programmes
(£18 billion over the period 1989/90 to 1994/5) which the companies are now
committed to. There has also been extensive investigation and re-evaluation of the
balance between in-house provision and outsourcing of various operational and
service tasks, notably with mains pipe-laying, but increasingly with other areas of
activity too (Ogden 1995*b*).

Diversification, which constitutes a third major area of activity where senior
managers may significantly affect overall company performance, has also been
influenced, albeit indirectly, by the presence of the regulatory framework. All the
new water plcs faced pressures as a consequence of their privatization to develop
corporate strategies that were distinctly different from those they had previously
embraced as public sector water authorities. The government had argued that privatization would encourage the water plcs 'to compete effectively in fields where
they can do so' and said that it 'would like to see the Water plcs expand their entrepreneurial activities, such as the provision of consultancy services, particularly
overseas' (Cmnd. 9734 1986, paras. 39, 78, 64). Investors and shareholders also
anticipated that the water plcs would be able to take profitable advantage of market
opportunities outside the regulated business of providing water services.
Management's interest in developing alternative sources of revenue and profits was
reinforced by the anticipated harsher financial climate generally expected to
emanate from the Director-General's 1994 review of the K factor and the prices
that water customers may be charged. Diversification was also facilitated by the
extent to which the companies had the means to do so: all the companies have
relatively low gearings, with consequent substantial potential borrowing capacity
at their disposal. Although the availability of financial resources is not sufficient
reason in itself, the opportunity this offers to diversify their activities has been
coupled with strong City expectations that the water plcs should use them to do
so.

In reacting to these pressures, the water plcs have undertaken a variety of initiatives which may be considered in terms of, firstly, redesigning the business and,
secondly, major initiatives. As regards the former, all the companies have reorganized their corporate structure. The pattern normally followed has been to establish a group holding company with a number of subsidiary companies, one of
which is the appointed business licensed by the Regulator to provide water and
sewerage services. Characteristic of the realignment process has been the emergence of new 'enterprise' companies based wholly or primarily on managers and
employees previously employed by the water authority. Typical examples include
scientific services, plumbing services, and engineering consultancy services. One
advantage of this realignment has been the opportunity to relocate outside the
realm of Ofwat's regulation various activities previously done by the water authority but not now deemed essential to providing water services. However, the
Director-General has imposed constraints on how far this process may be taken
by laying down guide-lines which define the activities to be regarded as within the

appointed business. The guide-lines also specify the information to be provided on transactions between the appointed business and other associated companies within the group to ensure that transfer pricing arrangements do not involve any cross-subsidy between the appointed business and other parts of the group (Ofwat 1993*a*).

The Director-General has also stated an interest in any diversification activity so that he can protect the interests of customers of water services. He has stated that diversification entails risks for customers in two ways. Firstly, if a financial venture undertaken by the group fails, it could jeopardize the ability of the appointed company to finance its functions. Secondly, there is the risk that the appointed company's performance may suffer through management time being channelled into diversified activity rather than running the appointed business (Ofwat 1992*a*). Consequently, following changes to the conditions of appointment, each board now has to certify that, in its opinion, 'there will be sufficient financial and management resources available to enable the appointed company to perform its functions for the next year' and that certification has to be repeated whenever a board 'becomes aware of any significant diversification' (Ofwat 1992*a*: 56). Although to date there is no reported example of formal intervention by the Director-General on these issues, the prospect of such a damaging eventuality no doubt influences senior managers' decisions about diversification activities.

In terms of major diversification initiatives, larger-scale acquisitions and in some instances joint ventures have been undertaken. However, so far all the companies have largely restricted themselves to activities which are associated in some way or another with their core business. One major area of diversification has been waste management. Although there are differences in some of the operational and technical skills required, there are sufficient similarities with the waste water business, particularly in the areas of liquid waste treatment and incineration, to make waste management attractive to water companies. In particular, the water plcs are expecting to achieve competitive advantages on the basis of reputations for dealing competently with waste products acquired through performing well in the regulated business of providing water and sewerage services.

The other major area of diversification is the international water business, where the emphasis has been on securing operating contracts, contracts for the design and construction of water treatment plants, and consultancy, which they have done with some considerable success (Ogden 1994*a*). In entering this arena, the water plcs have utilized their core competencies as the basis for developing the range of services deemed essential to compete effectively for international business. However, although these developments are viewed by senior managers optimistically in terms of future profit streams, to date the profit contribution from these activities is still relatively small.

A key element in all three major areas of management discretion, and indicative of the new imperatives senior managers are now subjected to, is the commitment to improving customer service. This commitment, a marked departure from previous practice, is primarily, but not only, a response to the fact that accounting for customers, and more particularly 'customer service', has become one of the new accounts of organizational performance required of the water plcs by Ofwat (Ogden 1994*b*). As well as his responsibilities for economic regulation, the Director-General is charged with responsibility for protecting customers. In addition to price regulation, ten new customer service committees have been established by Ofwat to represent the interests of customers and to regulate levels of service. The latter are monitored, and details of companies' performance are published by Ofwat. As Ofwat has stated, 'Monitoring the quality of service enables Ofwat, as well as customers, to make comparisons between companies and to identify those companies who are meeting customers' reasonable expectations and those who are not. The Director General will take into account each company's performance since 1989 when he resets their price limits in 1994' (Ofwat 1992*b*: 2).

Conscious of public scrutiny of their comparative performance, all the companies have been acutely aware of the need to improve their customer relations and services to customers, and have responded to the Director-General's concern with customer issues by introducing specialist customer relations departments and customer care programmes for employees, and internalizing the quality and customer service indicators used by Ofwat and identifying them as important business objectives in their own right. Developing good customer relations and improving customer service is also seen by senior managers as an important contribution to internal efficiency. Managers have argued that satisfied customers tend to pay their bills promptly, which is beneficial for turnover and cash flow, whereas dissatisfied customers do not pay their bills until they have had their problems sorted out. Having satisfied customers also reduces overheads; dissatisfied customers are seen to cost money, as their complaints need processing and responding, which requires well-trained staff (Ogden 1994*b*). Recognition as a customer-focused company was also valued in beneficial terms for opening up business opportunities in other markets outside regulated UK water services. Both in waste management and international contracts for providing water services managers believe a good reputation for customer service will provide a sound basis for their marketing strategy. As one senior manager at 'Beta' Water said: 'We have a view that what we want to create here is a model utility, the best of its kind, and if we do that it will provide a significant base for us to promote ["Beta"] Water in its pursuit of international and non-regulated business' (interview, quoted in Ogden 1994*b*).

Notwithstanding these benefits, it is clear that the main impetus to achieve and improve good customer relations stems mainly from the regulatory pressures exerted by the Director-General. To further their reputations in this field, some of the companies, e.g. Anglian (*Guardian*, 6 June 1994) and Yorkshire (*Guardian*, 8 June 1995) have recently announced rebates for customers alongside publication of their annual financial results. Wessex, in a more unusual step, have recently appointed two 'customer directors' to the board of its water services company with the specific brief to represent customer interests. These non-executive directorships are linked to the chairmanship of Wessex's two customer liaison panels, which are made up of representatives from organizations such as local councils and Citizens' Advice Bureaus. The liaison panels are elected every twelve months. Whether or not this is mere tokenism, it represents an acknowledgement of interests other than shareholders' as relevant to corporate governance.

5. Accountability of Senior Managers and their Rewards and Incentives

If privatization has enlarged the scope for discretion senior managers have in the water plcs to influence corporate performance, it has also provided the opportunity to introduce forms of reward and incentives not generally available in the public sector to encourage them to do so. With privatization remuneration packages for senior managers have both increased in size and changed in form. Table 12.1 provides details of salaries for chairmen and highest-paid directors for the period 1989–94. Just prior to privatization salaries of chairmen ranged from £37,000 at Northumbrian to £61,000 at North West, but by 1991 salaries (excluding pension contributions) had risen by an average of 156 per cent ranging from an increase at Thames of 226 per cent to an unusually low 38 per cent at Northumbrian. Salaries continued to increase throughout the 1991–4 period, but more modestly. A similar pattern is discernible in the case of highest-paid director. In all the companies except Yorkshire, a proportion of salary for most senior managers takes the form of a performance bonus. As Table 12.2 demonstrates, the amounts involved varied considerably. At North West, for example, the chairman received £55,000 in 1993 and £75,000 in 1994 in performance bonuses which constituted 23 per cent and 22 per cent respectively of salary; at the other end of the scale, Severn Trent's chairman got £8,400, 5 per cent of salary in performance bonus in 1994, and at Welsh the chairman and highest-paid director got 9 per cent of salary in performance bonus in 1994. In two cases in 1994, Northumbrian and Thames, no performance bonuses were paid as designated targets were not achieved. Performance criteria also varied considerably between the companies, with quality standards as defined by regulators being involved in four cases, along with more conventional financial measures of performance, such as earnings per share and profit levels. Chairmen and executive directors have also received substantial numbers of share options, and details of the numbers of share options under executive share options schemes held at the end of each year for 1990–4 by chairmen and chief executives (or equivalent) are shown in Table 12.3. These have proved in some instances to be highly lucrative. It is estimated (*Observer*, 14 May 1995) that the chief executive of Thames has made £307,874 in profits realized from shares sold, and the chairman of Southern has made £293,230. In both cases substantial numbers of share options remain to be exercised, which are estimated on the basis of the share price as at 25 April 1995 to be worth £217,112 and £291,622 respectively (ibid.).

Table 12.1. Salaries and bonuses of chairmen and highest-paid directors (£000s)
(excludes pension contributions)

	20 Nov. 1989	1990	1991	1992	1993	1994
Anglian						
Chairman	44	61	91	79	101	101
Highest-paid director	—	77	96	107	163	169
Northumbrian						
Chairman	37	31	51	76	91	54[ab]
Highest-paid director	—	50	82	110	117	135
North West						
Chairman	61	97	144	166	238	338
Highest-paid director	—	97	144	189	257	338
Severn Trent						
Chairman	49	88.7	149.5	143.7	179.3	173.6
Highest-paid director	—	108.2	158.8	148.2	195.4	218.1
Southern						
Chairman	44	46	142	169	170	169
Highest-paid director	—	59	142	169	170	169
South West						
Chairman	51	53	89	108	112	112
Highest-paid director	—	78	89	124	136	130
Thames						
Chairman	49	73	160	145	155	104[a]
Highest-paid director	—	157	209	199	215	247
Welsh						
Chairman	44	76	143	141	156	99[a]
Highest-paid director	—	82	143	141	156	139
Wessex						
Chairman	41	55	128	160	164	177
Highest-paid director	—	55	128	160	164	177
Yorkshire						
Chairman	55	75	119	143	156	156
Highest-paid director	—	75	119	143	156	156

[a] New chairman appointed.
[b] Eight months.

The scale of some of these remuneration packages has been the subject of much adverse press comment, both as part of a generalized concern about 'greed in the board rooms' (e.g. *Guardian*, 18 June 1994) and as an issue in its own right peculiar to the privatized utilities (e.g. *Observer*, 14 May 1995). This has led to calls, most vociferously voiced by Labour Party economic spokespersons, for regulatory intervention to curb alleged excesses. However, such intervention is currently outside the Regulator's terms of reference, and, as Claire Spottiswoode, Director-General of Ofgas, made clear when giving evidence to the House of Commons Select Committee on Employment, would not be a welcome addition to the Regulator's responsibilities (*Financial Times*, 16 April 1995). She also stated that, despite concern over the recent salary increase for Cedric Brown, the chief executive of British Gas, customers were insulated 'from the effect of pay increases

Table 12.2. Performance-related bonuses (£000s)

Water plc	1993		1994		Criteria for bonus
	Chairman	Highest-paid director	Chairman	Highest-paid director	
Anglian	None	24 (15)	None	25 (15)	Based on meeting investment targets, quality standards, levels of service, and financial targets
Northumbrian	a	8 (7)	a	b	Performance against key business targets
North West	55 (23)	56 (22)	75 (22)	Same c	Increase in profit before tax and return on capital employed
Severn Trent	22.6 (14)	24.6 (14)	8.4 (5)	36.9 (20)	Achievement against profit and earnings per share targets, and levels of service, water supply, and sewerage quality targets set by external regulators
Southern	28 (16)	Same c	22 (13)	Same c	Increase in company's earnings per share
South West	13 (12)	18 (13)	13 (12)	13 (10)	Earnings per share and achievement of other performance targets
Thames	b	b	b	b	Achieving target on earnings per share
Welsh	26 (17)	Same c	9 (9)	12 (9)	Performance based on profitability of the group
Wessex	19 (12)	Same c	28 (16)	Same c	Achievement of the group's profit target and an assessment of individual performance
Yorkshire	d		d		

Notes: Figures in parentheses indicate % of total salary as reported in Table 12.3.

a Does not participate.
b None: target(s) not achieved.
c Same = same individual.
d No performance-related bonus scheme in operation.

Table 12.3. Number of shares owned, and number of net balance of share options under executive share option schemes, at year end

Water plc	1990		1991		1992		1993		1994	
	Shares	Share options	Shares	Share options	Shares	Share options	Shares	Share options	Shares	Share options
Anglian										
Chairman	8,615	25,512	8,615	65,645	8,615	90,951	8,887	92,536	8,992	28,473
Group MD	786	30,631	786	65,748	786	104,858	5,075	77,986	1,063	88,607
Northumbrian										
Chairman	1,264[b]	38,314	1,264	38,314	1,364	71,419	4,493	33,105	[a]	[a]
Chief executive		38,314[b]	3,486	58,475	3,588	94,284	23,161	50,337	11,993	62,717
North West										
Chairman	8,362	122,250	8,362	171,700	8,362	216,700	55,911	94,450	5,469[c]	216,450[a]
Chief executive	4,200	143,750	4,200	157,000	42,000	204,250	4,200	235,499	[c]	[c]
Severn Trent										
Chairman	7,663	114,731	7,663	114,731	7,789	174,995	15,769	75,228	[a]	[a]
Chief executive	7,359	143,541	7,859	143,541	8,326	180,491	40,434	69,746	41,562	69,746
Southern										
Chairman	6,032	100,000	9,032	140,000	9,378	190,000	48,742	106,000	50,088	106,000
Group MD					10,384	130,000	49,440	57,000	51,075	72,000

Table 12.3. (Continued).

Water plc	1990 Shares	1990 Share options	1991 Shares	1991 Share options	1992 Shares	1992 Share options	1993 Shares	1993 Share options	1994 Shares	1994 Share options
South West										
Chairman	6,760		7,088	65,000	7,177	105,000	37,009	63,000	38,102	103,000
MD South West Water			2,000	65,000	2,089	112,000	7,212	76,000	7,344	106,000
Thames										
Chairman	11,263	90,000	11,263	172,000	11,576	199,334	49,617	109,334	3,540	a
Group chief executive	6,258	211,136	6,258	221,136	6,529	273,176	59,301	68,176	62,045	59,301
Welsh										
Chairman	5,980	90,337	6,264	186,544	6,264	180,408	6,564	180,408	5,500	a
Group MD	5,000	107,219	5,479	107,219	2,995	104,126	17,152	41,402	5,015	41,402
Wessex										
Chairman	33,110	76,173	33,110	106,654	33,193	146,654	56,603	117,231	37,162	117,231
Group MD	4,000	77,581	4,000	89,181	4,083	129,181	56,466	92,799	37,910	92,799
Yorkshire										
Chairman	6,263	64,499	9,153	86,929	10,415	107,308	75,252	35,611	77,305	35,611
Group MD	2,295	67,860	2,385	78,477	2,469	94,484	2,755	84,703	38,234	13,385

a New chairman.
b New chief executive.
c New chief executive appointed in Jan. 1996 was previously group finance director.

through the price setting process and that the question of pay increases was a matter for shareholders'. This view was endorsed by the report on pay for senior executives in the privatized utilities by the above-mentioned Select Committee (*Guardian*, 30 June 1995). The report said: 'Nothing in our inquiry has indicated that the interests of either customers or employees are adversely affected by present policies on executive pay.' Nevertheless, in a minority report the Labour members of the Committee again called for the utility regulators to use pricing policy to influence executive pay. However, to argue for regulatory intervention to curb 'excessive' pay increases is firstly to assume that the Regulator could define what was an 'acceptable' and 'non-excessive' level of remuneration; and secondly to acknowledge that existing corporate governance arrangements in the privatized water plcs are inadequate. The latter may consist of two possible arguments. To call upon the Regulator to exercise control over executives' pay may simply mean that shareholders are in some way or other failing to ensure that their interests are being properly represented when decisions over pay are made. It may, however, implicitly if not explicitly, also involve the argument that shareholders' interests are not the only legitimate consideration. The representation of, for example, customers' interests by the Regulator in deliberations over executives' pay, or indeed over any other issue of corporate governance, implies a move towards a 'stakeholder' approach to matters of corporate governance which is distinctly at odds with current accepted private sector arrangements. Whether or not there is any merit in the latter point, the criticisms made by the House of Commons Select Committee on executive pay cannot be attributed to some peculiarity in the corporate governance arrangements operating in the water plcs which renders shareholders unable to have their interests properly represented, since they comply with accepted private sector practice. Consequently, criticisms of the inadequacy of corporate governance arrangements in the water plcs are implicitly, if not explicitly, criticisms of private sector corporate governance arrangements in general.

6. The Water plcs and Cadbury's Recommendations on Corporate Governance

The accountability of senior managers in the water plcs and the rewards they receive are subject to the normal arrangements and procedures of private sector corporate governance provision. This includes comprehensive compliance with the recommendations of the Cadbury Committee. The water plcs welcomed the Cadbury Report (1992), and all have expressed their commitment to comply fully with the Code of Best Practice. Indeed all of them were already doing so in respect of most of the recommendations. North West Water, for example, stated in the 1993 Annual Report that the directors welcomed the Cadbury Report and that 'The company currently complies with almost all aspects of the code and will review the detailed requirements for full compliance during the next financial year.' Anglian Water in the 1993 Annual Report asserts that it 'fully supports the spirit and letter of the Cadbury Code'. Northumbrian's 1993 Annual Report states that Cadbury 'has recommended a number of measures intended to improve the quality of information given to shareholders and to improve Board accountability. We welcome these moves and will endeavour to see that the Northumbrian Water group continues to adopt the best practice recommended by such bodies.' There was already a high degree of compliance with the Code's recommendations. As Table 12.4 on the composition of boards indicates, all the companies had more than three non-executive directors in 1991 and continued to do so, except for 1993 in the case of Welsh Water. This was brought about by the following circumstances, as explained in the 1993 Annual Report: 'As a result of 2 non-executive directors assuming executive director responsibilities, the present number of non-executive directors has fallen below that recommended by Cadbury. The company is actively seeking to appoint further non-executive directors.' This was done and in 1994 Welsh Water reported 'full compliance' with the Code. In nearly all cases the positions of chief executive and chairman were held by different directors. Indeed Thames reports that it 'clearly separates the responsibilities of the chairman from those of the group chief executive' (1993 Annual Report), and Anglian reports that its Board 'has a chairman and managing director with a clear division of responsibility between them' (1993 Annual Report). Southern and South West, however, have had executive chairmen. In the case of Southern, the position changed in 1993 with the appointment of a group managing director. In the case of South West, Keith Court has continued as executive chairman. Although there is a non-executive deputy chairman, and the managing director of South West Water Services Limited, the main core business of South West Water plc, sits on the group board, this arrangement is not fully compliant with the Code.

All the companies have introduced Remuneration Committees and as Table 12.5 indicates have done so prior to Cadbury's Report. At Wessex, for example, the role of the remuneration committee is described as follows: 'it ensures the company's directors and senior executives are fairly rewarded for their individual contributions to the group's overall performance' and 'ensures the remuneration of the executive directors of the company is set by a committee of the Board which excludes the executive directors, (1992 Annual Report). In carrying these tasks it is clear that the remuneration committees are, as elsewhere in the private sector (see Chapter 3, by Ezzamel and Watson), influenced by comparisons with practice in other companies and have specialist advice to help them make such comparisons (see Table 12.5). Table 12.5 also details the composition of the remuneration committees demonstrating that in all the companies, with the exception of South West, they consist entirely of non-executive directors as recommended by Cadbury. South West's arrangements for its remuneration committee of the board are unusual in that the executive chairman is a member along with three non-executive directors. The situation at Thames requires some comment: the presence of the chairman on the remuneration committee during 1993–4 is explained by the fact that Sir Christopher Leaver, who was a non-

Table 12.4. Composition of boards

Water plc	1991			1992			1993			1994		
	Executive directors (no.)	Separation of chairman and chief executive	Non-executive directors (no.)	Executive directors (no.)	Separation of chairman and chief executive	Non-executive directors (no.)	Executive directors (no.)	Separation of chairman and chief executive	Non-executive directors (no.)	Executive directors (no.)	Separation of chairman and chief executive	Non-executive directors (no.)
Anglian	5	Yes	7	5	Yes	6	5	Yes	5	4	Yes	7
Northumbrian	3	Yes	4	5	Yes	6			6	3	Yes	5
North West	5	Yes	5	5	Yes	6	5	Yes	6	4	Yes	6
Severn Trent	6	Yes	6	5	Yes	7	5	Yes	7	5	Yes	5
Southern	3	No[a]	4	3	No[a]	4	5	Yes[b]	4	4	Yes[b]	5
South West	5	No[a]	7	5	No[a]	7	5	No[a]	7	5	No[a]	6
Thames	4	Yes	5	4	Yes	5	4	Yes	4	5	Yes	4
Welsh	3	Yes	4	3	Yes	4	5	Yes	2	5	Yes	4
Wessex	4	Yes	5	4	Yes	5	4	Yes	6	3	Yes	7
Yorkshire	5	Yes	4	5	Yes	4	4	Yes	5	6	Yes	5

[a] Ex-chairman.
[b] Group MD appointed.

Table 12.5. Remuneration committees (membership numbers are given where reported)

Water plc	1991	1992	1993	1994
Anglian	No information	Yes: all non-executive	5: non-executive	7: non-executive Takes independent specialist advice
Northumbrian	Yes: all non-executive	Yes: all non-executive	Yes: all non-executive	Yes: all non-executive Receives independent external advice from Hay Management Consultants and New Bridge Street Consultants
North West	No information	Yes	3: non-executive	Yes: non-executive Directors + independent specialist adviser in personnel management
Severn Trent	Yes: all non-executive	6: non-executive	5: non-executive	5: non-executive Take advice of outside independent consultants
Southern	Yes: all non-executive	2: non-executive	3: non-executive	3: non-executive
South West	3: non-executive + chairman	3: non-executive + chairman	3: non-executive + chairman	3: non-executive + chairman
Thames	Yes: chaired by non-executive	5: non-executive	5: non-executive	5: non-executive Takes appropriate external advice
Welsh	Yes: all non-executive	4: non-executive	2: non-executive	4: non-executive Takes independent specialist advice
Wessex	No information provided	4: non-executive (joint remuneration and audit committee)	4: non-executive	4: non-executive
Yorkshire	Yes	Yes	Yes	5: non-executive

executive director and member of the remuneration committee, became chairman by virtue of his position as deputy chairman on the unexpected death of Sir Roy Watts, the previous chairman. In the following year Sir Christopher Leaver retired and was replaced by Sir Robert Clarke, who had been a non-executive director with a seat on the remuneration committee.

The situation with audit committees was straightforward and, as Table 12.6 indicates, all companies had committees consisting only of non-executive directors (Table 12.6). In terms of length of service contracts for executive directors, all the companies fully complied with the Code of Best Practice, with three years being the norm. However, at Welsh it was eighteen months, and twenty-four

Table 12.6. Audit committees

Water plc	1991	1992	1993	1994
Anglian		Yes: non-executive	3: non-executive	Yes: non-executive
Northumbrian	Yes: all non-executive	Yes: all non-executive	Yes: all non-executive	Yes: all non-executive
North West	5: non-executive + chairman	5: non-executive + chairman	5: non-executive	5: non-executive
Severn Trent		4: non-executive	5: non-executive	5: non-executive
Southern	Yes: no details	3: non-executive + group finance director	3: non-executive	3: non-executive
South West	4: non-executive	5: non-executive	3: non-executive	4: non-executive
Thames	Yes: chaired by non-executive	3: non-executive	3: non-executive	3: non-executive
Welsh	Yes	2: non-executive	2: non-executive	3: non-executive
Wessex	No information provided	4: non-executive (joint remuneration and audit committee)	4: non-executive	4: non-executive
Yorkshire	Yes	Yes	Yes	5: non-executive

months at Northumbrian. At North West a director appointed in 1994 has a three-year contract, but the period of notice required declines evenly over time to a period of one year's notice on the second anniversary of his appointment. Thereafter one year's notice will apply. In all the companies the total emoluments of directors, and those of the chairman and the highest-paid UK director, are disclosed. As regards the latter, their salary and performance-related payments are separately identified. Although the basis for measuring performance for purposes of performance-related pay is indicated where applicable (see Table 12.2), no information is provided regarding the mechanics of how performance-related pay is calculated. However, this is typical of general private sector practice.

Although corporate governance arrangements in the water plcs comply with the best practice provisions recommended generally for the private sector, this is not necessarily an argument to condone the levels of salary and remuneration packages granted to senior executives in the water plcs. Cadbury's recommendations for improving corporate governance have attracted a number of criticisms (Keasey and Wright 1993) and in particular have been criticized for offering little reassurance that problems of 'excessive' executive pay where they occur will be satisfactorily remedied. They do little to alter what Forbes and Watson (1993) regard as the main problem: that 'it is not the lack of formal powers of the shareholders, but rather the lack of incentives to act and the difficulties in using what powers they have'. Moreover, the emphasis on non-executive directors to provide the appropriate monitoring and control of management presupposes they will be sufficiently independent of management and, as Ezzamel and Watson (1995) surmise, 'possess the power and incentives to act decisively in situations where executives appear not to be acting in shareholder interests', all of which are highly contentious (Cosh and Hughes 1987; Jensen 1989; Main and Johnston 1992, 1993; Chapter 3, by Ezzamel and Watson). More particularly, the evidence on the influence of remuneration committees suggests that they have little discernible effect on how far executive pay is tied to company performance, and that executive pay awards tend to be higher when determined by them (Main and Johnston 1993). Indeed remuneration committees may amount to little more than a new legitimization of the existing processes by which executive pay is determined. In the light of these considerations it is not surprising to find that the alleged impotence of current corporate governance practice to control executive pay is by no means confined to the privatized water plcs. Criticisms of the salary levels and remuneration packages of senior executives in other private sector plcs have been widespread (e.g. see *Guardian*, 18 June 1994; *Independent on Sunday*, 12 June, 21 August 1994) and were instrumental in the setting up of the Greenbury Committee on executive remuneration by the CBI.

Although it is too early to say, it is doubtful if the Greenbury Committee's recommended code of practice will do much to assuage the criticisms of directors' remuneration. Despite the good intentions of advocating greater transparency in the arrangements for determining directors' pay, and encouraging shareholders to take a more active interest in those arrangements, the Code of Practice seems to offer little that is not already available, or is likely to have any significant impact on the current situation. The underlying problem has remained largely unresolved: namely, how do you ensure that financial incentives, which although designed to encourage senior executives to act in ways which serve shareholders' interests are premissed on assumptions of self-interested behaviour, are not themselves abused by executives acting out of self-interest? The more financial incentives are emphasized as a means of motivating managers, the more likely they are to be abused. Present corporate governance arrangements generally seem unable to provide much of a restraint. There is certainly no reason to suppose that the corporate governance arrangements for monitoring directors' remunerations are any less effective in the water plcs than any other large private sector company.

7. Conclusion

Despite considerable public criticism of the salaries and remuneration of senior executives in the privatized water industry, this chapter has argued that it is misleading to think of their behaviour as simply opportunistic. Contrary to views expressed by leading industrialists that senior executives in the water industry do not operate in competitive conditions and its attendant implication that the financial success of the companies they manage is merely a function of their continued status as monopoly suppliers, the chapter has demonstrated that there are three important areas of managerial discretion whereby the activities and decisions of senior executives can have considerable effect on corporate profitability: relations with the Regulator, improving internal efficiency, and diversification. Moreover, it has been suggested that the scrutiny exercised by the Regulator, and the extent to which the publication of performance indicators required by the Regulator assists scrutiny by investors and City analysts, constitute in many ways a more active monitoring of managerial behaviour of senior executives than perhaps most private sector companies experience. With privatization the salaries and remuneration of senior executives are now determined by board remuneration committees in accord with standard private sector practice. Indeed the water plcs fully comply with the best standards of corporate governance as recommended by the Cadbury Committee, and shareholders enjoy the same opportunities as elsewhere in the private sector to monitor salaries and remuneration packages granted to senior executives. Consequently, criticisms of 'excessive' executive pay and perks in the water plcs cannot be sustained on the grounds that their corporate governance arrangements represent in some sense or other a deviant case. Rather, solutions to alleged problems of executive pay in the water industry lie not in terms of any further special regulatory intervention, but with reform of corporate governance arrangements in general in the private sector.

REFERENCES

Abromeit, H. (1988), 'British Privatisation Policy', *Parliamentary Affairs*, 41/1: 68–85.

Aylen, J. (1988), 'The Privatisation of the British Steel Corporation', *Fiscal Studies*, 9/3: 1–25.

Bishop, M., and Kay, J. (1988), *Does Privatisation Work?: Lessons from the UK* (London: Centre for Business Strategy, London Business School).

—— —— and Mayer, C.(1994), *Privatisation and Economic Performance* (Oxford: Oxford University Press).

—— —— —— (1995), *The Regulatory Challenge* (Oxford: Oxford University Press).

Cmnd. 9734 (1986), *White Paper on Privatisation of the Water Authorities in England and Wales* (London: HMSO).

Chambers, D. (1988), 'Managing Operations and the Relevance of Privatisation', in V. V. Ramanadham (ed.), *Privatisation in the UK* (London: Routledge).

Cosh, A., and Hughes, A. (1987), 'The Anatomy of Corporate Control: Directors, Shareholders and Executive Remuneration of Giant US and UK Corporations', *Cambridge Journal of Economics*, 11: 285–313.

Cowan, S. (1994), 'Privatisation and Regulation of the Water Industry in England and Wales', in M. Bishop, J. Kay, C. Mayer, and D. Thompson (eds.), *Privatisation and Economic Performance* (Oxford: Oxford University Press).

Day, P., and Klein, R. (1987), *Accountabilities: Five Public Services* (London: Tavistock).

Ezzamel, M., and Watson, R. (1995), 'An Empirical Investigation of the Relationship between Executive Remuneration and Corporate and Human Capital Charactistics', Paper presented at Conference on Beyond Accounting, Finance and Management, Waikato, New Zealand, July.

Forbes, W., and Watson, R. (1993), 'Managerial Remuneration and Corporate Governance: A Review of the Issues', *Accounting and Business Research*, 23: 331–8.

Grout, P. (1995), 'The Cost of Capital in Regulated Industries', in Bishop *et al.* (1993).

Harper, W. R. (1988), 'Privatisation in the Water Sector', in V. V. Ramanadham (ed.), *Privatisation in the UK* (London: Routledge).

Heald, D. (1989), 'The UK: Privatisation and its Political Context', in J. Vickers and V. Wright (eds.), *The Politics of Industrial Privatisation in Western Europe* (London: Weidenfeld & Nicolson).

—— and Steel, D. (1986), 'Privatising Public Enterprises: An Analysis of the Government's Case', in J. Kay, C. Mayer, and D. Thompson (eds.), *Privatisation and Regulation—The UK Experience* (Oxford: Clarendon Press).

Hills, J. H. (1986), *De-Regulating Telecoms: Competition and Control in the US, Japan and Britain* (London: Francis Pinter).

Hutton, W. (1995), *The State We're In* (London: Jonathan Cape).

Jackson, P. M., and Price, C. (1994), 'Privatisation and Regulation: A Review of the Issues', in P. M. Jackson and C. Price (eds.), *Privatisation and Regulation* (Harlow: Longman).

Jensen, M. C. (1989), 'The Eclipse of the Public Corporation', *Harvard Business Review* (Oct.), 61–74.

Kay, J., and Thompson, D. (1986), 'Privatisation: A Policy in Search of a Rationale', *Economic Journal*, 96: 18–32.

Keasey, K., and Wright, M. (1993), 'Issues in Corporate Accountability and Governance: An

Editorial', *Accounting and Business Research*, 23/91A: 291–303.

Littlechild, S. (1986), *Economic Regulation of Privatised Water Authorities* (London: Department of the Environment/HMSO).

Main, B. G. M., and Johnston, J. (1992), *The Remuneration Committee as an Instrument of Corporate Governance*, Occasional Paper No. 35 (Edinburgh: David Hume Institute, University of Edinburgh).

—— —— (1993), 'Remuneration Committees and Corporate Governance', *Accounting and Business Research*, 23: 351–62.

Mitchell, J. (1990), 'Britain: Privatisation as Myth', in J. J. Richardson (ed.), *Privatisation and De-Regulation in Canada and Britain* (Aldershot: Dartmouth).

MMC (Monopoly and Mergers Commission) (1981), *Report on Water Services Provided by Severn Trent Water Authority* (London: HMSO).

Ofwat (1991), *Cost of Capital: A Consultation Paper*, i and ii (Birmingham: Ofwat).

—— (1992*a*), *Annual Report 1991* (London: HMSO).

—— (1992*b*), *Report on Levels of Service for the Water Industry in England and Wales 1991–1992* (Birmingham: Ofwat).

—— (1993*a*), *Annual Report 1992* (London: HMSO).

—— (1993*b*), *Comparing the Cost of Water Delivered*, Research Paper No. 1 (Birmingham: Ofwat).

—— (1993*c*), *The Cost of Water Delivered and Sewage Collected 1992–1993* (Birmingham: Ofwat).

—— (1993*d*), *Levels of Service for the Water Industry of England and Wales 1992–1993* (London: HMSO).

—— (1993*e*), *Setting Price Limits for Water and Sewerage Services: The Framework and Approach to the 1994 Periodic Review* (Birmingham: Ofwat).

—— (1994*a*), *Annual Report 1993* (London: HMSO).

—— (1994*b*), *Future Charges for Water and Sewerage Services* (Birmingham: Ofwat).

Ogden, S. G. (1994*a*), 'The Development of Corporate Strategies within the Privatized Water plcs', Paper presented at the British Academy of Management Conference, University of Lancaster, Sept. 1994.

—— (1994*b*), 'Accounting for Organisational Performance', *The Construction of the Customer in the Privatised Water Industry*, Paper presented at Conference on Accounting and Accountability in the New Public Sector, University of Edinburgh, Dec. 1994.

—— (1995*a*), 'Transforming Frameworks of Accountability: The Case of Water Privatisation', *Accounting, Organizations and Society*, 20/2–3: 193–218.

—— (1995*b*), 'The Role of Accounting in Organizational Change', Paper presented at the British Accounting Association Conference, University of the West of England, Apr. 1995.

Thomas, D. (1986), 'The Union Response to De-Nationalisation', in J. Kay, C. Mayer, and D. Thompson (eds.), *Privatisation and Regulation—The UK Experience* (Oxford: Clarendon Press).

Utton, M. A. (1986), *The Economics of Regulating Industry* (Oxford: Blackwell).

Vass, P. (1993), 'Water Privatisation and the First Periodic Review', *Financial Accountability and Management*, 9/3: 209–24.

Veljanovski, C. (1987), *Selling the State: Privatisation in Britain* (London: Weidenfeld & Nicolson).

Vickers, J., and Wright, V. (1989), *The Politics of Industrial Privatisation in Western Europe* (London: Weidenfeld & Nicolson).

Vickers, J., and Yarrow, G. (1988), *Privatisation: An Economic Analysis* (Cambridge, Mass.:

MIT Press).

Water Services Association (1991), *The Cost of Capital in the Water Industry*, i, ii, iii (London: Water Services Association).

Wiltshire, K. (1988), *Privatisation: The British Experience* (London: Longman, Cheshire).

13

CORPORATE GOVERNANCE IN THE PUBLIC SECTOR: THE CASE OF THE NHS

Lynn Ashburner

1. Introduction

Good corporate governance is necessary if companies are to retain a competitive advantage, and essential if they are to survive. Within the public sector the issues faced by organizations differ significantly from those in the private sector in several ways. Competition and markets, where they exist in the public sector, are of a very different kind from those in the private sector, and the question of survival is often not an issue. The creation of quasi-markets and the introduction of competition since 1979 has brought many parts of the public sector closer to the private sector model, but key differences still remain.

Ensuring effective accountability within the public sector means that corporate governance is as important an issue as in the private sector. As Ranson and Stewart (1994) argue, the use of public money means that public organizations legitimately face even more stringent accountability mechanisms. In essence public services are funded largely through taxation and many provide a service where the government seeks to limit or control costs, whilst others, such as those in the criminal justice system and social care services, actually impose consumption on people. It is therefore problematic to view the consumer of public services as a 'customer' exercising choice. Services such as education and health are seen as 'merit' goods rather than 'private' goods and thus there are minimum limits below which the provision of such services would not be allowed to fall.

So, despite the separation of purchasing from providing, the use of competitive tendering, the creation of Next Steps agencies within the Civil Service, and the introduction of quasi-markets, such services remain essentially public. Although as competitive tendering has allowed some private sector companies to bid for the provision of services, and as the Next Step agencies continue to increase in number, the delivery of some public services can be seen to have become more distanced from the traditional structures and mechanisms which ensured direct accountability to government and ministers. As examples in the Prison Service and the Child Support Agency have shown, this has raised an interesting debate on the extent to which accountability rests with the chief executive or the minister.

The traditional public administration model is where public officials, employed by state organizations, implement and execute government policies determined by the political authorities within a framework of law. In such a structure, accountability clearly rests at government level. As Farnham and Horton (1993) note, despite the influx of private sector structures, processes, and ideas, and the consequent growth of managerialism within the public sector, the unique nature of public sector organizations which stems from the scope and impact of the decisions of managers and their fundamentally political character remains. Farnham and Horton go on to show how public organizations are created by government for primarily collectivist or political purposes and are ultimately accountable to the political representatives, whether the services are provided by the private sector, by an agency, or within the public sector.

So not only are the goals, ownership, and accountability factors different in public organizations but so are their criteria for success. In the private sector goals are largely economic or market in nature, whereas in the public sector there are central issues of equity, availability, and access. A very wide range of activities are covered within the public sector, from the nationalized industries, other public corporations, central government departments, local authorities, and non-departmental agencies to the National Health Service. None has developed as far as the NHS in the creation of boards, which resemble those in the private sector, to oversee the management and governance of their organizations.

Issues of probity, which fall within the remit of corporate governance, are of importance within both the private and the public sectors, although differences exist with regard to the form that board accountability takes. As shown in Chapter 1, good corporate governance is reliant upon the introduction and maintenance of mechanisms to promote behaviour and performance on the part of manager, which is in the interests of the organization's stakeholders. Even where such mechanisms exist, and even where there is control by the market and guide-lines in lieu of regulation, the ultimate factor is the extent to which the board takes account of these. This factor raises issues of the structure of boards as well as of the importance of recruitment and composition.

The problems prevalent in the private sector indicate the need for a reassessment of internal mechanisms, structure, and composition as well as external regulation, with regard to corporate governance. The study by Ashburner *et al.* (1993) of the development of boards within the NHS has produced in-depth data on board operations which serve to widen the focus and debate on corporate governance in general. The data produced show that even where there is strong external regulation, even when non-executive directors are numerous and totally independent, there remain important issues with regard to accountability and effectiveness.

Whilst the board of directors model in its various forms is used extensively in the private sector, its use within the public sector is still limited and of recent origin. The transference of such a variable and unproven model of corporate governance has no basis in comparative analysis of relative appropriateness. It reflects instead a fundamental political allegiance to private sector models in general. With the major stakeholders being the government and the public in general, rather than individual and institutional investors, the requirement for probity, for example, has been addressed more directly. The adapted models in use in the public sector therefore have a relevance for the study of corporate governance across both sectors. The strategic apex of public sector organizations have more commonly comprised 'authorities' with a composition of predominantly lay, generalist, or representative members, with the managers or administrators of the organization present merely to report and receive the approval of the authority.

Since 1979 the government has introduced a series of fundamental reforms within many parts of the public sector, the basis of which have been broadly either to transfer public sector organizations into the private sector or to introduce private sector models and personnel into the public sector. The central idea was to increase the level of managerialism in the face of what were seen to be static bureaucracies with powerful professional groups. The ideology which lies behind this most recent attempt at public sector restructuring is rooted in the concepts of the 'New Right' with its assumption of the superiority of the market and competition. This is discussed further in the next section. The adherence to markets as a basis of deciding the provision of services was in marked contrast to the previous forms of social planning. Underlying this philosophy was a belief that public services would, where possible, be made more efficient by transferring them to the private sector, and where this was not possible to introduce market-like mechanisms into the service.

Whilst there have been broadly comparable trends in the reform processes within different parts of the public sector, there are also many differences. Developments have occurred at different speeds and not all reforms are common across the sector. One outcome has been the increase in non-elected bodies (sometimes referred to as quangos) to run national and local enterprises often in the stead of the central and local authorities, which is of primary significance with regard to the issue of local accountability or democratic control. Not all of these bodies have followed the model of private sector boards as closely as have those in the health service.

This chapter examines the private–public comparison of what is required within a governance model and looks at the implications for the public sector of taking the private sector model. It assesses whether such a direct transference is appropriate, given the differences in the purpose of the two sectors and the inherent weaknesses of the private sector model. Next, there is an assessment of governance across the public sector which highlights the unique features required of such a system. Data from the recent study of boards in the health service are presented to show how the board model is operating with regard to governance issues and the role of the non-executive, and an attempt is made to assess effectiveness.

The chapter concludes by considering the implications of the experience of public sector boards for both the public and private sectors.

2. The Public–Private Comparison

The 1980s were associated politically with an increase in influence of the 'New Right' in Britain (Hayes 1994) and other developed countries. For the public sector this meant a dismantling of collectivism in an attempt to redefine the role of the state, and challenges to the social democratic principles and values which have dominated British politics since 1945. This occurred within the context of the slowing down of economic growth world-wide and the perception of the public sector as poorly managed and an increasing drain on resources. The philosophy of the New Right was that the creation of markets and privatization would bring both the efficient allocation of resources and choice to consumers and purchasers. There is little research evidence on the effectiveness of these reforms in achieving these objectives but early indications are that where they have had an impact it has been very marginal (Ashburner *et al.* 1994). Where privatization was not possible the aim was to make the public sector 'more business-like', with the transfer of private sector people, practices, and processes. Administrators became managers and where markets did not exist quasi-markets were introduced. There was no empirical evidence that this structure was appropriate for the public sector (Ashburner *et al.* 1994), but nevertheless it formed the basis of a widespread and sustained series of government policies affecting all parts of the public sector.

One element of these reforms is that previous forms of authorities with direct or indirect local authority influence and local democratic accountability have been removed and replaced by new non-elected bodies. In many areas such as health these have been modelled on the private sector board. Given the speed and extent of recent developments, those occurring within the health service are taken as the main comparator.

In discussing the role of boards, issues of financial probity and corporate governance have come to the fore in both the public and the private sectors. The private sector has no shortage of examples of failures in governance, with Guinness, BCCI, and the Maxwell affair, but the public sector, equally, is not immune, with the financial scandals in Wessex (Committee of Public Accounts 1993*a*) and West Midlands Health Authorities (Committee of Public Accounts 1993*b*). These reports showed that the common link was a loss of managerial control and accountability by the board over management, problems similar to those found in the private sector. The NHS management executive was also criticized for being very slow to realize something was wrong because of the weak line of accountability from the authorities to the centre. The important issues highlighted here are those of accountability and the balance of influence between the executive and the non-executive directors. The role of the non-executive is critical and becomes problematic if the expectation is that they should act in both a supportive and a 'policing' role. Whilst these are key elements of a board's operations, it is essential also to emphasize the importance of assessing effectiveness. The composition of the board and how it operates are critical for all of these issues.

It is possible to see that across sectors a governance model needs to be effective in addressing the issues of probity and accountability, as well as those pertaining to the efficient management of the organization. Whereas the private sector has the primary objective of making a profit, the public sector is equally focused on providing a certain level of service within a set budget. Both sectors therefore have a concern with strategy formulation as well as executive scrutiny. Although the need to make a profit can be presented as a 'simple' objective not shared with the public sector, the reality is less straightforward, with many companies recognizing the interests of customers, the environment, and staff. If we take Charkham's (1994) conception of the main role of the board being to strike a balance between conflicting interests, then this again could apply equally to both sectors. The difference lies in the notion of accountability. In the private sector, despite there being a number of stakeholders, the focus is almost exclusively on the interests or influence of the investor or shareholder. In the past within the public sector, governance structures have attempted to reflect the different levels of accountability, to the user and the community, as well as to the taxpayer and the government. The focus in the private sector is again predominantly on financial accountability, whereas in the public sector the predominant factor has historically been to deliver the required service in an equitable way. As Stewart and Ranson (1988) have pointed out, a major difference between the two sectors is the politicized context in which public sector bodies operate. What needs to be assessed is whether the requirements of governance in the public sector can be adequately addressed by these new boards. If the private sector board model is to be transferred into the public sector, then it is important to understand the similarities and differences in their purpose and what the implications are for the public sector. What follows is a brief review of what is known about the composition, role, and effectiveness of private sector boards.

The Composition of Private Sector Boards

The placing of a board of executive and non-executive directors at the top of organizations is intended to ensure that the actions of senior managers are monitored and that there are adequate levels of accountability. The Cadbury Report (1992) states simply that 'corporate governance is the system by which companies are directed and controlled'. The Report addresses some but not all of the issues raised by recent corporate failures and concerns about financial reporting. Charkham (1994) acknowledges the wide concern that the British board system is inadequate. There is in fact no legal requirement for companies to have a board of directors. The Companies Act 1985 requires only that there are at least two directors, but it does not require that they be managers, neither does it require there to be non-executives. The duties laid on these directors therefore make no distinction between executives and non-executives and relate foremost to the preparation of annual accounts and the requirement that they ensure that the business is 'properly managed'. Given that the role of the chair of the board is not a requirement by law, this position carries a considerable level of responsibility. There is responsibility not just for the running of the board and the setting of the agenda but for its size, composition, and balance. Given the power, as well as the ambiguity, of this role, it is frequently taken on by the chief executive in private sector companies. This should be an important issue, but although the Cadbury Report did state that there should be a separation of powers and the appointment of a non-executive chair, this fell short of a firm recommendation.

A review of board literature by FitzGerald and Pettigrew (1991) concludes that there is no fixed pattern of board composition. Figures from Bank of England surveys (1985, 1988) show that the average size of a British board was nine (between six and eleven) and that non-executives comprised 33 per cent in 1985 and 36 per cent in 1988. A Korn Ferry survey (1989) showed that very few of the non-executives were actually independent directors as 62 per cent were executive directors from the main board. This lack of an independent element was reinforced in 58 per cent of boards, where the chair was an executive, usually the chief executive, from within the organization. The pattern differs in the USA, where non-executives comprise 74 per cent of directors and the average board size is thirteen. However, executive chairs still predominate at 80 per cent (Lorsch and MacIver 1989). The Cadbury Report recommended that the influence of non-executives should be strengthened and that they should be independent, with no business or financial interests in the company. The new NHS boards have a majority of independent non-executive directors and clearly the issue of direct financial interest does not arise. The non-executives receive an honorarium, but this is a standard sum which is independent of the performance of the organization. Another Cadbury proposal is that non-executive directors should be capable of bringing independent judgement to bear on issues of strategy, performance, the use of resources, the making of key appointments, and standards of conduct. Were such recommendations to be followed, there would need to be a considerable shake-up of private sector boards in the UK.

The Role of Private Sector Boards

There is a diversity of forms of boards within the private sector, but despite their importance, relatively little is known about how they operate or what makes them effective. Most literature on the role of boards is prescriptive rather than descriptive and what research exists uses indirect reporting methodologies. Lorsch and MacIver's (1989) study was based upon extensive empirical evidence from directors in the US. This study identified the main functions of boards to be to oversee the management of the company, to review the company's performance, to oversee its social responsibilities, and to ensure compliance with the law. The majority of lists of board roles, besides being prescriptive, are also predominantly inward-looking. Pfeffer (1972) shows that boards also have an important role in facilitating relationships with external organizations as well as a ceremonial function. Such roles would have a particular relevance for public sector bodies with their interface with their clientele and community. Kovner's study (1974) of American hospital boards also stressed the importance of the outward-looking role for these boards in their relationship with their local community.

Lorsch and MacIver's list, like many others, does not specifically include a strategic role for the board. Tricker's (1984) definition, based on UK boards, highlighted three primary board activities: establishing strategic direction, monitoring and evaluating performance, and participating in executive action. More recent literature has tended to emphasize the board's strategic role (Charkham 1986; Zahra 1990). A survey by the Institute of Directors (Coulson-Thomas and Wakelam 1991) suggested that in the future, boards would spend less time on monitoring and more on initiating processes for change. This has important implications for the board's role in ensuring probity. If the board is to be more drawn into managerial roles such as strategy formulation, then a very clear understanding needs to be established concerning the extent of the role; otherwise the monitoring role and the independent evaluation of the strategy by the non-executives might be compromised. What this highlights is the existing ambiguity with regard to how one might define the board's strategic role and how this relates to the role of executives. Such issues are critical with regard to the effectiveness of the board in relation to organizational performance and probity.

The Cadbury Report largely continues in the tradition of self-regulation. However, it does propose that boards should establish what Cadbury calls 'effective audit committees' with a remit to monitor financial control and overall organizational performance. It is at this point that there is an emphasis on 'independent outsiders'. These bodies should also monitor the performance of the chief executive. This should require that performance criteria also need to be established for individuals, for the executive as a body, and for the board itself. It will be important to understand how such groups operate and how effective they are.

Assessment of Board Effectiveness

How boards interpret their roles and how they operate are key to their effectiveness. There is little evidence from the private sector on the form, content, and process of board meetings from which any measures of effectiveness or key variables might be established. The highlighting of the board's strategic role, as noted in the previous section, has been one implicit measure, but one that remains ambiguous. The concept of 'effectiveness' as applied to boards needs to go beyond ensuring that the organization has strategic direction and is managed effectively, or the implementation of wider policies, to include issues of probity and accountability. Charkham (1994: 4) establishes two basic principles of good corporate governance as, firstly, that management must have the freedom to drive the enterprise forward and, secondly, that it must exercise this freedom within a framework of effective accountability. If the public sector is to take on the models of the private sector, then it is important that both the strengths and weaknesses are known so that the latter can be avoided.

A major problem in the private sector, as already noted, is the lack of regulation, with, for example, no requirement in law for non-executive directors on boards, whether insiders or outsiders. Charkham (1994) sees a second major weakness as the strain placed upon non-executives, who share an equal level of responsibility but without the time and knowledge of the executives, and without any formal powers. He compares the British system unfavourably with that of Germany, where there is a dual board system, with an executive board and a supervisory board comprised of shareholder and employee representatives. The supervisory board has the formal powers since the executive board is required to inform and consult with it. See Chapter 11, by Clarke and Bostock, for more discussion.

Charkham's analysis of corporate governance in five countries concludes that despite there being some excellent boards in the UK, the limited legal requirements mean that there are also some of the worst. He states that the co-operative and supervisory roles of the non-executives are simply not consistent, that accountability is often nominal and not real, and that, as in the US system, there is the possibility that a powerful chief executive could dominate the board. He believes that the absence of access to information as of right allows for poor governance to continue and that the real problem for the US and the UK systems are that a lot of people do well from the present system and are therefore reluctant to change it.

The UK model of boards would not immediately appear to be one that recommends itself to other sectors, especially where the issues of accountability and probity in relation to the use of public monies are fundamental. The desire of public sector reforms to increase the level of managerialism in the face of bureaucracy and professional power can be met in the transfer of governance of public sector organizations from authorities with a lay and professional membership to boards with a strong management presence. But, as Charkham (1986) has so clearly shown, the empowerment of management is not necessarily the same as, nor even necessarily leads to, more effective boards. The over-powerful chief executive and the dominance of the executive are instead identified as weaknesses in the system when it comes to ensuring accountability and probity.

This raises the issue of whether the transference of private sector concepts and models is appropriate for the public sector, a debate concerned not only with the acknowledged weaknesses within the private sector systems but also with the fundamental differences in role and purpose between the public and private sectors.

3. The Public Sector Context

Public sector management as a discipline has emerged from the meeting of public administration theory and more general management literatures, based predominantly on the private sector. The precise form that this hybrid takes is still a matter of contention (Ferlie *et al.* 1996). Those from a public administrative tradition (Pollitt 1990; Hood 1991) continue to emphasize the significance of the differences between the two sectors and believe that managerial roles are not easily transferable from the private to the public sector. There are the different contexts of the two sectors, with one being market-driven and the other politically driven. There are also a series of distinctive conditions in the public sector which are not present in the private, such as the role of collective choice, the rights of citizenship, and the notions of equity, need, and justice (Stewart and Walsh 1992).

The use of the private sector board model in the public sector is part of a wider trend towards an increasing number of non-elected bodies to govern a wide range of organizations within the public sector. This has involved the removal of previous forms of authority with their direct or indirect forms of democratic control. Within the health service, reforms such as those of trust status, GP fundholding, and new organizational forms for commissioning were not statutory, but the structure and composition of the new boards was. Members of the boards were no longer there as representatives of different groups of health professionals and local authorities, or as lay members, but as direct appointments made or approved by the Secretary of State. The emphasis in recruitment was on business people from large private sector organizations rather than public sector managers or professionals.

Within the health service, the perception of a trade-off between managerial efficiency and the representation of different interest groups is long-established in the changing patterns of governance within the NHS (Ashburner and Cairncross 1993). There has been a history of tension and debate between different interest groups about who should be members of the bodies created to run the health service and how they should be appointed. The two main areas of conflict have been whether representation or personal capacity was the basis of appointment and which groups, if any, should be represented. The NHS, as created in 1948, was described by Klein (1983) as a compromise between those who sought to limit responsibility for the health service to elected local government representatives and the medical professionals themselves, with their continuing dominance. The most recent reforms actually represent the considerable rise to power of the newly created managerial group at the expense of both local authority and professional representatives.

The process of public sector reform focused on the health service with the publication in 1989 of the White Paper *Working for Patients* (Cmnd. 555). Earlier reforms had introduced the concept of general management (Griffiths 1983) into the NHS and were seen as the foundation upon which these later reforms to introduce concepts and models from the private sector were to be built. The central concept was the purchaser–provider split with the creation of markets and competition. Provider units would be given a degree of autonomy and become NHS trusts, whilst GPs would be given the opportunity to buy services direct from providers instead of having them bought solely by the local health authority. The changes to the composition and constitution of health authorities, and the setting up of a new form of body with the NHS trusts, were less publicized features of the reforms.

The model of the board chosen for the health service follows the recommendations of the Cadbury Report (1992) more closely than do most private sector boards. Non-executives not only comprise six of the eleven places but are all independent of the organization. Also, the positions of chair and chief executive are separated and the position of chair must be taken by a non-executive. A key difference however, is that far from the chair being the first among equals, as in the private sector, in the NHS their appointment by the Secretary of State and the inability of the non-executives to remove them makes them potentially very powerful figures. This has clear implications for the role of the chair in the implementation of government policies, especially where these might not be so readily embraced by management, and reflects a strong line of accountability to the Secretary of State, in contrast to the lack of any direct mechanisms for accountability to patients and the community. Overall the emphasis was placed on strengthening the role and influence of management. The thinking on composition may also have been influenced by research which had been critical of the effectiveness of the previous style of health authority with its range of different areas of representation, which had been seen to have resulted in a lack of corporate identity and role confusion (Day and Klein 1987). That factors other than composition might contribute to a lack of cohesion and effectiveness was not considered. Instead a more homogeneous group of executives and non-executives, predominantly from the private sector (Ashburner and Cairncross 1993; Ashburner 1994), was formed.

One fundamental difference between boards in the NHS and those in the private sector is that private company directors are accountable to shareholders, whereas in the NHS directors are accountable directly only to the Secretary of State. A second difference is the level of independence of action. For a main board in the private sector the divorce between ownership and control and largely ineffective shareholder meetings produces a high degree of autonomy. Boards in the NHS are more comparable with subsidiary boards, given the role of the Department of Health and centrally located executive in both policy decisions and control of resources. Another potential factor is the level of professional influence within public sector organizations, notably that of the medical profession in health care. Even though health professionals have ultimate responsibility for the care of individuals, and management can be seen as responsible for the collectivity of patients, there is a single hierarchy. Clinicians are integrated into the management hierarchy and decision-making processes, on both an individual and a structural level. Increasing numbers of clinicians are taking on managerial roles (Ashburner 1995), both in purchasing and in acute units, where the clinical directors are the main management layer between the executive and the directorates. It is at directorate level that the direct planning of health care provision and budgets is carried out.

The above factors, which include some constraints on the new health service boards' freedom to act, their limited base of membership, lack of direct public accountability, and the potential weaknesses in the model of the board transferred from the private sector, form the context within which the data from the study can be examined.

4. Empirical Data from NHS Boards

Ashburner *et al.* (1993) included the observation of the public and private parts of board meetings of eleven NHS boards over periods of between twelve and eighteen months by a group of one full-time and three part-time researchers. During each meeting data were recorded on both content and process of the proceedings, including information on who contributed and the nature of the contribution. This process was complemented by in-depth interviews with all board members and other key members of the organizations. In addition, a survey was carried out of every member of the new boards in England, during their first year of operation, comprising over 2,000 responses with a response rate of 69 per cent for regional, district, and family health service authorities and 62 per cent for trusts. This enabled extensive information to be assembled on profiles of members, how they were selected, and their experiences and attitudes.

Composition and Attitudes

The extent to which boards in the NHS are likely to be influenced by private sector patterns of board operations will depend in part on the composition of the boards and the experiences of the chairs and non-executives of the new bodies. Two-thirds of all non-executive members across all types of board were employed in the private sector (Ashburner and Cairncross 1993; Ashburner 1994). This represents a strong influence of private sector experience into the newly formed boards and a considerable strengthening of managerialism, with the inclusion of five executives on health service boards for the first time. The percentage of non-executives who were also directors in the private sector was highest on the trust boards. Over two-thirds of trust chairs and almost half of non-executives were private sector directors, compared with half of other NHS board chairs and a third of their non-executives.

When directors were asked in the questionnaire what special skills they brought to the boards, the majority included those of management and leadership, with 65 per cent of non-executives including 'management' and 52 per cent 'leadership'. Functionally the areas of finance, marketing, and personnel were the most common backgrounds of the non-executives. However, when asked about the attributes necessary for a non-executive, personal qualities were considered more important than specific skills, with 'common sense and good judgement' being assessed as essential or very important and coming top with 92 per cent. Second came 'sufficient time for board business' at 83 per cent, followed by 'an ability to work well in a group'. How these attributes could be assessed in the recruitment process is not clear. More surprisingly, 'experience of management in business' was rated by only 36 per cent of respondents, with even fewer (21 per cent) citing 'experience of management in the public sector'. Unsurprisingly, 72 per cent of chairs and 64 per cent of non-executives felt that the new NHS boards should be modelled on the private sector model. The responses of the executives were less emphatic, with only 28 per cent of trust chief executives, 63 per cent of other NHS board chief executives, and 57 per cent of other executives agreeing.

These replies raise the issue of what is meant by board effectiveness and the types of skills and experience that are relevant at board level to inform the decisions that need to be taken. Could the high level of homogeneity evidenced, which was seen to lead to a strong corporate identity, also be a disadvantage? Given the size and complexity of the NHS and all the different organizations within it, the focus on private sector management experience and the removal of the broad base of membership could be seen as reducing the depth and quality of debate, which might have an effect on managerial effectiveness. As on private sector boards, there are also no directors who have a direct representational role to key stakeholder groups. Such data would suggest that these new NHS boards are very likely to become more managerialist, but that this need not necessarily make them more effective or accountable.

Board Processes

In studying the processes within board meetings, an understanding of what can be judged 'effective' depends upon the purpose of the board, and its role and objectives. Whereas the health service reforms were specific about the issue of structure and composition, no reference was made to the role that these bodies were expected to take. During the first months after establishment, the research found that there was some ambiguity amongst both executive and non-executive directors regarding their precise role (Ashburner and Cairncross 1993). During the periods of observation, none of the boards studied in the first two years of the reforms took any time during or between meetings to address the issue of defining the board or individual roles more precisely. As the Department of Health increased the number of guide-lines on issues such as probity and the recruitment of new directors, boards slowly began to address indirectly issues relating to their role. As more hospitals took on trust status and formed boards, they built upon the experience of the earlier trusts. The 'third wave' trust studied showed a far greater awareness of the issues of setting board and individual objectives.

With the objective of the reforms to make the NHS more 'business-like', the role of the boards was interpreted by the research as enabling the new boards to become more strategic decision-making bodies. Without a definition of purpose there would be nothing for the board to measure its performance against. The analysis of the processes which occur at board meetings and any assessment of board effectiveness are based upon a number of prerequisites which have been identified as part of the research. These include the format of meetings, regular attendance by all directors, the amount and timing of available information, and the skills that individuals bring to their roles.

The survey revealed that the majority of boards met once a month and these meetings were subdivided in a variety of ways between public, private, and confidential agendas. Trusts alone were not required to hold any meetings in public aside from one separate annual public meeting. Extra meetings were held as required to discuss key items in more depth, and various subcommittees were set up in respect of certain key board roles, such as audit, remuneration, or complaints. The role played by informal meetings was not addressed by the research, but clearly these can play a critical role both in the level of involvement of the non-executives in debating issues with the executives and in their general learning-curve. The high level of regular attendance ensured that directors had greater knowledge of the agenda and the history of prior discussions on a topic.

What appeared on the board agendas and the quality of the information given to the non-executives are critical issues in board effectiveness. While the standard of data and its presentation varied between boards, there was little expression of dissatisfaction by non-executives as such issues were regularly discussed at board meetings. Limited secretarial support reduced the scope for 'executive summaries' to be produced from often very lengthy documents. The analysis of the content of board agendas highlighted the balance between operational or 'for information' items and those which were part of a strategic decision-making process. Critical here, for the non-executive's ability to monitor or influence executive decisions, was the stage in that process at which items were brought to the board.

Without a discussion on the role of the board, it was not possible for the boards studied to define clearly the criteria for inclusion of an item on the board's agenda, or what the balance should be between operational and strategic issues. The chief executives interviewed, at the outset of the study, all described how the setting of the agenda was an intuitive process. Towards the end many were able to specify more precisely the criteria for inclusion and the opening up of the agenda so that others could have items included. The questionnaire had shown that directors had identified both operational and strategic board roles as being important. For example, the role most frequently mentioned by respondents as 'very important' was the obligation to meet the health needs of the community, and the second was more strategically that of judging the priorities with regard to use of resources, while the third was longer-term: the determination of strategic objectives. The fourth and fifth most important roles were defined as ensuring that standards of care were determined and met and the monitoring of the organization's performance.

Somewhat as a contrast to these expressed expectations of directors, the majority of the time of the meetings observed was taken up with items for information and operational issues. A key operational issue vital for the monitoring of performance was finance and this, uniquely, appeared on every agenda, and at many meetings it was the item that took the greatest proportion of time. Most boards had one or two items per meeting that had strategic relevance. These ranged from the location of future services and the interpretation of central policy to decisions on possible rationing. What was significant was that such discussions seldom resulted in a decision being made, hence the focus on strategy formulation rather than strategic decision-making. It was also notable that over the three-year period of the study the balance of strategic items and discussion on most boards observed increased.

Board 'Effectiveness'

For the purposes of the study the level of board effectiveness was assessed by direct observation and the reported views of the board members in relation to several factors, such as their involvement in debate about future strategies rather than merely approving management decisions. Many boards were also beginning to introduce forms of measuring the performance of the board and its members, based upon the achievement of defined targets.

There are a number of key influences on board processes which have a direct bearing on board effectiveness. One such is the balance of influence of the executives and non-executives and the analysis of the contributions made at the board meetings studied. The inbuilt disadvantage suffered by non-executives in their lack of time and involvement when compared with the executives is exacerbated if the agenda is limited in scope and if items of strategic importance are not presented to the board until the decision-making process is complete. The non-executives will be less familiar with the issues, they have had no opportunity to comment during the formative stages, and possibly the range of potential options will have been reduced. The number of options presented to the non-executives in the formation of policy is an important dimension of board power, so that when the executives bring decisions to the board for approval their role is reduced to that of the 'rubber stamp'. Thus the setting and the timing of agenda items can form an indirect or a direct form of control over the board by the executive.

How effective boards are thus depends upon the willingness of the executives to open up the strategy formulation process to the board. In this the role of the chair can be crucial, since many chairs have a greater involvement in the organizations than do other non-executives. This is a clear example of how a separate and independent chair can enhance the effectiveness of the board. Just as the domination of a board by the chief executive can be a problem in reducing debate and non-executive contributions, so can the domination of a chair. There were examples of the former in our study, but not of the latter. Despite the ultimate power of the chair and non-executives with regard to the appointment of executives, it requires a powerful chair to ensure a balance of influence. The survey of directors showed that non-executives acknowledged that the executives had the greatest influence on the decision-making process at board level. However, there was also a measure of indirect control being exerted by the mere presence on a board of independent non-executives. Some executives said that the nature of the proposals they put forward was influenced by the fact that they would need board approval. Hence some proposals that they thought might be unacceptable were not considered and not put forward.

Despite the dominance of the executive, on a few occasions observed by the authors, the non-executives were successful at changing or rejecting an executive proposal. In one trust the non-executives reversed a decision not to spend money on signposting, and in a purchasing authority the non-executives were successful in changing the balance of resource allocation to ensure that more went to mental health.

Another factor critical to board effectiveness is the ability of the directors themselves. They need more than just knowledge of the organizations, since they need to be able to understand issues from across the functions and to take a corporate view. In the early stages of board formation this was as problematic for some of the executives new to their board role as it was for some of the non-executives. There was a tendency for people to contribute only in their own functional areas or to ask questions of clarification rather than being more probing. The type and extent of contributions cannot be generalized by role or background as these were more dependent upon individual personalities. It was notable that on the trust boards the executives appeared more willing to open up debate with the non-executives, even to the point of seeking advice. This could be related to several factors, such as the newness of the trust board compared with the other NHS boards which had developed out of the old authorities with their different way of working, and the relative newness of the trust executives to their board roles. Although some non-executives were willing to challenge the executives, this was always on detail rather than on the underlying assumptions or philosophy of the decision. The norms of politeness and consensus still predominated. The development of experience and confidence occurred as part of a natural learning curve for many directors, but not for all, and not as fast as on those boards where board and director development were specifically addressed.

It is problematic to assess the role and influence of the non-executives in the formulation of strategy since this is often an implicit rather than an explicit process, given the emergent nature of strategic decision-making. Another problem is the nature of the dual role of the non-executives. For the majority of the time the emphasis is on their supportive role, which places them in a role complementary to management. On many boards the non-executives were allocated specific roles that drew them into operational issues. This made it more problematic for them to 'stand back' and take on the monitoring and independent overview essential to ensure accountability and probity. Charkham (1994) also notes the incompatibility of the 'co-operative' and 'supervisory' roles.

How effectively non-executive directors are able to carry out these roles is dependent upon all the factors so far discussed. These factors are in the remit of individual boards to address but they are not necessarily recognized in the formal structures and mechanisms for accountability. They represent the prerequisites for board effectiveness and it is the cumulative effect of them all which is significant in understanding how boards can become more effective. If the issues of board roles and the boundaries between items which are the prerogative of managers and items which should come to the board are not openly discussed, then the influence of non-executives will remain weak.

5. Conclusion

In exploring how the private sector board model has been implemented within the public sector, several key conclusions can be drawn. Firstly, we need to understand whether this is the most appropriate model for the public sector. In this it is apparent that the regulations controlling the operation of NHS boards are far greater than those for the private sector. The former have gone beyond the Cadbury recommendations which private sector organizations are not required to fulfil. In this sense there has not been a direct transfer of the private sector model but an adaptation, and what has emerged can be seen as a hybrid form.

The issue of how effective such boards are needs to be understood in the context of their purpose. If they are to be effective bodies for ensuring accountability and probity, then the ability of the non-executive to hold the executive to account becomes the critical factor. Combined with this are issues about the nature of accountability. In the private sector this relates to the key stakeholders, who are predominantly the investors. In the public sector the notions of accountability go wider and include not just formal accountability upwards to the Department of Health, seen primarily in financial terms, but the more direct accountability to the public or local community for the expenditure of public monies and the provision of public services. Where the new structures acknowledge the importance of formal upwards accountability, they have been severely criticized for ignoring local or democratic accountability. This is not an issue local boards can fully address on their own account, despite attempts to be open and involve the public, since it is a statutory issue of structure and composition.

In relation to organizational effectiveness it is clear that the empowerment of management is not necessarily related to the effectiveness of the board and it can be counter-productive. Taken with the conclusion that, by itself, changing the structure and composition of health service boards would not lead to greater effectiveness, the issue of how the board defines its role becomes the central focus. For the position and power of the non-executives to be identified and the balance of power between management and the board established, there needs to be a clear definition of board roles. Here, the balance between the monitoring role and involvement in strategy formulation becomes critical, as does the balance of power between the executive and the non-executive directors. The board is the strategic apex and it sets the whole direction of the organization. Research on excellence has shown senior management competence in strategy development to be a key factor. Pearce and Shaker (1991) suggest that effective boards with an open, questioning style produce more effective organizational performance.

Any assessment of effectiveness relates separately to each defined board role. An increased effectiveness in one area may detract from another. Ultimately any increase in involvement of the board or non-executives into a more strategic role needs to be carefully balanced against the need for the non-executives to retain an independent stance so that they can objectively evaluate both the executive and the strategy. For the NHS in particular it is critical that the need for accountability and the representation of key stakeholders do not become secondary to the organizational 'success' factors, now that the only formal accountability is to the Department of Health and 'success' is judged predominantly in financial terms. The notion in the public sector that such bodies are either democratically accountable or managerially effective needs to be challenged if the development of boards is not to be limited by narrow thinking. There is an opportunity for the emergent hybrid form to integrate both of these requirements.

The developments and the experience of the NHS has shown how the effectiveness of boards can be improved if the relevant prerequisites are met. This can only happen once the issues of structure and composition have been addressed. But the introduction of formal mechanisms for accountability will only have a limited effect on overall board effectiveness. Private sector boards also need to focus on the issue of their roles and the development of their executive and non-executive directors to face the difficult challenges that lie ahead.

REFERENCES

Ashburner, L. (1994), 'The Composition of NHS Trust Boards', *Health Service Management Research*, 7/3: 154–64.

—— (1995), 'The Role of Clinicians in the Management of the NHS', in J. Leopold, M. Hughes, and I. Glover (eds.), *Beyond Reason? The National Health Service and the Limits of Management* (Aldershot: Avebury).

—— and Cairncross, L. (1993), 'Health Authority Members: Continuity or Change?', *Public Administration*, 71/3: 357–75.

—— and FitzGerald, L. (1994), 'Boards of Directors in Healthcare and Strategy Formulation Processes', Paper presented to the British Academy of Management Conference, Lancaster University, Sept.

Ashburner, L., Ferlie, E., and FitzGerald, L. (1993), *Boards and Authorities in Action*, Paper No. 11, Authorities in Action (Bristol: NHSTD).

—— —— —— (1994), 'Quasi-Markets and the Development of Competition in the NHS: An Initial Analysis of their Impact', Paper presented to the 24th Annual Conference of the Public Administration Committee of the Joint University Council, York University, Sept.

Bank of England (1985), 'Composition of Company Boards', *Bank of England Quarterly Bulletin* (June), 255–6.

—— (1988), 'Composition of Company Boards', *Bank of England Quarterly Bulletin* (May), 242.

Cadbury, A. (1992), *Report of the Committee on the Financial Aspects of Corporate Governance* (London: Gee).

Charkham, J. (1986), *Effective Boards* (London: Chartac).

—— (1994), *Keeping Good Company: A Study of Corporate Governance in Five Countries* (Oxford: Oxford University Press).

Cmnd. 555 (1989), *Working for Patients* (London: HMSO).

Committee of Public Accounts (1993a), *Wessex Regional Health Authority: Regional Information Systems Plan*, HC 658, 63rd report session 1992–3 (London: HMSO).

—— (1993b), *West Midlands Regional Health Authority: Regionally Managed Services Organisation*, HC 485, 57th report session 1992–3 (London: HMSO).

Coulson-Thomas, C., and Wakelam, A. (1991), *The Effective Board: Current Practice, Myths and Realities* (London: Director Books).

Day, P., and Klein, R. (1987), *Accountabilities: Five Public Services* (London: Tavistock).

Farnham, D., and Horton, S. (1993), 'Managing Private and Public Organisations', in Farnham and Horton (eds.), *Managing the New Public Services* (Basingstoke: Macmillan).

Ferlie, E., Ashburner, L., and FitzGerald, L. (1995), 'Corporate Governance and the Public Sector: Some Issues and Evidence from the NHS', *Public Administration*, 73/3: 375–92.

—— —— —— and Pettigrew, A. (1996), *The New Public Management in Action* (Oxford: Oxford University Press).

FitzGerald, L., and Pettigrew, A. (1991), *Boards in Action: Some Implications for Health Authorities*, Paper No. 2, Authorities in the NHS (Bristol: NHSTD).

Griffiths, R. (1983), *NHS Management Inquiry* (London: DHSS).

Hayes, M. (1994), *The New Right in Britain: An Introduction to Theory and Practice* (London: Pluto Press).

Hood, C. (1991), 'A Public Management for All Seasons?', *Public Administration*, 69: 3–19.

Klein, R. (1983), *The Politics of the National Health Service* (London: Longman).

Korn Ferry (1989), *International Boards of Directors Study* (London: Korn-Ferry).

Kovner, A. R. (1974), 'Hospital Board Members as Policy Makers: Roles, Priorities and Qualifications', *Medical Care*, 12/12: 971–82.

Lorsch, J., and MacIver, J. (1989), *Pawns or Potentates: The Reality of America's Corporate Boards* (Boston: Harvard Business School Press).

Pearce, J. A., and Shaker, A. Z. (1991), 'The Relative Power of CEOs and Boards of Directors: Associations with Corporate Performance', *Strategic Management Journal*, 12: 135–53.

Pfeffer, J. (1972), 'Size, Composition and Function of Hospital Boards of Directors: A Study of Organisational–environmental Linkage', *Administrative Science Quarterly*, 18: 349–64.

Pollitt, C. (1990), *Managerialism and the Public Services* (Oxford: Blackwell).

Ranson, S., and Stewart, J. (1994), *Management for the Public Domain: Enabling the*

Learning Society (London: Macmillan).

Stewart, J., and Ranson, S. (1988), 'Management in the Public Domain', *Public Money and Management* (Spring–Summer), 13–18.

——and Walsh, K. (1992), 'Change in the Management of Public Services', *Public Administration*, 70: 499–518.

Tricker, R. I. (1984), *Corporate Governance: Practices, Procedures and Powers in British Companies and their Boards of Directors* (Aldershot: Gower).

Zahra, S. A. (1990), 'Increasing the Board's Involvement in Strategy', *Long Range Planning*, 23/6: 109–17.

INDEX